Neuroeconomics, Judgment and Decision Making

MW00562475

This volume explores how and why people make judgments and decisions that have economic consequences, and what the implications are for human well-being. It provides an integrated review of the latest research from many different disciplines, including social, cognitive, and developmental psychology; neuroscience and neurobiology; and economics and business.

The book has six areas of focus: historical foundations, cognitive consistency and inconsistency, heuristics and biases, neuroeconomics and neurobiology, developmental and individual differences, and improving decisions. Throughout, the contributors draw out implications from traditional behavioral research as well as evidence from neuroscience. In recent years, neuroscientific methods have matured beyond being simply correlational and descriptive, into theoretical prediction and explanation, and this has opened up many new areas of discovery about economic behavior that are reviewed in the book. In the final part, there are applications of the research into cognitive development, individual differences, and the improvement of decisions.

The book takes a broad perspective and is written in an accessible way so as to reach a wide audience of advanced students and researchers interested in behavioral economics and related areas. This includes neuroscientists, neuropsychologists, clinicians, psychologists (developmental, social, and cognitive), economists, and other social scientists; legal scholars and criminologists; professionals in public health and medicine; educators; evidence-based practitioners; and policy-makers.

Evan A. Wilhelms is a PhD candidate in the Department of Human Development at Cornell University, and the Laboratory Leader in Dr. Valerie Reyna's Laboratory for Rational Decision Making. His research is on the topics of judgment and decision making, with implications for financial and health well-being in adolescents and adults. His work has appeared in the *Journal of Medicine and Philosophy* and *Virtual Mentor: American Medical Association Journal of Ethics*, as well as several edited volumes.

Valerie F. Reyna is Professor of Human Development and Psychology at Cornell University, Co-Director of the Cornell University Magnetic Resonance Imaging Facility, Co-Director of the Center for Behavioral Economics and Decision Research, and Past President of the Society for Judgment and Decision Making. Her research encompasses human judgment and decision making, numeracy and quantitative reasoning, risk and uncertainty, medical decision making, social judgment, and false memory.

FRONTIERS OF COGNITIVE PSYCHOLOGY

Series Editors
Nelson Cowan, *University of Missouri-Columbia*
David Balota, *Washington University in St. Louis*

Frontiers of Cognitive Psychology is a new series of cognitive psychology books, which aims to bring together the very latest research in the discipline, providing a comprehensive and up-to-date review of the latest empirical, theoretical, and practical issues in the field. Each volume will concentrate on a traditional core area of cognitive psychology, or an area which is emerging as a new core area for the future, and may include interdisciplinary perspectives from areas such as developmental psychology, neuroscience, evolutionary psychology, forensic psychology, social psychology, and the health sciences.

Published

Working Memory: The Connected Intelligence, Tracy Packiam Alloway & Ross G. Alloway (Eds)

Neuroeconomics, Judgment, and Decision Making, edited by Evan A. Wilhelms & Valerie F. Reyna

Forthcoming

New Methods in Cognitive Psychology, Daniel H. Spieler & Eric Schumacher (Eds)

Motivation and Cognitive Control, Todd S. Braver

Big Data in Cognitive Science, Michael N. Jones

Neuroeconomics, Judgment, and Decision Making

Edited by

Evan A. Wilhelms

and

Valerie F. Reyna

Psychology Press
Taylor & Francis Group
NEW YORK AND LONDON

First published 2015
by Psychology Press
711 Third Avenue, New York, NY 10017

and by Psychology Press
27 Church Road, Hove, East Sussex BN3 2FA

Psychology Press is an imprint of the Taylor & Francis Group, an informa business

Library of Congress Cataloging-in-Publication Data

Catalog record for this book has been requested.

ISBN: 978-1-84872-659-8 (hbk)
ISBN: 978-1-84872-660-4 (pbk)
ISBN: 978-1-315-76392-7 (ebk)

Typeset in New Caledonia
by Apex CoVantage, LLC

Printed and bound in Great Britain by TJ International Ltd., Padstow Cornwall

Contents

Illustrations

FIGURES

TABLES

Contributors

Alessandro Acquisti, PhD,
Heinz College, Carnegie Mellon
University, Pittsburgh, PA;
Co-director of the CMU Center
for Behavioral Decision Research,
Pittsburgh, PA

Donato Barbagallo, PhD,
Carnegie Mellon University,
Pittsburgh, PA; Politecnico di Milano,
Milan, Italy

Wändi Bruine de Bruin, PhD,
Leeds University Business School,
Leeds, UK; Centre for Decision
Research, Department of Engineering
and Public Policy, Carnegie Mellon
University, RAND Corporation,
Pittsburgh, PA

Priscila G. Brust-Renck, MA,
Department of Human Development,
Cornell University, Ithaca, NY

Anne-Sophie Chaxel, PhD,
Desautels Faculty of Management,
McGill University, Montreal, Quebec,
Canada

Jonathan C. Corbin, MA,
Department of Human Development,
Cornell University, Ithaca, NY

Natalie L. Denburg, PhD,
Carver College of Medicine, University
of Iowa, Iowa City, IA

Stephan Dickert, PhD,
Vienna University of Economics and
Business, Vienna, Austria; Linköping
University, Linköping, Sweden

Julie S. Downs, PhD,
Department of Social and Decision
Sciences, Carnegie Mellon University,
Pittsburgh, PA

Anna C. K. van Duijvenvoorde, PhD,
Department of Psychology, Leiden
University, the Netherlands; Leiden
Institute for Brain and Cognition,
the Netherlands; Department of
Psychology, University of Amsterdam,
the Netherlands

Ward Edwards,° PhD,
Department of Psychology,
University of Southern California,
Los Angeles, CA

Bernd Figner, PhD,
Radboud University, Nijmegen,
the Netherlands; Center for the
Decision Sciences, Columbia University,
New York, NY

Baruch Fischhoff, PhD,
Department of Engineering and Public Policy, Department of Social and Decision Sciences, Carnegie Mellon University, Pittsburgh, PA

Gary J. Gaeth, PhD,
Department of Marketing, University of Iowa, Iowa City, IA

Thomas E. Gladwin, PhD,
Radboud University, Nijmegen, the Netherlands; University of Amsterdam, Amsterdam, the Netherlands

William Hedgcock, PhD,
Department of Marketing, University of Iowa, Iowa City, IA

Rebecca K. Helm, LLM,
Department of Human Development, Cornell University, Ithaca, NY

Robin M. Hogarth, PhD,
Department of Economics & Business, Universitat Pompeu Fabra, Barcelona, Spain

Hilde M. Huizenga, PhD,
Department of Psychology, University of Amsterdam, the Netherlands; Cognitive Science Center Amsterdam, Amsterdam, the Netherlands

Brenda R. J. Jansen, PhD,
Department of Psychology, University of Amsterdam, the Netherlands; Cognitive Science Center Amsterdam, Amsterdam, the Netherlands

Irwin P. Levin, PhD,
Departments of Psychology and Marketing, University of Iowa, Iowa City, IA

Jordana M. Liberali, PhD,
Erasmus School of Economics, Erasmus University Rotterdam, Rotterdam, the Netherlands

Todd McElroy, PhD,
Department of Psychology, Appalachian State University, Boone, NC

Joowon Park, BA,
Johnson School of Management, Cornell University, Ithaca, NY

Andrew M. Parker, PhD,
RAND Corporation, Pittsburgh, PA

Valerie F. Reyna, PhD,
Departments of Human Development and Psychology, Human Neuroscience Institute, Cornell Magnetic Resonance Imaging Facility, Cornell University, Ithaca, NY

J. Edward Russo, PhD,
Johnson School of Management, Cornell University, Ithaca, NY

Roni A. Setton, BA,
Department of Human Development, Cornell University, Ithaca, NY

James Shanteau, PhD,
Department of Psychological Sciences, Kansas State University, Manhattan, KS

Paul Slovic, PhD,
Decision Research, Department of Psychology, University of Oregon, Eugene, OR

Emre Soyer, PhD, Faculty of Business, Ozyegin University, Istanbul, Turkey

Manoj Thomas, PhD,
Johnson School of Management,
Cornell University, Ithaca, NY

Daniel Tranel, PhD,
Department of Psychology,
University of Iowa,
Iowa City, IA

Daniel Västfjäll, PhD,
Decision Research, Department of
Behavioural Sciences and Learning,
Linköping University, Linkoping,
Sweden

Evan A. Wilhelms, MA,
Department of Human Development,
Cornell University, Ithaca, NY

Note: ° Posthumous authorship with longtime collaborator.

Introduction

Neuroeconomics, Judgment, and Decision Making

EVAN A. WILHELMS AND VALERIE F. REYNA

Neuroeconomics, judgment, and decision making encompass different disciplines, including social, cognitive, and developmental psychology; neuroscience and neurobiology; and economics and business. But, in this volume, they are all directed at understanding how and why people make judgments and decisions that have economic consequences, with broad implications for human well-being.

The origins of judgments, decisions, and all other economic behavior can be found in the brain. A comparatively small portion of the human brain is devoted to input from the environment—the occipital lobe for vision, olfactory lobe for chemical senses, the auditory cortex, and the somatosensory cortex. Smaller still is the region for generating our output back into our environment, largely limited to the motor cortex of the frontal lobe. From the remainder—in fact, the majority of the cerebral cortex—humans must interpret the input from their senses, process, calculate, weigh options, consider threats, plan for their futures, and select a course of action, all before finally taking that course of action with our words and deeds.

Psychologists investigate the latter topics, working in conjunction with other fields, to study normative (what people should do), descriptive (what people actually do), and prescriptive (how to help people do what they should) approaches to judgment and decision making. On the cutting edge of this research has been neurobiological inquiry, which allows these experts to discover and infer the biological causes of our decisions—bridging the aforementioned gap between input and output. This relatively new field of research has been called *neuroeconomics,* referring to research that uses neurobiological data to inform understanding of economic behavior and decision making. This field has capitalized on recently developed technology to investigate healthy people—whereas decades ago brain research depended largely on animals and patients with lesions.

A great deal of research in the field of judgment and decision making involves how people respond to numerical information, especially risks, probabilities, dollar amounts, and other attribute values. However, people are notoriously poor at processing numbers, and even experts exhibit biases and fallacies in numerical judgments and decisions (for a review, see Reyna, Nelson, Han, & Dieckmann, 2009). Thus, many effects found when investigating behavior in this field have been described in terms of heuristics and biases, that is, shortcuts and errors people make in their thinking. More recently, scholars instead emphasize the gains and benefits that come from intuitive thinking, such as when those with expert training are able to make better decisions based on less information.

Regardless of whether scholars emphasize errors or successes, research in judgment and decision making has important applications for improving practice in law, management, marketing, computer science, health care, and many other fields. Government agencies increasingly rely on research in decision making to make policy decisions and businesses increasingly rely on such research for management and marketing decisions. Knowing how people process numerical information about risks, and decide based on that information, is critical for the health and well-being of patients so that they are fully informed and may freely decide between treatment options. Readers interested mainly in such practical applications will find that this book provides a broad introduction to the field.

The main body of this book is divided into six parts representing the following areas of focus: historical foundations; cognitive consistency and inconsistency; heuristics and biases; neuroeconomics and neurobiology; developmental and individual differences; and improving decisions. Although the medium requires us to assign the chapters to one of these sections, many of them are broader than the heading would suggest, including themes covered in chapters from other sections.

In this volume, authors draw out implications from both behavioral evidence and neuroscientific evidence. Neuroscientific methods such as functional magnetic resonance imaging have opened the door to new questions about behavior and paths for cognitive psychology. Although much of the initial work has been merely correlational and descriptive—such as showing "what lights up" in the brain during specific decision tasks—the field has been maturing into theoretical prediction and explanation, as represented here.

The volume begins with a chapter contributed by a founder (and former president) of the Society for Judgment and Decision Making, James Shanteau, who offers some historical perspective on the source of our current research paradigms in judgment and decision making. In doing so, he focuses on five psychologists who have contributed to the field: Wilhelm Wundt, James McKeen Cattell, Edward Titchener, Edwin Boring, and Ward Edwards. He describes how the field of judgment and decision making has arrived at its current paradigms, methods, and theories, using research on domain experts as an illustration. Shanteau describes the assumption of the generalized normal adult human mind, and how it has influenced the field of judgment and decision making, including the study of heuristics and biases. From this perspective, he concludes that our current assumptions about normal human minds are insufficient to investigate populations such as domain experts, and offers analysis of how such research should proceed in the future.

The section that follows is on the subject of cognitive consistency and inconsistency, and it begins with a chapter by Anne-Sophie Chaxel and J. Edward Russo that introduces the topic of cognitive consistency. Beginning by reviewing seminal work on cognitive dissonance, including some major theories that preceded it—such as balance theory, congruity theory, and symmetry theory—they propose a unified framework to describe how people activate a goal of being consistent in their choices, how they become aware of any inconsistency or dissonance, and how they achieve consistency in their outcomes through cognitive processing. To illustrate these mechanisms, they introduce experimental manipulations that are designed to differentially prime the goal of consistency or the mindset of consistency. One such manipulation, for example, invokes a delay between a consistency prime and subsequent decision tasks, resulting in frustration of the goal of cognitive consistency. Ironically, the desire for consistency, a basic assumption of economic theory, produces biases and distortions.

The next chapter by Evan A. Wilhelms, Rebecca K. Helm, Roni A. Setton, and Valerie F. Reyna introduces fuzzy-trace theory as a theory of memory, reasoning, and decision making, explicating its predictions about people's forecasts of future well-being. First, they introduce the principles of fuzzy-trace theory, a novel dual-process theory based on memory representations. This theory predicts some paradoxical effects, such as increases in some biases and false memories with age from childhood to adulthood. The authors then briefly review some of the evidence for these effects, before applying the theory to make predictions about how people forecast future emotions. They review evidence in support of this new extension of the theory, specifically that people generally have accurate gist processing (and, hence, judgments) of the valence of their life experiences, but that more precise judgments such as degree of arousal or intensity of happiness rely on verbatim processing, which is more fragile and error-prone. Therefore, people's inconsistent judgments grow out of separate verbatim and gist dual processes, yielding disparate forecasts of their future emotions and well-being.

The next section on heuristics and biases begins with a short introduction to intuition, inhibition, and interference authored by Jonathan C. Corbin, Jordana M. Liberali, Valerie F. Reyna, and Priscila G. Brust-Renck. Applying a fuzzy-trace theory perspective, this chapter examines how reliance on gist and verbatim representations, interference, inhibition, and individual differences in cognitive ability (e.g., intelligence and working memory capacity) explains variability in judgment and decision making (with an emphasis on probability judgment and risky-choice framing effects). For example, the conjunction fallacy occurs when people judge an intersection of probabilistic events (i.e. both A and B occur) as more likely than one of the events separately (i.e. either A or B occurring). The classic example of this is the Linda problem, in which people rate the hypothetical character Linda as being more likely to be a feminist and a bank teller than any bank teller—based on a stereotypic description of Linda. In addition to explaining classic examples of biases such as this one, they also introduce recent research that has been done to identify how theories of memory representation and decision making—specifically fuzzy-trace theory—can explain and predict these biases. This chapter describes the role of intuition and interference in supporting biases, and covers the role of inhibition (as measured by intelligence tests and functional magnetic resonance imaging studies) in avoiding such biases. Finally, they will discuss research that has shown that inhibition does not always play a role in avoiding bias, and describe how fuzzy-trace theory accounts for such findings.

J. Edward Russo continues this section on biases by summarizing research on predecisional distortion of information. In this chapter, he explains the effect of bias toward a leading alternative, in which people form a preference early on in the process of making a decision (possibly unconsciously) and subsequently interpret new evidence as being in favor of that initial preference. This bias can occur even in the absence of previous beliefs about the options in the decision, separating it from other classic effects (such as belief bias). Russo reviews some evidence that this effect occurs, before considering whether it could be an artifact of the measurement method and under what conditions the effect could be eliminated. The chapter concludes by considering under what contexts this effect may be considered "rational," and by proposing other phenomena that may be partially explained by this bias.

The section on heuristics and bias ends with Manoj Thomas and Joowon Park's introduction to the precision effect. In this chapter, they discuss how unusually precise numbers—13,172.89 instead of 13,000—can induce biases. They propose a model that explains the occurrence of heuristic processing, called the discrepancy attribution model. In this model, when people expect round numbers and instead are presented with unusually precise numbers, a discrepancy arises in processing. They find that people tend to attribute the discrepancy to some salient factor of the decision context, as guided by naive lay theories about the context of the judgment or decision. Coming from a perspective of management and marketing, Thomas and Park illustrate the effects of this model through a brief review of literature on numerical precision, including the precision effect's influence on believability, perceived rarity, and confidence intervals. They conclude by integrating these findings with recent work on neuroscience, explaining how it applies to calculations of precise numbers.

The seventh chapter of this volume introduces a section on neuroeconomics and neurobiology, beginning with a chapter by Irwin P. Levin, Todd McElroy, Gary J. Gaeth, William Hedgcock, Natalie L. Denburg, and Daniel Tranel. In this chapter they discuss common tasks that are found in the judgment and decision-making literature, including the risky choice framing task. In this task, numerically equivalent information is treated differently depending on whether the choice is described as a gain or loss. Levin and colleagues introduce the neurological underpinnings of this classic effect by citing research implementing a variety of laboratory techniques including functional magnetic resonance imaging, eye tracking, and tracking of circadian rhythm and glucose levels. This research is placed in the context of dual-process theories—in which one process operates quickly and unconsciously, while the other operates slowly and deliberately. They summarize what this research implies for the biology behind risky decisions, and propose implications for future research.

This section continues with Thomas E. Gladwin and Bernd Figner's chapter on the neuroscience of dual-process theories. These theories, mentioned above, sometimes characterize the automatic and unconscious process as "hot," implying emotional impulsivity, and the deliberate and calculative system as "cold," implying calm rationality. In their chapter, they discuss some of these theories to clarify the terminology used, while reviewing many of the tasks that have been used to measure "hot" and "cold" executive function—including the Columbia Card Task. They also review recent criticisms of these theories based in neurological and physiological evidence, arguing that current definitions of these two processes may be insufficient, if in fact there is agreement on the definitions across dual-process theories at all. They conclude by presenting an alternative model for explaining behavior on these tasks—the reprocessing and reinforcement model of reflectivity.

The last chapter in this section on neuroeconomics and neurobiology is written by Stephan Dickert, Daniel Västfjäll, and Paul Slovic on the subject of the neuroeconomics of charitable giving. It has been a challenge for some time within social sciences to reconcile the fact that people are altruistic with the assumption of self-interest that explains other human behavior; the latter is also a core assumption of classical economic theory. Dickert and his colleagues review evidence regarding the circumstances under which people are more likely to help others and give charitably, placing this research in the context of dual-process theories. Specifically, they cover biases in the valuation of lives—when individual differences in beliefs, numeric ability, affective and other cognitive processes, cause people to imbue fewer lives with more value than a greater number of lives. They cover both the psychological and neuroeconomic explanations for why such a bias might occur.

The section that follows is on the topic of developmental and individual differences, and begins with a chapter by Anna C. K. van Duijvenvoorde, Brenda R. J. Jansen, and Hilde M. Huizenga on changes in decision strategies that occur between childhood and adulthood. The focus of this chapter is on the use of different decision strategies through development—including both integrative and heuristic strategies—as well as the influence of affect and control on decisions. They take a perspective that incorporates developmental psychology, judgment, and decision making, as well as neuroimaging research. In assessing developmental changes in strategies and control, they associate them with development of cortical and subcortical brain regions, concluding by discussing individual differences in decision making and the research paradigms that characterize them.

The second chapter in this section is written by Wändi Bruine de Bruin, Andrew M. Parker, and Baruch Fischhoff, and is a review of developmental differences in decision making across the lifespan. They first consider how decision-making competence should be defined, based on the integration of normative criteria, beliefs, values, and metacognition. They then review evidence of differences across the lifespan in each of these criteria for decision-making competence, comparing adolescents to adults, and young adults to older adults. Building on this evidence, they review several studies that develop and validate an individual-differences measure of decision-making competence. Overall, they describe skills that contribute to the ability to make decisions and to see how those skills vary with age, while drawing implications for improving decision making through decision aids, training, and communications.

The final section of the book applies the research discussed earlier to improving decisions. The first of the chapters in this section is written by Julie S. Downs,

Donato Barbagallo, and Alessandro Acquisti on how judgments and decision making can be improved in the context of information security. They frame choices regarding sharing banking information online in terms of declarative knowledge about risks and procedural knowledge about how to evaluate them. They then propose a model regarding how this knowledge interacts with perceptions of severity and susceptibility to risk, costs of taking action, and the effectiveness of different strategies to predict whether people will share sensitive information with malicious websites. They find that declarative knowledge is associated with identifying which strategies are best, though procedural knowledge predicts effectiveness in protection against risks.

This section concludes with a chapter from Robin M. Hogarth and Emre Soyer, and is about simulating outcomes to improve decisions. They begin by reviewing information processing in the human cognitive system, emphasizing mechanisms that allow people to overcome processing limitations. Then, using an experimental paradigm in which people make probabilistic judgments, they delineate judgment tasks across two dimensions: whether the structure of the task is clear to the individual or opaque; and whether people acquire information about the task through experience or through a description. They then review how this paradigm could be applied to a variety of experimental tasks ranging from classical judgment tasks, investment decisions, and predicting the chance of winning a competition. They conclude that experientially simulating outcomes results in more accurate responses.

It has been our goal in inviting these contributors to draw from the work of internationally renowned scholars who represent the diverse perspectives that one is likely to find working in the field. This volume is intended to be a resource for senior undergraduates, graduate students, researchers, and practitioners, and is suitable as a core text or supplementary readings in advanced courses and seminars in psychology, economics, or business.

AUTHOR NOTE

Preparation of this manuscript was supported in part by the National Institutes of Health from the National Cancer Institute award R21CA149796 and from the National Institute of Nursing Research award RO1NR014368–01 to the second author. Correspondence concerning this article should be addressed to Evan A. Wilhelms, Department of Human Development, G77, Martha Van Rensselaer Hall, Cornell University, Ithaca, NY 14853. Email: eaw97@cornell.edu; Phone: 440-941-3826.

REFERENCES

Reyna, V. F., Nelson, W., Han, P., & Dieckmann, N. F. (2009). How numeracy influences risk comprehension and medical decision making. *Psychological Bulletin, 135*, 943–973. doi:10.1037/a0017327.

Part I

Historical Foundations

1

Decision Making by Experts

Influence of Five Key Psychologists

JAMES SHANTEAU AND WARD EDWARDS

Psychological studies involving experts date back to the earliest days of experimental psychology. Research on domain experts has also been a fundamental part of the history of judgment and decision making (JDM). The purpose of this chapter is to look at how domain experts have been viewed in the psychological literature. The focus will be on an unappreciated historical bias derived from a misinterpretation of the foundations of experimental psychology.

This chapter will first focus on the contributions of five historically significant psychologists: Wilhelm Wundt, James McKeen Cattell, Edward Titchener, Edwin Boring, and Ward Edwards. The discussion will turn on the impact of an overlooked assumption—the assumption of the generalized normal adult human mind (abbreviated as GNAHM)—that arises from this history. The chapter concludes with an analysis, drawn from the ideas of Wundt and Edwards, about where research on experts should go in the future.

Much research done today investigates judgment-and-decision-making phenomena involving normal adult minds. This emphasis on normality reflects some unrecognized assumptions about the human mind, namely, that methods and theories are assumed to be generalizable to most people. However, the study of outliers, such as experts, has revealed some of the most intriguing aspects of human behavior. In this chapter, we review the work of five foundational thinkers whose research on expertise provides insight into the source of pivotal assumptions that guide contemporary research in neuroeconomics, judgment, and decision making.

JAMES McKEEN CATTELL

The first study of the psychological processes of domain experts appears to have been conducted in 1886 by James McKeen Cattell as part of his doctoral degree under Wilhelm Wundt, the founder of experimental psychology. Cattell investigated individual differences using "association times" (reaction times) for two skilled observers with different domain expertise. One (B) was "a teacher of mathematics" and the other (C) "busied himself more with literature" (Cattell, 1887, p. 31); thus they had expertise in contrasting domains. Cattell asked both observers to answer common questions, some oriented toward math, some oriented toward literature, and others oriented toward unrelated fields. The questions were designed to "call to mind facts with which (both observers) were familiar" (Cattell, 1887, p. 71).

The results revealed that mean reaction times over all questions were similar for the two observers: .42 seconds for B and .44 seconds for C. However, there was an interaction between question type and domain of expertise. The results from Cattell's study show a 2×2 crossover—expertise in a domain leads to faster response times for questions in that domain. As Cattell put it, "C knows quite as well as B that $5 + 7 = 12$, yet he needs 1/10 sec longer to call it to mind. B knows quite as well as C that Dante was a poet, but needs 1/10 sec longer to think of it." In other words, expertise has an impact on the rate of thinking above and beyond simply getting the right answer.

In another research phase, Cattell assessed "the time it takes to form a judgment or opinion" (1887, p. 69), e.g., deciding which of two eminent men was thought to be greater. The results again showed a 2×2 crossover. Expertise in a domain leads to faster judgments or choices. "In judging as to the relative greatness of eminent men, the times were shortest . . . if the (observer) had already compared the men together" (Cattell, 1887, p. 72). Cattell (1887, p. 73) saw this research as just the beginning and concludes: "I think it . . . desirable to still further increase the number of experiments."

Despite this promising beginning, there was little effort to follow up this line of research. Important questions about the effects of expertise on the speed of decision making remain unexplored. Other aspects of decision making by experts also received little attention. Moreover, few theories were advanced and few unique methodologies were developed to study the behavior of experts. One purpose of this chapter is to explore a previously unappreciated reason for the paucity of research. To understand this reason, however, it is first necessary to look at the efforts of three major historical figures in the development of experimental psychology.[1]

WILHELM WUNDT

There is little dispute that Wilhelm Wundt is the founder of experimental psychology. "Wundt is the founder because . . . he brought the empirical methods of physiology to the questions of philosophy and also created a new, identifiable role—that of psychologist" (Leahey, 1987, p. 182). Wundt made his vision clear in his seminal book, *Principles of Physiological Psychology* (1873), noting that it was his intention to establish psychology as a new domain of science.[2]

Wundt argued that the goal for psychology should be "the construction of explanations of experience and the development of techniques for objectifying experience" (Blumenthal, 1975, p. 1081). Experiences to be analyzed ranged from memory and perception to social psychology and language. In his research, Wundt advocated the use of "internal perception." Although this methodology has often been labelled *introspection*, "Wundt did not use the kind of qualitative introspection in which subjects describe in detail their inner experiences. . . . The majority of Wundt's studies involved objective measurements that used a variety of sophisticated laboratory equipment. . . . Wundt then inferred information about conscious processes and elements from these objective measures" (Schultz & Schultz, 1987, pp. 65–66).

The "subjects" in Wundt's laboratory were far from the naive students commonly used now in research. Instead, highly trained observers (frequently Wundt himself or his graduate students) "were presented with carefully controlled, sensory events and required to describe their mental experiences" (Schultz & Schultz, 1987, p. 65). To yield valid observations, Wundt insisted that certain rules be enforced: the observer had to be "master of the situation . . . all observations were to be repeated many times; and finally experimental conditions were to be varied systematically" (Hothersall, 1984, p. 88). As Wundt argued, "we learn little about our minds from casual, haphazard self-observation . . . It is essential that observations be made by trained observers under carefully specified conditions for the purpose of answering well-defined question" (Wundt, 1904, p. 7). Wundt dismissed self-observation as "contemplative meditation that led only to fruitless debates and the grossest self-deceptions" (1904, p. 7). Therefore, psychological insights came from skilled observers, not naive subjects. Indeed, Wundt would likely disagree with the reliance on student subjects in research today.[3]

Wundt chose the term *voluntarismus* (voluntarism) for his school of psychology. To understand causality, Wundt used the concepts of *purpose, value,* and *future anticipation.* His "central mechanism of psychological causality was apperception, which in modern terms translates roughly to selective attention" (Blumenthal, 1980, p. 30). Attention was more than just selective: "the mind is a creative, dynamic, volitional force . . . It must be understood through an analysis of its activity—its processes" (Hothersall, 1984, p. 89). Moreover, "the act of choice constituted . . . a special case of 'volitional activity.' . . . This is the basis on which the later forms of volition, i.e. choice and decision, develop" (Danzinger, 1980b, p. 96). In short, Wundt developed a dynamic process theory of choice based on the concept of will operating selectively on goals, values, and future prospects.

Wundt's view of psychology is surprisingly modern. As Fancher (1979, p. 148) concluded, current psychologists will "find that their studies of such cognitive phenomena as information processing, selective inattention, and perceptual masking are much in the tradition of Wundt's studies." According to Wundt (1892, p. 495), "the fundamental character of mental life . . . in all its phases it is process; an active, not passive, existence." Thus, it can be argued that Wundt would have been comfortable with the focus of much of modern cognitive research.[4]

The numbers associated with Wundt are truly phenomenal: he taught over 24,000 students, supervised 186 doctoral students, including 16 from North

America. Many of the early psychology laboratories in the USA were founded by Wundt's students. "Wundt so influenced the first generation of American psychologists that the majority of American students of psychology [today] can probably trace their historical lineage back to him" (Boring & Boring, 1948). Ward Edwards received his degree under Boring, who was a student of Titchener, who studied with Wundt. In other words, with Edwards you could *shake the hand that shook the hand that shook the hand that shook the hand of Wundt.*

EDWARD TITCHENER

Wundt's most vocal advocate in the USA was Edward Titchener. After spending two years with Wundt, Titchener considered himself to be a true Wundtian — he "accepted Wundt's psychology without reservation" (Hothersall, 1984 p. 103). "Titchener pronounced himself to be Wundt's loyal follower and true interpreter. He proclaimed Wundt as the source of his psychology and the precursor who validated his credentials" (Anderson, 1980, p. 95). American psychologists seldom felt the need to read Wundt in German because all they needed to know was provided by Titchener. (Of course, few Americans can read academic German.) Furthermore, what little was available in English often contained serious translation errors. It is noteworthy that "many more of Wundt's books were translated into Russian — even into Spanish — than were ever translated into English" (Blumenthal, 1980, p. 28).

It was believed that Titchener's approach to psychology was essentially a mirror image of that of Wundt — if you knew Titchener, you knew Wundt. However,

> recent research on Wundt's writings casts doubt on this conclusion . . . Evidence suggests that [Titchener] altered Wundt's positions to make them appear compatible with his own, to lend credibility to his own views by asserting that they were consistent with those of psychology's founder. Titchener . . . elected to translate only those portions of Wundt's publications that supported his own approach to psychology. . . . For 100 years, texts in the history of psychology, and teachers of the history courses, have been compounding and reinforcing the error under the imprimatur of [Titchener's] alleged expertise.
>
> (Schultz & Schultz, 1987, pp. 58–59)

Titchener named his system of psychology *structuralism* because of his emphasis on "discovering the elemental structure of consciousness" (Benjamin, 1988, p. 209). "Although Wundt recognized elements or contents of consciousness, his overriding concern was their organization into higher-level cognitive processes through the principle of apperception" (Schultz & Schultz, 1987, p. 85). While Wundt emphasized the whole, Titchener focused on the parts — a view he adapted from James Mill (Danziger, 1980a). Wundt never described his psychology as structuralism. Indeed, after Wundt's death, his students named his movement *Ganzheit Psychology* or "holistic psychology."

Titchener considered subjects "to be a recording instrument, objectively noting the characteristics of the object being observed. Human subjects were nothing more than impartial and detached machines" (Schultz & Schultz, 1987, p. 91).

Titchener talked about mechanized observation: "the method of psychology is the same as the method of physics . . . strictly impartial and unprejudiced" (Titchener, 1910, p. 23). He often referred to his subjects as reagents: "a reagent is generally a passive agent, one that is applied to something to elicit certain reactions" (Schultz & Schultz, 1987, p. 91).

In contrast, Wundt's subjects played a more active role. One of Wundt's rules was that highly trained observers had to be "master of the situation" (Schultz & Schultz, 1987, p. 91). To yield valid introspections, Wundt's subjects controlled the situation, whereas Titchener's subjects were passive observers.[5]

Titchener's (1923) view of the appropriate content of behavioral research was narrow. He was interested in "pure psychology" with no room for comparative (animal) psychology, mental testing, educational psychology, industrial psychology, or social psychology. These fields were considered impure because subjects in these settings could not use introspection. When discussing why he opposed animal research, Titchener (1916, p. 267) argued, "if animals thought, they could undoubtedly use their vocal organs for speech; and since they do not talk, they cannot either be thinking." This is in contrast to Wundt's more expansive views of psychology.

> There are other source of psychological knowledge . . . in which we may trace the operation of determinate psychical motives: chief among them are language, myth and custom . . . They are dependent upon universal psychological laws; and the phenomenon that are referable to those laws form the subject-matter of a special psychological discipline, ethnic psychology.
>
> (Wundt, 1904, p. 4)

In most respects, Titchener presented a view of psychology that differed radically from Wundt's. Although Titchener made numerous contributions to psychology, he was not an accurate spokesman for Wundt. "If one were now to take the trouble to compare the psychological system of Titchener with . . . Wundt, one would be able to establish that one was dealing with two quite distinct psychological systems, the one calling itself structuralism, and the other voluntarism" (Danzinger, 1980a, pp. 73–74).

EDWIN G. BORING

During his 33-year career, 58 students received their PhD under Titchener. Some became major figures in the years following Titchener's death in 1927. Three of these (Karl M. Dallenbach, Madison Bentley, and Margaret Floy Washburn) are still known today. But Titchener's best known and "most loyal student" was Edwin Boring (Benjamin, 1988, p. 210). Boring had a distinguished career at Harvard where he became "the historian" of experimental psychology.

It is through Boring that most American psychologists learned about Wundt.

> Titchener's inaccurate version of Wundt's system influenced contemporary psychologists not only because of the status Titchener achieved . . . but also because of the

visibility attained by his student, E. G. Boring. . . . Thus, generations of students have been offered a portrait of Wundtian psychology that may be more myth than fact, more legend than truth.

(Schultz & Schultz, 1987, p. 59)

According to Blumenthal (1975), many "myths of origin" about Wundt can be traced directly to Boring's two editions of the *History of Experimental Psychology* (1929, 1950).[6] For nearly 70 years, Americans relied on Boring to tell Wundt's story. However, Boring's accounts were heavily slanted toward Titchener's perspective. One example concerns Wundt's focus on *volition* as a motivational mechanism. Titchener (1908) largely dismissed this theme: "Without giving supportive citation, Boring (1950) states that Wundt had opposed the implication of an active volitional agent in psychology" (Benjamin, 1988, p. 197). Mischel (1970) argued that volition is, in fact, central to Wundt's approach. As another example, Titchener (1921, p. 169) held that the ten volumes of *Völkerpsychologie* were the result of Wundt's weakness for "troublesome subjects of a certain sort," a view reflected in Boring's accounts.

The 1950 edition of Boring's history of experimental psychology is credited with playing a major role in establishing the legitimacy of psychology. It was published at a time when "psychology [was] hungry for scientific respectability" (Gillis & Schneider, 1966, p. 230). The argument for legitimacy had three elements:

1. a scientific tradition dating back to Wundt that establishes the historical precedents of research psychology;
2. an emphasis on statistical analyses based on (mis)reading of Fisher, Neyman-Pearson, and other statisticians; and
3. the institutionalization of the "classical experimental design" involving a comparison between experimental and control groups (Gillis & Schneider, 1966).

Together, they provided a myth of origin for psychology.[7]

Hebb (1972, p. 291) says the 1950 Boring history book is "commonly considered the standard work, and beautifully clear in its exposition, this book is thoroughly misleading in its emphasis . . . on Wundt and Titchener." It seems clear now that the typical American view of Wundt is incorrect, largely because of the impact of Boring's accounts. Blumenthal (1979, p. 40) concludes that Wundt was the "founding father of psychology that most psychologists have never known." It is no wonder that Max Wundt (Wundt's son) described the picture of his father's work as "nothing more than a caricature" (Hothersall, 1984, p. 99).

Still, Boring can be seen as a product of his times. "Boring's description of Wundt was probably the most intelligible and most acceptable one for the great majority of American psychologists. For them, it served to crystallize a then coherent explanation of the history of psychology . . . that justified the course of psychology's progress" (Blumenthal, 1980, p. 40). Indeed, Boring's accounts were more accurate than others who attempted to justify themselves by contrasting their approaches with a caricature of Wundt.

GENERALIZED NORMAL ADULT HUMAN MIND

One central belief of Titchener involved the Generalized Normal Adult Human Mind (or GNAHM). According to Boring (1929, p. 407), "Titchener interest lay in the generalized, normal, adult mind that had also been Wundt's main concern." Later writers reflected this theme: Wundt's "classical concept [was] that the major goal in psychology was to form generalizations about the normal human adult mind" (Helmstadter, 1964, p. 4). And, "like Wundt, [Titchener] was interested in 'the generalized human mind.' . . . psychology may gather its material from many sources, but its aim is to understand the generalized human mind" (Heidbreder, 1933, p. 125–126). This theme is also reflected by Anastasi (1968), Kendler (1987), Maloney and Ward (1976), Sargent and Stafford (1965), and Watson (1968).

What are the origins of GNAHM? Boring (1929) cites Wundt. Edwards (1983) cites Wundt and Titchener. Others (e.g., Fancher, 1979) cite a German intellectual tradition of concern for the human mind in general. The first author's search of a number of volumes by and about Wundt (e.g., Rieber, 1980) revealed no mention of the term. However, given that Wundt published over 491 papers with a total of 53,735 published pages (Boring, 1950), it is virtually impossible to prove that he never used the phrase. However, it is clear that Titchener referred to the concept repeatedly. "Psychology . . . is concerned with the normal, human, adult mind" (Titchener, 1916, p. 2).

Regardless of the origins, the belief in GNAHM has become so widespread that it has become the accepted norm for psychological investigations. Today, few researchers realize that there are any alternatives. They fail to recognize that this unstated conjecture colors nearly every aspect of their research perspective. Thus, the methods, analytic procedures, and theories used to study psychological processes are assumed to be generalizable to most, if not all, humans (i.e. undergraduates provide as good a source as any to examine behavior). Thus, GNAHM leads to research paradigms based on investigation of psychological phenomena involving "typical students."

As a result, experimental psychology developed neither the methods nor the theories to deal with outliers, such as experts. To the contrary, studies of expertise generally reflect GNAHM thinking. The behaviors that have been found to characterize student subjects become the starting point for research on experts. While this strategy sometimes can be revealing, it often overlooks some of the most intriguing aspects of expert behavior.[8]

As a consequence, researchers have not developed separate paradigms for investigating domain experts. Instead, theories and methods were borrowed from studies of students. Because these paradigms are often ill suited to the study of experts, it should not be surprising to find that understanding of experts has not advanced at the same rate as understanding of nonexpert subjects.

In fact, the methods and approaches used to study experts were borrowed primarily from paradigms created for other purposes. Few (if any) of the concepts used in judgment and decision-making studies were developed with experts in mind. As a consequence, expertise has been investigated using approaches designed to study typical GNAHM behavior. It should not be surprising, therefore, to find that conclusions from studies on experts tend to parallel those of nonexperts.

That is not to say that paradigms originally developed within the GNAHM perspective cannot be adapted to study expert behavior. As shown below, it is possible to use such approaches to provide insights into expertise. The key is not the approach, per se. Rather, it is how researchers use an approach—any technique can be used appropriately in some situations and misused in others (Shanteau, 1977).

Before continuing, it is essential to comment on the definition of "expert." Shanteau (1992a) argued that experts should be viewed as those who have risen to the top of a domain, i.e. they are the best at what they do. In most domains experts gain their knowledge from a combination of formal training and on-the-job experience. What has yet to be determined, however, is how these two forms of knowledge combine and whether there is an interaction with tasks (Lopes, personal communication, 1997).

TRADITIONAL JDM RESEARCH USING PSYCHOMETRIC ANALYSES

In the 1950s and 1960s, systematic research on domain experts began with psychometric analyses of validity and reliability conducted using clinical psychologists, e.g., Goldberg (1959) had 22 subjects (4 practicing clinicians, 10 student interns, and 8 naive subjects) examine 30 Bender–Gestalt protocols (a test for cortical brain damage). For all groups, accuracy/validity was 65 to 70 percent, where 50 percent is chance.

In an analysis of reliability, Oskamp (1962) found a correlation of .44 for repeated judgments of the same cases by clinicians. In related research, Oskamp (1965) reported that confidence of clinical psychologists increased as more information was available: Confidence ratings for increasing amounts of information were 33, 39, 46, and 53 percent, respectively. However, the accuracy remained unchanged at 26, 23, 28, and 28 percent, where 20 percent is chance. Further, no difference was found between expert clinicians and students. The conclusion from such psychometric studies is:

1. Clinicians' judgments are lacking in accuracy and consistency.
2. More information increases confidence but not accuracy.
3. There is little difference in the judgments of clinicians and novices.

(Goldberg, 1968)

Similar validity and reliability results were obtained for other expert domains, such as medical doctors (Einhorn, 1974), parole officers (Carroll & Payne, 1976), and court judges (Ebbesen & Konecni, 1975). Also, related research has shown that experience is often unrelated to judgment ability (Meehl, 1954) and that experts often perform little better than novices. Thus, these psychometric studies suggest a universal GNAHM result: Both experts and novices show the same poor performance.

Einhorn (1974) argued that reliability is a necessary condition for expertise. There are two ways to define reliability. The first involves *intra-judge* correlations (also known as *internal consistency* or *stability*): that is, when asked to judge the same case, an expert should make the same judgment. The other involves *inter-judge* correlations (also known as *between-subject reliability* or *consensus*): different experts looking at the same case should arrive at the same judgment.[9]

Empirically, the correlations for repeated judgments of the same case by individual experts ranged between .4 and .5. Similar levels of internal consistency have been reported for other types of domain experts, such as licensed grain judges (Trumbo, Adams, Milner, & Schipper, 1962).

These sorts of results led to the GNAHM conclusion that experts are not reliable. When similar analyses were conducted with expert auditors, however, the correlations were considerably better. For instance, Ashton (1974) observed a mean correlation of over .8 between two presentations of 32 cases involving internal control. Researchers looking at other tasks have reported even higher results. Despite differences in task and experimenters, the findings are surprisingly consistent— between .8 and .9.

Even more impressive levels of internal consistency can be seen for livestock judges. The r-values obtained by Phelps (1977) for four top swine judges ranged from .95 to .97 for judgments of overall breeding quality. Average r values for other livestock tasks ranged from .8 to near 1.00 (perfect). Thus, livestock judges show quite high levels of intra-judge reliability.

Stewart, Roebber, and Bosart's (1997) study of weather forecasters yielded the highest internal consistency levels yet observed. Weather experts were found to have nearly perfect reliability for 24-hour temperature forecasts. Slightly lower values were obtained for 24-hour precipitation forecasts. It appears, therefore, that internal consistency for weather forecasters is near perfect.

Besides internal consistency, Einhorn (1974) also argued that experts should agree with each other. Estimates of *inter-judge* reliability (consensus) values revealed average between-judge correlation values of less than .40 for stockbrokers (Slovic, 1969) and clinical psychologists (Goldberg & Werts, 1966). Somewhat higher values were observed by Einhorn (1974) for medical pathologists. Despite the impressively high internal consistency found for livestock judges, Phelps (1977) observed an average between-judge correlation of only .50. These values are similar enough to each other to support a GNAHM argument of mediocre inter-judge consensus across skill levels and domains.

However, results for expert auditors are noticeably higher. Kida (1980) asked 27 audit partners to judge 40 profiles based on five accounting ratios; the average inter-judge correlation was .76. Similar findings were reported by Ashton (1974) for judged strength of internal controls and by Libby, Artman, and Willingham (1985) for judgments of control reliance.

Inter-auditor reliability has been observed to increase as a function of experience. In a study of materiality judgments, Krogstad, Ettenson, and Shanteau (1984) compared 11 accounting students with 10 audit seniors (mid-level professionals) and 10 audit partners; the mean correlations showed a systematic increase from .66 to .76 to .83. Similar results were reported by Messier (1983) in a study of partners with different levels of experience. The highest recorded levels of inter-judge reliability were observed for weather forecasters. Stewart et al. (1997) reported measures of consistency that approached 1.0 for 24-hour temperature forecasts and were slightly lower for 24-hour precipitation forecasts.[10]

Given the high intra-judge and inter-judge correlations observed for auditors and especially for weather forecasters, it is clear that low reliability for expert judges is not a GNAHM conclusion. Some tasks reveal high levels of agreement, both within and across experts.

TRADITIONAL JDM RESEARCH USING LINEAR MODELS

Use of linear regression methods for modelling judgment began in the 1950s (Hammond, 1955; Hoffman, 1960).[11] Much of this early research involved modelling use of the Minnesota Multiphasic Personality Inventory (MMPI) by psychologists for diagnostic purposes (Meehl, 1954). Clinicians claimed that proper use of the 11 MMPI scales required extensive training and experience and that simple linear models (such as a sum of weighted scores) could not capture the richness of the diagnostic process. These claims were challenged in a series of studies showing that:

1. Judgments of experienced clinicians were little better than graduate students (Oskamp, 1967).
2. Statistical diagnosis based on linear regression models outperformed diagnoses made by clinicians (Goldberg, 1969).
3. Diagnoses derived from regression models of the clinicians' own judgments outperformed the clinicians (Goldberg, 1970).
4. The performance of clinicians could be matched by a model that simply added the 11 scores using equal weights (Dawes & Corrigan, 1974).

This work inspired similar research that presented an unflattering view of the abilities of experts.

Common sense implies that the greater knowledge of experts should be reflected in the models of their judgments. However, research has shown that linear models of expert judgments are based on relatively little information. Despite the presence of numerous relevant cues, Hoffman, Slovic, and Rorer (1968) were able to model the judgments of medical radiologists using two to six cues (also see Einhorn, 1974). Ebbesen and Konecni (1975) found only one to three cues were needed to model the bail set by court judges for defendants. Slovic (1969) was able to model stockbrokers' judgments using six to seven cues. Thus, despite the availability of additional information in each case, models of experts in these studies were based on surprisingly few cues. This suggests that experts may make important decisions without adequate attention to all the relevant information. If so, it should not be surprising to find that expert decisions were often viewed as seriously flawed (Dawes, 1988).

In all, the evidence from traditional research revealed that linear models of experts and nonexperts alike contained a small number of significant predictor cues. "A robust finding in research on human judgment is that relatively few cues account for virtually all of the systematic variance" (Reilly & Doherty, 1989, p. 123).

Since the expectation of greater information use by experts was not confirmed, the GNAHM conclusion was drawn that experts are limited decision makers.

INFORMATION-USE HYPOTHESIS

It makes sense that experts should be able to access more information than nonexperts. JDM researchers have interpreted this conjecture to imply that greater expertise should be reflected by a larger number of cues in linear models. Moreover, models of experts should contain more variables than models of novices. This was labelled the Information-Use Hypothesis by Shanteau (1992b).

Is this GNAHM-based conjecture correct? A cursory examination of the literature suggests mixed support. Sometimes models of experts have been found to be based on relatively large numbers of variables, e.g., analyses of livestock judges led to models with 8 to 11 significant cues (Phelps & Shanteau, 1978). But, other studies reported that agricultural expertise could be described with relatively few cues (Trumbo, Adams, Milner, & Schipper, 1962).

One explanation for this seeming contradiction lies in the distinction between relevant and irrelevant information; prior research has not evaluated the degree of relevance of the cues used by experts. But ignoring irrelevant information is exactly what an expert should do, even if it leads to fewer significant cues. Thus, the information-use hypothesis must be modified to state that experts should only be influenced by information that is the most relevant or diagnostic.

Support for this modified information-use perspective was obtained in studies of auditors. Ettenson, Shanteau, and Krogstad (1987) compared the materiality judgments of a proposed account adjustment made by 11 audit managers and 11 accounting students. Multiple regression analyses revealed 2.7 significant cues (out of 8) for managers and 2.6 for students. Although the models contained similar numbers of cues, the pattern of cue weights was quite different. For expert auditors, most weight was placed on one cue with little weight given to other cues. For students, the weighting distribution was flatter: similar weights were given to the various cues. Students failed to recognize that one cue was by far the most relevant. Although the number of significant cues did not differentiate between experts and novices, the ability to identify critical cues did.

Bamber, Tubbs, Gaeth, and Ramsey (1991) compared 94 experienced auditors and 97 inexperienced auditors. Both groups were asked to review two audit cases and to revise their assessment after receiving two additional pieces of information, one relevant and one irrelevant. Both groups responded with appropriate assessment revisions after seeing relevant information. However, inexperienced auditors made an adjustment after seeing irrelevant information, whereas the judgments of experienced auditors were largely unchanged.

The evidence from studies of experts in auditing and elsewhere is consistent: judgments of novices can often be modelled with as many (or sometimes more) cues as experts. These findings do not support the information-use hypothesis — the judgments of experts do not always seem to be based on more information than nonexperts. However, experts do differ from novices in the *type* of information used. What distinguishes an expert is his or her ability to discriminate what is diagnostic from what is nondiagnostic. Nonexperts lack the ability to separate relevant from irrelevant information. It is the type of information used, not the amount, that distinguishes experts and novices (Jacavone & Dostal, 1992).

Prior decision researchers failed to recognize that relevance is *context* dependent. What is diagnostic in one context may be nondiagnostic in another. Only an experienced decision maker can determine what is relevant (and what is not) for a given situation. That is why they are considered experts and why it is so hard for others (including researchers) to understand what they are doing. Thus, the ability to evaluate the diagnosticity of information in a given context is critical to expertise.

TRADITIONAL JDM RESEARCH USING HEURISTICS AND BIASES

In the early 1970s, Tversky and Kahneman developed a paradigm that has dominated the JDM literature since. They argued that humans make use of heuristics rules as mental shortcuts to reduce the cognitive complexity of making probabilistic judgments. "In general, these heuristics are quite useful, but sometimes they lead to severe and systematic errors [biases]" (Tversky & Kahneman, 1974, p. 1124). To demonstrate the application of heuristics, such as *representativeness,* they developed various empirical demonstrations that produced behavior that deviated from normative or correct answers. For instance, they found that student subjects often *ignore base rates* or prior information in making judgments.

The method commonly used to study heuristics and biases involves having undergraduates answer statistics questions presented as word problems. In the well-known *cab problem,* for example, verbal descriptions are provided of prior odds and the likelihood ratio (Kahneman & Tversky, 1972). The correct answer can be computed from an application of Bayes Theorem. Estimates of the posterior odds reveal that subjects behaved as if they *ignored base rates.*

Similar findings have been observed for other word problems. For instance, consider the *lawyer–engineer* problem: "Dick is a 30-year-old man. He is married with no children. A man of high ability and high motivation, he promises to be quite successful in his field. He is well liked by his colleagues." The description was designed to be uninformative about Dick's occupation. When asked whether Dick was more likely to be an engineer or a lawyer, most students judged probability to be .5, even when they were told the overall proportion of engineers was .7 or .3. In other words, students ignored base rate.

Tversky and Kahneman (1974) argued that heuristics and biases are *universal cognitive illusions,* even for experts: "here is much evidence that experts are not immune to the cognitive illusions that affect other people (Kahneman, 1991, p. 1165)." Similarly, Tversky (quoted in Gardner, 1985, p. 360) stated, "whenever there is a simple error that most laymen fall for, there is always a slightly more sophisticated version of the same problem that experts fall for." Thus, Kahneman and Tversky drew the GNAHM conclusion that biased behavior from the use of heuristics applies to both students and experts.[12]

Is the GNAHM argument that experts ignore base rates just like students correct? This question has been studied extensively in auditing. Using a variation of the lawyer–engineer problem, Joyce and Biddle (1981) reported that 132 auditors underutilized base rate information in judging management fraud. They found, however, that professional auditors did better than students. In a follow-up study, however, Holt (1987) concluded that it was the wording of the problem, rather than the use or misuse of base rates, that led to the Joyce and Biddle conclusion.

To see if task familiarity influenced reliance on base rates, Kida (1984) evaluated 73 audit partners and managers; "most auditors attended to both base rates and indicant [case specific] data" (Smith & Kida, 1991, p. 475). Thus, "auditors' behaviors correspond more closely to normative principles than the behaviors of naive student subjects. This increased attention to base rates by auditors seems to be present primarily for tasks that appear to be familiar to them" (Smith & Kida, 1991, p. 480).

To examine the use of heuristics by experts, Shanteau (1989) reviewed 20 studies of audit judgment. These studies examined one or more of the heuristics proposed by Tversky and Kahneman. Overall, the results were often surprisingly close to normative. Consider the following examples: Bamber (1983) found that auditor managers were not only sensitive to the reliability of information, they often overcompensated. Kinney and Uecker (1982) observed results contrary to the anchoring-and-adjustment heuristic in two experiments. Biddle and Joyce (1982) failed to find the effects predicted by the availability heuristics. Gibbins (1977) reported 40 percent of auditors' responses followed representativeness, about half made the normative response, and the remainder were inconsistent with either. Comparable findings were observed by Waller and Felix (1987) and Abdolmohammadi and Wright (1987).

Despite these results, many audit researchers nonetheless emphasized the presence of heuristics. When Biddle and Joyce (1982) failed to support anchoring and adjustment, they concluded, "some as yet unidentified heuristic was at work" (p. 189). Similarly, Ashton (1983, p. 35) states, "despite the mixed nature of the overall results in the heuristics area, findings such as these suggest that auditors often have difficulty understanding the implications of sample information." The possibility that auditors may not have used common heuristics apparently was not considered.

These cases reflect a tendency in auditing (and other areas) to define success of a study by whether biases are observed or not. This "bias" toward emphasizing poor decision behavior also has been reported in psychology (Christensen-Szalanski & Beach, 1984). Shanteau (1989, p. 170) concluded that "heuristics and biases research . . . has been of limited relevance for auditing research."

Smith and Kida (1991) examined 25 studies of heuristics and biases in the accounting and auditing literature. They considered research on each of the heuristics proposed by Kahneman and Tversky. With anchoring and adjustment, for instance, they concluded that auditors show considerable bias when presented with unfamiliar, student-like problems. "However, when the experimental tasks were more analogous to typical audit judgments, and hence more familiar to the [expert] subjects, anchoring results were often not found or were significantly mitigated" (Smith & Kida, 1991, p. 477).

Looking at auditing studies of representativeness, Smith and Kida report: "In experiments asking [accounting] students to perform abstract and unfamiliar tasks, the results more strongly support the earlier findings in the heuristics literature, whereas in experiments asking experienced auditors to complete familiar, job-related tasks, the results . . . correspond more closely to normative principles than the behaviors of naive student subjects" (1991, p. 480).

Smith and Kida concluded the "biases found readily in other research are not evident in judgements of professional auditors" (1991, p. 485). Based on the reviews conducted by both Smith and Kida (1991) and Shanteau (1989), it seems clear that effects observed for students in studies of heuristics and biases do not necessarily generalize to auditing experts.

Similar conclusions have been drawn in other domains. For instance, Schwartz and Griffin (1986, p. 82) reported that use of heuristics in medical decision making is limited. "Decision heuristics . . . appear more likely to create biases in the psychology laboratory than in the [medical] clinic." Other investigators arrived at similar conclusions (Anderson, 1986; Cohen, 1981; Edwards, 1983; Edwards & von Winterfeldt, 1986; Gigerenzer & Hoffrage, 1995; Jungermann, 1983; Shanteau, 1978; Wallsten, 1983; Wright, 1984). As Smith and Kida (1991, p. 486) conclude,

> the use of a particular heuristic or the presence of a bias depends on the decision maker studied, the task performed, and the match between the two. . . . Accordingly, findings from heuristic studies that use students performing generic tasks of limited consequence do not necessarily generalize well to this expert decision making context.

However, not all experts are immune to use of heuristics. Although quite knowledgeable about their fields, some domain experts seem unable to translate that knowledge into appropriate decisions. As with naive students, judgments of probability present a particular difficulty for many experts. For instance, Slovic and Monahan (1995) found that both expert clinicians and naive participants were inappropriately influenced by scale format in making assessments of probability of danger from mental patients.

Obviously, more research is needed to determine the conditions under which experts may be expected to perform well. One possibility (Slovic, personal communication, 1997) is that experts do well in repetitive tasks where there is high-quality feedback—such as weather forecasting and auditing. In contrast, experts do poorly when probability forecasts are required where there is low-fidelity feedback, such as clinical psychology and legal judgment. There is clearly a need to develop an assessment of task characteristics to make some sense out of such differences.

WILHELM WUNDT AND WARD EDWARDS

What direction should JDM research on expertise take to address the questions raised here? For answers, we will turn first to directions laid down a century ago by Wundt. Then we will consider a more modern set of ideas by Ward Edwards.

It is worth recalling that Wundt stressed the role of *skilled participants* in behavioral research. He had no interest in studying the behavior of naive subjects.

While this might be considered an extreme position today, it has merit. If we want to gain maximum insight into a task, we should work with those who have the best perspective on the task. For most tasks in decision making, that implies conducting research with individuals who have the most experience, which often means experts.

Wundt's methodology involved objective measures of internal perception under controlled conditions involving sophisticated laboratory equipment. Our goal today is the same as Wundt's: to make inferences about conscious processes from objective measurements. Wundt's emphasis on *apperception* or selective attention also seems appropriate to understanding how (and when) experts achieve superior performance. Recently, many investigators have concluded that the superiority of domain experts depends on their ability to focus on relevant information (Benner, Tanner, & Chesla, 1996; Ettenson, Shanteau, & Krogstad, 1987; Jacavone & Dostal, 1992; Mosier, 1997; Phelps & Shanteau, 1978; Schwartz & Griffin, 1986; Shanteau, 1992b). One goal in future research should be to learn how experts make these discriminations and to find ways to enhance the process.

As with so much in the judgment-and-decision-making research, Edwards was the first to note the significance of the concerns expressed here. In 1983, he saw the danger to JDM research by overreliance on GNAHM thinking. According to Edwards, investigators operated as if "any individual's mind was as much a representative of the 'generalized normal adult human' as any other" (1983, p. 507). Thus,

> studies of unmotivated subjects and use of non-expert subjects are enshrined in psychological tradition. . . . I have been in disagreement with this line of research and thought for some time, and now I regret my own role in starting it off in the early 1960's. . . . it is time to call a halt.
>
> (1983, p. 508)

Edwards offered two messages. "One is that psychologists have failed to heed the urging of Egon Brunswik (1955) that generalizations from laboratory tasks should consider the degree to which the task . . . resembles or represents the context to which the generalization is made" (1983, p. 509). This parallels Wundt's *principle of psychic relations*—the significance of any mental event is dependent upon context. In short, decisions and choices must be studied in context.

Edwards' second message is that

> experts can in fact do a remarkably good job of assessing and working with probabilities. Two groups of studies seem to show this. One is concerned with weather forecasters. . . . A second group of studies seems to say that physicians also work well with probabilistic reasoning tasks of kinds familiar to them.
>
> (1983, p. 511)

Edwards drew three conclusions:

> One is that, as a practical matter, the rejection of human capacity to perform probabilistic tasks is extremely premature. . . . Obviously, the experimenters themselves, using

tools and expertise, were able to perform such tasks rather well. . . . A second conclusion is that the 'generalized normal adult human mind' is simply the wrong target for research on human intellectual performance. We must recognize that minds vary, that tools can help, that expertise can help.

(1983, p. 511)

His final conclusion is

that we have no choice but to develop a taxonomy of intellectual tasks themselves. Only with the aid of such a taxonomy can we think with reasonable sophistication about how to identify among the myriad types of experts and the myriad types of tasks . . . just exactly what kinds of people and tasks deserve our attention.

(1983, p. 512)

These arguments remain as challenges for JDM researchers today and in the future.

ACKNOWLEDGMENTS

The work described in this chapter was stimulated from a suggestion by Ward Edwards (1927–2005) in 1992. Prior to his death, he provided valuable input at every step as these ideas developed. In a very real sense, therefore, this project is a direct result of Ward's efforts to advance understanding of decision research generally and expertise specifically.

However, the first author's interaction with Edwards predates this project by many years. Our first contact was in 1970 when the first author was a postdoc at the University of Michigan. Shortly after arriving in Ann Arbor, Edwards invited him to give a presentation about a study Shanteau had conducted on probability revision. The results showed that, contrary to the typical version of Bayes Theorem, subjects were averaging present and prior probabilities. Edwards was the first to grasp the meaning of the results. He then offered an alternative version of Bayes that was consistent with averaging.

This example illustrates three of Edward's most valuable traits. First, he consistently provided enthusiastic encouragement to young researchers in judgment and decision making. Second, he understands and promotes new ideas and research directions. And third, he offers insightful reinterpretations that force you to think more deeply.

AUTHOR NOTES

This research was supported, in part, by Grant 96-12126 from the National Science Foundation and by support from the Institute for Social and Behavioral Research at Kansas State University to the first author and by support from the Social Science Research Institute at University of Southern California to the second author. We are grateful to Paul Slovic and Lola Lopes for their helpful comments on the manuscript. We are also indebted to Gerd Gigerenzer and Franz Samelson for their insights into the misconceptions of Wilhelm Wundt held by most psychologists.

The first author would particularly like to thank Franz Samelson, Professor Emeritus at Kansas State University. He provided much of the source material used in the chapter, as well as key insights into the early work of James McKeen Cattell.

NOTES

1. Cattell plays a curious role in this history. After completing his studies with Wundt, he worked for a time in England with Francis Galton (Charles Darwin's half cousin), the originator of research on individual ability. It is sometimes assumed that Cattell was originally inclined to follow Wundt in the study of GNAHM behavior, but that Galton convinced him to investigate individual differences instead. The reality, as the opening section shows, was that Cattell (1885) was already interested in individual differences at the time he was a student in Germany (Sokal, 1981). It is also noteworthy that some of Wundt's other students went on to have productive careers in fields as varied as psychopathology, classical conditioning, perception, child psychology, physiology, applied psychology, psycholinguistics, comparative psychology, statistics, education, and social psychology. These are all fields divergent from Wundt's emphasis on perception and sensation. As Murphy (1929, p. 173) stated, "Wundt's students began even while still with him the study of problems which were both envisaged and prosecuted with originality and relative independence." Thus, Cattell's lifelong focus on individual differences was well within the tradition of Wundt's students pursuing their own objectives.

2. By the mid 19th century, the adjective *phsysiologischen* (physiological) came to mean "experimental." Thus, there was discussion of "physiological pedagogy," "physiological aesthetics," and "physiological psychology" (Blumenthal, 1980). Wundt was inspired by research methods of physiologists, such as Müller and Helmholtz. However, "Wundt saw psychology as a separate science in which it was not necessary to refer to physiological processes. . . . Hence, his psychology was not physiological psychology in the current sense of that term" (Watson, 1979, p. 131).

3. As Gigerenzer notes (personal communication, 1994), the "subjects" in Wundt's research were PhDs or professors. "The longstanding Wundtian tradition (was) that experimental subjects had to be experts." So an argument can be made that the first studies using experts were in fact conducted by Wundt. However, Cattell appears to have been the first to conduct research that examined the domain knowledge of experts. In contrast, Wundt asked his subjects to use their experience to gain further insights into basic psychological processes, such as perception.

4. Wundt's long academic career can be divided into three parts. In the 1860s and 1870s, he studied attention, learning, memory, reaction time, and mental associations in addition to perception. "Out of this work came what is often considered the most important book in the history of psychology, '*Grundzüge der Physiologischen Psychologie*' (*Principles of Physiological Psychology*), published in two parts in 1873 and 1874" (Schultz, 1969, p. 45). In his middle career, during the 1880s, Wundt turned his efforts to philosophical psychology, with books entitled *Logic, Ethic,* and *System of Philosophy.* Starting in the 1890s, Wundt's final project was to create social psychology (Miller, 1962, p. 23). He did this through 10 volumes on *Völkerpsychologie* (*Ethnic Psychology*) covering the study

of languages, art, myths, social customs, law, morals, and culture. Thus, Wundt's actual career was far broader than the narrow stereotypic view typically taught to American psychology students.

5. Titchener was responsible for other "myths of origin" concerning Wundt. Titchener advocated a methodology based on introspective techniques under carefully controlled conditions. "To ensure his students' accuracy in describing their consciousness experiences, Titchener drilled them in what he called 'hard introspective labor.' Certain introspections were defined as correct, and certain others as in error, with the final authority being Titchener himself" (Hothersall, 1984, p. 105). Titchener considered most ordinary untrained (or common-sense) observations "worthless;" they were "usually inaccurate" and almost involved what he called the *stimulus error*—confusing the mental process with the object being observed.

Although Titchener attributed his methodology to Wundt, "Titchener's form of introspection was quite different from Wundt's. . . . Titchener used detailed, qualitative, subjective reports of the subjects' mental activities during the act of introspection" (Schultz & Schultz, 1987, p. 90). This contrasted with Wundt's reliance on laboratory instruments and his focus on objective quantitative measurements, such as reaction time. Wundt's label for his technique is *selbst-beobachtung* or "self-observation." This term is often translated as "introspection," an unfortunate choice because it implies "a type of armchair speculation, which was certainly not what Wundt meant" (Hothersall, 1984, p. 88). He dismissed introspection as "contemplative mediation that led only to pointless debate and the grossest self-deception" (Wundt, 1904, p. 7).

6. This reflects a trend noted by psychohistorian Samelson (1974) for social scientists to create "myths of origins" to justify present positions as being the inevitable course of history. Obviously, psychology is not immune to the development of, and belief in, these myths.

7. See Gigerenzer (1993) for a discussion of how psychologists misinterpreted the arguments of statisticians, e.g., the current reification of null hypothesis significance testing in psychology.

8. As pointed out by Cronbach (1960) in his essay, "The Two Disciplines of Scientific Psychology," a schism separates two branches of behavioral research. On the one hand, laboratory researchers focus on controlled experimentation looking for global effects—the "Wundt tradition." On the other hand, individual difference researchers examine variations of behavior within designated groups—the "Galton tradition." Investigators from both perspectives view the breach as having historical justification. The following excerpt from Kelly (1967, pp. 87–88) discusses the schism:

> The early experimental psychologists were primarily concerned with discovery of general laws to describe the exact relationships between variables. . . . In their search for general laws, they were looking for relationships that are true for all persons. To the extent that individual differences among subjects showed up in the results of an experiment, they were regarded as errors rather than phenomena of intrinsic interest. Even today, the most widely used statistical technique—analysis of variance—for inferring that a true difference exists between groups of subjects tests the differences of means and overlooks marked individual differences among the members of each group.
>
> By contrast, following the lead of Galton in England and James McKeen Cattell in the United States, another group of psychologists became intrigued with the range of variety of individual differences, the origins of such differences, and the relation among these differences. Unfortunately, there was all too little communication between the two groups of psychologists. Each tended to develop its own theories, methods, and body of knowledge.

Both approaches, however, accepted the basic GNAHM argument. Experimental researchers focus on average results; outlier behavior is generally excluded from the group averages. Individual difference researchers, while sensitive to subject variation, focus on distributions of scores; normal distributions are assumed with an emphasis on modal behavior. In their own ways, both experimental and individual difference researchers are concerned about the characteristics of groups of subjects. In this partition, there is no clear home for research on experts.

9. The question of validity (accuracy) will not be pursued because correct answers seldom, if ever, exist in the domains under consideration. Indeed, the concept of a *gold standard* or other absolute point of reference rarely applies to tasks performed by experts; in fact, we often rely on experts precisely because we do not have correct answers (Gigerenzer & Goldstein, 1996; Shanteau, 1992a).
10. Theoretically, inter-judge correlations should not be higher than the intra-judge correlations. Due to the rounding of results, however, some reported inter-judge correlations are slightly higher than comparable values for intra-judge correlations.
11. In what appears the first regression analysis of expert judgment, Wallace (1923) reanalyzed data that Hughes (1917) collected on corn judges. Using a precursor of path analysis, Wallace found that experts relied primarily on ear length; however, kernel weight was most predictive of yields. Despite its historical precedence, this application of the linear model to the study of experts was not followed up.
12. It should be pointed out that base rates or prior information are vitally important for expertise. For an expert to ignore base rates would be a most serious error. To concentrate only on case-specific information is equivalent to making decisions without using past knowledge or experience. This contradicts one of the most fundamental characteristics of experts. Use of prior experience is a defining ingredient of expertise. Indeed, the words "expert" and "experience" have the same Latin root. Thus, when an expert ignores base rates, there is every reason to question his or her competence.

REFERENCES

Abdolmohammadi, M., & Wright, A. (1987). An examination of the effects of experience and task complexity on audit judgments. *Accounting Review, 62(3)*, 1–13.

Anastasi, A. (1968). *Psychological testing* (3rd ed.). New York, NY: Macmillan.

Anderson, N. H. (1986). A cognitive theory of judgment and decision. In B. Brehmer, H. Jungermann, P. Lourens, & G. Sevón (Eds.), *New directions in research on decision making* (pp. 63–108). Amsterdam: North-Holland Press.

Anderson, R. J. (1980). Wundt's prominence and popularity in his later years. *Psychological Research, 42(6)*, 87–101.

Ashton, R. H. (1974). An experimental study of internal control judgments. *Journal of Accounting Research, 12(3)*, 143–157.

——(1983). *Research in audit decision making: Rationale, evidence, and implications.* Vancouver: Canadian Certified General Accountants' Monograph 6.

Bamber, E. M. (1983). Expert judgment in the audit team: A source reliability approach. *Journal of Accounting Research, 21(2)*, 396–412.

Bamber, E. M., Tubbs, R. M., Gaeth, G., & Ramsey, R. J. (1991). Characteristics of audit experience in belief revision. In *USC audit judgment symposium.* Los Angeles, CA: University of Southern California.

Benjamin, L. T., Jr. (1988). *A history of psychology: Original sources and contemporary research.* New York, NY: McGraw-Hill.

Benner, P., Tanner, C. A., & Chesla, C. A. (1996). *Expertise in nursing practice: Caring, clinical judgment, and ethics.* New York, NY: Springer.

Biddle, G. C., & Joyce, E. J. (1982). Heuristics and biases: Some implications for probabilistic inference in auditing. In *Symposium on audit research IV.* Urbana, IL: University of Illinois.

Blumenthal, A. L. (1975). A reappraisal of Wilhelm Wundt. *American Psychologist, 30,* 1081–1086.

——(1979). The founding father we never knew. *Contemporary Psychology, 24(7),* 449–453.

—— (1980). Wilhelm Wundt and early American psychology: A clash of cultures. In R. W. Rieber (Ed.), *Wilhelm Wundt and the making of a scientific psychology* (pp. 121–142). New York, NY: Plenum Press.

Boring, E. G. (1929). *A history of experimental psychology.* New York, NY: Appleton & Co.

——(1950). *A history of experimental psychology* (2nd ed.), New York, NY: Appleton.

Boring, M. D., & Boring, E. G. (1948). Masters and pupils among the American psychologists. *American Journal of Psychology, 61,* 527–34.

Brunswik, E. (1955). Representative design and probabilistic theory in a functional psychology. *Psychological Review, 62(3),* 193–217.

Carroll, J. S., & Payne, J. W. (1976). The psychology of parole decision processes: A joint application of attribution theory and information-processing psychology. In J. S. Carroll & J. W. Payne (Eds.), *Cognition and social psychology* (pp. 13–32). Hillsdale, NJ: Erlbaum.

Cattell, J. M. (1885). The inertia of the eye and the brain. *Brain, 8,* 295–312.

——(1886). The time it takes to see and name objects. *Mind, 11,* 63–65.

——(1887). Experiments on the association of ideas. *Mind, 12,* 68–74.

Christensen-Szalanski, J. J. J., & Beach, L. R. (1984). The citation bias: Fad and fashion in the judgment and decision making literature. *American Psychologist, 39(1),* 75–78.

Cohen, L. J. (1981). Can human irrationality be experimentally demonstrated? *Behavior and Brain Sciences, 4,* 317–331.

Cronbach, L. J. (1960). The two disciplines of scientific psychology. *American Psychologist, 12(11),* 671–684.

Danziger, K. (1980a). Wundt and the two traditions of psychology. In R. W. Rieber (Ed.), *Wilhelm Wundt and the making of a scientific psychology* (pp. 73–88). New York, NY: Plenum.

—— (1980b). Wundt's theory of behavior and volition. In R. W. Rieber (Ed.), *Wilhelm Wundt and the making of a scientific psychology* (pp. 89–105). New York, NY: Plenum Press.

Dawes, R. M. (1988). *Rational choice in an uncertain world.* San Diego, CA: Harcourt Brace Jovanovich.

Dawes, R. M., & Corrigan, B. (1974). Linear models in decision making. *Psychological Bulletin, 81(2),* 95–106.

Ebbesen, E., & Konecni, V. (1975). Decision making and information integration in the courts: The setting of bail. *Journal of Personality and Social Psychology, 32(5),* 805–821.

Edwards, W. (1983). Human cognitive capacities, representativeness, and ground rules for research. In P. Humphreys, O. Svenson, & A. Vari (Eds.), *Analyzing and aiding decision processes* (pp. 507–513). Budapest: Akademiai Kiado.

Edwards, W., & von Winterfeldt, D. (1986). On cognitive illusions and their implications. *Southern California Law Review, 59(2),* 401–451.

Einhorn, H. (1974). Expert judgment: Some necessary conditions and an example. *Journal of Applied Psychology, 59(5),* 562–571.

Ettenson, R., Shanteau, J., & Krogstad, J. (1987). Expert judgment: Is more information better? *Psychological Reports, 60(1),* 227–38.

Fancher, R. E. (1979). *Pioneers of psychology*. New York, NY: Norton.

Gardner, H. (1985). *The mind's new science: A history of the cognitive revolution*. New York, NY: Basic Books.

Gibbins, M. (1977). Human inference, heuristics, and auditors' judgment processes. In *CICA Auditing Research Symposium* (pp. 516–524). Toronto: CICA.

Gigerenzer, G. (1993). The superego, the ego, and the id in statistical reasoning. In G. Keren & C. Lewis (Eds.), *A handbook for data analysis in the behavioral sciences: Methodological issues* (pp. 311–339). Hillsdale, NJ: Erlbaum.

Gigerenzer, G., & Goldstein, D. G. (1996). Reasoning the fast and frugal way: Models of bounded rationality. *Psychological Review, 103(4)*, 650–669.

Gigerenzer, G., & Hoffrage, U. (1995). How to improve Bayesian reasoning without instruction: Frequency formats. *Psychological Review, 102(4)*, 684–704.

Gillis, J., & Schneider, C. (1966). The historical preconditions of representative design. In K. R. Hammond (Ed.), *The psychology of Egon Brunswik* (pp. 204–236). New York, NY: Holt.

Goldberg, L. R. (1959). The effectiveness of clinician's judgments: The diagnosis of organic brain damage from the Bender-Gestalt Test. *Journal of Consulting Psychology, 23*, 25–33.

—— (1968). Simple models or simple processes? Some research on clinical judgments. *American Psychologist, 23(7)*, 483–496.

—— (1969). The search for configural relationships in personality assessment: The diagnosis of psychosis vs. neurosis from the MMPI. *Multivariate Behavioral Research, 4(4)*, 523–536.

—— (1970). Man vs. model of man: A rationale, plus some evidence, for a method of improving clinical inferences. *Psychological Bulletin, 73*, 422–432.

Goldberg, L. R., & Werts, C. E. (1966). The reliability of clinicians' judgments: A multitrait-multimethod approach. *Journal of Consulting Psychology, 30(3)*, 199–206.

Hammond, K. R. (1955). Probabilistic functioning and the clinical method. *Psychological Review, 62(4)*, 255–262.

Hebb, D. O. (1972). *Textbook of psychology* (3rd ed.). Philadelphia, PA: W. B. Saunders.

Heidbreder, E. (1933). *Seven psychologies*. New York, NY: Appleton-Century Co.

Helmstadter, G. C. (1964). *Principles of psychological measurement*. New York, NY: Appleton.

Henrich, J., Heine, S. J., & Norenzayan, A. (2010). The weirdest people in the world? *The Behavioral and brain sciences, 33(2–3)*, 61–83; discussion 83–135.

Hoffman, P. J. (1960). The paramorphic representation of clinical judgment. *Psychological Bulletin, 57(2)*, 255–262.

Hoffman, P., Slovic, P., & Rorer, L. (1968). An analysis of variance model for the assessment of configural cue utilization in clinical judgment. *Psychological Bulletin, 69(5)*, 338–349.

Holt, D. L. (1987). Auditors and base rates revisited. *Accounting, Organizations, and Society, 12(fall)*, 571–578.

Hothersall, D. (1984). *History of psychology*. Philadelphia, PA: Temple University Press.

Hughes, H. D. (1917). An interesting corn seed experiment. *Iowa Agriculturalist, 17*, 424–425.

Jacavone, J., & Dostal, M. (1992). A descriptive study of nursing judgment in assessment and management of cardiac pain. *Advances in Nursing Science, 15*, 54–63.

Joyce, E. J. (1976). Expert judgment in audit program planning. *Journal of Accounting Research, 14*, 29–60.

Joyce, E. J., & Biddle, G. C. (1981). Are auditors' judgments sufficiently regressive? *Journal of Accounting Research, 19(2)*, 329–349.

Jungermann, H. (1983). The two camps of rationality. In R. W. Scholz (Ed.), *Decision making under uncertainty* (pp. 627–641). Amsterdam: Elsevier.

Kahneman, D. (1991). Judgment and decision making: A personal view. *Psychological Science, 2(3),* 142–145.

Kahneman, D., & Tversky, A. (1972). Subjective probability: A judgment of representativeness. *Cognitive Psychology, 3(3),* 430–454.

Kelly, E. L. (1967). *Assessment of human characteristics.* Belmont, CA: Brooks/Cole.

Kendler, H. H. (1987). *Historical foundations of modern psychology.* Philadelphia, PA: Temple University Press.

Kida, T. (1980). An investigation into auditors' continuity and related qualification judgments. *Journal of Accounting Research, 18(2),* 506–523.

—— (1984). The effect of causality and specificity on data use. *Journal of Accounting Research, 22(1),* 145–152.

Kinney, W. R., & Uecker, W. (1982). Mitigating the consequences of anchoring in auditor judgments. *The Accounting Review, 57(1),* 55–69.

Krogstad, J. L., Ettenson, R. T., & Shanteau, J. (1984). Context and experience in auditors' materiality judgments. *Auditing: A Journal of Practice & Theory, 4,* 54–73.

Leahey, T. H. (1987). *A history of psychology: Main currents in psychological thought* (2nd ed.). Englewood Cliffs, NJ: Prentice-Hall.

Libby, R., Artman, J. T., & Willingham, J. J. (1985). Process susceptibility, control risk, and audit planning. *The Accounting Review, 60(April),* 212–230.

Maloney, M. P., & Ward, M. P. (1976). *Psychological assessment: A conceptual approach.* New York, NY: Oxford University Press.

Meehl, P. (1954). *Clinical versus statistical prediction: A theoretical analysis and a review of the evidence.* Minneapolis, MN: University of Minnesota Press.

Messier, W. F. (1983). The effect of experience and firm type on materiality/disclosure judgments. *Journal of Accounting Research, 21(fall),* 611–618.

Miller, G. A. (1962). *Psychology: The science of mental life.* New York, NY: Harper & Row.

Mischel, T. (1970). Wundt and the conceptual foundations of psychology. *Philosophical and Phenomenological Research, 31(1),* 1–26.

Mosier, K. L. (1997). Myths of expert decision making and automated decision aids. In C. Zsambok & G. Klein (Eds.), *Naturalistic decision making* (pp. 319–330). Hillsdale, NJ: Erlbaum.

Murphy, G. (1929). *An historical introduction to modern psychology.* New York, NY: Harcourt, Brace & Co.

Oskamp, S. (1962). The relationship of clinical experience and training methods to several criteria of clinical prediction. *Psychological Monograph, 76* (25).

—— (1965). Overconfidence in case-study judgments. *Journal of Consulting Psychology, 29(June),* 261–265.

—— (1967). Clinical judgment from the MMPI: Simple or complex? *Journal of Clinical Psychology, 23(4),* 411–415.

Phelps, R. H. (1977). Expert livestock judgment: A descriptive analysis of the development of expertise. Unpublished dissertation. Manhattan, KS: Kansas State University.

Phelps, R. H., & Shanteau, J. (1978). Livestock judges: How much information can an expert use? *Organizational Behavior and Human Performance, 21(2),* 209–219.

Reilly, B. A., & Doherty, M. E. (1989). A note on the assessment of self-insight in judgment research. *Organizational Behavior & Human Performance, 21(2),* 123–131.

Rieber, R. W. (1980). *Wilhelm Wundt and the making of a scientific psychology.* New York, NY: Plenum.

Samelson, F. (1974). History, origin myth and ideology: "Discovery" of social psychology. *Journal for the Theory of Social Behavior, 4(2)*, 217–231.

Sargent, S. S., & Stafford, K. R. (1965). *Basic teachings of the great psychologists* (rev ed.). Garden City, NY: Dolphin Books.

Schultz, D. P. (1969). *A history of modern psychology.* San Diego, CA: Harcourt.

Schultz, D. P., & Schultz, S. E. (1987). *A history of modern psychology* (4th ed.). San Diego, CA: Harcourt Brace Jovanovich.

Schwartz, S. & Griffin, T. (1986). *Medical thinking: The psychology of medical judgment and decision making.* New York, NY: Springer-Verlag.

Shanteau, J. (1977). Correlation as a deceiving measure of fit. *Bulletin of the Psychonomic Society, 10(2)*, 134–136.

——(1978). When does a response error become a judgmental bias? *Journal of Experimental Psychology: Human Learning and Memory, 4(6)*, 579–581.

——(1989). Cognitive heuristics and biases in behavioral auditing: Review, comments, and observations. *Accounting, Organizations, and Society, 14(1/2)*, 165–177.

——(1992a). Competence in experts: The role of task characteristics. *Organizational Behavior and Human Decision Processes, 53(2)*, 252–266.

——(1992b). How much information does an expert use? Is it relevant? *Acta Psycholgica, 81(1)*, 75–86.

Shanteau, J., & Stewart, T. R. (1992). Why study expert decision making? Some historical perspectives and comments. *Organizational Behavior and Human Decision Processes, 53(2)*, 95–106.

Slovic, P. (1969). Analyzing the expert judge: A descriptive study of a stockbroker's decision processes. *Journal of Applied Psychology, 53(August)*, 255–263.

Slovic, P., & Monahan, J. (1995). Probability, danger, and coercion: A study of risk perception and decision making in mental health law. *Law and Human Behavior, 19(1)*, 49–65.

Smith, J. F., & Kida, T. (1991). Heuristics and biases: Expertise and task realism in auditing. *Psychological Bulletin, 109(3)*, 472–489.

Sokal, M. M. (1981). *An education in psychology: James McKeen Cattell's journal and letters from Germany and England, 1880–1888.* Cambridge, MA: MIT Press.

Stewart, T. R., Roebber, P. J., & Bosart, L. F. (1997). The importance of the task in analyzing expert judgment. *Organizational Behavior and Human Decision Processes, 69*, 205–219.

Titchener, E. B. (1908). *The psychology of feeling and attention.* New York, NY: Macmillan.

——(1910). *A textbook of psychology.* New York, NY: Macmillan.

——(1916). *A beginner's psychology.* New York, NY: Macmillan.

——(1921). Wilhelm Wundt. *American Journal of Psychology, 32*, 161–178.

——(1923). *An outline of psychology.* New York, NY: Macmillan.

Trumbo, D., Adams, C., Milner, M., & Schipper, L. (1962). Reliability and accuracy in the inspection of hard red winter wheat. *Cereal Science Today, 7*, 62–71.

Tversky, A., & Kahneman, D. (1974). Judgment under uncertainty: Heuristics and biases. *Science, 185(4157)*, 1124–1131.

Wallace, H. A. (1923). What is in the corn judge's mind? *Journal of the American Society of Agronomy, 15(7)*, 300–324.

Waller, W. S., & Felix, W. L., Jr. (1987). Auditors' covariation judgment. *The Accounting Review, 62*, 275–292.

Wallsten, T. S. (1983). The theoretical status of judgmental heuristics. In R. W. Scholz (Ed.), *Decision making under uncertainty* (pp. 21–38). Amsterdam: North-Holland.

Watson, R. I. (1968). *The great psychologists: From Aristotle to Freud* (2nd ed.). Philadelphia, PA: J. B. Lippincott Co.

——(1979). *Basic writings in the history of psychology*. New York, NY: Oxford.

Wright, G. (1984). *Behavioral decision theory: An introduction*. Beverly Hills, CA: Sage.

Wundt, W. (1873). *Grundzüge der physiologischen psychologie*. Leipzig: Engelmann.

——(1892). *Vorlesungen über die menschen und theirseele* (trans. M. S. Creighton & E. B. Titchener). *Lectures on human and animal psychology*. New York, NY: Macmillan.

——(1904). *Principles of physiological psychology* (4th ed.) (trans. E. B. Titchener). New York, NY: Macmillan.

Part II

Cognitive Consistency and Inconsistency

2

Cognitive Consistency

Cognitive and Motivational Perspectives

ANNE-SOPHIE CHAXEL AND J. EDWARD RUSSO

Theories of cognitive consistency emerged over a half century ago and have since generated numerous variations and controversies. Past research typically focused on understanding circumstances in which inconsistencies arise and how people recover from them. In the present chapter, we first review the seminal paradigm of cognitive dissonance theory and the major theories it spawned. We then integrate this past work into a unified framework. We subsequently build on this current framework and draw on new theoretical and methodological advances in social and cognitive psychology to extend it. We propose that cognitive consistency can be both a goal, or a desired outcome that people are motivated to reach, and also a cognitive procedure that helps to achieve that goal. In other words, we posit that for consistency to be attained, an associated cognitive procedure must work in parallel to restructure units of information into a consistent interpretation. Recognizing this dual nature of cognitive consistency, we propose different methods for priming cognitive consistency as a goal and as a cognitive procedure. Successful priming was verified by a lexical decision task and by self-reported activation levels. To confirm the goal–cognitive procedure distinction, a delay was inserted after the priming manipulations. For all observed effects, the delay produced the standard temporal pattern of an increase when consistency is a goal and a decrease when it is a cognitive procedure. The value of the two methods is then demonstrated by predicted increases in two biases: the predecisional distortion of information and selective perception.

 ew people would disagree that individuals strive for consistency in its fundamental sense of a coherent understanding of their surroundings. The alternative, some level of incoherence, ranges from discomforting to alarming. For basic tasks like early humans' survival-oriented predictions, seeking consistency in the surrounding environment must have been critical. For intellective tasks that are commonly faced today, like decisions and judgments, finding consistency between incoming information and what individuals already know would seem to be essential to successfully integrating that information (Nickerson, 2008; Thagard, 2006).

Consistency theories presume the existence of an interconnected system or network of beliefs in one or more domains that interact with each other. Beliefs can complement each other (e.g., "I am for gun control" and "I believe the Second Amendment should be interpreted more narrowly"), or conflict with each other (e.g., "I am for gun control" and "I believe that guns are needed for self-defense"). When they conflict, cognitive instability arises. This instability is presumed to create a state of discomfort that drives a change in one or both of the beliefs, in order to restore some of the lost cognitive balance within the system.

Cognitive consistency theories emerged in the 1950s, at least under that label, and flourished during the next two decades. However, as measured by the number of consistency-related publications, they then declined drastically. By 1983, Abelson could title an article, "Whatever Became of Cognitive Consistency?" Because of several shifts in research focus, this decline was more apparent than real. The term "cognitive consistency" almost disappeared only because the phenomenon itself was interpreted from different perspectives and given different labels, such as "dissonance," "balance," and "coherence."

In this chapter, our first objective is to provide an integrative overview of cognitive consistency theories, without focusing on any one specific label. Our conceptualization incorporates not only the causes, moderators, and consequences of an inconsistency between beliefs but also makes more explicit the processes associated with the perception of an inconsistency. Our second objective stems from the recognition that the variety and richness of consistency theories have not been matched by methods for testing these theories. To this end we introduce two priming methods that enable tests of the role of cognitive consistency in phenomena of interest. We empirically validate these methods and then demonstrate their potential value by applying them to the phenomenon of expectations' influence on perception.

COGNITIVE CONSISTENCY THEORIES

The common ancestor of all theories of cognitive consistency is Gestalt theory (Wertheimer, 1922, 1923). It focused on the formation of perceptual units that are based on the functional principle of holism, or the requirement that the individual units form a coherent whole. When they do not, even if due only to a single unusual or unexpected component, attention is automatically drawn to that component and an active process of comprehension begun. Analogously, cognitive consistency theories have postulated that beliefs are part of a system of dynamic relationships that should be coherent and that a dissonant belief will elicit discomfort, which the individual will try to reduce.

The seminal idea that systems of beliefs naturally strive for consistency was manifest, over time, in four main research streams. We label them, in historical order, cognitive consistency, self-theory, meaning maintenance, and individual differences. All four theoretical perspectives focus on understanding when inconsistencies occur and how people deal with them. After briefly reviewing the main emphasis of each stream, we proffer an integrative framework augmented by a new emphasis on process.

The Cognitive Consistency Stream

The major works within the cognitive consistency stream are balance theory (Heider, 1946, 1958), congruity theory (Osgood & Tannenbaum, 1955), symmetry theory (Newcomb, 1953), and the theory of cognitive dissonance (Festinger, 1957, 1964). Balance, congruity, and symmetry theories all focus on structures of liking and disliking among people. They demonstrate how people tend to dislike interpersonal conflict or even ambivalence. In each of these theories, consistency was seen as a desirable end-state that individuals strive to achieve.

The first of these, Heider's balance theory (Heider, 1946, 1958), described potential relationships within a simple system composed of two people, p and o, and a social entity of mutual interest, x. The resulting triad was said to be consistent if any set of affective relations among p, o, and x is balanced (p likes o, o likes x, p likes x; or p dislikes o, p dislikes x, o likes x; or p dislikes o, p likes x, o dislikes x; or p likes o, p dislikes x, o dislikes x). Conversely, the triad was said to be inconsistent if the set of relations among elements of the triad is unbalanced by reversing any one of the relationships above. In any of the latter cases, a tension emerges and p is driven to restore a state of affective balance by modifying his or her attitude toward o or x.

This seminal idea was further enriched by both the congruity theory of Osgood and Tannenbaum (1955) and the symmetry theory of Newcomb (1953). Osgood and Tannenbaum's domain of interest was persuasion and communication. As a result, Heider's triad (p, x, o) was associated in congruity theory with an audience, a message source, and a concept. The mechanism is the same as in Heider's theory: An audience that has inconsistent preferences for the message source and the concept (for instance, liking the source but disliking its message) is driven to restore balance. Congruity theory refined balance theory in two ways. First, instead of being only directional (like or dislike), as in Heider's work, the measurement of the attitudes of p toward x and o was quantified on a semantic differential scale. The second change required that, to restore balance, both the attitudes toward o and x change, not only one or the other.

Newcomb (1953) then enabled the extent of attitude change of the individual p toward o and x to depend on the strength of p's liking of o. In other words, Newcomb defended the idea that a tension toward symmetry makes the two individuals p and o defined in Heider's work likely to communicate in order to align their attitudes toward x. As a result, the drive to restore consistency within the social (i.e. multiperson) system was predicted to be higher as the bonds between o and p became stronger.

The last and best known theory in this seminal stream is Festinger's theory of cognitive dissonance (1957). For Festinger, dissonance, an uncomfortable state, is triggered when an individual holds two cognitions that are inconsistent. Four phenomena illustrate this idea. The first is the free-choice paradigm (e.g., Brehm, 1956), in which the positive aspects of a rejected alternative and the negative aspects of a chosen alternative comprise the dissonant elements of a decision. A decision creates commitment to a chosen alternative, which results in a motivational drive to reduce dissonant elements in order to avoid the discomfort associated with dissonance. Second is the belief-disconfirmation paradigm, which observes attitude change, and in particular proselytism, within a group whose beliefs are disconfirmed by an external event (e.g., Festinger, Riecken, & Schachter, 1956). Third is the effort-justification paradigm (e.g., Aronson & Mills, 1959), which states that dissonance can arise between the effort invested in a task and its actual outcome (for instance, going through a severe initiation to be accepted within a group that ends up being boring). Individuals would then change their attitude toward the outcome in order to make it consonant with the invested effort (e.g., seeing the group as not boring after all). Last is the induced-compliance paradigm (e.g., Festinger & Carlsmith, 1959), in which participants are asked to behave in a counter-attitudinal way (e.g., writing a counter-attitudinal essay) and then change their attitudes to better fit their required behavior.

While Heider, Newcomb, Osgood, and Tannenbaum focused exclusively on affective and social representations, Festinger broadened the scope of consistency theories by explicitly including cognitive representations. Dissonance was not seen only as arising from an affective inconsistency between people and objects or beliefs, but also from the conflict between two or more beliefs within the same individual. This version of cognitive dissonance became the dominant theory from which all revisions derived.

The Self-Theory Stream

The apparent disappearance of cognitive consistency theories from research in the early 1970s to which we alluded above was explained by a reinterpretation of cognitive consistency through the lens of the self-concept. The five theoretical perspectives in this stream were all major revisions of Festinger's theory. They tended to focus on the two questions: Is cognitive dissonance a motivational state, that is, a "force directed toward goal fulfillment" (Liberman & Dar, 2009, p. 278)? What is the role played by self-beliefs in the experience of dissonance?

Two of the five theories dismiss all motivational underpinnings to the experience of dissonance. According to the *self-perception view* (Bem, 1967), people infer their attitudes (which are malleable) from their behavior. As a result, people change their attitudes after a behavior that is discrepant with their previous attitudes not because they experience a discomfort-driven need for consistency but because they adjust their attitudes on the basis of their behavior. According to impression management theory (Tedeschi, Schlenker, & Bonoma, 1971), people in dissonance studies neither experience dissonance nor actually change their attitude toward the target object. Instead, they just want to appear coherent to the experimenter. These two accounts, which radically reinterpret Festinger's results, reject the status of cognitive dissonance as a motivational state. However, their acceptance has been hindered by their trouble explaining why arousal mediates the relationship between an inconsistency episode and behavioral consequences (Croyle & Cooper, 1983; Elliot & Devine, 1994; Zanna & Cooper, 1974).

Three less radical reinterpretations of Festinger's (1957) cognitive dissonance theory complete the self-theory stream. The self-consistency view (Aronson, 1968) postulated that people think and behave in a way that is consistent with their conception of themselves. The overarching goal is to achieve consistency between well-founded self-beliefs and incoming information (both cognitive and affective). Using this basic idea, Aronson (1968) emphasized that cognitive dissonance is more likely to occur when the inconsistency challenges our self-view as stable, competent, and moral. Aronson was followed by two related theories, Cooper and Fazio's "New Look" theory (1984), and Steele's self-affirmation theory (1988). According to the New Look view, dissonance is triggered when a behavior represents a violation of societal or normative standards that drives aversive consequences. In the classic instructed compliance paradigm, participants lie to a confederate by saying that a dull task is interesting and then experience dissonance between their behavior (saying "the task is interesting") and their corresponding belief (they know full well that the task is actually dull). In contrast, New Look theorists see dissonance arising because the participant feels personally responsible for deceiving the confederate. Finally, according to the self-affirmation view, a discrepant behavior threatens a sense of self-worth. As a result, when dissonance is experienced, people are motivated to restore their personal integrity by focusing on other positive aspects of the self, such as important values and positive social comparisons. In the boring task scenario above, lying threatens the self-integrity of the participant, who is then more likely to engage in compensatory actions to regain self-esteem.

In subsequent years, researchers focused on understanding how self-beliefs trigger self-expectations about one's thoughts and behavior, which may in turn conflict with an actual state of the self (Thibodeau & Aronson, 1992). The central role of expectations in the experience of dissonance was also highlighted by Stone and Cooper (2001), who proposed a self-expectancy framework that was intended to integrate self-consistency, New Look, and self-affirmation theories. They proposed that dissonance begins when people exhibit a behavior and then assess that behavior against self-standards. These standards can be personal (self-beliefs in the self-consistency and self-affirmation theories) or normative (as in the New Look theory).

The Meaning Maintenance Stream

The idea that a violation of expectations drives a motivational force for reconciling the perceived mismatch was reinterpreted by Heine, Proulx, and Vohs (2006). This stream of research emphasizes the following questions: "Why do we seek to relate objects to each other and to the self?" and "Why do we retain mental representations that are internally consistent?"

Heine et al. (2006) introduced a revised consistency model that focuses on the maintenance of meaning. In this revised model, people are assumed to expect and prefer a world that is meaningful and predictable. As a result they hold mental representations that are composed of expected relations between elements of thoughts and which are intended to give meaning to the world. When meaning is threatened, individuals work toward its restoration. In other words, if an expected relation is disconfirmed or challenged, such as by an inconsistency between expectations and experience, meaning is threatened. This, in turn, triggers a reaffirmation process, also labeled "fluid compensation" (McGregor, Zanna, Holmes, & Spencer, 2001; Steele, 1988). This model shares the same foundation as cognitive consistency and self-theories yet is differentiated by the inclusion of the maintenance of meaning as the driving force.

The Individual Differences Stream

This last of the four cognitive consistency streams focuses on individual differences. Are there stable differences in the extent to which people strive to reconcile dissonant beliefs, feelings, and behaviors, and, if so, can those differences be assessed?

An early attempt to assess individual differences in aversion to cognitive inconsistency is the need for consistency (NfC) scale of Cialdini, Trost, and Newsom (1995). This scale has been applied mainly to social phenomena. For instance, one of the consequences of a strong NfC is that individuals tend to orient their attention to the past more than to the present, in order to achieve a better match between past behavior and a current choice (Cialdini et al., 1995). Another consequence of a high preference for consistency is a stronger inclination to punish transgressions of laws (e.g., Nail, Bedell, & Little, 2003). High-NfC individuals give greater weight to prior entry variables (e.g., previous expectations, commitments, choices) and adjust their subsequent responses accordingly. Low-NfC individuals give less weight to the implications of such variables in their judgments.

A UNIFIED FRAMEWORK

The Existing Framework

We have argued that the apparent disappearance of the early cognitive consistency theories was, in fact, a dispersed evolution into different research streams. Each focused on specific contexts and, partly as a consequence, on specific features of cognitive consistency. We now integrate the various research streams into the unified framework depicted in Figure 2.1.

Shown in bold are the three basic elements of any dissonance theory: the triggering inconsistency, the resulting dissonance, and the individual's response. From the three research streams that followed cognitive dissonance, we draw four moderators (Baron & Kenny, 1986). That is, these four factors affect the strength of the relation between the initiating cause (an episode of inconsistency) and the immediate consequence (felt dissonance).

Maybe the most straightforward of these moderators is individual differences, as illustrated by the work of Cialdini (1995). The more individuals are averse to inconsistencies, the more likely they are to experience dissonance when confronted by one.

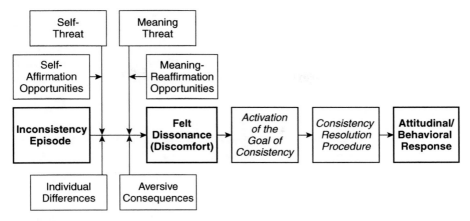

Figure 2.1   Conceptual framework.

The second moderator is the New Look theory's aversive consequences. Because they have been shown to increase the predictive power of cognitive dissonance theory sometimes but not always (Aronson, Fried, & Stone, 1991; Fried & Aronson, 1995; Stone, Aronson, Crain, Winslow, & Fried, 1994), we also consider them to be a moderator of the strength of the main effect of the inconsistency on felt dissonance.

The third element is self-consistency theory's threat to the self. This theory has usually been considered a competing explanation of Festinger's results and, in practice, has nearly replaced cognitive dissonance theory.[1]

However, Aronson himself claimed that his intention was only to show conditions under which the predictive power of the original theory was stronger rather than conditions necessary to the experience of dissonance: "dissonance is greatest and clearest when it involves not just any two cognitions but, rather, a cognition about the self and a piece of our behavior that violates that self-concept" (1992, p. 305). In other words, self-beliefs do not need to be involved to experience dissonance, but the impact of the inconsistency episode on the felt dissonance is stronger when it threatens the self. Again, this is the definition of a moderator. Furthermore, as already noted by Stone and Cooper (2001) in a framework focused on self-theories, when self-affirmation opportunities are made salient (for instance, by reaffirming core values), the impact of the self-threat on the felt dissonance is weaker. This makes such self-affirmation opportunities a moderator of the impact of self-threat on felt dissonance.

The fourth and last moderator is the presence of a meaning threat. Because dissonance theories have never been explicitly discussed by Heine et al. (2006), this is the most speculative aspect of our framework. The question is whether inconsistency is triggered *only* when meaning is threatened (which would make it a necessary condition) or is triggered more strongly when meaning is threatened (which would make it a moderator). If meaning disruption was a necessary condition for feeling dissonance, it would then disqualify inconsistencies that do not directly threaten meaning, such as a mismatch between two existing cognitive elements (e.g., "I am a smoker" and "Smoking causes cancer"). It seems both fairer and more conservative to think that expectations and experience are two types of cognitive elements that may impact the strength of the feeling of discomfort. Thus, we also place meaning threat as a moderator of the relationship between the inconsistency episode and felt dissonance.

In 1992, Aronson (p. 307) stated:

> In the past few years, a plethora of minitheories has sprung up . . . Each of these theories is a worthy and interesting effort at combining cognition and motivation, but each has a limited scope; in my judgment, with a little work, every one of them can be contained under the general rubric of dissonance theory.

Compatible with Aronson's view, our proposed framework claims that a single direct effect (an inconsistency episode) accounts for cognitive dissonance, as stated in the earliest version of the theory. However, we fully recognize that the strength of the effect may vary with the type of conflicting cognitive elements, including attitudes, behaviors, beliefs (notably self-beliefs and expectations), and experience. Situations that decrease one's sense of self-worth, produce aversive social consequences, or threaten one's sense of meaning may also contribute to a stronger feeling of dissonance.

We now turn to extending our basic framework by explicating the process by which consistency influences attitude/beliefs and behaviors. We believe not only that process is important to any adequate theory but also that its consideration can lead to the kind of experimental paradigms that may provide novel tests of the theory.

Extending the Framework

For 50 years, the existing literature has focused on identifying the conditions that enable or increase dissonance (as conceptualized by Festinger) and, as a result, when attitude change would occur. In this section we address three questions that have received far less attention. First, what are the alternative conceptualizations of cognitive consistency? Second, how does cognitive consistency affect information processing, that is, what is its downstream impact on cognition? Finally, what are the available methods for measuring and manipulating the level of consistency that individuals strive for? To this purpose, we propose to extend the existing conceptual framework by adding an explicit process to it. We introduce and support this extension by offering answers to the three questions above in the form of propositions.

First, regarding the conceptualizations of cognitive consistency, we propose that consistency may be a cognitive goal (Proposition 1). Then, we claim that the goal of cognitive consistency's downstream impact on cognition is to trigger a specific cognitive procedure, or mindset, designed to increase the internal state of consistency (Proposition 2). Finally, we propose new methods to elevate and measure levels of cognitive consistency (Proposition 3).

Proposition 1: Cognitive Consistency Is a Goal   In every theory reviewed above, an inconsistency generates a striving to restore consistency. As Tannenbaum (1968, p. 344) stated, "some degree of consistency and equilibrium . . . [is] essential for reasons of parsimony and economy of effort, as well as to allow for the predictability of, and hence adaptability to, subsequent encounters." We posit that this amounts to assuming that consistency is a desirable end-state or, equivalently, a goal. When an inconsistency is detected, we engage in cognitive actions to return to a more acceptable level of cognitive consistency (a level that may vary between situations and individuals).

Research over the past ten years has revealed a great deal about the nature and behavior of goals (e.g., Ferguson & Porter, 2009; Foster, Liberman, & Friedman, 2007). Goals are cognitive constructs represented in memory that motivate and direct action. Although controversy remains over the definition of a goal, we shall adopt the common view, that a goal is a "cognitive representation of a desired end-point that impacts evaluations, emotions, and behaviors" (Fishbach & Ferguson, 2007, p. 491). Goals contain information about their end-states that can vary in abstractness (consistency being an abstract goal) and include a variety of behaviors, plans, and objects that enable one to reach the end-state. For instance, the achievement goal might include context-specific planning behaviors, such as a study schedule to help achieve success on an exam. Similarly, the cognitive consistency goal might include cognitive procedures that may help its successful achievement.

Proposition 2: The Goal of Consistency Has an Associated Cognitive Procedure, or Mindset, for Achieving It   The research streams reviewed here all focus on understanding how inconsistencies arise and how people recover from them. Yet as early as the 1960s, a different and entirely parallel stream of research in cognitive psychology emerged, focusing on understanding how a consistency property governed the cognitive system. In 1968, McGuire lamented that the existing cognitive consistency theories studied consistency as an end and not as a means for throwing light on thought processes (as he claimed they should). This disinclination to follow in the steps of earlier cognitive consistency theorists did not come from a disagreement with the content of their research, but from a different view on what topic is "most deserving of attention" (McGuire, 1968, p. 141):

> I have obviously been rather disappointed and regretful about the main directions which consistency theory has taken . . . Where I would have taken the need for consistency for granted and used it to map the cognitive system, the subsequent work has largely taken the cognitive system for granted, and tried to clarify the need for consistency. It has sidestepped the cognitive structure question.

McGuire's research agenda contributed to subsequent research on coherence-driven mechanisms of constraint satisfaction (e.g., Read & Miller, 1994; Shultz & Lepper, 1996; Simon & Holyoak, 2002; Spellman, Ullman, & Holyoak, 1993; Thagard, 1989). These models describe how belief systems are modified by incoming information in order to eliminate inconsistencies. In coherence-driven theories of constraint satisfaction, consistency is seen not only as a desirable end-state but also, or even foremost, as a property of the cognitive system that organizes our current thoughts and processes incoming information. In other words, a cognitive consistency goal is seen as associated to a specific cognitive procedure that, as much as possible, eliminates inconsistencies and settles systems of beliefs into consistent states. This conceptualization matches the concept of mindset as a cognitive procedure or sequence of actions.[2] (For a review, see Wyer & Xu, 2010.)

A mindset is defined as a cognitive or behavioral procedure that is associated with a particular goal. For instance, Xu and Wyer (2008) studied the comparison mindset, that is, the cognitive procedure associated with the goal of comparing objects. A characteristic of mindsets is that, once activated, they are more likely to be used subsequently, even in a different domain, and even without the activation of their associated goal. Xu and Wyer (2008) have shown that comparing animals makes people more likely in a subsequent task to complete a purchase because they have automatically started to compare the available products. Similarly, we propose that the goal of consistency is associated to a specific cognitive procedure, or mindset of consistency, by which disparate elements are connected to form a more coherent entity. Furthermore, once activated, it is more likely to remain active in the short term and thereby be used in a new domain and independently of the activation of the goal of consistency.

Propositions 1 and 2 have implicitly argued that consistency theories rely on two dimensions: a motivational dimension and a cognitive dimension. The motivational element (goal activation driven by an inconsistency) directly triggers a process stored in memory that can reconcile the inconsistent elements (mindset activation). The process by which the mindset operates then, in turn, drives an attitudinal and/or behavioral change. This change may or may not be sufficient to attain the goal. If it is not, the goal remains active and prompts further cognitive actions, until the goal is attained or is abandoned.

These two propositions naturally prompt the question of the relation between the goal and mindset conceptualizations of consistency. A mindset is a procedure activated by a goal as a means to achieve it. When a goal is frequently activated, its subsequent mindset becomes closely associated with it. Then this goal–mindset association can be activated bidirectionally so that activating the mindset also activates its associated goal (Wyer & Xu, 2010). This is necessarily only speculative in the domain of cognitive consistency. However, it need not remain so. We suggest that understanding how the goal and mindset versions of consistency operate may best be achieved empirically.

Proposition 3: Consistency Levels Can Be Elevated and Measured   Our

third focus is methods. Obviously new methods can enable tests that were impossible before their development, and it is just such methods that we introduce now. However, we also recognize that the influence of methods, though often powerful, is sometimes not obvious. We earlier quoted Greenwald and Ronis' (1978, p. 56) plaint that cognitive dissonance research was occluded by the "self" stream. Here is the continuation of their words, "The ego-related cognitive processes, being relatively easy to observe, may have pulled the theory in their direction. Had effort been directed instead at achieving more precise methods of testing the original dissonance formulation, perhaps more support for it would have been obtained." Fortunately, we now have methods that were not available decades ago.

PRIMING CONSISTENCY AS A GOAL

The most familiar goal-activation methods involve some form of semantic priming. Participants' exposure to goal-related words leads them to engage in goal-congruent behavior. For instance, solving scrambled sentences with words related to achievement activates concepts related to achievement and subsequently impacts behavior (Fishbach & Ferguson, 2007). This method has already been successfully applied in research on consistency (Russo, Carlson, Meloy, & Yong, 2008). More precisely, participants were subliminally primed with concepts related to consistency (e.g., "congruence," "compatible"), which in turn impacted how participants processed information in a second and unrelated task. However, we note that the power of semantic priming to always drive a motivational state has recently been questioned (Sela & Shiv, 2009). Semantic methods may sometimes prime only the semantic network associated to the target goal without inducing a real motivation to pursue that goal.

The priming of an actual motivational state requires a difference between the actual state and a desired state (Miller, Galanter, & Pribram, 1960; Sela & Shiv, 2009; Zeigarnik, 1967). A behavioral task that triggers such a discrepancy should prime the goal to reduce it. This amounts to behavioral (rather than semantic) priming of a goal. Note that this is actually what is done in all cognitive dissonance studies. For instance, participants in an induced-compliance paradigm write a counter-attitudinal essay, which is a behavior that creates a state of inconsistency and motivates participants to restore consistency.

If a motivation to reach the goal is successfully primed, then the goal activation increases when a delay frustrates goal attainment (Bargh, Gollwitzer, Lee-Chai, Barndollar, & Troetschel, 2001; Fishbach & Ferguson, 2009; Förster et al., 2007):

> When [a goal] has been activated, the person will increase his or her efforts for a while until the goal has been met (. . .). In contrast, when mere semantic knowledge (. . .) has been activated, that activation should rapidly decay over time such that the person may quickly show less evidence of that activated knowledge in perception or judgment.
>
> (Fishbach & Ferguson, 2009, p. 493)

Thus, a test of successful goal activation should include two measurement times, one immediately after the priming and one after a delay of a few minutes. The delay condition is expected to yield greater activation than the no-delay condition.

Interestingly, long before the current study of goals had rigorously identified the impact of a delay, Walster and Berscheid (1968) dedicated an entire chapter in *Theories of Cognitive Consistency: A Sourcebook* to the effects of time on cognitive consistency. They highlighted how inserting a delay between the experimental manipulation and the measurement of the dependent variable actually decreased the variability in the data:

> A delay between the manipulation of dissonance and the measurement of the resulting dissonance reduction was incorporated into many dissonance studies. Researchers found that such a delay increased their predictive ability. Since time is not itself an independent variable in any of the consistency theories, this delay is not necessary theoretically. But in practice such a delay is often essential.
>
> (Walster & Berscheid, 1968, p. 599)

Without the benefit of what we now know about the temporal pattern of goal activation, Walster and Berscheid seem to have described consistency as a goal including the value of a delay to strengthening the manipulation.

PRIMING CONSISTENCY AS A MINDSET

Activating consistency as a mindset means finding a task that requires the repeated use of a procedure that achieves consistency (Wyer & Xu, 2010). Repetition of such a task should build momentum for that consistency-achieving process. Then, when subsequently presented with an unrelated task that can be completed by applying a consistency mindset (i.e. procedure), performance in this second task should be elevated. One plausible priming manipulation is solving a set of anagrams. As participants repeatedly rearrange letters to make a legitimate word (e.g., EBLTA to TABLE), they may be engaged in a consistency-based process that activates more general consistency-oriented procedures. More specifically, the required cognitive restructuring activated by the anagram task (obtained by rearranging disparate letters into a consistent string of letters) may in turn activate the restructuring procedure needed to process information in a consistent manner. In other words, the objective of the anagram task is not to activate cognitive consistency per se but to activate a cognitive restructuring procedure by which disparate elements (letters or units of information) are reorganized to produce a new interpretation.

A mindset also has a characteristic temporal pattern of activation, but one that differs from that of a goal. A delay of a few minutes is more likely to cause the activation to dissipate, although at an unknown rate. As a consequence, if consistency is a mindset and its activation is measured twice, the delay condition should exhibit weaker results than the no-delay condition. We have seen that the reverse pattern, stronger results after a delay, should be observed when consistency is activated as a motivational state (i.e. as a goal). Thus, the temporal pattern of activation distinguishes goal activation from mindset activation.

MEASURING THE ACTIVATION LEVEL OF CONSISTENCY

In addition to the advances in priming methods, we also have at our disposal at least two methods that confirm that consistency has been primed and can follow its activation level over time. Those are reaction times (Abad, Noguera, & Ortells, 2003; de Groot, 1985; Neely, 1991), and Carlson's direct assessment method (Carlson et al., 2014).

Reaction times verify the effectiveness of a priming method by checking whether participants respond faster to goal-related than neutral words. This method relies on the network of concepts associated to the goal. If a goal is primed, then the entire network is activated, which results in faster reaction times to closely connected concepts like related words.

Carlson's method for assessing goal activation requires that individuals report their level of goal activation on a continuous scale (from 0 "not at all active" to 100 "maximally active"), and they do this when interrupted while performing some task. Carlson et al. (2012) have shown that the method's success requires both online measurement (i.e. direct self-reports during, not after, the task) and the use of a continuous scale (rather than an all-or-none response in which participants report a goal as having been active or not).

EMPIRICAL RESULTS

Four studies tested the claim that cognitive consistency can be primed both as a goal (a motivational state) and as a mindset (a cognitive procedure). Further, all four tested the two characteristic temporal patterns, namely that the activation of a goal should be elevated after a delay, while the activation of a mindset should decline after a delay. The four studies employed the same two-factor design, three levels of priming method (goal activation, mindset activation, and no activation/control) × two levels of delay (delay, no delay/control). The only change across studies was the focal task, which was predicted to be affected by the priming of cognitive consistency. The first three experiments served to validate the two priming methods, while the fourth illustrated their application to a well-known phenomenon.

Several attempts at priming consistency as a goal led to the adoption of a conundrum, a problem that requires participants to resolve two seemingly inconsistent facts. One such conundrum is, "Why do we criticize traders for being overpaid but accept football players and movie stars' salaries?" The expected inability to provide a fully satisfactory answer should activate the goal of consistency. More importantly, because that goal has not been achieved, it remains active during any immediately subsequent task (Förster et al., 2007; Zeigarnik, 1967).

In order to activate cognitive consistency as a mindset, we sought a task in which participants repeatedly face an inconsistency that they can successfully resolve by employing the same procedure each time. Several attempts led us to use a series of anagrams, each of which requires the reordering of a deranged set of letters into a common, easily recognized word (e.g., RACHI to CHAIR). A set of anagrams was pretested to be easy enough to solve that nearly every participant would fully succeed. Although the detailed steps to solution differ from anagram to anagram, the set of tactics is roughly the same, such as try Y at the end, place C and H together, etc. (Novick & Sherman, 2003).

After finding the two priming tasks, we also needed a filler task that could create a delay of several minutes. In the following Experiments 1, 3, and 4, participants saw a five-minute silent film, an extract of Charlie Chaplin's *The Kid*. In Experiment 2, participants were instructed to "Describe one interesting thing you did last week. Your challenge is to enable the reader to experience, through your words, what you yourself did."

Experiment 1 used reaction times in a word-naming task. Participants were required to read aloud a series of common words as quickly as possible. Response times measured the accessibility of the concepts associated with those words. Two categories of six words each were presented. The target category was consistency, represented by the words "agreement," "coherence," "compatible," "congruence," "consistent," and "fitting." A control category displayed neutral words ("above," "collection," "deepen," "kitchen," "overcome," "underline").

Experiment 2 used the Carlson et al. (2013) method described above to directly assess the activation of the consistency goal. The focal task, as in Carlson et al. (2013), was a binary choice between two products. Participants were asked to read units of information (product attributes) and to report their current leader in the choice process and to evaluate the information they read. During this choice task, participants were interrupted twice and asked to report the activation levels of the consistency and three other distractor goals.

Experiment 3 tested the effectiveness of our two priming methods with a phenomenon already shown to be affected by the consistency goal, the distortion of information during a binary choice (Russo, Carlson, Meloy, & Yong, 2008; and see Russo in this volume). Information distortion is defined as the biased evaluation of new information to support an emerging preference or belief (Russo & Chaxel, 2010; Russo, Medvec, & Meloy, 1996). Specifically, during a choice process, as one alternative naturally emerges as the tentative leader, individuals typically interpret incoming information as favoring this leader more than they should. If our methods successfully prime consistency, this downstream effect on information distortion should show an increase.

Experiment 4 applied the goal and mindset-activation methods to a phenomenon that has been hypothesized to be driven, in part, by cognitive consistency, the impact of expectations on perception (or "selective perception"; Coppin, Delplanque, Cayeux, Porcherot, & Sander, 2010; Klaaren, Hodges, & Wilson, 1994). Participants saw the title, main actors, and a synopsis of the plot for four movie trailers that had not yet been released. Based on this information, they were asked to rate how much they expected to like each movie's trailer on a scale from 0 (not at all) to 100 (very much). After watching all four movie trailers, participants rated how much they actually liked each one on the same scale. The criterion for the effect of consistency was a decline in a measure of disagreement, the absolute value of the difference between the rated expectation and actual liking.

In all four experiments, we expect significant differences between controls and the stronger version of each method, the goal-activation condition with a delay and the mindset-activation condition without a delay. In addition, there should be the predicted difference in the response to the delay, an increase for goal priming and a decrease for mindset priming. The data obtained in each experiment are displayed in Figure 2.2.

In Experiment 1, a two-way ANOVA including planned comparisons was performed on the within-participant difference in reaction time between words related to consistency and control words, with prime (goal/mindset/control) and delay (yes/no) as factors. First, as predicted, the biggest effects (lower response times) were produced by goal priming with a delay ($M_{goal\text{-}delay}$ = 22.6 milliseconds vs. $M_{control\text{-}delay}$ = 107.7 milliseconds; t (52) = 3.21; p < .01) and mindset priming without a delay ($M_{mindset\text{-}nodelay}$ = −25.7 milliseconds vs. $M_{control\text{-}nodelay}$ = 87.5 milliseconds; t (52) = −4.08;

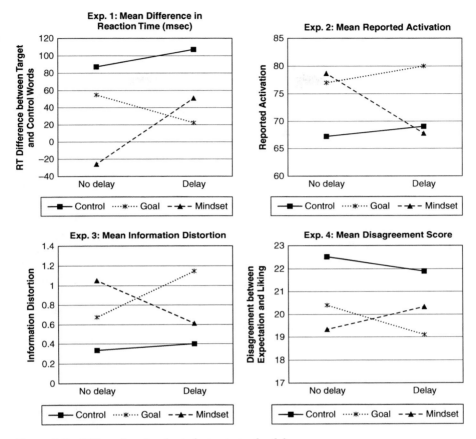

Figure 2.2   Effect of goal and mindset priming by delay.

one-sided $p < .01$).[3] The second prediction was the temporal pattern of a delay-induced increase for goal priming and decrease for mindset priming. The means conformed to this pattern. For statistical power we tested the predicted interaction among the four relevant values (using a one-sided statistical test; Ott & Long-necker, 2001). The crossover interaction (shown in Figure 2.2) was statistically reliable, $F(1, 32) = 6.26$, one-sided $p < .05$. Thus, the greater accessibility of consistency-related words verified that cognitive consistency was successfully activated as both a goal and a mindset, with the predicted temporal pattern confirming the distinction between them.

The effects observed in Experiment 2 paralleled those of Experiment 1. For both priming methods participants reported reliably higher levels of consistency (on a scale from 0 to 100) than their respective controls. For goal activation, $M_{goal\text{-}delay} = 80.0$ vs. $M_{control\text{-}delay} = 68.9$; $t(57) = 1.78$; $p < .05$. For mindset activation, $M_{mindset\text{-}nodelay} = 78.7$ vs. $M_{control\text{-}nodelay} = 66.2$; $t(60) = 1.90$; $p < .05$. Finally, the reported goal activation increased with the delay, while the opposite temporal pattern was observed for the mindset activation, with their interaction again statistically reliable (F (1,117) = 2.93, $p < .05$).

Similar to the pattern observed in Experiments 1 and 2, the mean information distortion observed in Experiment 3 was significantly higher when activated as a goal by the conundrum ($M_{\text{goal-delay}}$ = 1.15 vs. $M_{\text{control-delay}}$ = .40; t (38) = 2.27; $p < .05$) and when activated as a mindset by the anagrams ($M_{\text{mindset-nodelay}}$ = 1.05 vs. $M_{\text{control-nodelay}}$ = .33; t (38) = 2.19; $p < .05$). The predicted temporal pattern was also found, with the effect of the goal activation greater with a delay and vice versa for the mindset activation (F (1,136) = 4.30, $p < .05$).

Finally, the same 3 × 2 ANOVA and planned comparisons were performed for Experiment 4 testing for cognitive consistency as a driver of selective perception. Again, the results exhibited the pattern observed in all three earlier studies. Most importantly, the mean disagreement score between expectation ratings and liking scores was significantly lower (after a delay) when the goal of consistency was activated by the conundrum ($M_{\text{goal-delay}}$ = 19.1 vs. $M_{\text{control-delay}}$ = 21.9; t (158) = 1.66; $p < .05$). Similarly, when the anagrams activated consistency as a mindset (without a delay) disagreement between the expected and reported liking of the movie trailers was reliably lower ($M_{\text{mindset-nodelay}}$ = 19.4 vs. $M_{\text{control-nodelay}}$ = 22.5; t (158) = 1.83; $p < .05$). The now familiar temporal pattern was found again, though not reliably so. Although the goal needed a delay to become more active, while the same delay reduced the effectiveness of the anagrams to prime consistency as a mindset, their interaction was not statistically reliable, $F(1,316) = 0.95, p > .15$. We can only speculate on why a nonsignificant effect of a delay might have occurred. Recall that participants had to watch all four movie trailers before they rated them. This effectively inserted an additional delay of about three minutes immediately after the prime, altering the delay conditions from the designed times of zero and five minutes to actual times of three and eight minutes. This alteration may have blunted the manipulation of no delay versus delay.

CONCLUSION

Russo et al. (2008) showed that cognitive consistency can be primed as a semantic construct. This chapter proposed that consistency can also be conceptualized and primed as a motivational state (a goal) and as a procedure (a mindset). This means that we now have two methods for activating cognitive consistency and, therefore, two methods for testing claims that consistency contributes to a hypothesized effect or for discovering consistency-driven phenomena that were not thought to be affected by consistency. The present results also contribute to showing that the usual findings of cognitive dissonance cannot be explained merely by a potential method artifact (Chen & Risen, 2010).

Maybe just as important, the methods may enable a more thorough explanation of cognitive consistency itself. Is it always a goal? In contrast, is it only sometimes a mindset, possibly only when the goal-achieving process has been repeated often enough to become firmly associated with the goal? Can cognitive consistency also be viewed as characteristic of the structure of a belief system, and as a measure of that structure (i.e. the degree of consistency among beliefs)?

Finally, what other phenomena might be explained, at least in part, by the desire for cognitive consistency? We see cognitive consistency as a force for reconciling different beliefs. What activating consistency does is strengthen this force. Thus, one natural class of phenomena that might be driven by the desire for consistency is that where an existing belief confronts new information. Possibilities include the correspondence bias (Gilbert & Malone, 1995), the endowment effect (Kahneman, Knetsch, & Thaler, 1990), and the prior belief effect (Lord, Ross, & Lepper, 1979). Of course, these applications are speculative. Our hope is that what is necessarily speculation at present might, through the application of new priming methods, be informed empirically.

NOTES

1. Greenwald and Ronis (1978, p. 56) not only recognized the "evolution" of dissonance theory into the self-threat stream, but questioned it: "Perhaps the only victim of the evolutionary process is the original version of dissonance theory, which has effectively been discarded. But has it ever really been proven wrong? Consider the possibility that dissonance researchers abandoned portions of the original theory because their experiments inadvertently tapped self-protective cognitive processing instead of, or in addition to, dissonance reduction. The ego-related cognitive processes, being relatively easy to observe, may have pulled the theory in their direction."
2. Alternative types of mindsets are also reviewed by Wyer and Xu (2010).
3. All statistical tests are one-sided.

REFERENCES

Abad, M. J. F., Noguera C., & Ortells J. J. (2003). Influence of prime–target relationship on semantic priming effects from words in a lexical decision task. *Acta Psychologica, 113(3)*, 283–295.

Abelson, R. P. (1983). Whatever became of consistency theory? *Personality and Social Psychology Bulletin, 9(1)*, 37–64.

Aronson, E. (1968). Dissonance theory: Progress and problems. In R. P. Abelson, E. Aronson, W. J. McGuire, T. M. Newcomb, M. J. Rosenberg, & P. H. Tannenbaum (Eds.), *Cognitive consistency theories: A sourcebook* (pp. 5–27), Chicago, IL: Rand McNally.

——(1992). The return of the repressed: Dissonance theory makes a comeback. *Psychological Inquiry, 3(4)*, 303–311.

Aronson, E., Fried, C., & Stone, J. (1991). AIDS prevention and dissonance: A new twist on an old theory. *American Journal of Public Health, 81*, 1636–1638.

Aronson, E. & Mills, J. (1959). The effect of severity of initiation on liking for a group. *Journal of Abnormal and Social Psychology, 59(2)*, 177–181.

Bargh, J. A., Gollwitzer, P.M., Lee-Chai, A., Barndollar, K., & Troetschel, R. (2001). The automated will: Nonconscious activation and pursuit of behavioral goal. *Journal of Personality and Social Psychology, 81(6)*, 1014–1027.

Baron, R. M., & Kenny, D. A. (1986). The moderator–mediator variable distinction in social psychological research: Conceptual, strategic, and statistical considerations. *Journal of Personality and Social Psychology, 51(6)*, 1173–1182.

Bem, D. J. (1967). Self-perception: An alternative interpretation of cognitive dissonance phenomena. *Psychological Review, 74(3)*, 183–200.

Brehm, J. W. (1956). Postdecision changes in the desirability of alternatives. *Journal of Abnormal and Social Psychology, 52(3)*, 384–389.

Carlson, K. A., Tanner, R. J., Meloy M. G., & Russo J. E. (2014). Catching nonconscious goals in the act of decision making. *Organizational Behavior and Human Decision Processes, 123(1)*, 65–76.

Chen, M. K., & Risen, J. (2010). Choice affects and reflects preferences: Revisiting the free-choice paradigm. *Journal of Personality and Social Psychology, 99(4)*, 573–594.

Cialdini, R. B., Trost, M. R., & Newsom, T. J. (1995). Preference for consistency: The development of a valid measure and the discovery of surprising behavioral implications. *Journal of Personality and Social Psychology, 69(2)*, 318–328.

Cooper, J., & Fazio, R. H. (1984). A new look at dissonance theory. In L. Berkowitz (Ed.), *Advances in experimental social psychology* (pp. 229–262). Hillsdale, NJ: Erlbaum.

Coppin, G., Delplanque, S., Cayeux, I., Porcherot, C., & Sander, D. (2010). I'm no longer torn after choice: How explicit choices implicitly shape preferences of odors. *Psychological Science, 21(4)*, 489–493.

Croyle, R. T., & Cooper, J. (1983). Dissonance arousal: Physiological evidence. *Journal of Personality and Social Psychology, 45(4)*, 782–791.

De Groot, A.M. (1985), Word-context effects in word naming and lexical decision. *Quarterly Journal of Experimental Psychology: Human Experimental Psychology, 37A(2)*, 281–297.

Elliot, A. J., & Devine, P. G. (1994). On the motivational nature of cognitive dissonance: Dissonance as psychological discomfort. *Journal of Personality and Social Psychology, 67(3)*, 382–394.

Ferguson, M. J., & Porter S. C. (2009). Goals and (implicit) attitudes. In G. B. Moskowitz & H. Grant (Eds.), *The psychology of goals* (pp. 454–460). New York, NY: Guilford.

Festinger, L. (1957). *A theory of cognitive dissonance.* Evanston, IL: Row, Peterson.

——(1964). *Conflict, decision, and dissonance.* Palo Alto, CA: Stanford University Press.

Festinger, L., & Carlsmith, J. M. (1959). Cognitive consequences of forced compliance. *Journal of Abnormal and Social Psychology, 58(2)*, 203–210.

Festinger, L., Riecken, H. W., & Schachter, S. (1956). *When prophecy fails.* New York, NY: Harper & Row.

Fishbach, A., & Ferguson, M. F. (2007). The goal construct in social psychology. In A. W. Kruglanski & E. T. Higgins (Eds.), *Social psychology: Handbook of basic principles* (pp. 490–515). New York, NY: Guilford Press.

Förster, J., Liberman, N., & Friedman, R. (2007). Seven principles of goal activation: A systematic approach to distinguishing goal priming from priming of non-goal constructs. *Personality and Social Psychology Review, 11(3)*, 211–233.

Fried, C. B., & Aronson, E. (1995). Hypocrisy, misattribution, and dissonance reduction. *Personality and Social Psychology Bulletin, 21(9)*, 925–933.

Gilbert, D. T., & Malone, P. S. (1995). The correspondence bias. *Psychological Bulletin, 117(1)*, 21–38.

Greenwald, A. G., & Ronis, D. L. (1978). Twenty years of cognitive dissonance: Case study of the evolution of a theory. *Psychological Review, 85(1)*, 53–57.

Heider, F. (1946). Attitudes and cognitive organization. *Journal of Psychology, 21(1)*, 107–111.

——(1958). *The psychology of interpersonal relations.* New York, NY: Wiley.

Heine, S. J., Proulx, T., & Vohs, K. D. (2006). The meaning maintenance model: On the coherence of human motivations. *Personality and Social Psychology Review, 10(2)*, 88–110.

Kahneman, D., Knetsch, J. L., & Thaler, R. H. (1990). Experimental tests of the endowment effect and the Coase theorem. *Journal of Political Economy, 98(6)*, 1325–1348.

Klaaren, K. J., Hodges, S. D., & Wilson, T. D. (1994). The role of affective expectations in subjective experience and decision-making. *Social Cognition, 12(2)*, 77–101.

Liberman, N., & Dar, R. (2009). Normal and pathological consequences of encountering difficulties in monitoring progress toward goals. In G. B. Moskowitz & H. Grant (Eds.), *The psychology of goals* (pp. 277–303). New York, NY: Guilford.

Lord, C. G., Ross L., & Lepper, M. R. (1979). Biased assimilation and attitude polarization: The effects of prior theories on subsequently considered evidence. *Journal of Personality and Social Psychology, 37(11),* 2098–2109.

McGregor, I., Zanna, M. P., Holmes, J. G., & Spencer, S. J. (2001). Compensatory conviction in the face of personal uncertainty: Going to extremes and being oneself. *Journal of Personality and Social Psychology, 80(3),* 472–488.

McGuire, W. J. (1968). Personality and attitude change: An information processing theory. In A. G. Greenwald, T. C. Brock, & T. M. Ostrom (Eds.), *Psychological foundations of attitudes* (pp. 171–196). San Diego, CA: Academic Press.

Miller, G. A., Galanter, E., & Pribram, K. H. (1960). *Plans and the structure of behavior.* New York, NY: Holt, Rinehart & Winston.

Nail, P. R., Bedell, K. E., & Little, C. D. (2003). Should President Clinton be prosecuted for perjury? The effects of preference for consistency, self-esteem, and political party affiliation. *Personality and Individual Differences, 35(8),* 1821–1823.

Neely, J. H. (1991). Semantic priming effects in visual word recognition: A selective review of current findings and theories. In D. Besner & G. W. Humphreys (Eds.), *Basic processes in reading: Visual word recognition* (pp. 264–336). Hillsdale, NJ: Erlbaum.

Newcomb, T. T. (1953). An approach to the study of communicative acts. *Psychological Review, 60(6),* 393–404.

Nickerson, R. S. (2008). *Aspects of rationality: Reflections on what it means to be rational and whether we are.* New York, NY: Psychology Press.

Novick, L. R., & Sherman, S. J. (2003). On the nature of insight solutions: Evidence from skill differences in anagram solution, *The Quarterly Journal of Experimental Psychology, 56(2),* 351–382.

Osgood, C. E., & Tannenbaum, P. H. (1955). The principle of congruity in the prediction of attitude change. *Psychological Review, 62(1),* 42–55.

Read, S. J., & Miller, L. C. (1994). Dissonance and balance in belief systems: The promise of parallel constraint satisfaction processes and connectionist modeling approaches. In R. C. Schank & E. J. Langer (Eds.), *Beliefs, reasoning, and decision making: Psycho-logic in honor of Bob Abelson* (pp. 209–235). Hillsdale, NJ: Erlbaum.

Russo, J. E., Carlson, K. A., Meloy, M. G., & Yong, K. (2008). The goal of consistency as a cause of information distortion. *Journal of Experimental Psychology, 137(3),* 456–470.

Russo, J. E., & Chaxel, A. S. (2010). How persuasive messages can influence behavior without awareness. *Journal of Consumer Psychology, 20(3),* 338–342.

Russo, J. E., Meloy, M. G., & Medvec, V. H. (1996). The distortion of information during decisions. *Organizational Behavior and Human Decision Processes, 66(1),* 102–111.

Sela, A., & Shiv, B. (2009). Unraveling priming: When does the same prime activate a goal versus a trait? *Journal of Consumer Research, 36(3),* 418–433.

Shultz, T. R., & Lepper, M. R. (1996). Cognitive dissonance reduction as constraint satisfaction. *Psychological Review, 103(2),* 219–240.

Simon, D., & Holyoak, K. J. (2002). Structural dynamics of cognition: From consistency theories to constraint satisfaction. *Personality and Social Psychology Review, 6(4),* 283–294.

Spellman, B. A., Ullman, J. B., & Holyoak, K. J. (1993). A coherence model of cognitive consistency: Dynamics of attitude change during the Persian Gulf War. *Journal of Social Issues, 49(4),* 147–165.

Steele, C. M. (1988). The psychology of self-affirmation: Sustaining the integrity of the self. In L. Berkowitz (Ed.), *Advances in experimental social psychology* (pp. 261–302). San Diego, CA: Academic Press.

Stone, J., Aronson, E., Crain, L., Winslow, M., & Fried, C. (1994). Creating hypocrisy as a means of inducing young adults to purchase condoms. *Personality and Social Psychology Bulletin, 20(1),* 116–128.

Stone, J., & Cooper, J., (2001). A self-standards model of cognitive dissonance. *Journal of Experimental Social Psychology, 37(3),* 228–243.

Tannenbaum, P. (1968). Summary: Is anything special about consistency? In R. P. Abelson, E. Aronson, W. J. McGuire, T. M. Newcomb, M. J. Rosenberg, & P. H. Tannenbaum (Eds.), *Theories of cognitive consistency: A sourcebook* (pp. 343–346). Chicago, IL: Rand McNally.

Tedeschi, J. T., Schlenker, B. R., & Bonoma, T. V. (1971). Cognitive dissonance: Private ratiocination or public spectacle? *American Psychologist, 26(8),* 685–695.

Thagard, P. (1989). Explanatory coherence. *Behavioral and Brain Sciences, 12(3),* 435–467.

—— (2006). Evaluating explanations in law, science and everyday life. *Current Directions in Psychological Science, 15(3),* 141–145.

Thibodeau, R., & Aronson, E. (1992). Taking a closer look: Reasserting the role of the self-concept in dissonance theory. *Personality and Social Psychology Bulletin, 18(5),* 591–602.

Walster, E., & Berscheid, E. (1968). The effects of time on cognitive consistency. In R. P. Abelson, E. Aronson, W. J. McGuire, T. M. Newcomb, M. J. Rosenberg, & P. H. Tannenbaum (Eds.), *Theories of cognitive consistency: A sourcebook,* Chicago, IL: Rand McNally.

Wertheimer, M. (1922). Untersuchungen zur Lehre von der Gestalt I. Prinzipielle Bemerkungen. *Psychologische Forschung, 1,* 47–58.

—— (1923). Untersuchungen zur Lehre von der Gestalt II. *Psychologische Forschung, 4,* 301–350.

Wyer, R. S., & Xu, A. J. (2010). The role of behavioral mind-sets in goal-directed activity: Conceptual underpinnings and empirical evidence. *Journal of Consumer Psychology, 20(2),* 107–112.

Xu, A. J., & Wyer, R. S. (2008). The comparative mind-set: From animal comparisons to increased purchase intentions. *Psychological Science, 19(9),* 859–864.

Zanna, M. P., & Cooper, J. (1974). Dissonance and the pill: An attributional approach to studying the arousal properties of dissonance. *Journal of Personality and Social Psychology, 29(5),* 703–709.

Zeigarnik, B. V. (1967). On finished and unfinished tasks. In W. D. Ellis (Ed.), *A sourcebook of Gestalt psychology.* New York, NY: Humanities Press.

3

Fuzzy-Trace Theory Explains Paradoxical Dissociations in Affective Forecasting

EVAN A. WILHELMS, REBECCA K. HELM,
RONI A. SETTON, AND VALERIE F. REYNA

People often make decisions based on forecasts of subjective well-being—predictions for how they expect to feel about different outcomes in the future. In this chapter, we briefly introduce the principles of fuzzy-trace theory, a dual-process model of decision making, and integrate the relevant neuroscience literature in order to consider how assessments of subjective well-being are stored in terms of gist and verbatim representations. Fuzzy-trace theory posits that people tend to rely on the simplest gist necessary when making decisions. When applied to subjective well-being, this means that people will generally base emotional forecasts on categorical gist representations, unless cued to make a verbatim judgment. That is, people will rely on meaningful information about valence and discrete emotions (often based on gist representations) as a default mode of processing. We predict that this reliance on gist representations is beneficial such that it generally leads to accurate predictions of valence, and that recollection or prediction of more precise judgments (such as degree of arousal or intensity of happiness) is subject to more interference, and thus more inaccuracy.

P eople will often base important decisions on what emotions they expect to feel as a result of the decision. These decisions could be selecting between monetary gambles (Mellers & McGraw, 2001), considering unsafe sexual risks (Richard, Van der Plight, & De Vries, 1996), or selecting between consumer brands (Rosenzweig & Gilovich, 2012; Shiv & Huber, 2000). Other life choices, such as what career to pursue, whom to marry, and where to live, may also be influenced by these forecasts of emotional reactions, and the accuracy of those predictions can have a permanent influence on one's well-being (Wilson & Gilbert,

2003). In addition, measures of subjective well-being are found to be predictive of measures of objective well-being, such as physical health and longevity (Diener, 2000). It would thus be beneficial to make accurate judgments of what will make us happy and satisfied in our future lives and to understand how and why these judgments often become inaccurate.

Recent research has investigated the role that affective forecasting—people's predictions about their future emotions—plays in several other decision-making paradigms. For example, one recent study has found that loss aversion in gambling tasks was at least partially the result of people overestimating the impact the loss would have on their emotions compared to an equivalent gain, when in fact, if they lost the gamble, the loss did not have the impact they predicted (Kermer, Driver-Linn, Wilson, & Gilbert, 2006). Further work has connected affective forecasts to neurobiological mechanisms. For example, when participants make predictions of how much they will enjoy future events while undergoing functional imaging, they show less activity in the ventromedial prefrontal cortex (vmPFC) than when they made similar judgments about events in the present (Mitchell, Schirmer, Ames, & Gilbert, 2011). As this region is associated with thinking about oneself and introspection, it suggests that people are less prone to self-referential simulation in making these predictions about the future. Furthermore, the extent of the decrease in vmPFC activity predicted impatient decisions in temporal discounting tasks that pit smaller sooner against larger later rewards, consistent with a lower ability to project the future self.

In this chapter, we introduce fuzzy-trace theory (FTT) as a theory of memory and reasoning based in memory representations. We introduce its foundational principles and review some reasoning errors and paradoxical effects that it predicts, such as developmental reversals (that children outperform adults on cognitive tasks). We then discuss how these few principles can be extended to predict how people will make judgments of their happiness and well-being, as it applies to making evaluations of their emotional states in the present, remembering emotions of the past, and forecasting emotions in the future. Finally, we apply these principles to the literature on affective forecasting to show how these theoretical predictions explain apparent contradictions.

FUZZY-TRACE THEORY

We begin this chapter with an introduction to the foundational principles of FTT. We describe the principles of FTT in turn and provide illustrative supporting evidence in Table 3.1.

FTT is a theory of memory and reasoning which is grounded in research on how people represent, retrieve, and process information when they make decisions (Reyna, 2012). It is based on two categories of mental representations of stored knowledge. The first category consists of gist representations, vague qualitative representations that capture the bottom-line meaning of a problem or situation. The second category is verbatim representations, precise representations of the surface detail of information such as numerical information and precise wording (Reyna & Brainerd, 2011). For example, a 49-year-old woman who is told that

Table 3.1 Illustrative findings supporting principles of FTT.

Principle	Stimuli	Task	Finding	Sources
I. Independent encoding, storage, and retrieval of gist versus verbatim representations of experience.	Numerical inputs, such as Farmer Brown has eight cows, seven sheep, four pigs, and two horses.	Recall verbatim numbers of animals; make gist judgments of relative magnitude.	Being able to remember verbatim numbers did not help children remember either the global gist (most or least) or the pairwise gist (more or less) of numbers, and manipulations that improved verbatim memory did not improve gist memory. Providing additional evidence which enhanced gist memory impaired verbatim memory.	Brainerd & Gordon 1994
II. Fuzzy-processing preference (default reliance on gist-based processing, or intuition, in reasoning, judgment, and decision making)	Four different environmental issue scenarios, framed either positively (human lives, animal lives, or acres of forest saved) or negatively (lives lost or acres of forest damaged).	Participants were asked to choose between a sure option and a risky option in different task types. One type (called Type 4) was identical to the classic framing problem (called Type 1) but hid the zero complements. For example, in Type 1, the risky option in the gain frame would be: *If the release of fish is implemented, there is a ⅓ probability that all of the twelve fish species will survive and a ⅔ probability that none of them will survive.* In Type 4, the risky option in the gain frame would be: *If the release of fish is implemented, there is a ⅓ probability that all of the twelve fish species will survive.*	Although Type 1 and Type 4 problems were identical, framing was found in Type 1 but not Type 4. This suggests a fuzzy-processing preference. In Task 1 people treat the gain frame as saving some fish vs. either saving some fish or saving none and treat the loss frame as either losing some fish or losing some fish vs. losing none (causing them to prefer the sure option in the gain frame and the risky option in the loss frame). In Task 4 people treat the gain frame as some will be saved vs. some will be saved and the loss frame as some will die vs. some will die.	Kühberger & Tanner 2010

(Continued)

Table 3.1 (*Continued*)

Principle	Stimuli	Task	Finding	Sources
III. Developmental increase in false memory created by acceptance of gist-consistent distractors.	Deese–Roediger–McDermott (DRM) paradigm presentation of a list of related words	Reviewed fifty-five studies in which participants were asked to either recall or recognize as many words from previously presented DRM lists as possible.	Subjects falsely remember words that are associates of words that were presented. Fifty-three of the fifty-five experiments reviewed showed developmental increases in false recall and/or recognition from childhood to adulthood.	Brainerd, Reyna, & Zember 2011
IV. Greater experience produces greater reliance on gist-based processing.	Nine decision problems about nine hypothetical patients at three levels of cardiac risk.	Participants responded to each patient description, according to guidelines for unstable angina. For each patient, participants had to make five judgments of risk or probability and a triage decision.	Physicians relied on fewer dimensions of information than medical students. Physicians were better at discriminating levels of risk according to external correspondence criteria but violated internal coherence criteria. They achieved better discrimination by processing less information and made sharper all-or-none distinctions among decision categories.	Reyna & Lloyd 2006
V. Developmental reversals in decision making.	Sixty decision problems about human lives and other valued outcomes divided into two stimulus sets. Each subject got thirty problems (fifteen in the gain frame and fifteen in the loss frame), equally divided among three truncation conditions (complete, nonzero complement present, and zero complement present).	Participants were asked to choose between a sure option and a risky option, depending on what they would prefer in real life.	Intelligence agents exhibited larger decision biases than college students, treating equivalent outcomes differently based on superficial differences in wording. Post-college adults occupied a middle ground.	Reyna, Chick, Corbin, & Hsia 2013

her lifetime risk for developing breast cancer is 22.2 percent would encode the verbatim number (22.2 percent) along with a separate representation of the gist of the information (such as "That is really bad" or "My risk is high"; Reyna, 2008). It is important to note that people routinely extract and encode hierarchies of gist from information, rather than a single-gist representation. These hierarchies vary in their level of precision, from categorical to ordinal (for example, in a probability judgment task, "The blue jar has some winning tokens," "The blue jar has more winning tokens than the red jar," "The blue jar has more than 20 or 30 winning tokens, but I don't know exactly how many"; Rivers, Reyna, & Mills, 2008).

According to FTT, an individual who learns new information encodes gist and verbatim representations of words, numbers, sentences, or events in parallel and stores them separately (Reyna & Kiernan, 1994). An individual would store verbatim traces of the actual experience (e.g., hearing the words "spaniel" and "Chicago") and independently store gist traces, using past experience and knowledge to extract the bottom-line meaning of the experience (e.g., "dog," "city"). Gist and verbatim representations are then retrieved independently (Brainerd & Reyna, 2004; Reyna, 2005). The proposition of independent storage and retrieval is supported by evidence of dissociations between measures of verbatim and gist representations. For example, one empirical study found that being able to remember verbatim numbers did not help remembering either the global gist (most or least) or the pairwise gist (more or less) of numbers, and manipulations that improved verbatim memory did not improve gist memory (Brainerd & Gordon, 1994; Reyna & Brainerd, 1995).

Semantic meaning is vital to gist processing since gist-based representations, by definition, require the extraction of bottom-line meaning from information. Verbatim memories support feelings of vivid item-specific recollection of targets, whereas feelings of nonspecific resemblance are supported by gist memories (Reyna, Mills, Estrada, & Brainerd, 2007). A person's memory of particular facts depends on which is retrieved. Memory errors can be increased by relying on gist representations or decreased by enhancing verbatim representations. On the one hand, if "ill," "hospital," and "nurse" are all words presented to a participant, someone relying on a gist-based representation may remember the words as being medically related and might, therefore, falsely recognize the word "doctor." On the other hand, a participant relying on a verbatim representation might specifically remember the words "ill," "hospital," and "nurse" by rote rehearsal, and would be less likely to falsely recognize "doctor" (Brainerd & Reyna, 2005). Under predictable conditions, as when gist memories are repeatedly cued, retrieval of strong gist memories can support illusory feelings of vivid item-specific recollection, a phenomenon known as phantom recollection. Thus, verbatim memory is used to both accept information identical to the stimulus from which it was encoded and reject gist items that were only meaning-consistent (Reyna & Kiernan, 1995). Gist memory, however, is more enduring than verbatim memory, which is subject to greater interference. After a delay, gist memory is used to accept both presented items and meaning-consistent gist items (Reyna & Kiernan, 1994, 1995).

These memories—or mental representations—are used whenever people process information, as in decision making and reasoning. Across tasks, FTT posits that adults have a fuzzy processing preference. This preference means that although they encode both gist and verbatim representations, they use the simplest gist they can to reason or make decisions. In contrast, children and adolescents are less likely to have a mature understanding of the gist of a situation and, furthermore, are more likely to focus on more precise representations toward the verbatim end of the gist–verbatim hierarchy. Adolescent processing of decisions, for example, more closely resembles a calculation of a mathematics problem, in which they are more likely to weigh risks and benefits in a specific situation (Wilhelms & Reyna, 2013). Laboratory experiments in children, adolescents, and adults have confirmed this developmental pattern (e.g., Reyna & Ellis 1994; Reyna, Estrada, DeMarinis, Myers, Stanisz, & Mills, 2011; Reyna & Farley, 2006).

As individuals develop and acquire greater expertise in a domain, their decisions are increasingly based on the gist, or meaning, of information, as opposed to its verbatim details (Reyna & Brainerd, 2011), and the preference to operate on the crudest level of the hierarchy of gist increases. In other words, adults begin with the lowest (categorical) level of gist and only proceed to higher (more precise) levels if the lower levels do not provide an answer (Reyna, 2012).

This gist-based processing is more sophisticated because it is based on meaning rather than literal information, and a mature understanding of the gist of a situation can lead to better decision making. In contrast, research has shown that verbatim-based processing in adolescents is associated with risky decision making (Reyna & Farley, 2006). As an example, adolescents may be willing to risk HIV because the probability of transmission is low while mature adults with a gist understanding of what is at stake would have an immediate, categorical response to not expose themselves to the risk. A study of decision making in physicians showed that when they make decisions in their domain of expertise, more knowledgeable individuals (in this case, cardiologists) process fewer dimensions of information and do so more qualitatively (consistent with using gist representations) than those with less knowledge and training and yet are better at discriminating levels of risk (Reyna & Lloyd, 2006).

GIST AND DEVELOPMENT WITH AGE AND EXPERTISE

Before applying the principles of FTT to predictions about memory for emotional states, judgments and forecasts of emotional states, and subjective well-being, we illustrate how these principles have been applied to predict other judgments. Because FTT predicts a developmental pattern of gist and verbatim processing in which verbatim processing is relied on more readily before gist processing, differences between adolescent and adult judgment can demonstrate how reliance on gist representations can result in one judgment while verbatim representations can result in another. We briefly discuss some of the evidence for developmental patterns of gist and verbatim processing to inform and guide predictions of how the same basic principles about gist and verbatim processing can be applied to subjective well-being (SWB).

A number of reasoning biases that have been shown to increase with age— referred to as *developmental reversals*—are explained by FTT's proposition that verbatim and gist processing operate independently and in parallel. Examples of developmental reversals include age increases from childhood to adulthood in framing biases (i.e. inconsistencies in preferences for gambling depending on wording), the representativeness heuristic (i.e. a mental shortcut that produces reasoning fallacies), and false memories (e.g., Brainerd, Reyna, & Zember, 2011; Reyna & Brainerd, 1994).

As adolescents continue to grow in age and experience, they begin to increasingly rely on gist-based processing (and less on verbatim processing), slowly moving toward the categorical end of the continuum, to a fuzzy processing preference. The developmental shift from verbatim to gist processing from adolescence to adulthood is paralleled by developmental differences that occur at the level of the brain. Synaptic "pruning" of weak or unused synapses, resulting in a significant reduction of gray matter, occurs in conjunction with increased myelination of axons to facilitate speed and efficiency of information transfer during childhood and adolescence (Chick & Reyna, 2012; Giedd et al., 2012). Increased myelination and the development of longer connections (e.g., between the prefrontal cortex and parietal, subcortical, and association areas; Asato, Terwilliger, Woo, & Luna, 2010; Klingberg et al., 1999; Mukherjee & McKinstry, 2006) could support an increased capacity to integrate information (Chick & Reyna, 2012; Reyna & Brainerd, 2011). However, this development does not always lead to improvement in memory and reasoning performance in laboratory tasks. Quite the contrary, an increased reliance on gist processing with age has been shown to make adults more susceptible to semantically based memory and reasoning errors, as observed in Deese–Roediger–McDermott (DRM) paradigm tasks (Brainerd, Reyna, & Zember, 2011) and framing tasks (Reyna, Chick, Corbin, & Hsia, 2013), among other tasks. Such "intelligent" errors are evidence for the shift to gist processing predicted by FTT. These developmental reversals, so called because they reverse the traditional assumptions about developmental improvements in accuracy, belie the overall advantages to the fuzzy processing preference that have been demonstrated in multiple contexts, such as protection against potentially catastrophic risk taking (e.g., Mills, Reyna, & Estrada, 2008).

The shift from verbatim to gist processing with age not only explains the aforementioned developmental reversals but also results in the gradual development of sophisticated processing for a mature understanding of situations. Maturing brain networks that can integrate information (as described above) enable the processing of fewer, higher quality aspects of information (in less time) for overall better decision making as adolescents approach adulthood (Reyna, Chapman, Dougherty, & Confrey, 2012).

Neuroimaging evidence supports the idea that adolescents rely on more deliberation in their decision making. For example, one such study has shown that adolescents take longer to deliberate over risky decisions that they ultimately reject, such as deciding whether it is a good idea to set one's hair on fire (Baird & Fugelsang, 2004; Reyna & Farley, 2006). Although subjects gave safe and healthy answers in the end (e.g., saying "no" to the prospect of setting one's hair on fire and "yes" to eating a salad), neuroimaging data showed that this delay was correlated with activation in areas associated with deliberation (e.g., parts of the prefrontal

cortex) in adolescents, whereas neuroimaging data of adults, who made the decision faster, showed activation in areas associated with imagery (fusiform gyrus)
and gut responses (insula). These results are consistent with FTT's prediction that
adolescents use an alternative mechanism to make decisions—relying more on
quantitative verbatim representations to make decisions rather than the qualitative, meaningful representations used by adults.

RISK PERCEPTION AND RISK TAKING

Research has been done in applying the principles of FTT to the field of public health (e.g., sexual risk taking, such as initiation of sex and number of sexual
partners), in particular adolescent risk perception and risk taking. As examples,
experimental findings showed that the relation between estimates of personal risk
and self-reported risk taking could be reversed, as predicted by FTT, by changing wording of questions to elicit verbatim versus gist processing. That is, asking
respondents to estimate highly specific risks numerically elicits specific verbatim
memories of instances of risk taking, whereas asking global questions with simple
response categories ("low" or "high" risk) about beliefs elicits gist processing; the
former creates positive correlations and the latter negative correlations between
risk perception and risk taking (e.g., Mills et al., 2008; Reyna et al., 2011).

This work has generally supported FTT's prediction that adolescents rely more
on verbatim deliberation in making risky decisions and risk assessments than on
gist representations. Showing how adolescents differ from adults in this domain
can illustrate the differences in verbatim and gist processing that will inform predictions about judgments of SWB. In particular, there is evidence that supports the
idea that different types of representation elicited by slightly different questions
produce opposing judgments and that reliance on gist representations could result
in better real-world outcomes. Both of these effects will be relevant to discussion
of SWB judgments.

Gist-based processing can have a protective effect in that it discourages risk
taking, in comparison to verbatim-based processing. When relying on gist-based
processing, an individual will make decisions based on simple bottom-line extrac-
tions of meaning, such as "unprotected sex risks AIDS," then apply simple values
or principles to those representations, such as "avoid risk" or "better to be safe than
sorry." Quantitative verbatim thinking, however, involves a risk–benefit trade-off
that often results in risk taking since the benefits of risky behavior are often high
and the risks are often low. For example, the risk of HIV infection from a single act
of unprotected sex is low, compared to the perceived potential benefits, especially
when considering the risk of a single act relative to the cumulative risk of repeating
that act multiple times (Mills, Reyna, & Estrada, 2008). In contrast, the gist of HIV
risk would be that the risk of HIV is categorically "bad" and unprotected sex should
therefore be avoided.

In the context of framing, adolescents displayed reverse framing when potential
gains were high (i.e. when a higher magnitude gain was found in the gamble)
leading to risk-seeking behavior in the gain frame (Reyna et al., 2011). The sensitivity to reward magnitude in adolescents supports the FTT prediction that they

are using quantitative deliberation rather than categorical principles (such as "risk is bad") to make decisions.

The developmental literature points to an asymmetry in the development of reward and cognitive-control mechanisms that interact with the differences in processing between adults and adolescents described above. More specifically, dopaminergic pathways in the ventral striatum, activated in response to motivation and reward sensitivity, have been found to develop earlier in adolescence and young adulthood than those in the prefrontal cortex, which are implicated in cognitive control and inhibition (Somerville, Jones, & Casey, 2010). Within the ventral striatum, the nucleus accumbens has been shown to respond monotonically to reward magnitude in both adolescents and adults, with adolescents especially sensitive to a high magnitude of rewards (Chick & Reyna, 2012). The developmental delay between reward and cognitive-control systems is thought to drive risk taking (Reyna & Brainerd, 2011). Peaks in sensation seeking (Romer, 2003; Steinberg et al., 2008) and temporal discounting (Green et al., 1996; Reyna & Farley, 2006) during adolescence support this hypothesis. A growth in white matter, which connects frontal areas and subcortical reward systems, occurs in adolescence and is thought to facilitate the development of inhibition and self-control (Casey et al., 2008; Galvan et al., 2007) to counter risk-taking behavior. FTT incorporates this research on cortical control and adds to it the predictions regarding development of gist processing, based in synaptic pruning and increased myelination (as previously discussed). Mature adults therefore resist risk taking not only because they have increased self-control but also because they intuitively grasp the gists of risky situations and efficiently retrieve simple risk-avoidant values, which, in turn, augments self-control.

Studies of decision making and behavioral intentions confirm the protective effect of gist-based processing and global risk avoidance (Reyna & Farley, 2006). For example, as briefly noted above, presenting alternative measures of risk perception that varied the cues presented (specific or global) and the level of precision required in the response (verbatim or gist) showed that thinking categorically about risk and endorsing simple global values such as "avoid risk" were associated with reduced risk taking. In contrast with global questions such as "are risks of having sex low, medium, or high?" specific questions that required verbatim judgment such as "are you likely to get pregnant or get someone pregnant in the next month?" were associated with judgments that reflected risky behavior (Mills, Reyna, & Estrada, 2008). Endorsement of the absolute categorical gist principle, "No risk is better than some risk" but not the relative principle "Less risk is better than more risk" was associated with behavioral intentions to take fewer risks. For example, adolescents were more than twice as likely to be sexually active (61 percent compared to 30 percent) if they endorsed the relative principle but not the absolute one than if they endorsed the absolute principle but not the relative one (Mills, Reyna, & Estrada, 2008). Furthermore, measures of gist thinking have consistently predicted real-life risky behaviors and behavioral intentions in adolescent framing studies (Reyna, Estrada et al., 2011). That is, gist-based thinking was associated with health-protective ideation and behavior. Naturally, gist processing can produce greater risk taking under circumstances in which that preference reflects insight about the gist of one's options.

MORE ACCURACY FROM FEWER CHARACTERISTICS

FTT also predicts that, in some contexts, gist processing results in decision makers being able to make more accurate decisions based on fewer characteristics. Under predictable conditions, succinct gist representations applied to judgments will be more accurate compared to considering a long list of verbatim details. This paradox will be particularly relevant to judgments of global well-being (such as life satisfaction, as we shall see below). A brief discussion of how some experts and others can make better decisions based on considering less detail can inform our predictions of how people make global forecasts and judgments of SWB.

According to FTT, as people become more knowledgeable, their information processing becomes more gist-based. It takes experience to know which details to ignore when making a decision, so more experienced decision makers can base decisions on fewer dimensions of information, rather than all of the details that less experienced decision makers may consider. This principle can be illustrated by a study examining variations in domain-specific expertise in unstable angina by comparing judgments and decisions of medical students, family-practice physicians, emergency-medicine physicians, internal-medicine physicians, cardiologists, and nationally recognized expert cardiologists (each of which received medical training in making decisions relating to unstable angina; Reyna & Lloyd, 2006). The study showed differences in knowledge to be associated with differences in risk perception and risk tolerance, which in turn predicted differences in decision making. Specifically, more knowledgeable individuals could reliably discriminate low-risk from high-risk patients. Those with higher levels of knowledge processed fewer dimensions of information, relying on only one dimension of risk, and made sharper distinctions among decision categories. Those with less knowledge relied on more dimensions of risk and were more likely to hedge their decision making by choosing intermediate levels of care. This finding illustrates that experts achieved better discrimination by processing less information. Similar findings come from data in a study that assessed deviation from protocol in case studies by emergency medical technicians (EMTs) trained in basic or advanced life support (Lazar, 2012). Despite precise knowledge of clinical protocols (89 percent correct in control conditions), EMTs with advanced training and more experience deviated from protocol more than EMTs with basic training in cases specifically manipulated such that a deviation from protocol in accordance with the gist of clinical scenarios (as opposed to surface features of symptoms) was desirable. In accordance with FTT, although these experienced EMTs clearly had the verbatim, declarative knowledge, they relied more on gist processing compared to less experienced EMTs.

Studies on deliberation in decision making also provide support for the idea that gist-based processing can result in more accurate decision making. For example, studies have shown that in certain circumstances more accurate decisions were made in the absence of attentive deliberation (Dijksterhuis, Bos, Nordgren, & van Baaren, 2006). In one task, participants read information about hypothetical cars. Each car was characterized by either 4 or 12 attributes in order to test the effect of different levels of cognitive load. The best car had 75 percent positive attributes compared to 50 percent or 25 percent for the other cars. Half of the participants were asked to deliberate about which was the best car for four minutes. The other half were given a distracting task and then asked to pick the best car. When making the decision regarding cars about which they had heard 12 characteristics (the higher cognitive load), participants who had an interference task had lower verbatim memory for the details of the cars, and, hence, were forced to rely on the gist. Gist processors chose the best car significantly more often than those who had time to deliberate about the details of the cars (Dijksterhuis, Bos, Nordgren, & van Baaren, 2006; see also Fukukura, Ferguson, & Fujita, 2013). Thus, deliberation about complex details (i.e. verbatim processing of information) can have a detrimental effect on the accuracy of decision making, as shown in earlier work on FTT in which boosting memory for detail lowered reasoning performance (e.g., see Reyna & Brainerd, 1995).

Therefore, although increased reliance on gist processing can lead to certain developmental reversals, it results in more mature decision making in two main ways. First, it has a protective effect against risk taking, promoting reliance on categorical principles of risk avoidance rather than a trade-off between risks and benefits. Second, it can allow individuals to make more accurate decisions based on fewer dimensions of information. This effect occurs because gist-based processing focuses on the most important aspects of information, ignoring surplus information that can safely be ignored.

FTT AND MEMORY FOR EMOTION

As shown above, FTT describes judgments as reliant on memory representations, with adults showing a preference for reliance on gist representations in their decisions. This is also true when people make judgments about their own SWB. These judgments can be made about emotions and well-being in the present, about memories of emotions in response to past events, and predictions of emotions and well-being about future events. In fact, forecasts of the future tend to rely on our memories of similar experiences from the past; both simulating future events and recalling past events activates the same core neural network (Schacter, Addis, & Buckner, 2008; Wilson & Gilbert, 2003). In order to make predictions regarding whether forecasts and memories of emotional states will be accurate, it is important to consider how both emotions and assessments of well-being are stored in gist and verbatim memory representations.

A useful delineation for discussing how emotions are experienced is the distinction between valence and arousal. Valence refers to the evaluation of an emotion as positive or negative (good or bad), whereas arousal refers to the intensity of the emotion. As the hierarchy of gist in which representations are stored is roughly parallel with scales of measurement (in which the simplest gists are stored as categorical distinctions, followed by ordinal distinctions, followed by more fine-grained, verbatim distinctions), memory for the valence of an experience—an all-or-none distinction—is stored in the most simple and categorical of gist representations (Rivers, Reyna, & Mills, 2008). Because memory for valence is stored as a categorical gist memory and because intuition is defined as gist-based processing in FTT, memories for valence form the basis of intuitive judgments (e.g., of well-being). This theoretically motivated hypothesis is supported by neurological evidence that links damage to the amygdala (though not adjacent medial-temporal damage) with a deficit in encoding the gist of stimuli, while sparing the memory for details (Adolphs, Tranel, & Buchanan, 2005). Additionally, evidence has shown that the enduring memory of the positive valence can contribute to a preference for a stimulus after only a brief exposure; long-term retention of valence is further evidence that valence is encoded as gist (Monahan, Murphy, & Zajonc, 2000; Zajonc, 2001). Thus, the valence stored in the gist representation of an experience or stimulus is central to its meaning (Osgood, Suci, & Tannenbaum, 1957), and this stored valence drives other judgments about the experience as well.

States of arousal, however, can be encoded differently than the simple categorical valence of an experience and seem to affect how information is encoded during the experience (Rivers, Reyna, & Mills, 2008). For example, negatively valenced arousal has been associated with enhanced memory for the gist but with attenuated memory for visual detail of stimuli (Adolphs, Denburg, & Tranel, 2001). Again, this effect was mediated by the amygdala, such that those with right unilateral amygdala damage did not show the relationship between memory for detail and arousal. However, it was also found in young adults that while negative arousal enhances gist memory, it also enhances memory for central details that are pertinent to the gist of the stimuli, while leaving memory for peripheral details unaffected (Kensinger, Garoff-Eaton, & Schacter, 2006). The right amygdala was also associated with memory for visual detail (Kensinger, Garoff-Eaton, & Schacter, 2007). These effects have generally shown that the level of arousal of an emotional experience focuses processing on the gist of the experience, as well as the details that inform that gist, such that these elements are enduringly retained in memory.

This body of work has informed FTT's predictions that the experienced valence of an emotional experience is encoded as a categorical gist representation (as either positive or negative, good or bad) and that these gists will endure in memory and subsequently be relied on for judgments and decisions. One's level of arousal at the time of encoding an emotional experience, however, can result in a greater focus on the gist of the experience and a de-emphasis on peripheral details, subsequently enhancing the memory for the gist. This effect of arousal is predicted because verbatim memories have been shown to be sensitive to interference, such as that produced by stress and strong emotion (Rivers et al., 2008). As people tend to rely on these gists for most judgments, this will include judgments of future or past well-being. As Wilson and Gilbert (2003) noted, making predictions about the emotions of future experiences is based on recalling feelings from the past. It is important, then, to briefly consider how such judgments are assessed in literature on SWB and affective forecasting, in order to see how memory representations will influence those judgments and predictions.

ASSESSING HAPPINESS AND SWB

SWB can be analyzed as multiple components. One simple definition would be the momentary experience of positive affect or happiness (Wilson & Gilbert, 2003). These moments aggregate such that general measures of positive affect can also be assessed, defined as the frequency of experiencing positive affect or pleasant emotions in comparison to negative (Diener, 2000). There are also global components of SWB, such as life satisfaction, defined as global judgments of one's life, as well as global judgments within specific domains (e.g., work or family).

Studies of SWB and affective forecasting tend to use self-report scales and measures to assess these constructs. Though some longer scales exist—such as the PANAS (Positive And Negative Affect Schedule; Watson, Clark, & Tellegen, 1988)—much of the recent work in affective forecasting has used single-item measures of happiness (Wilson & Gilbert, 2003). These items could specifically ask how happy people are now, or how happy people are in general these days, and are often assessed through experience sampling, in which participants respond to short surveys in real time as they go about their daily activities. The scale of measurement can also vary. Satisfaction has been measured with a seven-item response scale ranging from "delighted" to "terrible" when asked the question "How do you feel about your life as a whole?" (Andrews & Withey, 1976), whereas more recent work has assessed momentary happiness with real-time reports using the question "How are you feeling right now?" on a continuous scale from 1 to 100 (Killingsworth & Gilbert, 2010).

The scales of measurement used in assessing judgments of well-being and happiness are relevant to making predictions about how individuals will remember their own reported emotional reactions in addition to how they will then predict their emotional responses to future events. FTT predicts that the precision of the representation used in a given task (i.e. a gist or verbatim representation) is influenced by the requirements of the response format (Mills, Reyna, & Estrada, 2008). Specifically, the response format of the question can alternatively induce activation of verbatim or gist representations: A categorical choice, such as choosing an item you prefer, activates the most simple gist representations while exact values, such as naming a specific price you would pay for an item, activates verbatim representations. This prediction is supported by evidence that found that altering response formats—such as ordering preferences (as opposed to choosing between options) and expressing magnitude of the preference on an exact numerical scale—changed reported preferences (Fischer & Hawkins, 1993). This prediction has also accounted for preference reversals based on changes in response format (Reyna & Brainerd, 2011). FTT also predicts that subjects will tend to rely on the least precise representation necessary for the task. Therefore, if a task requires a person to provide merely a judgment of valence—such as assessing whether a stimulus is positive or negative, or recalling whether a past experience was happy or sad—a simple categorical gist representation may be used to provide a response. If a task requires a more specific judgment—such as rating one's level of arousal, or recalling a specific intensity or duration of a past happy experience—a more specific representation of their judgment may be required. As previously discussed, these more precise verbatim representations are subject to inference over time, and if the required verbatim representation is not available for the task, subjects will reconstruct their response based on gist.

FTT can provide predictions regarding the accuracy of SWB memories and predictions from these principles. Memories for categorical emotional content, including simple judgments of valence and some discrete emotional states, will tend to be robust and endure over time as gist representations. These gist representations will also form the basis of predicted judgments of well-being and happiness, as simulating and forecasting the future has been found to rely largely on the same neural networks as recalling the past (Schacter et al., 2012). Whether these forecasts are accurate will depend on the response format of the questions. If people are asked to recall or predict the valence or categorical emotional state they have experienced or will experience, people will generally be accurate, as this judgment elicits a categorical gist memory that tends to be robust over time. Exceptions will tend to occur when people do not have relevant experience to make predictions. However, when tasks require precise values, such as specific numeric ratings of happiness, people will activate specific verbatim representations that are subject to greater interference over time. This will result in less consistency between forecasts, ratings in the moment, and recollections of emotions regarding a specific stimulus or event. If the ratings in the moment are the standard against which accuracy is based, then the forecasts and recollections of those judgments will be inaccurate in comparison. Contrary to momentary emotional reactions, global assessments of well-being will tend to be based on enduring gist representations and thus be stable over time; inaccuracies in forecasts and memories will tend to arise from misleading verbatim details. Although FTT has not been applied previously to explain effects in affective forecasting, evidence from this literature supports these aforementioned predictions, as we discuss below.

JUDGMENTS OF VALENCE BASED ON GIST

The existing literature on affective forecasting has not interpreted evidence according to how changes in response format can elicit activation of different memory representations, and some of the findings can thus appear paradoxical. However, interpreting this evidence in terms of whether verbatim or gist representations are activated allows insight into explaining how people arrive at their judgments and forecasts, and can also allow additional predictions to be made about judgments of SWB. Evidence from affective forecasting literature has generally supported the prediction that people will forecast their emotions based on gist memory unless given a specific cue to do otherwise. This often results in accurate forecasts when subjects predict the valence of emotion or specific emotional states, but less accuracy when having to predict verbatim judgments of intensity or arousal.

Demonstrations of accuracy when predicting valence can be found in a study in which subjects had to predict their reactions to winning or losing a date in a dating game (Wilson, Wheatley, Kurtz, Dunn, & Gilbert, 2002). Subjects were given computer-simulated expectations of being matched with someone in the dating game (ranging from 1.5 percent to 98.5 percent) and were asked to predict their future moods if they were to have won or lost. Although there were variations in how good or bad they expected to feel (as influenced by their expectations), subjects were uniformly accurate at predicting whether their responses would be positive or negative. If errors do occur in predicting the valence of a future emotion, it is likely to be the result of the individual having no previous experience with the context of the future judgment (e.g., a child trying a new food; Wilson & Gilbert,

2003). In other words, the individual has no gist representation of past experiences on which to draw to project into the future (Schacter, Addis, & Buckner, 2008). In general, however, people tend to be accurate at making categorical judgments about future emotional states, such as judgments of valence.

People also tend to be accurate about another sort of categorical forecast of emotion: predicting discrete emotional states. One study demonstrated this by assigning participants to either a forecasting condition or an experiencing condition (Robinson & Clore, 2001). Those in the forecasting condition read several one- or two-sentence descriptions, each about a photo, and rated whether the actual photo would elicit a variety of discrete emotions (e.g., anger, happiness, embarrassment, etc.). Those in the experiencing condition, however, saw the actual photos and made the same ratings regarding their actual experiences with the photo. Mean appraisal ratings and mean emotional ratings were highly convergent between the two conditions, meaning that the general pattern of predicted emotional reaction was highly consistent with experienced reaction. When inaccuracies were found (typically in the rated intensity of the emotion), they reflected the generalized beliefs of the participants in the forecasting condition, supporting the prediction that such judgments are based on participants' encoded gists.

Thus, people tend to be accurate in forecasting both valence and discrete emotional categories of future experience when basing these judgments on gists of past experience, but, ironically, are less accurate at precise predictions (see below). Only if they lack relevant knowledge, such as if they have never personally experienced a situation, and thus have no memories on which to draw, will they be less accurate at forecasting.

PRECISE JUDGMENTS BASED ON VERBATIM DETAIL

Errors in prediction of emotions become more frequent as the judgment required for the prediction becomes more precise. When people are asked to give a specific rating to their level of happiness or intensity of arousal, people will draw on verbatim representations that are subject to greater interference over time. In the absence of the accurate verbatim representations, such as when making a forecast of one's happiness level in a future situation, people will tend to rely on gists, in this case often a theory of events based on the cue or question. This will result in less consistency between forecasts of happiness, present ratings of happiness, and recollections of happiness. If the ratings in the moment are the standard against which accuracy is based, then the forecasts and recollections of those judgments will be inaccurate in comparison. These errors can be decreased if, at the time of forecast, the person is prompted with the verbatim cues that match the future situation.

One study that demonstrates this effect compared predicted to experienced happiness in response to the participants' team winning or losing an upcoming football game (Wilson, Wheatley, Meyers, Gilbert, & Axsom, 2000). Participants were asked to make predictions about how happy they would be—on a continuous scale from 1 to 9—if their teams won or lost on the day after the game. Half of these participants made predictions after completing a diary in which they were also asked to report what they would be doing on the days following the game (e.g., studying, socializing with friends, etc.), with an estimate of how long. Those whose team won predicted a greater intensity of happiness than they experienced compared to their baseline happiness, and those whose team lost predicted less intensity of happiness than they experienced compared to baseline. This illustrates that people tend to be inaccurate when making a quantitative instead of categorical forecast of well-being. Forecasts seem to be based on a theory of events, an expected gist that winning will make them happy. However, this effect did not occur for the condition in which participants were also asked to make quantitative judgments of the time spent doing various activities in the days following the game before making predictions of their happiness. The report of happiness on the days following the win was more likely to be based on verbatim memory of actual experience, and when people were given specific verbatim cues regarding likely events that would occur in the days following the game, people's predictions of experienced happiness were more accurate.

Other studies have replicated the same basic effect that people make inaccurate forecasts regarding the intensity of emotional responses, usually predicting greater intensity than is experienced, reflecting forecasts based on a gist of a theory of events. Another such example was conducted based on the outcome of a recent presidential election (Wilson, Meyers, & Gilbert, 2002). Three months before the election, Democratic participants were asked to predict their happiness if Bill Clinton were to win. They were also asked to report their happiness right after his actual re-election in 1996, and to recall their happiness from right after his re-election three months later. Predictions of happiness beforehand were found to be much higher than happiness actually experienced, illustrating the same bias in judgment displayed above. These same participants also displayed a retrospective durability bias, in which they also recalled being happier than they had been (in essence reverting back to their predicted level of happiness). Both of these effects can be described as a result of reliance on gist in judgments: When asked about happiness given a supported candidate's win (either in the future or the past), people report a strong positive reaction because that judgment fits the expected gist of the event (the theory of events). However, a report of happiness on the day of the win is based on verbatim memory of actual experience, and thus overall intensity of happiness is less influenced by the recent positive event.

Patterns of recalling and predicting judgments of happiness such as these—in which people overestimate the rated intensity of an emotional experience if they are not currently experiencing it—have been referred to as the impact bias (Wilson & Gilbert, 2013). Briefly summarized, the impact bias is the overestimation of the impact that events will have on our emotions, both regarding estimations of duration and intensity. This is generally understood to be a result of making judgments of emotional experience without the rich contextual details that accompany a concurrent emotional experience (Robinson & Clore, 2002). This results in distant future predictions becoming more simplistic and categorical (gist-based) while predictions of the immediate future have more of the detail and complexity that is readily available in one's current context (Liberman, Sagristano, & Trope, 2002). FTT predicts that these details will not be stored long-term in memory and will therefore not be used in making judgments or estimates of well-being for contexts in the future or past, as this past evidence has supported.

GLOBAL JUDGMENTS BASED ON GIST

Global judgments of well-being, such as overall happiness and life satisfaction, tend to be based on enduring gist representations, contrary to momentary emotional reactions to a specific stimulus or context. Thus, when making forecasts about global judgments of well-being, different patterns of accuracy of these forecasts can emerge. Like forecasts and memories of valence, people will base global judgments of well-being on encoded gists, whether it be a forecast or a memory. For global judgments made in the present—such as how happy a person has been "overall these days"—people still rely on the same global gists. The specific question itself asks for a global judgment, which will elicit gist representations according to FTT. Thus, when forecasting or recalling these judgments, reliance on those gists will result in greater accuracy, as people will tend to rely on the same representations when making forecasts, judging based on recent experience or by recalling a memory. Unlike the previously discussed research, then, giving a cue that focuses attention on verbatim details of the experience can mislead forecasts. Some recent research has supported these theoretical predictions.

In one such study, college undergraduates were asked to predict the overall happiness they would experience after random assignment to one of several college dorms (Dunn, Wilson, & Gilbert, 2003). In this housing lottery, many of the social features would remain constant across the various possible outcomes—that is, roommates and blockmates (friends who enter the housing lottery together) will generally be assigned together in the lottery. The participants on average were all able to recognize that the social features of their housing assignments would have a greater effect on their overall happiness than the physical details of the locations (e.g., room size, location of dormitory). They were correct in this assessment; happiness correlated with the quality of the social features but did not relate to the quality of the physical features. In this sense, the participants did have an accurate gist understanding of what results in their global well-being. However, when asked specifically about how happy they would be based on their assigned dormitory, which amounts only to a difference in physical features that has little influence on their overall happiness, participants overestimated the effect this would have on their happiness. The cue in the question about specific dormitories deflected processing toward details, distracting them from the essential gist, that having their friends around is what contributes to well-being, focusing their attention on irrelevant verbatim detail. People who did not get the housing assignment they rated most highly were happier than they thought they would be, and those who got their desired dorm were not as happy. A second experiment changed the order of the questions, asking the participants about which factors had a greater effect on their happiness before asking them to make a prediction. This increased the accuracy of their judgments. The participants in this case had the important gist understanding of what causes their overall happiness in mind, by being primed by the important social factors that would stay the same, instead of answering based on the comparatively irrelevant detail of the location of their dorm.

A growing body of research also supports the idea that focusing attention on verbatim details as opposed to gist—as in the physical aspects of housing assignments in the previous study—can have detrimental effects on judgment (Fukukura, Ferguson, & Fujita, 2013). For example, one study, as discussed above, either gave participants four minutes to deliberate over the details of possible cars to buy, or four minutes of a buffer task (anagram-solving) to distract them from the details of the cars (Dijksterhuis, Bos, Nordgren, & van Baaren, 2006). Those in the distracted condition tended to pick the car with more positive features as their favorite. In a similar study, people were given a choice of cell phones after writing for three minutes on either *how* people purchase cell phones or *why* people purchase cell phones—a standard method for inducing concrete versus abstract levels of construal, respectively (Fukukura, Ferguson, & Fujita, 2013). By manipulating the level of abstraction, the level of detail was manipulated, with those writing about *how* including more detail than those writing about *why*. The traditional interpretation is that this is a manipulation of construal level, as the greater detail represents a lower level of construal, whereas the abstraction associated with writing about *why* represents higher construal. People who wrote about *why* people purchase cell phones were more likely to choose the phone with objectively better characteristics than those who wrote about *how*. However, this effect of construal level was actually found to be completely moderated by gist memory for traits of the phone; people who wrote about why people purchase phones were better able to recall the gist of which phones scored highest on a variety of characteristics (but not necessarily details), and this measure of gist memory predicted purchasing the best phone. This result suggests that it is the reliance on these gist representations of options that results in choosing the option that will result in the highest satisfaction, as opposed to construal levels per se.

Recent work has suggested that less focus on verbatim detail can also have an effect on SWB as well. Hsee, Zhang, Cai, and Zhang (2013) recently conducted a series of studies in which a higher earning rate of rewards—in this case, chocolates—resulted in people earning more than they could eat, referred to as "overearning." When given a cap of the amount of chocolates they can earn, however, they reported being more happy with the outcome. In fact, ratings of happiness were negatively correlated with earnings. This effect can be interpreted as the cap on earnings distracting participants from a verbatim detail—specifically the rate of earning—resulting in higher well-being overall.

The argument that global measures of SWB (such as life satisfaction) and more ephemeral measures of SWB (such as daily happiness) are supported by different memory representations supports predictions that these different measures share different relationships with explanatory variables. This can be counterintuitive and paradoxical given that, generally, life satisfaction and daily happiness are correlated. For example, in a nationwide survey of more than 145,000 people, life satisfaction was associated with income and education, whereas daily happiness was predicted more so by care giving, loneliness, health, and smoking (Kahneman & Deaton, 2010). Although in this study life satisfaction and daily happiness were generally positively correlated, the separate activation of gist and verbatim representations for responding to these questions predicts that some variables will positively relate to one and negatively relate to the other. For example, frequent spending may lead to an increase in daily happiness but a decrease in overall life satisfaction. Separating judgments of SWB by the representations that underlie those judgments, such that global judgments of life satisfaction are supported by gist representations and momentary judgments of happiness are supported by verbatim representations, allows additional predictions to be made about how these measures can differentially predict outcomes.

CONCLUSIONS

In this chapter we have discussed an alternative theoretical perspective, FTT, which explains and predicts empirical results in the judgment and decison-making literature to be the result of varying memory representations. We then applied these principles to make predictions regarding judgments of subjective well-being—including happiness and life satisfaction—that people may subsequently use to guide choices. We also briefly looked at the evidence in support of these predictions. The theoretical predictions and empirical evidence support the hypothesis that categorical judgments of emotions and global judgments of well-being are supported by gist memory representations. Therefore, people will be more accurate if they rely on these gist representations for their predictions. In contrast, specific ratings of intensity of emotion appear to be supported more by the verbatim details of the context of the experience. Because these verbatim details are subject to greater interference over time, memories of these details will be less accurate and recall of past judgments of momentary happiness will be less accurate as well. As forecasts of future judgments of happiness are based on these memories, these forecasts will be inaccurate if the predictions are made in the absence of any verbatim details from the context of the experience.

Past work on affective forecasting has placed the results in the context of construal level theory (Wilson & Gilbert, 2003). This theory has been used to explain differences in preferences between near-future events and distant-future events through differences in the levels of concrete details (Liberman, Sagristano, & Trope, 2002; Trope & Liberman, 2003). The theory does not predict, however, any greater accuracy with higher levels of construal (i.e. fewer details). This would put it at a disadvantage in predicting some of the effects reviewed above, such as when people pick preferable cars or better phones when distracted from the details. Instead, as was described above, level of detail or abstraction has an effect on choice through changes in gist memory representation, as those who focused on why people choose phones organized the information into cohesive gist memories that improved decisions. Drawing predictions from FTT also permits predictions regarding real-world outcomes. For example, it may be that focusing on global representations of well-being (such as life satisfaction or global happiness) as opposed to more ephemeral representations (such as momentary happiness) predicts improvements in more objectively-defined outcomes, such as health, education, or financial state.

Global representations of well-being based on gist may have additional impact through a much more simple mechanism: People spend a great deal of time not focused on the details of their present environment. In a recent study of real-time reports of well-being from about 500 people, 46.9 percent of samples taken included a report of mind-wandering (Killingsworth & Gilbert, 2010). This suggests that much of the time, people are not focused on the details of their current activities, and a good portion of this is likely to be because of reminiscing about the past or daydreaming about the future. If people spend much of their daily lives focused on the global gists that form the basis of overall happiness and life satisfaction instead of the verbatim detail of their experience, then it may be more important to focus people on enduring gist representations than judgments of specific levels of intensity of happiness when it comes to guiding people's choices about their futures. As Daniel Kahneman summarized regarding predictions of future happiness, "nothing in life is as important as you think it is, while you are thinking about it" Kahneman, 2011, p. 402). This may be because asking about intensity of in-the-moment happiness is the wrong question to ask—long-term happiness in retrospect, the digested gist of experience, may be what ultimately matters for well-being (Kahneman, 2011, p. 402).

AUTHOR NOTE

Preparation of this chapter was supported in part by the National Institutes of Health under Awards R21CA149796 and R01NR014368–01 to V. F. Reyna. The content is solely the responsibility of the authors and does not necessarily represent the official views of the National Institutes of Health.

REFERENCES

Adolphs, R., Denburg, N. L., & Tranel, D. (2001). The amygdala's role in long-term declarative memory for gist and detail. *Behavioral Neuroscience, 115(5)*, 983–992.

Adolphs, R., Tranel, D., & Buchanan, T. W. (2005). Amygdala damage impairs emotional memory for gist but not details of complex stimuli. *Nature Neuroscience, 8(4)*, 512–518.

Andrews, F. M., & Withey, S. B. (1976). *Social indicators of well-being.* New York, NY: Plenum Press.

Asato, M. R., Terwilliger, R., Woo, J., & Luna, B. (2010). White matter development in adolescence: A DTI study. *Cerebral Cortex, 20(9)*, 2122–2131.

Baird, A. A., & Fugelsang, J. A. (2004). The emergence of consequential thought: Evidence from neuroscience. *Philosophical Transactions of the Royal Society of London, Series B: Biological Sciences 359(1451)*, 1797–1804.

Brainerd, C. J., & Gordon, L. L. (2004). Development of verbatim and gist memory for numbers. *Developmental Psychology, 30(2)*, 163–177.

Brainerd, C. J., Holliday, R. E., & Reyna, V. F. (2004). Behavioral measurement of remembering phenomenologies: So simple a child can do it. *Child Development, 75(2)*, 505–522.

Brainerd, C. J., & Reyna, V. F. (1998). Fuzzy-trace theory and children's false memories. *Journal of Experimental Child Psychology, 71(2)*, 81–129.

—— (2004). Fuzzy trace theory and memory development. *Developmental Review, 24(4),* 396–439.

—— (2005). *The science of false memory.* New York, NY: Oxford University Press.

Brainerd, C. J., Reyna, V. F., & Kneer, R. (1995). False-recognition reversal: When is similarity distinctive? *Journal of Memory and Language, 34(2),* 157–185.

Brainerd, C. J., Reyna, V. F., & Zember, E. (2011). Theoretical and forensic implications of developmental studies of the DRM illusion. *Memory and Cognition, 39(3),* 365–380.

Brainerd, C. J., Wright, R., Reyna, V. F., & Mojardin, A. H. (2001). Conjoint recognition and phantom recollection. *Journal of Experimental Psychology: Learning, Memory, and Cognition, 27(2),* 307–327.

Casey, B. J., Getz, S., & Galvan, A. (2008). The adolescent brain. *Developmental Review, 28(1),* 42–77.

Ceci, S. J., & Bruck, M. (1998). The ontogeny and durability of true and false memories: A fuzzy trace account. *Journal of Experimental Child Psychology, 71(2),* 165–169.

Chick, C. F., & Reyna, V. F. (2012) A fuzzy-trace theory of adolescent risk-taking: Beyond self-control and sensation seeking. In V. F. Reyna, S. Chapman, M. Dougherty, & J. Confrey (Eds.), *The adolescent brain: Learning, reasoning, and decision making* (pp. 379–428). Washington, DC: American Psychological Association.

Davidson, D. (1995). The representativeness heuristic and conjunction fallacy effect in children's decision-making. *Merrill-Palmer Quarterly, 41(3),* 328–346.

Deese, J. (1959). On the prediction of occurrence of particular verbal intrusions in immediate recall. *Journal of Experimental Psychology, 58(1),* 17–22.

Diener, E. (2000). Subjective well-being: The science of happiness and a proposal for a national index. *American Psychologist, 55(1),* 34–43.

Dijksterhuis, A., Bos, M. W., Nordgren, L. F., & van Baaren, R. B. (2006). On making the right choice: The deliberation-without-attention effect. *Science, 311(5763),* 1005–1007.

Dunn, E. W., Wilson, T. D., & Gilbert, D. T. (2003). Location, location, location: The misprediction of satisfaction in housing lotteries. *Personality and Social Psychology Bulletin, 29(11),* 1421–1432.

Figner, B., Knoch, D., Johnson, E. J., Krosch, A. R., Lisanby, S. H., Fehr, E., et al. (2010). Lateral prefrontal cortex and self-control in intertemporal choice. *Nature Neuroscience, 13(5),* 538–539.

Fischer, G. W., & Hawkins, S. A. (1993). Strategy compatibility, scale compatibility, and the prominence effect. *Journal of Experimental Psychology: Human Perception and Performance, 19(3),* 580–597.

Fukukura, J., Ferguson, M. J., & Fujita, K. (2013). Psychological distance can improve decision making under information overload via gist memory. *Journal of Experimental Psychology: General, 142(3),* 658–665.

Galvan, A., Hare, T., Voss, H., Glover, G., & Casey, B. J. (2007). Risk-taking and the adolescent brain: Who is at risk? *Developmental Science, 10(2),* F8–F14.

Giedd, J. N., Stockman, M., Weddle, C., Liverpool, M., Wallace, G. L., Lee, N. R., Lalonde, F., & Lenroot, R. K. (2012). Anatomic magnetic resonance imaging of the developing child and adolescent brain. In V. F. Reyna, S. B. Chapman, M. R. Dougherty, & J. Confrey (Eds.), *The adolescent brain: Learning, reasoning, and decision making* (pp. 15–35). Washington, DC: American Psychological Association.

Gilbert, D. T., & Wilson, T. D. (2009). Why the brain talks to itself: Sources of error in emotional prediction. *Philosophical Transactions of the Royal Society of London. Series B, Biological Sciences, 364(1521),* 1335–1341.

Gilovich, T., Griffin, D. W., & Kahneman, D. (2002). *The psychology of intuitive judgment: Heuristic and biases.* Cambridge: Cambridge University Press.

Green, L., Myerson, J., Lichtman, D., Rosen, S., & Fry, A. (1996). Temporal discounting in choice between delayed rewards: The role of age and income. *Psychology and Aging, 11(1),* 79–84.

Hsee, C. K., Zhang, J., Cai, C. F., & Zhang, S. (2013). Overearning. *Psychological Science, 24(6),* 852–859.

Jacobs, J. E., & Klaczynski, P. A. (2002). The development of judgment and decision making during childhood and adolescence. *Current Directions in Psychological Science, 11(4),* 145–149.

Jacobs, J. E., & Potenza, M. (1991). The use of judgment heuristics to make social and object decisions: A developmental perspective. *Child Development, 62(1),* 166–178.

Kahneman, D. (2011). *Thinking, fast and slow.* New York, NY: Farrar, Straus & Giroux.

Kahneman, D., & Deaton, A. (2010). High income improves evaluation of life but not emotional well-being. *Proceedings of the National Academy of Sciences of the United States of America, 107(38),* 16489–16493.

Kahneman, D., & Tversky, A. (1973). On the psychology of prediction. *Psychological Review, 80(4),* 237–251.

Kensinger, E. A., Garoff-Eaton, R. J., & Schacter, D. L. (2006). Memory for specific visual details can be enhanced by negative arousing content. *Journal of Memory and Language, 54(1),* 99–112.

—— (2007). How negative emotion enhances the visual specificity of a memory. *Journal of Cognitive Neuroscience, 19(11),* 1872–1887.

Kermer, D. A., Driver-Linn, E., Wilson, T. D., & Gilbert, D. T. (2006). Loss aversion is an affective forecasting error. *Psychological Science, 17(8),* 649–653.

Killingsworth, M. A., & Gilbert, D. T. (2010). A wandering mind is an unhappy mind. *Science, 330(6006),* 932.

Klingberg, T., Vaidya, C. J., Gabrieli, J. D. E., Moseley, M. E., & Hedehus, M. (1999). Myelination and organization of the frontal white matter in children: A diffusion tensor MRI study. *NeuroReport, 10(13),* 2817–2821.

Kühberger, A., & Tanner, C. (2010). Risky choice framing: Task versions and a comparison of prospect theory and fuzzy-trace theory. *Journal of Behavioral Decision Making, 23(3),* 314–329.

Lazar, A. N. (2012). Desirable deviations in medical decision making in the pre-hospital setting: A fuzzy-trace theory approach. Unpublished master thesis. Cornell University, Ithaca, NY.

Liberman, N., Sagristano, M. D., & Trope, Y. (2002). The effect of temporal distance on level of mental construal. *Journal of Experimental Social Psychology, 38(6),* 523–534.

Mellers, B. A., & McGraw, A. P. (2001). Anticipated emotions as guides to choice. *Current Directions in Psychological Science, 10(6),* 210–214.

Miller, G. A. (1956). The magical number seven, plus or minus two: Some limits on our capacity for processing information. *Psychological Review, 63(2),* 81–97.

Mills, B., Reyna, V. F., & Estrada, S. (2008). Explaining contradictory relations between risk perception and risk taking. *Psychological Science, 19(5),* 429–433.

Mitchell, J. P., Schirmer, J., Ames, D. L., & Gilbert, D. T. (2011). Medial prefrontal cortex predicts intertemporal choice. *Journal of Cognitive Neuroscience, 23(4),* 1–10.

Monahan, J. L., Murphy, S. T., & Zajonc, R. B. (2000). Subliminal mere exposure: Specific, general, and diffuse effects. *Psychological Science, 11(6),* 462–466.

Mukherjee, P., & McKinstry, R. C. (2006). Diffusion tensor imaging and tractography of human brain development. *Neuroimaging Clinics of North America, 16(1),* 19–43.

Odegard, T. N., Holliday, R. E., Brainerd, C. J., & Reyna, V. F. (2008). Attention to global-gist processing eliminates age effects in false memories. *Journal of Experimental Child Psychology, 99(2),* 96–113.

Osgood, C. E., Suci, G., & Tannenbaum, P. (1957). *The measurement of meaning*. Champaign, IL: University of Illinois Press.

Reyna, V. F. (1991). Class inclusion, the conjunction fallacy, and other cognitive illusions. *Developmental Review, 11(4)*, 317–336.

—— (2008). A theory of medical decision making and health: Fuzzy trace theory. *Medical Decision Making, 28(6)*, 850–865.

—— (2012). A new intuitionism: Meaning, memory, and development in fuzzy trace theory. *Judgment and Decision Making, 7(3)*, 332–359.

Reyna, V. F., & Adam, M. B. (2003). Fuzzy-trace theory, risk communication, and product labeling in sexually transmitted diseases. *Risk Analysis: An Official Publication of the Society for Risk Analysis, 23(2)*, 325–342.

Reyna, V. F., & Brainerd, C. J. (1993). Fuzzy memory and mathematics in the classroom. In G. M. Davies & R. H. Logie (Eds.), *Memory in everyday life* (pp. 91–119). Amsterdam: North-Holland/Elsevier Science Publishers.

—— (1994). The origins of probability judgment: A review of data and theories. In G. Wright & P. Ayton (Eds.), *Subjective probability* (pp. 239–272). New York, NY: Wiley.

—— (1995) Fuzzy-trace theory: An interim synthesis. *Learning and Individual Differences, 7(1)*, 1–75.

—— (2011). Dual process in decision making and developmental neuroscience: A fuzzy-trace model. *Developmental Review, 31(2–3)*, 180–206.

Reyna, V. F., Chapman, S. B., Dougherty, M., & Confrey, J. (2012). *The adolescent brain: Learning, reasoning and decision making*. Washington, DC: American Psychological Association.

Reyna, V. F., Chick, C. F., Corbin, J. C., & Hsia, A. N. (2013). Developmental reversals in risky decision making: Intelligence agents show larger decision biases than college students. *Psychological Science, 25(1)*, 76–84.

Reyna, V. F., & Ellis, S. C. (1994). Fuzzy trace theory and framing effects in children's risky decision making. *Psychological Science, 5(5)*, 275–279.

Reyna, V. F., Estrada, S. M., DeMarinis, J. A., Myers, R. M., Stanisz, J. M., & Mills, B. A. (2011). Neurobiological and memory models of risky decision making in adolescents versus young adults. *Journal of Experimental Psychology: Learning, Memory, and Cognition, 37(5)*, 1125–1142.

Reyna, V. F., & Farley, F. (2006). Risk and rationality in adolescent decision making: Implications for theory, practice, and public policy. *Psychological Science in the Public Interest, 7(1)*, 1–44.

Reyna, V. F., & Kiernan, B. (1994). Development of gist versus verbatim memory in sentence recognition: Effects of lexical familiarity, semantic content, encoding instructions and retention interval. *Developmental Psychology, 30(2)*, 178–191.

—— (1995). Children's memory and metaphorical interpretation. *Metaphor and Symbolic Activity, 10(4)*, 309–331.

Reyna, V. F., & Lloyd, F. J. (2006). Physician decision making and cardiac risk: Effects of knowledge, risk perception, risk tolerance and fuzzy processing. *Journal of Experimental Psychology: Applied, 12(3)*, 179–195.

Reyna, V. F., Mills, B. A., Estrada, S. M., & Brainerd, C. J. (2007). False memory in children: Data, theory, and legal implications. In M. P. Toglia, J. D. Read, D. F. Ross, & R. C. L. Lindsay (Eds.), *The handbook of eyewitness psychology: Memory for events* (pp. 473–510). Mahwah, NJ: Erlbaum.

Richard, R. J., Van der Plight, J., & De Vries, N. K. (1996), Anticipated affect and behavioral choice. *Basic and Applied Social Psychology, 18(2)*, 111–129.

Rivers, S. E., Reyna, V. F., & Mills, B. (2008). Risk taking under the influence: A fuzzy-trace theory of emotion in adolescence. *Developmental Review, 28(1)*, 107–144.

Robinson, M. D., & Clore, G. L. (2001). Simulation, scenarios, and emotional appraisal: Testing the convergence of real and imagined reactions to emotional stimuli. *Personality and Social Psychology Bulletin, 27(11)*, 1520–1532.

Roediger, H. L., III, & McDermott, K. B. (1995). Creating false memories: Remembering words not presented on lists. *Journal of Experimental Psychology: Learning, Memory, and Cognition, 21(4)*, 803–814.

Romer, D. (2003). *Reducing adolescent risk: Toward an integrated approach*. Thousand Oaks, CA: Sage Publications.

Rosenzweig, E., & Gilovich, T. (2012). Buyer's remorse or missed opportunity? Differential regrets for material and experiential purchases. *Journal of Personality and Social Psychology, 102(2)*, 215–223.

Schacter, D. L., Addis, D. R., & Buckner, R. L. (2008). Episodic simulation of future events: concepts, data, and applications. *Annals of the New York Academy of Sciences, 1124(1)*, 39–60.

Schacter, D. L., Addis, D. R., Hassabis, D., Martin, V. C., Spreng, R. N., & Szpunar, K. K. (2012). The future of memory: Remembering, imagining, and the brain. *Neuron, 76(4)*, 677–694.

Shiv, B., & Huber, J. (2000). The impact of anticipating satisfaction on consumer choice. *Journal of Consumer Research, 27(2)*, 202–216.

Somerville, L. H., Jones, R. M., & Casey, B. J. (2010). A time of change: Behavioral and neural correlates of adolescent sensitivity to appetitive and aversive environmental cues. *Brain and Cognition, 72(1)*, 124–133.

Steinberg, L., Albert, D., Cauffman, E., Banich, M., Graham, S., & Woolard, J. (2008). Age differences in sensation seeking and impulsivity as indexed by behavior and self-report: Evidence for a dual systems model. *Developmental Psychology, 44(6)*, 1764–1778.

Trope, Y., & Liberman, N. (2003). Temporal construal. *Psychological Review, 110(3)*, 403–421.

Tversky, A. (1969). Intransitivity of preferences. *Psychological Review, 76(1)*, 31–48.

Tversky, A., & Kahneman, D. (1983). Extensional versus intuitive reasoning: The conjunction fallacy in probability judgment. *Psychological Review, 90(4)*, 293–315.

——(1986). Rational choice and the framing of decisions. *Journal of Business, 59(4)*, 251–278.

Watson, D., Clark, L. A., & Tellegen, A. (1988). Development and validation of brief measures of positive and negative affect: The PANAS scales. *Journal of Personality and Social Psychology, 54(6)*, 1063–1070.

Wilhelms, E. A., Corbin, J. C., & Reyna, V. F. (in press). Gist memory in reasoning and decision making: Age, experience, and expertise. In V. Thompson & A. Feeney (Eds.), *Reasoning as memory*. New York, NY: Psychology Press.

Wilhelms, E. A., & Reyna, V. F. (2013). Fuzzy trace theory and medical decisions by minors: Differences in reasoning between adolescents and adults. *Journal of Medicine and Philosophy, 38(3)*, 268–282.

Wilson, T. D., & Gilbert, D. T. (2003). Affective forecasting. *Advances in Experimental Social Psychology, 35*, 345–411.

——(2013). The impact bias is alive and well. *Journal of Personality and Social Psychology, 105(5)*, 740–748.

Wilson, T. D., Meyers, J., & Gilbert, D. T. (2001). Lessons from the past: Do people learn from experience that emotional reactions are short-lived? *Personality and Social Psychology Bulletin, 27(12)*, 1648–1661.

Wilson, T. D., Wheatley, T. P., Kurtz, J. L., Dunn, E. W., & Gilbert, D. T. (2004). When to fire: Anticipatory versus postevent reconstrual of uncontrollable events. *Personality and Social Psychology Bulletin, 30(3)*, 340–351.

Wilson, T. D., Wheatley, T., Meyers, J. M., Gilbert, D. T., & Axsom, D. (2000). Focalism: A source of durability bias in affective forecasting. *Journal of Personality and Social Psychology, 78(5)*, 821–836.

Woodzicka, J. A., & LaFrance, M. (2001). Real versus imagined gender harassment. *Journal of Social Issues, 57(1)*, 15–30.

Zajonc, R. B. (2001). Mere exposure: A gateway to the subliminal. *Current Directions in Psychological Science, 10(6)*, 224–228.

Part III

Heuristics and Biases

4

Intuition, Interference, Inhibition, and Individual Differences in Fuzzy-Trace Theory

JONATHAN C. CORBIN, JORDANA M.
LIBERALI, VALERIE F. REYNA, AND
PRISCILA G. BRUST-RENCK

According to fuzzy-trace theory, individuals rely on two memory representations of information to make judgments and decisions—verbatim representations, which are detailed and specific, and gist representations, which are meaningful and intuitive. Fuzzy-trace theory posits a third process of monitoring and inhibition, which allows for improved decision making in the face of task interference. First, this chapter reviews the role of interference and intuition in judgment and decision making—particularly output interference (i.e. verbatim interference) and interference from gist representations (e.g., reliance on compelling, intuitive stereotypes rather than relevant statistical information). Next, we discuss the role of inhibition in avoiding common judgment and decision-making biases. Specifically, inhibition is reviewed through the perspectives of developmental psychology, individual differences (e.g., working memory), and neuroeconomics, highlighting converging results from each area. Finally, we discuss conditions in which inhibition fails to prevent biases in judgment and decision making.

Judgment and decision-making research has focused on systematic biases, which challenge broad assumptions about human rationality. However, individuals vary in the degree to which they display these biases (e.g., Bruine de Bruin, Parker, & Fischhoff, 2007; Stanovich & West, 2008). The current chapter approaches individual differences in judgment and decision making through the lens of fuzzy-trace theory (FTT), a theory of memory, decision making, and neuroeconomics, which has been shown to account for a number of judgment-and-decision-making phenomena (Reyna & Brainerd, 2011; Reyna & Zayas, 2014). Furthermore, we take an individual-differences approach in explaining the role of inhibition in avoiding bias.

First, we discuss the role of intuition in judgment and decision making from the perspective of FTT (see Chapter 3 for a brief introduction). Specifically, this chapter focuses on meaningful intuition, or gist (Reyna, 2012), as opposed to other conceptions of intuition that emphasize mindless associations (which involves stimulus–response pairings; e.g., Robinson & Roediger, 1997). According to FTT, individuals encode multiple independent memory representations of a stimulus simultaneously, ranging from very detailed, concrete representations (i.e. verbatim representations) to qualitative representations, which are meaningful (i.e. gist representations; Reyna, 2012). An example would be representing the chance of rain on any given day. A verbatim representation for a chance of rain would be the exact numeric quantity (e.g., 20 percent, 20/100, ⅕, etc.). The gist consists of meaningful qualitative distinctions such as "a low probability of rain" or, categorically, "It is not going to rain today." Whereas verbatim representations are concrete (the difference between a 10 percent and 40 percent chance of rain is equal to the difference between a 35 percent and a 65 percent), gist representations rely on context and meaningful distinctions (both a 10 percent and 40 percent chance of rain mean that rain is unlikely whereas the difference between 35 percent and 65 percent could mean the difference between leaving the umbrella at home and bringing it to work).

Furthermore, gist representations are robust to interference whereas verbatim representations are not (Brainerd, Aydin, & Reyna, 2012; Gorfein & MacLeod, 2007; Reyna, Mills, Estrada, & Brainerd, 2006). For example, if you are told that there is a 20 percent chance of rain, and then immediately are given a phone number to remember, it will become increasingly difficult to recall 20 percent if asked about the chances of rain later, but it will be easy to recall that the chance was low. Given that gist representations are meaningful and outlast verbatim representations, individuals generally rely on them to make judgments and decisions.

We therefore review research that demonstrates how task interference can lead to biased judgments and decisions. Specifically, we examine the role of output interference (i.e. tasks involving multiple mental operations; Dempster, 2002; Reyna, 1995) in biasing judgments (Reyna, 1995; Wolfe & Reyna, 2010), as well as how the retrieval of an inappropriate gist can interfere with the retrieval of task-appropriate verbatim (or alternate gist) representations (Reyna, Chick, Corbin, & Hsia, 2013; Wolfe & Reyna, 2010).

FTT also posits a third process of monitoring and inhibition, which accounts for individual differences with respect to the ability to inhibit compelling gists that can lead to decision biases (Reyna, 1995; Reyna & Brainerd, 1995). Although gist reliance can lead to some predictable biases (Reyna et al., 2013), research has demonstrated that a number of measures of cognitive ability predict individuals' likelihood of overcoming these biases (Del Missier, Mäntylä, Hansson, & Bruine de Bruin, 2013; Stanovich & West, 1998; Toplak et al., 2013). The results in the individual difference literature are also supported by developmental work (Reyna, 2004) as well as neuroeconomics (Reyna, Estrada, DeMarinis, Myers, Stanisz, & Mills, 2011).

Finally, we will discuss limitations of the ability to inhibit compelling gists that lead to biased decision making. Many judgment and decision-making tasks are set up so that gist and verbatim representations of the tasks lead to conflicting responses which can cue relevant reasoning principles (and therefore inhibition can play a role in combating interference; Toplak et al., 2013). Although inhibition is useful when combating interference, some types of problems do not cue an appropriate reasoning principle and therefore do not set up a conflict between intuitive and normative judgments or decisions (Stanovich & West, 2008).

INTERFERENCE IN JUDGMENT AND DECISION MAKING

Processing Interference

Given that verbatim representations are more susceptible to interference as compared to gist (Brainerd, Aydin, & Reyna, 2012), judgments and decisions that require precision are more likely to suffer when faced with processing interference (Wolfe & Reyna, 2010). In probability judgment, ratio bias (otherwise known as the numerosity effect; Reyna & Brainerd, 2008) occurs when individuals bias their decisions toward comparing numerators in a ratio and ignore the relevant denominators. This effect can be seen in tasks whereby adults are given two containers of marbles, one in which there is one black marble and nine white marbles and another in which there are ten black marbles and 90 white marbles, and they are asked from which container they would choose if they are rewarded for getting a black marble. Even with identical ratios (1:10), adults will generally prefer the container with more black marbles (i.e. a larger numerator; Pacini & Epstein, 1999; Reyna & Brainerd, 2008). Although this example does not demonstrate a judgment error (because ratios are equal), failing to inhibit one's initial judgment based on numerators (and thus ignoring denominators) can lead to judgment errors. For example, a minority of adults choose the incorrect container for similar problems in which the container with the larger numerator also has a smaller overall ratio—such as a choice between a container with 1 black marble and 9 white marbles (10 percent chance of a black marble) or a container with 8 black marbles and 92 white marbles (80 percent chance of a black marble; Denes-Raj & Epstein, 1994; Kirkpatrick & Epstein, 1992; Pacini & Epstein, 1999; Reyna & Brainerd, 1994; Stanovich & West, 2008).

Although a minority of adults demonstrated the bias in the previously discussed problem, probability-judgment tasks that involve increased amounts of output interference (i.e. requiring more mental steps to reach the correct conclusion) can lead to more common errors. A real-world example of a conditional probability task can be found when adults were asked to judge the probability of having a disease given a pretest probability of 10 percent, an 80 percent chance of having the disease with a positive result, and an 80 percent chance of not having the disease with a negative result. When asked whether the probability of having the disease given a positive test result is closer to 70 percent or 30 percent, a majority of adults (including a sample of physicians) chose 70 percent when the correct answer is 30 percent (Reyna, 2004; Reyna & Adam, 2003). In these types of problems, individuals are losing track of individual classes (i.e. true positives, true negatives, false positives, and false negatives) with respect to the overall base rate (i.e. 10 percent), and therefore they neglect the relevant denominator. Unlike previous examples, the added interference generated by keeping track of classes leads to a greater likelihood of judgment error. When the source of interference (confusion regarding overlapping classes) is removed by presenting individuals with 2×2 tables that separate out each individual class, performance greatly improves (Wolfe & Reyna, 2010), supporting the prediction that these judgment errors occur due to simple mental bookkeeping errors as opposed to knowledge deficits. Finally, deficits in memory capacity have also been ruled out as a cause of these judgment errors (Reyna & Brainerd, 2008).

DECISIONS BASED ON GIST

Given the susceptibility of verbatim traces to interference, it is not surprising that many judgments and decisions are based on gist. Furthermore, if a task encourages retrieval of a salient gist representation, decision makers will rely on the easily retrieved gist, rather than the more precise verbatim representation.

A well-studied reasoning error in probability judgment that incorporates both processing interference and interference from a salient gist can be found in the classic conjunction fallacy task used by Tversky and Kahneman (1983) called the "Linda Problem." The conjunction fallacy occurs when the probability of two events co-occurring is judged to be more likely than the probability of one of those events alone. In the "Linda Problem," participants were given a brief description of Linda in which she was described in terms that would easily bring to mind the stereotype that Linda was a feminist (e.g., she was a philosophy major and concerned with social justice in college). Then they are asked to judge how likely it is that Linda is a "bank teller," and how likely it is that she is a "feminist bank teller." Most people judge "feminist bank teller" as more likely than bank teller alone, exhibiting the conjunction fallacy.

In the same way as the previous judgment errors, FTT predicts that people demonstrate the conjunction fallacy because they focus on the numerator, "feminists" who are bank tellers, ignoring the larger class of bank tellers that includes feminists plus nonfeminists, which would be the appropriate denominator (Reyna & Brainerd, 2008; Wolfe & Reyna, 2010). Furthermore, this problem contains an appealing gist (the stereotypes that paint the picture of Linda as a feminist). Therefore, participants tend to follow the "garden path" created by the gist of Linda and judge that the conjunction is more likely than the whole.

Class-inclusion errors, such as the Linda Problem, are made more compelling by the presence of salient gist representations and by failure to retrieve reasoning principles that are known and understood according to FTT (Reyna, 1991, 2008; Reyna & Mills, 2007). Class-inclusion confusion is especially likely to produce errors when a compelling gist such as a visually or emotionally salient detail, a story, or a stereotype draws a person away from the relevant data in the direction of considering extraneous information, such as the stereotype elicited by the description of Linda (Reyna, 1991; Reyna & Brainerd, 2008).

To illustrate this prediction, consider an example of a disjunction fallacy (Brainerd, Reyna, & Aydin, 2010; Sloman, Rottenstreich, Wisniewski, Hadjichristidis, & Fox, 2004). Assume the following hypotheses: Ha = a person will be victim of a homicide by an acquaintance next year; Hs = a person will be victim of a homicide by a stranger next year; and Ha *or* Hs = the person will be victim of a homicide by an acquaintance *or* a stranger next year. The probability that the person will be a victim of a homicide by an acquaintance *or* a stranger next year (P(Ha or Hs)) is, by definition, equal to or greater than the probability that the person will be victim of a homicide by an acquaintance (Ha) next year or the probability that the person will be victim of a homicide by a stranger (Hs) next year. In other words: P(Ha) ≤ P(Ha or Hs) ≥ P(Hs).

Regarding these hypotheses, a disjunction fallacy is said to occur if the probability of the disjunction event of being a victim of a homicide by either a stranger or acquaintance (P(Ha or Hs)) is considered to be less probable than either one individually. In other words, P(Ha) > P(Ha or Hs) < P(Hs). This usual disjunctive fallacy, in which the probability of the disjunction event is rated to be less likely than one of the two individual events, is actually a subset of the larger class of subadditivity errors (even though, logically, it should be additive). More generally, logic and probability theory dictate that for every P(A) and P(B) where P(A) ≥ P(B): $0 \leq P(A) \leq 1.0$; $0 \leq P(B) \leq 1.0$; $0 \leq P(A \wedge B) \leq P(B)$; $P(A) \leq P(A \vee B) \geq P(A) + P(B) - P(A \wedge B)$. All other responses are *fallacious* and violate the basic assumption of internal consistency, one of the axioms of classical probability theory and support theory (Tversky & Koehler, 1994).

The previous examples of judgment fallacies due to output interference and misleading gists can also be extended to the realm of risky decision making. One specific example can be found in the risky-choice framing effect. In the framing effect, decisions framed in terms of gains tend to elicit risk avoidance, whereas decisions framed as losses elicit risk seeking (e.g., Levin, Schneider, & Gaeth, 1998; Reyna, 2012). In a classic example of this effect, the Asian Disease Problem (Tversky & Kahneman, 1986), participants were told that 600 lives were at risk of dying from a disease. They were asked to choose between two options to combat this disease, which were framed either in terms of people being saved (gains, A vs. B) or people dying (losses, C vs. D):

A. 200 people saved for sure.
B. ⅓ chance 600 people saved, ⅔ chance 0 people saved.
C. 400 people die for sure.
D. ⅓ chance 0 people die, ⅔ chance 600 people die.

Although the outcomes were the same across frames (A = C and B = D), overall, framing the problem in terms of gains encourages choosing the sure option (option A), whereas framing the problem in terms of losses encourages choosing the risky option (option D). These shifting risk preferences violate a fundamental axiom of expected utility theory, that of descriptive invariance (i.e. preferences should be consistent regardless of how a decision is superficially described, provided the options are objectively identical; Tversky & Kahneman, 1986).

According to FTT, framing effects are due to the gist representation of the problem, which consists of a categorical comparison between the sure option of "saving some" to the risky option of "saving some vs. saving none" in the gain frame which leads to a preference for "saving some." This representation is not *ad hoc*; according to FTT, people use the simplest representation (categorical gist) before trying other more fine-grained representations (e.g., ordinal representations; Mills, Reyna, & Estrada, 2008). Similar representational assumptions yield a preference for the risky option of "losing some vs. losing none" over losing some for sure in the loss frame, leading to the opposite preference (e.g., Kühberger & Tanner, 2010; Reyna & Brainerd, 1995). Furthermore, FTT predicts indifference when verbatim traces are relied on (given that expected vales are equal, i.e. ⅓ of 600 saved = 200 saved or ⅔ of 600 lost = 400 lost). Research has consistently supported both predictions, showing that when the gist of the framing problem was emphasized by presenting only the part of the problem that emphasizes the qualitative some vs. none distinction (i.e. 200 saved vs. ⅔ chance 0 saved), larger framing effects were found as compared to the standard problem (Kühberger & Tanner, 2010; Reyna & Brainerd, 1991; Reyna et al., 2013). Furthermore, indifference between options was found when only the verbatim aspect of the problem was emphasized by eliminating the categorical contrast with a zero outcome (e.g., 200 saved vs. ⅓ chance 600 saved). Therefore, eliminating the categorical gist distinction allowed for the reliance on verbatim traces.

INDIVIDUAL DIFFERENCES AND INHIBITION

Thus far, we have explicated the role of gist representations in some judgments and decisions. Specifically we have highlighted instances in which reliance on these representations leads to errors in probability judgment and inconsistent decision making due to processing interference and misleading gist. This section is dedicated to the third process which is outlined by FTT—that of inhibition. Specifically, we will focus on research that has demonstrated that individuals do vary systematically in their ability to inhibit interference and retrieve the appropriate memory representations and reasoning principles and avoid errors in judgment and decision making. For the purposes of this chapter we focus on studies that examine the role of inhibition in decision making from a number of angles, including studies showing developmental differences, individual differences in cognitive ability (such as intelligence and working memory capacity; Dempster, 1992; Dempster & Corkhill, 1999), and neuroimaging research.

Fuzzy-trace theory predicts that individuals who are better able to withstand processing interference are less likely to make incorrect judgments in probability-judgment tasks. Specifically, in ratio bias tasks inhibition is relied on in order to avoid falling prey to denominator neglect, in which one bases their judgment on a comparison between numerators. Regarding individual difference in the susceptibility to ratio bias (or numerosity effect), Stanovich and West (2008) found that adults higher in cognitive ability (as measured by SAT scores) were indeed less likely to demonstrate this bias. Furthermore, in a developmental study involving children ranging from second graders to ninth graders, Toplak, West, and

Stanovich (2013) demonstrated that the ratio bias decreased as children got older. This decline in bias with age was fully mediated by measure of cognitive ability (specifically the Wechsler Abbreviated Scales of Intelligence; Wechsler, 1999). This result supports FTT's prediction that the improvements with age are due to the increase in one's ability to inhibit prepotent responses with age (Reyna, 2004; Reyna & Mills, 2007).

Although one may expect the results for individual differences and ratio bias to easily extend to the conjunction fallacy (given that both tasks involve processing interference), the evidence appears to be more complicated. Given that conjunction fallacy tasks generally involve an alluring and misleading gist (e.g., the stereotype of Linda as a feminist in the previously discussed "Linda Problem"), there is an added level of interference in these tasks. Specifically, FTT predicts that the ability to inhibit processing interference does improve with age, but also predicts that gist memory (i.e. the ability to form meaningful connections between pieces of information to make a coherent inference) also increases with age (Reyna, 2013). Therefore, FTT predicts increases in conjunction errors with age for these types of problems.

The prediction for increases in errors with age for conjunction problems involving appealing stereotypes has been borne out in numerous studies (Davidson, 1995; Jacobs & Potenza, 1991). However, when conjunction problems do not contain appealing gists (e.g., the description of Linda is neutral), once more, reasoning improves with age (De Neys & Vanderputte, 2011; Klaczynski, 2001; Kokis, Macpherson, Toplak, West, & Stanovich, 2002; but see Reyna & Brainerd, 2008, for some important caveats about tasks). Again, this developmental pattern has been shown to be mediated by measures of cognitive ability (Toplak et al., 2013).

In research focusing on adult performance on conjunction problems that include misleading gists (e.g., compelling stereotypes), manipulations meant to help adults inhibit their initial responses to probability-judgment tasks (e.g., encouraging them to re-examine their judgments) also decrease errors (Brainerd & Reyna, 1990, 1995; Reyna & Brainerd, 1995). Finally, individual-differences research measuring cognitive ability in adult samples has also found that those higher in cognitive ability are less likely to demonstrate the conjunction fallacy (Liberali et al., 2012; Stanovich & West, 1998). Therefore, even with processing interference, and the lure of a compelling gist, individuals can retrieve the relevant reasoning principle (i.e. the likelihood of a subordinate class cannot be more probable than that of its parent class) and then inhibit responses that violate that principle.

Thus far we have demonstrated the role of inhibition in improving judgments in the face of both processing and gist-based interference. A similar example from the area of risky decision making can be found in the literature on between-subjects vs. within-subjects risky-choice framing effects. As previously discussed, framing effects are a result of reliance on categorical gist as opposed to precise verbatim representations. Studies that have employed within-subject designs, wherein subjects receive both gain and loss frames, measure whether participants reverse their own preferences between equivalent frames. Therefore, when subjects notice that they have received equivalent problems (i.e. they recognize the equivalency between frames, e.g., out of 600 lives total, 200 lives saved is equal to 400 people dying) and retrieve the relevant reasoning principle, preferences should remain consistent regardless of how equivalent information is presented (i.e. descriptive invariance). Individual-differences research has demonstrated that adults higher in cognitive ability are less likely to fall prey to these within-subject framing effects, presumably because they remember the previous problems better (Bruine de Bruin et al. 2007; Del Missier et al., 2013; Parker & Fischhoff, 2005; Reyna, Lloyd, & Brainerd, 2003; Stanovich & West, 1998, 1999).

Recent neuroscience and neuroeconomics research adds support for the role of inhibition in avoiding judgment errors related to interference (Reyna & Huettel, 2014). For example, De Neys, Vartanian, and Goel (2008) gave participants base-rate tasks in which they were asked to make probability judgments in which a stereotype conflicted with statistical information. These tasks were modeled after Tversky and Kahneman's (1973) classic base-rate problems in which participants must judge whether an individual is a lawyer or engineer after being told that the sample consists of 70 lawyers and 30 engineers and are given a description of this individual that is consistent with stereotypes about engineers (Adam & Reyna, 2005; Reyna & Adam, 2003). According to FTT, the fundamental processes leading to errors in base-rate problems are similar to conjunction problems in that they both stem from neglecting denominators and being led astray by the lure of a stereotype (i.e. gist) (e.g., Reyna, 2004; Reyna & Mills, 2007). Results supported their prediction that the right lateral prefrontal cortex (rlPFC), an area of the brain involved in inhibition (see Aron, Robbins, & Poldrack, 2004), was more active in participants who were able to inhibit alluring gist representations and rely on base rates (i.e. 70 lawyers out of 100) when making judgments. Similarly, the rlPFC has also been related to smaller framing effects (De Martino, Kumaran, Seymour, & Dolan, 2006; Zheng, Wang, & Zhu, 2010), thus adding support to the prediction that one mechanism through which individuals reduce framing effects in order to make consistent decisions is through inhibition.

IMPULSIVITY AND INTUITION AS DISTINCT CONSTRUCTS

Although much of the current chapter has focused on ways in which gist representations support biased decision making, FTT posits that gist is a developmentally advanced process of representing information (Reyna, 2012), which can lead to superior decision making under risk as compared to verbatim representations (Reyna & Farley, 2006; Reyna et al., 2011). Gist representations consist of connecting the dots between presented information and combining them with background knowledge to create a meaningful (and more easily remembered) representation. Although putting together the information given in a typical conjunction fallacy problem may lead to a misleading stereotype (e.g., Linda is a feminist), this same mechanism can result in improved diagnosis by medical experts (e.g., combining individual symptoms in a meaningful way; Reyna & Lloyd, 2006).

It is important to note that FTT distinguishes memory representation from impulsivity (Reyna, 2013). An example of an impulsive reliance on verbatim memory can be found in problems like "If it takes 5 machines 5 minutes to make 5 widgets, how long would it take 100 machines to make 100 widgets?" whereby individuals tend to give the incorrect answer of 100 minutes (Frederick, 2005). Instead of considering the relation between time and number of widgets, they rely on mindless verbatim matching (Liberali, Furlan, Reyna, Stein, & Pardo, 2012). An example of dissociation of gist representation from impulsivity can be found in research that has demonstrated that using analogies that reflect correct reasoning principles that are relevant to conjunction fallacy problems can improve performance. For example, describing the relationship between a set and a subset by comparing the description in a conjunction problem (e.g., bank tellers and feminist bank tellers) with that of baseball fans and left-handed baseball fans can help individuals retrieve the relevant reasoning principles and avoid the conjunction fallacy (Wolfe & Reyna, 2010). In contrast, the previously discussed manipulation of using 2 × 2 tables does have a larger effect than such analogies (the latter mainly affect representations and, thus, reduce semantic errors) because it reduces class-inclusion interference that would then need to be inhibited. Using a 2 × 2 table that represents each class of events (e.g., class of bank teller or not and class of feminist or not) separately reduces interference from overlapping classes (see Reyna & Brainerd, 2008).

WHEN HIGHER COGNITIVE ABILITY FAILS TO PREDICT BETTER JUDGMENT AND DECISION MAKING

So far, we have relied on evidence from individual-differences research and neuroscience to demonstrate the role of interference in judgment and decision making and the role of inhibition in avoiding bias. What each of the previously discussed phenomena have in common thus far is that each type of judgment or decision involves pitting an intuitive answer against a normatively correct one. In ratio bias problems, individuals are led astray by comparing the sizes of the numerators when in fact they should be focusing on comparing proportions. The conjunction fallacy and base-rate problems are similar to ratio bias (in that they involve denominator neglect) but include a salient gist, which further leads individuals away from accurate judgments. Finally, in framing problems, individuals will rely on categorical gist rather than focusing on the fact that gain and loss versions are numerically equivalent, and therefore decisions should be consistent across problems.

Inhibition allows reasoners to combat interference, retrieve relevant reasoning principles, and avoid bias. There is even evidence that those individuals who fail to inhibit their intuitions and demonstrate biases at least recognize (unconsciously) that there is a conflict present in these types of problems (De Neys, 2012). Although inhibition plays a large role in these decisions, it is not present when decisions do not involve an obvious conflict between intuition and a normative reasoning principle (De Neys, Vartanian, & Goel, 2008; Handley, Capon, Beveridge, Dennis, & Evans, 2004).

A simple manipulation that eliminates the previous pattern between cognitive ability and superior judgment and decision making is to compare responses between subjects as opposed to within. In conjunction problems, when comparing participants that only judge the likelihood of the conjunction (e.g., "feminist bank teller") to participants who only judge the likelihood of the parent class (e.g., "bank teller") one finds that overall the group getting the conjunction rates the likelihood as higher compared to the group judging the likelihood of the parent class. In fact, research has shown that the former relationship between cognitive ability and bias disappears in the context of the between-subjects version of the task (Stanovich & West, 2008).

The same effect described above can also be found for risky-choice framing problems. When framing problems are given between-subjects, the need for consistent decision making across frames is no longer apparent and individuals rely on categorical gist for their decisions. According to FTT, between-subjects framing effects are actually an indicator of advanced processing. Specifically, given a single framing problem (i.e. out of 600 total choose between 200 saved vs. $\frac{1}{3}$ chance 600 saved and $\frac{2}{3}$ chance 0 saved), reliance on the verbatim numerical information is unhelpful ($200 = \frac{1}{3} \times 600$). However, in this one-time decision, the categorical gist offers a helpful interpretation (in this example, either some saved or none saved). This contrasts with within-subject framing, in which there are multiple framing problems in each frame (gain and loss), thereby putting consistency at stake. The data support this prediction in that the previous relation between cognitive ability and framing disappears (Corbin, McElroy, & Black, 2010; Stanovich & West, 2008). Again, if any relationship exists, data suggest that it may be in the opposite direction, with those with higher cognitive ability showing larger framing effects (indicating a higher likelihood of gist reliance) than those with lower cognitive ability (Reyna et al., 2011, 2013). This illustrates that people use different mechanisms when framing problems are given within-subjects as opposed to between-subjects.

Research in neuroscience has found support for the role of the anterior cingulate cortex (ACC) in the detection of conflicts between intuitive and statistical information in judgment problems. Specifically, in the previously discussed De Neys et al. (2008) study, participants were given base-rate problems in which there was no conflict between statistical and intuitive information (in addition to the traditional base-rate problems). Activation of the ACC was only apparent in base-rate problems in which a conflict existed. It is important to differentiate conflict detection from inhibition however, given that ACC activation was found even when participants neglected base rates (avoiding the error required inhibition). Further support for the role of the ACC in conflict detection has been found in framing studies, in which activation in the ACC has also been related to reduction in framing (although conflict monitoring and inhibition have not been cleanly separated in these studies; De Martino et al., 2006; Zheng et al., 2010).

CONCLUSION

The current chapter overviews the FTT approach to judgment and decision making, with a particular emphasis on roles played by memory, interference, and inhibition (see Chapter 3 for review). Relying on these basic processes, FTT can account for the fact that many biases are not due to a lack of knowledge but instead occur because of interference. Furthermore, we have explored the role of inhibition in combating interference and have described converging results from a number of areas of research, which support this model. Also, we have made an important distinction between memory representation and impulsivity, demonstrating how cuing gist can be a source of interference (relying on stereotypes which conflict with relevant statistical information) but also can support inhibition (invoked after cuing appropriate reasoning principles using analogies). Finally, we have shown how decisions can be presented in ways that circumvent one's ability to use inhibition—for example, presenting framing problem between- as opposed to within-subjects—by failing to cue conflicts between intuitive gist and normative reasoning principles.

Fuzzy-trace theory provides a broad theoretical framework that has been applied to a wide range of areas, ranging from basic memory research to judgment and decision making (Reyna, 2012; Reyna & Brainerd, 1995). This theoretical perspective relies on a set of specific and distinct fundamental processes (i.e. gist and verbatim memory, interference, and inhibition) which account for why some judgments and decisions can go awry, to predict when some individuals may be more or less biased, and shed light on ways of improving judgments and decisions. As this chapter demonstrates, these concepts also hold an important position in both behavioral economics and neuroeconomics in increasing our understanding of how memory, cognitive ability, and inhibition relate to decision making, what neurological processes underlie these relationships, as well as under what circumstances we can expect to see them play a role.

AUTHOR NOTE

Preparation of this chapter was supported in part by the National Institutes of Health under Awards R21CA149796 and R01NR014368–01 to V. F. Reyna. The content is solely the responsibility of the authors and does not necessarily represent the official views of the National Institutes of Health.

REFERENCES

Aron, A. R., Robbins, T. W., & Poldrack, R. A. (2004). Inhibition and the right inferior frontal cortex. *Trends in Cognitive Sciences, 8(4),* 170–177.

Brainerd, C. J., Aydin, C., & Reyna, V. F. (2012). Development of dual-retrieval processes in recall: Learning, forgetting, and reminiscence. *Journal of Memory and Language, 66(4),* 763–788.

Brainerd, C. J., & Reyna, V. F. (1990). Inclusion illusions: Fuzzy-trace theory and perceptual salience effects in cognitive development. *Developmental Review, 10(4),* 365–403.

Bruine de Bruin, W., Parker, A.M., & Fischhoff, B. (2007). Individual differences in adult decision-making competence. *Journal of Personality and Social Psychology, 92(5),* 938–956.

Corbin, J., McElroy, T., & Black, C. (2010). Memory reflected in our decisions: Higher working memory capacity predicts greater bias in risky choice. *Judgment and Decision Making, 5(2),* 110–115.

Davidson, D. (1995). The representativeness heuristic and the conjunction fallacy effect in children's decision making. *Merrill-Palmer Quarterly, 41(3),* 328–346.

De Martino, B., Kumaran, D., Seymour, B., & Dolan, R. J. (2006). Frames, biases, and rational decision making in the human brain. *Science, 313(5787),* 684–687.

De Neys, W. (2012). Bias and conflict: A case for logical intuitions. *Perspectives on Psychological Science, 7(1),* 28–38.

De Neys, W., & Vanderputte, K. (2011). When less is not always more: Stereotype knowledge and reasoning development. *Developmental Psychology, 47(2),* 432–441.

De Neys, W., Vartanian, O., & Goel, V. (2008). Smarter than we think: When our brains detect that we are biased. *Psychological Science, 19(5),* 483–489.

Del Missier, F., Mäntylä, T., Hansson, P., Bruine de Bruin, W., Parker, A., & Nilsson, L. G. (2013). The multifold relationship between memory and decision making: An individual-differences study. *Journal of Experimental Psychology: Learning, Memory, and Cognition, 39(5),* 1344–1364.

Dempster, F. N. (2002). The rise and fall of the inhibitory mechanism: Toward a unified theory of cognitive development and aging. *Developmental Review, 12(1),* 45–75.

Dempster, F. N., & Corkill, A. J. (1999). Individual differences in susceptibility to interference and general cognitive ability. *Acta Psychologica, 101(2),* 395–416.

Denes-Raj, V., & Epstein, S. (1994). Conflict between intuitive and rational processing: When people behave against their better judgment. *Journal of Personality and Social Psychology, 66(5),* 819–829.

Frederick, S. (2005). Cognitive reflection and decision making. *Journal of Economic Perspectives, 19(4),* 25–42.

Gorfein, D. S., & MacLeod, C. M. (2007). *Inhibition in cognition.* Washington, DC: APA Press.

Handley, S. J., Capon, A., Beveridge, M., Dennis, I., & Evans, J. S. B. T. (2004). Working memory, inhibitory control and the development of children's reasoning. *Thinking and Reasoning, 10(2),* 175–195.

Jacobs, J. E., & Potenza, M. (1991). The use of judgment heuristics to make social and object decisions: A developmental perspective. *Child Development, 62(1),* 166–178.

Kahneman, D., & Tversky, A. (1973). On the psychology of prediction. *Psychological Review, 80(4),* 237–251.

Kirkpatrick, L. A., & Epstein, S. (1992). Cognitive-experiential self-theory and subjective probability: Further evidence for two conceptual systems. *Journal of Personality and Social Psychology, 63(4),* 534–544.

Klaczynski, P. A. (2001). Analytic and heuristic processing influences on adolescent reasoning and decision-making. *Child Development, 72(3),* 844–861.

Kokis, J. V., Macpherson, R., Toplak, M. E., West, R. F., & Stanovich, K. E. (2002). Heuristic and analytic processing: Age trends and associations with cognitive ability and cognitive styles. *Journal of Experimental Child Psychology, 83(1),* 26–52.

Kühberger, A., & Tanner, C. (2010). Risky choice framing: Task versions and a comparison of prospect theory and fuzzy-trace theory. *Journal of Behavioral Decision Making, 23(3),* 314–329.

Levin, I. P., Schneider, S. L., & Gaeth, G. J. (1998). All frames are not created equal: A typology and critical analysis of framing effects. *Organizational Behavior and Human Decision Processes, 76(2),* 149–188.

Liberali, J. M., Reyna, V. F., Furlan, S., Stein, L. M., & Pardo, S. T. (2012). Individual differences in numeracy, with implications for biases and fallacies in probability judgment. *Journal of Behavioral Decision Making, 25(4),* 361–381.

Pacini, R., & Epstein, S. (1999). The relation of rational and experiential information processing style, basic beliefs, and the ratio-bias phenomenon. *Journal of Personality and Social Psychology, 76(6),* 972–987.

Parker, A. M., & Fischhoff, B. (2005). Decision-making competence: External validation through an individual-differences approach. *Journal of Behavioral Decision Making, 18(1),* 1–28.

Rabinowitz, F. M., Howe, M. L., & Lawrence, J. A. (1989). Class inclusion and working memory. *Journal of Experimental Child Psychology, 48(3),* 379–409.

Reyna, V. F. (1991). Class inclusion, the conjunction fallacy, and other cognitive illusions. *Developmental Review, 11(4),* 317–336.

—— (1995). Interference effects in memory and reasoning: A fuzzy-trace theory analysis. In F. N. Dempster & C. J. Brainerd (Eds.), *Interference and inhibition in cognition* (pp. 29–59). San Diego, CA: Academic Press, Inc.

——(2004). How people make decisions that involve risk: A dual process approach. *Current Directions in Psychological Science, 13(3),* 60–66.

——(2008). Theories of medical decision making and health: An evidence-based approach. *Medical Decision Making, 28(6),* 829–833.

——(2012). A new intuitionism: Meaning, memory, and development in fuzzy-trace theory. *Judgment and Decision Making, 7(3),* 332–359.

——(2013). Intuition, reasoning, and development: A fuzzy-trace theory approach. In P. Barrouillet & C. Gauffroy (Eds.), *The development of thinking and reasoning* (pp.193–220). Hove: Psychology Press.

Reyna, V. F., & Brainerd, C. J. (1994). The origins of probability judgment: A review of data and theories. In G. Wright & P. Ayton (Eds.), *Subjective probability* (pp. 239–272). Oxford: Wiley.

——(1995). Fuzzy-trace theory: An interim synthesis. *Learning and Individual Differences, 7(1),* 1–75.

——(2008). Numeracy, ratio bias, and denominator neglect in judgments of risk and probability. *Learning and Individual Differences, 18(1),* 89–107.

——(2011). Dual processes in decision making and developmental neuroscience: A fuzzy-trace model. *Developmental Review, 31(2),* 180–206.

Reyna, V. F., Chick, C. F., Corbin, J. C., & Hsia, A. N. (2013). Developmental reversals in risky decision-making: Intelligence agents show larger decision biases than college students. *Psychological Science, 25(2),* 76–84.

Reyna, V. F., Estrada, S. M., DeMarinis, J. A., Myers, R. M., Stanisz, J. M., & Mills, B. A. (2011). Neurobiological and memory models of risky decision making in adolescents versus young adults. *Journal of Experimental Psychology: Learning, Memory, and Cognition, 37(5),* 1125–1142.

Reyna, V. F., & Farley, F. (2006). Risk and rationality in adolescent decision-making: Implications for theory, practice, and public policy. *Psychological Science in the Public Interest, 7(1),* 1–44.

Reyna, V. F., & Lloyd, F. J. (2006). Physician decision-making and cardiac risk: Effects of knowledge, risk perception, risk tolerance, and fuzzy processing. *Journal of Experimental Psychology: Applied, 12(3),* 179–195.

Reyna, V. F., & Mills, B. A. (2007). Interference processes in fuzzy-trace theory: Aging, Alzheimer's disease, and development. In C. MacLeod & D. Gorfein (Eds.), *Inhibition in cognition* (pp. 185–210). Washington, DC: APA Press.

Reyna, V. F., Mills, B. A., Estrada, S. M., & Brainerd, C. J. (2006). False memory in children: Data, theory, and legal implications. In M. P. Toglia, J. D. Read, D. F. Ross, & R. C. L. Lindsay (Eds.), *The handbook of eyewitness psychology: Memory for events* (pp. 473–510). Mahwah, NJ: Erlbaum.

Reyna, V. F., & Zayas, V. (2014). *The neuroscience of risky decision making.* Washington, DC: APA Press.

Robinson, K. J., & Roediger, H. L., III (1997). Associative processes in false recall and false recognition. *Psychological Science, 8(3),* 231–237.

Sloman, S., Rottenstreich, Y., Wisniewski, E., Hadjichristidis, C., & Fox, C. R. (2004). Typical versus atypical unpacking and superadditive probability judgment. *Journal of Experimental Psychology: Learning, Memory, and Cognition, 30(3),* 573–582.

Stanovich, K. E., & West, R. F. (1998). Individual differences in framing and conjunction effects. *Thinking and Reasoning, 4(4),* 289–317.

—— (1999). Individual differences in reasoning and the heuristics and biases debate. In P. Ackerman, P. Kyllonen, & R. Roberts (Eds.), *Learning and individual differences: Process, trait, and content determinants* (pp. 389–407). Washington, DC: APA Press.

——(2008). On the relative independence of thinking biases and cognitive ability. *Journal of Personality and Social Psychology, 94(4),* 672–695.

Toplak, M. E., West, R. F., & Stanovich, K. E. (2013). Rational thinking and cognitive sophistication: Development, cognitive abilities, and thinking dispositions. *Developmental Psychology.*

Tversky, A., & Kahneman, D. (1973). Availability: A heuristic for judging frequency and probability. *Cognitive Psychology, 5(2),* 207–232.

—— (1983). Extensional versus intuitive reasoning: The conjunction fallacy in probability judgment. *Psychological Review, 90(4),* 293–315.

—— (1986). Rational choice and the framing of decisions. *Journal of Business, 59(4),* S251–S278.

Tversky, A., & Koehler, D. J. (1994). Support theory: A nonextensional representation of subjective probability. *Psychological Review, 101(4),* 547–567.

Wechsler, D. (1999). *Wechsler Abbreviated Scale of Intelligence (WASI).* San Antonio, TX: The Psychological Corporation.

Wolfe, C. R., & Reyna, V. F. (2010). Semantic coherence and fallacies in estimating joint probabilities. *Journal of Behavioral Decision Making, 23(3),* 203–223.

Zheng, H., Wang, X. T., & Zhu, L. (2010). Framing effects: Behavioral dynamics and neural basis. *Neuropsychologia, 48(11),* 3198–3204.

5

The Predecisional Distortion
of Information

J. EDWARD RUSSO

The phenomenon of predecisional distortion of information is produced when decision makers interpret new evidence in favor of an alternative that is currently leading in attractiveness. This effect was long presumed not to exist because before a decision was completed decision makers could not know which alternative to support. However, once decision making is appreciated as a process during which a tentative preference emerges, that currently leading alternative is recognized as providing the direction necessary to the existence of predecisional distortion. Empirical evidence demonstrates that this bias can occur even in the absence of previous beliefs about the available alternatives, separating it from other classic effects (such as belief bias). The predecisional distortion of information is nearly always observed, at least when using the stepwise evolution-of-preference paradigm to track the choice process over time. It has been found in decisions made by auditors, entrepreneurs, prospective jurors, and physicians. By providing an initial advantage to one alternative, an adversary can use predecisional distortion to manipulate the decision maker's chosen alternative. Although the effect survives such manipulations intended to eliminate it as a financial payment for accurate information evaluation, it is eliminated through knowing attribute values before choice, through simultaneous instead of sequential presentation of alternatives, and in group decisions so long as there remains disagreement over the leading option. This bias has been shown to derive from the goal of cognitive consistency, specifically from the desire to see new information as consistent with the current, tentative preference.

T he focus of this chapter is the biased evaluation of information toward supporting the leading alternative during a decision, a phenomenon known as the predecisional distortion of information. During a decision, the alternative that is currently (and tentatively) leading in overall attractiveness receives additional support because new information tends to be interpreted in its favor.

This phenomenon should be distinguished from the familiar bias created by a prior belief, such as jurors' predisposition toward or against guilt in a criminal trial or citizens' position for or against capital punishment. Even in the complete absence of a prior position or preference, new information is distorted to support the leading alternative as soon as one emerges. The chapter has two main goals, communicating the core findings of the research on this bias and drawing implications from those findings to cognitive psychology.

The biased evaluation of information to support the currently leading alternative during a decision (i.e. the predecisional information distortion) was long presumed not to exist. Only a negative response seemed possible to the question: Before a decision has been made, how could a decision maker know which alternative to support? In contrast, there was general acceptance of a post-decision bias to favor the chosen alternative, especially a bias in which information is sought (or "searched for") but also in the evaluation of all the information acquired. However, the predecisional period was supposed to be free from the stain of such a bias. Frey (1986, p. 44) expressed the consensus of scholars, "Prior to a decision, people should be relatively unbiased in their seeking and evaluation of information."[1] Both because of such pronouncements and an obvious negative answer to the question above, most researchers presumed the impossibility of information distortion (ID) to support a preferred alternative *during* the choice process.

However, what if the choice process does not suddenly change from no preference whatsoever to a firm preference at the time of decision? What if it is better described as the gradual emergence of a preference? In other words, once any information becomes available to decision makers, it is evaluated to identify a preference or to clarify an existing one. The emerging preference is tentative, and it is qualified by the degree of commitment to it. While that commitment is still developing, a preference might better be labeled as only a leaning toward one alternative. That is, during a decision a preference emerges that is tentative and reversible and possesses a level of commitment that is initially moderate but grows by degrees. In contrast, the highest level of commitment defines a decision itself as in, "a decision is the identification of and commitment to a course of action" (Russo & Carlson, 2002, p. 371). Thus, depending on the level of commitment, a preference can range from a weak, tentative leaning to a firm, final decision.

Even a leaning toward one alternative that is tentative and weak satisfies a sine qua non for ID to occur. It identifies a direction in which to distort new information. While there can be no ID until such a preference emerges (because lacking it there is no direction in which to distort new information), once an emerging preference exists, distortion can and generally does occur.

EMPIRICAL EVIDENCE

If ID can occur in principle, how might its presence be determined empirically? I shall focus on a method known as the stepwise evolution of preference which tracks the choice process over time (Meloy & Russo, 2004; Russo, Medvec, & Meloy, 1996). However, there are other methods that should be acknowledged even if they shall not be reviewed here, particularly the methods associated with theories of spreading activation and connectionist models (e.g., Glöckner & Betsch, 2008; Holyoak & Simon, 1999; Read & Simon, 2012).

Returning to the stepwise evolution of preference method, consider a binary choice between two winter coats. A unit of information is an attribute, like materials, warmth, water protection, or workmanship, that contains the available information for both alternatives in a 50–100-word narrative. The water-protection attribute might read as follows:

> Coat H has a Pureforce® outer layer shield that keeps out rain and snow, especially in high wind environments. Although the Pureforce® shield does not have as much breathability as some other outer layers on the market today, the coat is one of the most water-resistant because its seams are hot-taped. Coat R employs a Hydrobloc® shell with a two-layer Monsoon™ membrane, a new material designed for maximum water resistance. Its layers are carefully aligned to let your body breathe while keeping the moisture out.

In order to track the progress of the choice, participants are asked for two responses after each attribute. First, they rate the diagnosticity of the information on a scale whose endpoints are "strongly favors Coat H" and "strongly favors Coat R" and whose midpoint is "favors neither coat." This scale might range from 1 to 9, with a midpoint of 5. The numerical rating reflects the evaluation of the diagnosticity of an attribute or, said differently, the degree of preference for one option relative to the other that the decision maker (subjectively) extracts from the information in the current attribute. A control group provides an unbiased estimate of the same diagnosticity or relative preference. It is used to create attributes whose mean evaluation is neutral (close to 5 on a 1–9 scale).

For their second response, participants identify which alternative is leading and by how much. For instance, participants might move a slider on a scale whose endpoints are labeled "Absolutely sure to choose Coat H" and "Absolutely sure to choose Coat R." The side of the midpoint identifies which alternative is leading, and the distance from the midpoint to the relevant endpoint indicates the current strength of that leaning (e.g., Chaxel, Russo, & Kerimi, 2013). Alternatively, the choice might be described as a horse race, and the decision maker is requested to state which "horse" (i.e. coat) is leading at this point in the race (i.e. decision). Then the decision maker expresses the likelihood that the leading "horse" will win the race "after all the information has been seen" (on a scale from 50 to 100). This requires two distinct responses to identify the leading alternative and, separately, its strength (Russo, Meloy, & Medvec, 1998).

To compute the bias that is ID, the two progress-tracking responses are used as follows. The first one, the decision maker's perceived diagnosticity, is compared to the control group's unbiased estimate of the same attribute's diagnosticity. Then the absolute difference between them is signed positively if it is directed toward favoring the leading alternative and negatively if toward the trailing alternative. For instance, on the 1–9 diagnosticity scale, if the observed rating of the current attribute is 6, the absolute difference from the midpoint (the control group's unbiased evaluation) would be signed +1 if Coat R had been leading and −1 if Coat H had been leading. In order to make the observed values of ID comparable across studies that used different scales for rating diagnosticity (attribute evaluation), the proportion of the maximum possible distortion is reported. In the above example, the maximum ID is 4, namely from the midpoint of 5 to either endpoint of the scale. Thus, a mean ID of 0.50 would become 12.5 percent of the maximum.

Table 5.1 summarizes all the studies that have used the stepwise evolution of preference method under the additional condition that there is no prior preference at the start of the choice. These are the purest cases, where nothing but the ID from an emerging preference should occur. I do not report studies in which one alternative has been "endowed" with a prior preference unless a control condition meets the criterion of no prior preference (and then only the control data are included). The overarching result from the studies in Table 5.1 is the consistent presence of ID. This presence occurs both for binary choice and for the evaluation of a single option (Bond, Carlson, Meloy, Russo, & Tanner, 2007). Its magnitude varies considerably, from 5 percent to 40 percent of the maximum, but its existence

Table 5.1   Results of studies using the stepwise evolution of preference method to assess information distortion.

Study	Type of Subjects	Number of Subjects	Alternatives	Mean Observed Proportion of Maximum Distortion	P Value of Observed Mean Distortion	Notes
Russo, Medvec, & Meloy 1996	Students	58	Restaurants Inns	17.0% 10.3%	<.05 <.10	Only the first attribute considered. Leading alternative based on a decision-irrelevant "endowment"
Russo, Meloy, & Medvec 1998	Students	16–18	Backpacks Health clubs Restaurants Running shoes	19.0% 22.2% 33.0% 12.7%	<.001 <.001 <.001 <.01	
Meloy 2000	Students	34	Restaurants	8.0%	<.05	Number of subjects is approximate
Russo, Meloy, & Wilks 2000	Students Auditors	70 90	Dry cleaners Dry cleaners	25.2% 17.8%	<.001 <.001	

(Continued)

Table 5.1 (*Continued*)

Study	Type of Subjects	Number of Subjects	Alternatives	Mean Observed Proportion of Maximum Distortion	P Value of Observed Mean Distortion	Notes
			Restaurants	17.8%	<.001	For an important professional dinner, not a personal dinner
			Clients	15.5%	<.001	
	Sales reps	76	Dry cleaners	22.8%	<.001	
			Restaurants	34.2%	<.001	For an important professional dinner, not a personal dinner
			Clients	20.0%	<.001	
Carlson & Russo 2001	Students	126	Civil legal case	14.8%	<.001	
		122	Criminal case	23.2%	<.001	
	Prospective jurors	148	Civil case	31.0%	<.001	
Meloy & Russo 2004	Students		Honeymoon resorts and college courses	23.0%	<.01	
		32	College courses and employees	40.0%		*P* Value not reported; the condition where ID is given served as a control in a larger design
Carlson & Pearo 2004	Students	85	Backpacks	15.2%		Significance not reported but assured in personal communication
	Graduate students and university staff	117	Wines	8.8%		Significance not reported but assured in personal communication
Meloy, Russo, & Miller 2006	Students	42	Restaurants and resorts	10.0%		

(*Continued*)

Table 5.1   (*Continued*)

Study	Type of Subjects	Number of Subjects	Alternatives	Mean Observed Proportion of Maximum Distortion	*P* Value of Observed Mean Distortion	Notes
		42	Scholarship	5.0%		*P* value not reported; the condition where ID is given served as a control in a larger design
			Applicants	6.8%		*P* value not reported; the condition where ID is given served as a control in a larger design
Russo, Carlson, Meloy, & Yong 2008	Students	44	Restaurants	13.2%	<.01	
			Pasta sauces	16.2%	<.001	
Russo & Chaxel 2010	Students		Vacation resorts	11.7%		*P* value not reported; the condition where ID is given served as a control in a larger design
Russo & Yong 2011	Students	191	Hotel investment and vehicle safety	12.8%	<.001	Binary choice and single evaluation combined; verbal and numerical formats combined
Boyle, Hanlon, & Russo 2012	Students	42	Entrepreneur venture	33.2%	<.001	

is nearly always confirmed. ID has also been recently shown for multiple alternatives (Blanchard, Carlson, & Meloy, 2014).

Two other results, not reflected in the table, speak to the uniform presence of predecisional distortion. First, this bias is systematically related to the strength of the emerging preference. Specifically, it is a linear function of the commitment to the currently leading alternative as assessed by the estimated likelihood that the leader will be the eventual choice once all the information has been seen (e.g., Carlson & Russo, 2001; Kostopoulou, Russo, Keenan, Delaney, & Douiri, 2012; Russo, Meloy, & Medvec, 1998). That is, the stronger is the commitment to the emerging preference, the greater is the ID of the next unit of information. Second, decision makers are unaware of their own distortion (e.g., Russo, Carlson, & Meloy, 2006; Russo, Meloy, & Wilks, 2000; Russo & Yong, 2011). Their self-reports of the presence of distortion have always failed to correlate with the magnitude of the observed ID. I believe that this is one reason why ID persists. If people were aware of it at the time they were biasing their evaluations, they would try to stop. Essentially, they are talking themselves into supporting the currently leading alternative merely because it is leading.

Several studies are disqualified from the table because the participants began with an installed initial preference. Nonetheless, this excluded work reveals at least three additional results. First, studies by DeKay and his collaborators reveal that decision makers distort even precise numerical values that would seem to be fixed and difficult to adjust toward supporting whichever alternative is leading (DeKay, Patino-Echeverri, & Fischbeck, 2009; DeKay, Stone, & Miller, 2011; DeKay, Stone, & Sorenson, 2012; Miller, DeKay, Stone, & Sorenson, 2013). Second, these same studies show that ID occurs in the context of risky choices, thereby extending the results beyond preferential choice. Both of these results are echoed by Russo and Yong (2011) who demonstrate that the ID of numerical values (13 percent of the maximum) is not even lower than the ID of those numbers' verbal equivalents (12.5 percent). Third, DeKay et al. (2011, 2012) and Miller et al. (2013) showed that ID mediates the effect of an initial preference on its final choice. That is, mediation analysis directly links ID to the option chosen and to the strength of preference for that chosen option. This mediation has also been found by Boyle, Russo, and Kim (2014) in decisions made by both American and Korean entrepreneurs.

IS ID AN ARTIFACT OF ITS MEASUREMENT METHOD?

The stepwise evolution of preference method requires that decision makers identify their currently leading alternative at multiple times during the decision process. It seems plausible that requiring decision makers to report that leader might increase their awareness of it and, quite possibly, their commitment to it. Russo et al. (1998) addressed this issue of a method-induced demand effect by omitting the identification of the current leader, the second of the progress-tracking questions that follow each attribute. When this leader identification was omitted, the overall mean ID (i.e. aggregated over the four pairs of alternatives that are listed separately in Table 5.1) declined from 22.2 percent to 10.5 percent of the scale. That is, the measured ID lost over 50 percent of its magnitude. However, not all of this decrease could be attributed to reporting the leading alternative. Because the leader was not identified by the decision maker, the experimenters had to infer it from the evaluations of all preceding attributes. For instance, if a decision maker rated the first three attributes as 6, 6, and 5 on the 1–9 rating scale of attribute evaluation or diagnosticity, the estimated cumulative preference for Coat R would be +2 (+1 from each of the first two attributes because the unbiased attribute evaluation was 5, the neutral midpoint of the scale). In contrast, if the same three attributes received ratings of 6, 3, and 5, the cumulative preference was computed as −1. However, in the latter case, how reliable is the apparent reversal of preference after Attribute 2? In either of these two hypothetical situations it is difficult to be certain of the preference after the second attribute, and this uncertainty often increased with more attributes. In addition, the summation of deviations from the midpoint necessarily assumed that decision makers gave equal weight to all attributes, an unjustifiably strong assumption. As a consequence, the inference as to which alternative was leading was almost certainly in error some of the time. Therefore, the observed decline in ID was due both to a possible artifact from requiring an explicit report of the leading alternative (that strengthened the commitment to it) and to the unavoidable error in assessing ID because the leader could not be accurately determined. Although these two contributors to the large decline in ID could not be separated, requiring the explicit identification of the leading alterative almost certainly elevated ID.

One limitation of the Russo et al. (1998) attempt to identify the measurement-driven demand effect is the absence of a test for this effect's impact on the actual choice. That is, if there is a demand effect, eliminating it by eliminating the intermediate responses that track the choice process should lead to a significant impact on the final choice. Carlson, Meloy, and Russo (2006) did exactly this: removed all intermediate responses in one condition and then compared the final choice with and without them. They found no difference, suggesting no demand effect at all or, at least, no influence of such an effect on choice. Miller et al. (2013) and Russo and Chaxel (2010) also found no effect on choice of the same absence of intermediate responses. The results of the two kinds of studies that have tried to answer the question of whether the tracking of the choice process creates a demand effect leave the question open. One possible resolution is that although such an effect exists, it is small enough not to have much influence on the ultimate choice.

CAN THE DISTORTION OF INFORMATION BE ELIMINATED?

ID can be eliminated, but not easily, even by what would seem to be obviously efficacious tactics. Offering a financial incentive for an accurate choice did not even reduce ID (Meloy, Russo, & Miller, 2006). Neither did targeting the monetary incentive to the estimation of each attribute's diagnosticity (i.e. precisely where the distortion occurs). Holding decision makers accountable reduced ID for sales representatives but not for public auditors (Russo et al., 2000). The latter acted as if they were always accountable. Finally, switching from selecting the better of two alternatives to rejecting the worse of two substantially reduced ID, by 53 percent in Study 1 and 61 percent in Study 2a of Meloy and Russo (2004). This effect was traced to the incompatibility between the negative posture of rejecting the worse alternative and the overall positive attractiveness of those same options. When decision makers were placed in the compatible situation of rejecting the worse of two *un*attractive alternatives, their ID was nearly equal to the case of selecting the better of two attractive ones.

Eliminating ID while individuals decide between two options has been achieved twice. If decision makers have knowledge of the attribute values before a choice, ID is reduced almost to zero (Carlson & Pearo, 2004). Furthermore, these researchers showed that ID was reduced only for the attributes whose values were known in advance and not for the others that were encountered for the first time. Second, ID can also be eliminated by switching the information format from sequential to simultaneous presentation (Carlson et al., 2006). When decision makers access attributes in a sequence, the currently leading alternative drives the distortion of the next attribute; but simultaneous presentation of all information for one alternative followed by all the information for the second alternative prevents the formation of ID.

The only other situation in which ID has been totally eliminated is a group decision in which conflicting preferences were installed (Boyle, Hanlon, & Russo, 2012). Four-person groups with conflicting initial preferences exhibited no ID so long as that conflict persisted. As soon as a tentative preference for one alternative was agreed on by all four individuals, ID emerged, increased rapidly, and exhibited a significantly higher level (49.8 percent) than for individuals performing the same task (33.2 percent; Table 5.1). Unfortunately, there seems to be no way to create within one individual the same conflict that is so beneficial to ID reduction in groups.

ARE THERE ANY INDIVIDUALS WHO EXHIBIT NO ID?

The good news is that one group has been found that shows zero distortion. Kostopoulou et al. (2012) studied physicians who made diagnoses based on medical cues. Of the 102 physicians, 15 exhibited no distortion as assessed by the double criterion of a very low mean ID (< 1 percent of the diagnosticity scale) and a near zero slope of the linear relation between confidence in the current diagnostic leaning and the ID of the next medical cue. The reason why these 15 physicians were distortion-free is unclear. Compared to those who exhibited ID, they were more experienced, but not significantly so. (Over all physicians, those with at least ten years of experience distorted significantly less, 10.4 percent, than did the less experienced, 15.6 percent.) Only further work can reveal the reason for the absence of ID in the small subgroup of physicians and any possible generality beyond this domain. Nonetheless, it is encouraging to know that some professionals can overcome the tendency to distort new information toward supporting their currently preferred belief.

WHAT CAUSES ID?

A natural candidate for the cause of ID is the desire to support the leading alternative. This goal drives similar information biases *post*decisionally, particularly the biased search for information to support the chosen option, also known as selective exposure to information (Fischer & Greitemeyer, 2010; Hart, Albarracin, Eagly, Brechan, Lindberg, & Merrill, 2009). ID is the predecisional version of the well-known postdecisional defense of the chosen option. However, the predecisional situation may be different because decision makers are unaware of ID. It seems implausible at best that decision makers could be using ID to deliberately support the leading alternative if they are unaware that they are distorting at all. Further, if they were aware, they would prefer to avoid it (Chaxel, Russo, & Kerimi, 2013).[2] Thus, we rule out an explicit desire to support the leading alternative as a cause of ID.

One cause of ID has been identified, the goal of cognitive consistency. This is the desire for two beliefs to be consistent with each other. In the case of ID, the first belief is the tentative preference for one alternative over the other; the second is the interpretation and evaluation of the next attribute of information. When Russo, Carlson, Meloy, and Yong (2008) activated the goal of cognitive consistency, they found a corresponding increase in ID. Further, when decision makers reported their activation levels of cognitive consistency and three other goals, only the former correlated with the magnitude of those individuals' ID. These results clearly identify the goal of consistency among beliefs as one cause of ID, but only as one cause. It does not bar the possibility that other causes also contribute to the presence or magnitude of ID.

Cognitive consistency is a less common type of goal, a process goal (van Osselaer et al., 2005). This contrasts with the more common outcome goals that are achieved by a desired outcome of a process. In decision making, typical outcome goals are aspects of the alternatives, like high gas mileage in an automobile, fewer calories in a meal, and more prestige in the journal for a submitted research paper. These goals tend to be as numerous and varied as the content of the alternatives themselves. Process goals are far less numerous but apply more widely to many decisions (and to other tasks as well). For example, process goals like minimizing the effort needed to make a decision or avoiding unpleasant feelings during the process of deciding may be active in many tasks, both decision and nondecision.

Because cognitive consistency is a process goal, it is not motivated by a desired outcome and, therefore, it is not susceptible to motivated reasoning (Kunda, 1990). Cognitive consistency does not choose sides. It does not care which belief has to change in order to accommodate the other, only that the two beliefs be made consistent. Although ID is a change in the evaluation of new information toward supporting the emerging preference, it sometimes happens that the new information so strongly supports the trailing alternative that the decision maker switches leaders. Thus, the goal of cognitive consistency can be achieved either by biasing the evaluation of the new information to support the current leader or by changing this tentative leader. Such indifference to the process outcome distinguishes process from outcome goals. It bears repeating that, even though ID is directional in that it supports the leading alternative, it is driven by the nondirectional (process) goal of cognitive consistency. The existence of systematic ID reflects the fact that in the conflict between the two beliefs of current leader and new information, the former usually, but not always, dominates.

IMPLICATIONS

Interpretation of Primacy Effects

ID is a primacy effect, but of a less common kind (Bond et al., 2007). Primacy is usually interpreted as a change of importance. Thus, in a comparison between two job candidates in which past performance is the first information seen, primacy means that this first attribute receives more "weight" (i.e. importance) in the decision than if it is encountered later. In contrast, primacy may also derive from a change in the inherent value of the decision-relevant information. If the second information encountered is experience, the perceived value of experience may change depending on whether the past performance was strong or weak. If strong, then greater experience is positive; but if the past performance was weak, greater experience suggests that the candidate failed to improve even with more time to do so. Thus, the value of experience changes as a function of past performance, quite possibly with no change in its importance. This interaction between two units of information is sometime labeled configural primacy. A thoughtful, empirically rich debate over the existence of a genuine change of value transpired between, inter alia, Anderson (1971, 1973) and Hamilton and Zanna (1974).

ID falls in the change-of-value class of primacy effects. Yet even in this category, it is different from the interaction between two attributes. That interaction is stable, as in how past performance interacts with experience. Instead, ID is a temporary change of perceived value in which that change is driven solely by the leading alternative. If the other alternative had been leading, the next attribute would likely have been distorted in the opposite direction, that is, would have exhibited a different interaction.

One possible reason for the dominance of importance-based interpretations of primacy is that importance weights are considered more malleable than the corresponding "scale values." It seems more plausible to view a primacy effect as due to a change in the importance of information like job candidates' experience than to see the value of, say, four years of experience changing. Indeed, at first consideration, it may seem impossible for a decision maker to place a different value on four years just because it is seen second versus first. In several ID studies, verbal protocols were informally collected in order to reveal participants' reasoning during the evaluation of an attribute. In particular, my colleagues and I wondered how it was possible for participants to distort information that was numerically precise. For instance, in one decision between two restaurants, an authoritative guidebook's ratings of food quality were provided on a 1–7 scale, 5.1 for Restaurant K and 5.3 for Restaurant T. When Restaurant T was leading immediately prior to encountering the guidebook's ratings, participants said something like, "That [information] favors T." That is, they acknowledged, rather straightforwardly, the support for their current leader. However, when Restaurant K was leading, the participants were confronted with disconfirming attribute information. Then they made statements like, "They're almost equal" and "That difference is so small that it hardly matters." That is, these participants discounted the leader-disconfirming information by dismissing it completely. It should also be noted that the verbal protocols occasionally revealed a change of importance weight. For example, if the trailing restaurant had more convenient parking or a shorter travel time, participants sometimes dismissed these attributes as "just not that important." Thus, in spite of numerically clear values, individuals found a way to justify the bias in valuation that constitutes ID. This change-of-value phenomenon has appeared repeatedly in the decision literature (e.g., Wallsten, 1981; see also Svenson, 1992).

However, it seems not to have been pursued or formally modeled to the extent that change of importance has.

RATIONALITY AND THE BAYESIAN CALCULUS

Is ID rational? One way to answer this question is to consider the preferential analog of the Bayesian framework for likelihood. In the Bayesian calculus for likelihoods, prior probability (i.e. degree of belief in the likelihood of an event) is combined with an observed datum to yield an updated posterior probability. A necessary condition of the Bayesian calculus is independence of the prior and the datum. Consider the preferential analog of the same calculus. The prior preference (the current leader) is updated by new information (the Bayesian datum) to yield an updated preference. In the preferential version of the Bayesian framework, ID amounts to a violation of independence between the prior preference and the new information. That violation occurs because the evaluation of the new information is influenced by the prior preference, which we have already recognized as a change-of-meaning type of primacy effect. Interestingly, this same violation of independence was also discovered by Boulding, Kalra, and Staelin (1999) in the context of modeling the joint effect of prior expectation and actual experience on overall customer satisfaction.

To return to the question of rationality, let us distinguish between local or myopic rationality and global or overall rationality. If any argument is to be made for the rationality of ID, it is at the local level. When trying to evaluate the impact of new information on the relative preference of two options, the case can be made that it is rational to use all the information available. This includes the current preference. Thus, it may be myopically rational to let the current preference contribute to the evaluation of a new unit of information. Of course, this influence is not globally rational in that it can lead to inferior choices (Russo et al., 2006) and, more dangerously, to being manipulated by an individual who controls the order of information and desires a decision maker to choose an option preferred by this individual (Russo & Chaxel, 2010). Thus, ID is not rational in that it risks an inferior decision. Yet it may possess the appeal of myopic rationality when the immediate task is to evaluate new information.

THE INFLUENCE OF A HEAD START

Recognizing that ID is one form of primacy raises the issue of the influence of an initial preference on the final decision. If a preselected alterative has its most favorable attribute placed as the first information that decision makers encounter, then it is likely to become the initial leader. Subsequent attributes may well be distorted toward supporting that leader, at least for many individuals, resulting in a choice proportion significantly higher than if the attributes had been seen in a neutral order. Thus, ID might be used to affect the eventual choice by controlling the order of information.

Carlson et al. (2006) presented information favoring one of two alternatives as either the first or fourth attribute out of six. The totality of the information was net neutral, favoring neither alternative when combined over all six attributes. (However much the first attribute favored one alternative, the fourth attribute favored the other alternative by an equal amount.) Nonetheless, the alternative that was favored by the first attribute was selected in 70 percent of the choices. Carlson et al. (2006) also showed that the proportion of times an inferior alternative was chosen could be increased from .16 to .30 by placing the one attribute that favored this alterative in the first position. Russo et al. (2006) went a step further and showed that the choice of a self-identified inferior alternative could be raised above .50 (to .62) by employing the same tactic of making its most favorable attribute the first information that decision makers see. Finally, Carlson, Meloy, and Miller (2013; see also Carlson, Meloy, & Lieb, 2009) showed that even when decision makers switch away from an initial leader, that alternative retains a subtle attraction (manifest as ID to support it) and is chosen at a rate above a neutral baseline.

Manipulating the chosen alternative can be achieved not only by controlling the order of decision-relevant information but also by using other information to create an equivalent head start. Russo et al. (1996) "endowed" one option, either a restaurant or an inn, with a history irrelevant to the criteria for choice. For instance, one of the innkeepers "has helped to secure accommodations for the participant's parents during a weekend when all of the local hostelries were booked" (Russo et al., 1996, p. 104). The endowed alternatives were selected on 80 percent of the choices, even though the decision-relevant information was neutral. Russo and Chaxel (2010) used two commercials to instantiate an initial preference for one of two beach resorts. Both advertisements had won awards, but one was judged to be more compatible with the category of resorts. The advertising-favored resort was chosen 68 percent of the time, even though, again, the attribute information comparing the two resorts was neutral. Furthermore, and even though decision makers explicitly acknowledged the direct influence of the commercials on their choice, they were unaware of the commercials' indirect impact via their distorted evaluation of the attributes.

The effect of a head start in the above studies suggests that in any task in which one alternative is "leading," ID may create a primacy effect. Candidate tasks include diagnosis (Kostopoulou et al., 2012), hypothesis identification (Jahn & Braatz, 2012; Whitman & Woodward, 2011), and problem solving in general. Indeed, might ID occur in any task where there is a focus on one possibility over others, possibly caused by no more than an initial availability?

COMMITMENT TO AN EMERGING PREFERENCE

One result that has been found uniformly across ID studies is that confidence in the current leader systematically drives the magnitude of the distortion of the next information. If confidence in the leader is considered equivalent to commitment to that alternative, then the finding is that greater commitment leads to greater ID. This presumed role of commitment was tested by finding a tactic for increasing commitment to the leading alternative without changing the information-based value of that option. Polman and Russo (2012) accomplished this by requiring their participants to expend more effort to indicate the leader after each attribute. Using pencil and paper, decision makers either checked a box to identify that leader (control condition) or had to completely darken an area about an inch square that took approximately ten seconds (high-commitment condition). The result was significantly more ID in the high-commitment condition, from 8.2 percent of the maximum to 16.8 percent in Experiment 1 and from 8.8 percent to 16.2 percent in Experiment 2. A different manipulation, allowing decision makers to view information that they had previously used, had the same effect on ID as a direct increase in commitment (Miller et al., 2013). As these authors write, "[A]pparently, reminding participants of the basis for their current leaning reinforced or strengthened that leaning, which in turn increased the distortion of later information (Miller et al., 2013, p. 672).

The influence of the extent of commitment to a leading alternative suggests that this factor might play a role in explaining related phenomena. Consider whether there exists a predecisional search bias. This is a search that favors information that confirms the current preference over information that disconfirms it; it is the search correspondent of the predecisional evaluation bias that is ID. The bulk of the literature reports the presence of such a search bias (e.g., Fischer, Lea, Kastenmuller, Greitemeyer, Fischer, & Frey, 2011; Fraser-Mackenzie & Dror, 2009; Young, Tiedens, Jung, & Tsai, 2011). However, at least two studies have reported no such bias (Carlson & Guha, 2011; Chaxel et al., 2013). Might the difference in these results be explained by commitment? When the predecisional search bias has been found, the procedure typically asks participants to make a tentative choice. Formally, that choice is entirely reversible when later information is acquired. However, might there be a substantial enough felt commitment to such an expression of preference that decision makers are motivated to defend it (Fischer & Greitemeyer, 2010)? One empirical approach to addressing this question is to use a more subtle method for identifying the leading alternative, one that should require less commitment. Then the presumed lower commitment should result in the decline of the confirming search bias. Guha and Carlson used the horse-race metaphor described above in the choice between two winter coats. This metaphor makes clear that the expressed preference may well change as more information is acquired and should induce less commitment than a tentative choice. In a method that went even further, the decision makers in Chaxel et al. (2013) used only a slider on a scale unmarked except for the endpoints which were labeled "strongly favors" one or the other alternative. The leading option was determined by which half of the scale the slider rested on. Both Guha and Carlson (2011) and Chaxel et al. (2013) found no predecisional search bias. Although there is yet to be a direct comparison between the more explicit method of an announced tentative choice for expressing the current leader and less explicit methods (like the horse race and slider), it seems plausible that different commitment may explain their opposite results.

RESEARCH PARADIGMS OF JUDGMENT AND DECISION MAKING

The main stream of research in judgment and decision making has flowed out of the rational criteria of economics and statistics. These criteria enabled the considerable success and dominant status of the anomalies paradigm over the past 40 years. Just as important, though less well recognized, is the methodological paradigm associated with anomalies research, namely the nearly complete restriction to input–output data. These data should be contrasted with the process paradigm, in which the decision process is traced over time and with some form of intermediate observation (Schulte-Mecklenbeck, Kuehberger, & Ranyard, 2011). These observations may be relatively complete, such as those in a verbal protocol (Ericsson & Moxley, 2011; Russo & Dosher, 1983), the sequence of eye fixations (Russo, 2011), or of manual information acquisitions (Willemsen & Johnson, 2011). More commonly, however, process data are selected intermediate responses, such as the two after each attribute in the stepwise evolution of preference method and the "online" report of goal activations in Carlson, Tanner, Meloy, and Russo (2012; see also Russo et al., 2008). The experimental method associated with ID clearly falls in the process paradigm.

The work on the predecisional distortion of information points to the value of treating seriously the decision process qua process (Johnson, Schulte-Mecklenbeck, & Willemsen, 2008). Besides the development of a preference during a decision (Lichtenstein & Slovic, 2006; Payne, Bettman, & Johnson, 1993), other changes include the relative activity of competing goals (e.g., Carlson et al., 2013) and affect, both positive and negative (e.g., Luce, Bettman, & Payne, 1997). One of the frequent concomitants of the process perspective is a shift from all-or-none dichotomies to a more complex understanding of decision behavior. This is what happened when preference was seen as emerging during the decision process rather than not existing at all until the decision was made. In this vein, Keren and Schul (2009) argue broadly against "two-system theories" in favor of more complex, and often continuous, views of behavior.

EPILOGUE

A Bit of History

Some readers may be interested in the unplanned path to the discovery of ID. The purpose of Russo et al. (1996), the first study of ID, was to test whether the known finding of postdecisional distortion of new information would occur when the commitment to one alternative was not created by a decision but rather by a source irrelevant to the decision criteria. Thus, in a choice between two restaurants, one was "endowed" by noting that its owner had contributed to a charity raffle the year before. This act, which we would now label a head start, should be independent of the quality of the dining experience at the restaurant. Nonetheless, the data showed that it did affect the evaluation of the first attribute, as we thought that it might. Note that this effect was determined relative to a control group that made the same decision with the same information (including the same first attribute), except without any endowment. We did not trust any effect on the evaluation of the second attribute, because it might have been influenced both by the endowment and also by the evaluation of the first attribute. Thus, the focus of testing was entirely on the first attribute.

The observed result, the effect of an irrelevant endowment on the first attribute, achieved the purpose of the study and would normally have been its end. However, recall the control group. Someone asked whether the second attribute in the control condition might be affected by whichever alternative was leading after the first one, just as the first attribute had been affected by the endowment in the experimental condition. Data analyses revealed that it was. Therefore, the leading alternative seemed to have the power to influence the evaluation of the next information, whether that leader was established by an endowment or by an earlier attribute. This is the predecisional distortion of information. Thus, full disclosure reveals that Russo et al. (1996) stumbled upon ID, and they could not legitimately claim to have predicted it beforehand. In fact they did not, stating the finding as "Attribute 2's evaluation for the unendowed participants exhibited a substantial, unexpected distortion in favor of the alternative preferred on Attribute 1" (Russo et al., 1996, p. 106).

The Natural Conflict between Experimental Paradigms

As noted above, ID research occurs in the process paradigm, in contrast to the input–output paradigm in which most decision-making studies are conducted. What happens when the paradigms clash, specifically when reviewers see ID work through the lens of the more common input–output paradigm? When the second and most important of the early ID manuscripts, Russo et al. (1998), was submitted for publication, it was recommended for rejection by all three reviewers. Furthermore, the reviewers unanimously agreed on the same compelling reason for rejection, that "there is nothing new here." Fortunately, each one identified a different familiar phenomenon, all drawn from the input–output paradigm, according to which ID was merely another unnecessary illustration. I do not recall the exact three, but over time the following have been offered as input–output phenomena that include ID as no more than a specific example: attitude extremity and polarization, cognitive dissonance, confirmation bias, the desirability bias (wishful thinking), the halo effect, and the prior belief effect. If ID research is viewed through the lens of the input–output paradigm, it may well appear to be very similar to one or more of these phenomena. That is, if the process component of ID research is stripped away and it is seen only as an input–output phenomenon, it may quite reasonably appear to fit an effect that is well known. Sensitive to the unusual combination of reviewers' complete agreement ("reject") and complete disagreement ("just another example of [three different phenomena]"), the editor offered the opportunity to explain why there was, in fact, something new in ID. Although this explanation was judged satisfactory, it illustrated the challenge of work carried out using one paradigm being evaluated from the perspective of a different one.

AUTHOR NOTE

The author thanks Kurt Carlson, Michael DeKay, Sophie Chaxel, Meg Meloy, David Weiss, and Catherine Wiggins for helpful feedback on earlier drafts.

NOTES

1. Earlier scholars did recognize the presence of a predecisional information bias. In their analysis of voting decisions, Lazarsfeld, Berelson, and Gaudet (1944) state that "[p]eople selected political material in accord with their own taste and bias. Even those who had not yet made a decision [on their vote] exposed themselves to propaganda, which fit their not-yet-conscious political predispositions" (pp. 79–80). Although this early research was confined to information search and did not explicitly include the interpretation or evaluation of that information, it did accept the possibility of a predecisional bias. That acceptance seems to have been completely excised from the research in psychology only a decade or so later (e.g., Festinger, 1957, 1964).
2. This is not to say that decision makers do not deliberately seek disconfirming information. They do, often wisely. However, while the search for information known to favor (or disfavor) one alternative is conscious and strategic, the predecisional distortion of information is a nonconscious and unintended bias in the evaluation of information. Chaxel et al. (2013) find that this bias is generally considered unacceptable, while a disconfirming search is generally acceptable.

REFERENCES

Anderson, N. H. (1971). Two more tests against change in meaning in adjective combinations. *Journal of Verbal Learning and Verbal Behavior, 10(1)*, 75–85.
——(1973). Serial position curves in impression formation. *Journal of Experimental Psychology, 97(1)*, 8–12.
Blanchard, S., Carlson, K. A., & Meloy, M. G. (2014). Biased predecisional processing of leading and non-leading alternatives. *Psychological Science, 25(3)*, 812–816.
Bond, S. D., Carlson, K. A., Meloy, M. G., Russo, J. E., & Tanner, R. J. (2007). Information distortion in the evaluation of a single option. *Organizational Behavior and Human Decision Processes, 102(2)*, 240–254.
Boulding, W., Kalra, A., & Staelin, R. (1999). The quality double whammy. *Marketing Science, 18(4)*, 463–484.
Boyle, P. J., Hanlon, D., & Russo, J. E. (2012). The value of task conflict to group decisions. *Journal of Behavioral Decision Making, 25(3)*, 217–227.
Boyle, P. J., Russo, J. E., & Kim, Y. (2014). The act of decision making as a source of entrepreneurs' unwarranted confidence. Working paper, January.
Carlson, K. A., & Guha, A. (2011). Leader-focused search: The impact of an emerging preference on information search. *Organizational Behavior and Human Decision Processes, 115(1)*, 133–141.
Carlson, K. A., Meloy, M. G., & Lieb, D. (2009). Benefits leader reversion: How a once preferred product recaptures its standing. *Journal of Marketing Research, 46(6)*, 788–797.
Carlson, K. A., Meloy, M. G., & Miller, E. G. (2013). Goal reversion in consumer choice. *Journal of Consumer Research, 39(5)*, 918–930.
Carlson, K. A., Meloy, M. G., & Russo, J. E. (2006). Leader-driven primacy: Using attribute order to affect consumer choice. *Journal of Consumer Research, 32(4)*, 513–518.
Carlson, K. A., & Pearo, L. (2004). Limiting predecisional distortion by prior valuation of attribute components. *Organizational Behavior and Human Decision Processes, 94(1)*, 48–59.
Carlson, K. A., & Russo, J. E. (2001). Jurors' distortion of evidence in legal trials. *Journal of Experimental Psychology: Applied, 7(2)*, 91–103.

Carlson, K. A., Tanner, R. J., Meloy, M. G., & Russo, J. E. (2014). Catching goals in the act of decision making, *Organizational Behavior and Human Decision Processes, 123(1)*, 65–76.

Chaxel, A.-S., Russo, J. E., & Kerimi, N. (2013). Preference-driven biases in decision makers' information search and evaluation. Manuscript submitted for publication, Desautels Faculty of Management, McGill University.

DeKay, M. L., Patino-Echeverri, D., & Fischbeck, P. S. (2009). Distortion of probability and outcome information in risky decisions. *Organizational Behavior and Human Decision Processes, 109(1)*, 79–92.

DeKay, M. L., Stone, E. R., & Miller, S. A. (2011). Leader-driven distortion of probability and payoff information affects choices between risky prospects. *Journal of Behavioral Decision Making, 24(4)*, 394–411.

DeKay, M. L., Stone, E. R., & Sorenson, C. M. (2012). Sizing up information distortion: Quantifying its effect on the subjective values of choice options. *Psychonomic Bulletin and Review, 19(2)*, 349–356.

Ericsson, K. A., & Moxley, J. (2011). Thinking aloud protocols: Concurrent verbalizations of thinking during performance on tasks involving decision making. In M. Schulte-Mecklenbeck, A. Kuehberger, & R. Ranyard (Eds.), *A handbook of process methods for decision research* (pp. 89–114). New York, NY: Psychology Press.

Festinger, Leon (1957). *A theory of cognitive dissonance*. Evanston, IL: Row, Peterson.

——(1964). *Conflict, decision and dissonance*. Palo Alto, CA: Stanford University Press.

Fischer, P., & Greitemeyer, T. (2010). A new look at selective-exposure effects. *Psychological Science, 19(6)*, 384–389.

Fischer, P., Lea, S., Kastenmuller, A., Greitemeyer, T., Fischer, J., & Frey, D. (2011). The process of selective exposure: Why confirmatory information search weakens over time. *Organizational Behavior and Human Decision Processes, 114(1)*, 37–48.

Fraser-Mackenzie, P., & Dror, I. E. (2009). Selective information sampling: Cognitive coherence in evaluation of a novel item. *Judgment and Decision Making, 4(4)*, 307–316.

Frey, D. (1986). Recent research on selective exposure to information. In L. Berkowitz (Ed.), *Advances in Experimental Social Psychology* (pp. 41–80). New York, NY: Academic Press.

Glöckner, A., & Betsch, T. (2008). Modeling option and strategy choices with connectionist networks: Towards an integrative model of automatic and deliberate decision making. *Judgment and Decision Making, 3(3)*, 215–228.

Hamilton, D. L., & Zanna, M. P. (1974). Context effects in impression formation: Changes in connotative meaning. *Journal of Personality and Social Psychology, 29(5)*, 649–654.

Hart, W., Albarracin, D., Eagly, A., Brechan, I., Lindberg, M. J., & Merrill, L. (2009). Feeling validated versus being correct: A meta-analysis of selective exposure to information. *Psychological Bulletin, 135(4)*, 555–588.

Holyoak, K. J., & Simon, D., (1999). Bidirectional reasoning in decision making by constraint satisfaction. *Journal of Experimental Psychology: General, 128(1)*, 3–31.

Jahn, G., & Braatz, J. (2012). Memory indexing of sequential symptom processing in diagnostic reasoning. Unpublished manuscript, Department of Psychology, University of Greifswald.

Johnson, E. J., Schulte-Mecklenbeck, M., & Willemsen, M. C. (2008). Process models deserve process data: Comment on Brandstatter, Gigerenzer, and Hertwig (2006). *Psychological Review, 115(1)*, 263–273.

Keren, G., & Schul, Y. (2009). Two is not always better than one: A critical evaluation of two-system theories. *Perspectives on Psychological Science, 4(6)*, 533–550.

Kostopoulou, O., Russo, J. E., Keenan, G., Delaney, B. C., & Douiri, A. (2012). Information distortion in physicians' diagnostic judgments. *Journal of Medical Decision Making, 32(6)*, 831–839.

Kunda, Z. (1990). The case for motivated reasoning. *Psychological Bulletin, 108(3)*, 480–498.

Lazarsfeld, P., Berelson, B., & Gaudet, H. (1944). *The people's choice: How the voter makes up his mind in a presidential campaign.* New York, NY: Columbia University Press.

Lichtenstein, S., & Slovic, P. (2006). *The construction of preferences.* Cambridge: Cambridge University Press.

Luce, M. F., Bettman, J. R., & Payne, J. W. (1997). Choice processing in emotionally difficult decisions. *Journal of Experimental Psychology: Learning, Memory, and Cognition, 23(2)*, 384–405.

Meloy, M. G., & Russo, J. E. (2004). Binary choice under instructions to select versus reject. *Organizational Behavior and Human Decision Processes, 93(2)*, 114–128.

Meloy, M. G., Russo, J. E., & Miller, E. G. (2006). Monetary incentives and mood. *Journal of Marketing Research, 43(2)*, 267–275.

Miller, S. A., DeKay, M. L., Stone, E. R., & Sorenson, C. M. (2013). Assessing the sensitivity of information distortion to four potential influences in studies of risky choice. *Judgment and Decision Making, 8(6)*, 662–677.

Payne, J. W., Bettman, J. R., & Johnson, E. J. (1993). *The adaptive decision-maker.* Cambridge: Cambridge University Press.

Polman, E., & Russo, J. E. (2012). Commitment to a developing preference and predecisional distortion of information. *Organizational Behavior and Human Decision Processes, 119(1)*, 78–88.

Read, S. J., & Simon, D. (2012). Parallel constraint satisfaction as a mechanism for cognitive consistency. In B. Gawronski & F. Strack (Eds.), *Cognitive consistency: A fundamental principle in social cognition* (pp. 66–86). New York, NY: Guilford Press.

Russo, J. E. (2011). Eye fixations as a process trace. In M. Schulte-Mecklenbeck, A. Kuehberger, & R. Ranyard (Eds.), *A handbook of process methods for decision research* (pp. 43–64). New York, NY: Psychology Press.

Russo, J. E., & Carlson, K. A. (2002). Individual decision making. In R. Wensley & B. Weitz (Eds.), *Handbook of marketing* (pp. 371–408). Thousand Oaks, CA: Sage.

Russo, J. E., Carlson, K. A., & Meloy, M. G. (2006). Choosing an inferior alternative. *Psychological Science, 17(10)*, 899–904.

Russo, J. E., Carlson, K. A., Meloy, M. G., & Yong, K. (2008). The goal of consistency as a cause of information distortion. *Journal of Experimental Psychology: General, 137(3)*, 456–470.

Russo, J. E., & Chaxel, A.-S. (2010). How persuasive messages can influence choice without awareness. *Journal of Consumer Psychology, 20(3)*, 338–342.

Russo, J. E., & Dosher, B. A. (1983). Strategies for multiattribute binary choice. *Journal of Experimental Psychology: Learning, Memory and Cognition, 9(4)*, 676–696.

Russo, J. E., Medvec, V. H., & Meloy, M. G. (1996). The distortion of information during decisions. *Organizational Behavior and Human Decision Processes, 66(1)*, 102–110.

Russo, J. E., Meloy, M. G., & Medvec, V. H. (1998). The distortion of product information during brand choice. *Journal of Marketing Research, 35(4)*, 438–452.

Russo, J. E., Meloy, M. G., & Wilks, T. J. (2000). Predecisional distortion of information by auditors and salespersons. *Management Science, 46(1)*, 13–27.

Russo, J. E., & Yong, K. (2011). The distortion of information to support an emerging evaluation of risk. *Journal of Econometrics, 162(1)*, 132–139.

Schulte-Mecklenbeck, M., Kuehberger, A., & Ranyard, R. (Eds.) (2011). *A handbook of process methods for decision research.* New York, NY: Psychology Press.

Svenson, O. (1992). Differentiation and consolidation theory of human decision making: A frame of reference for the study of pre- and post-decision processes. *Acta Psychologica, 80(1–3)*, 143–168.

Van Osselaer, S. M. J., Suresh, R., Campbell, M. C., Cohen, J. B., Dale, J. K., Herr, P.M., Janiszewski, C., & Tavassoli, N. T. (2005). Choice based on goals. *Marketing Letters, 16(1)*, 335–346.

Wallsten, T. J. (1981). Physician and medical student bias in evaluating diagnostic information. *Journal of Medical Decisions Making, 2(2)*, 145–164.

Whitman, J. C., & Woodward, T. S. (2011). Evidence affects hypothesis judgments more if accumulated gradually than if presented instantaneously. *Psychonomic Bulletin and Review, 18(6)*, 1156–1165.

Willemsen, M., & Johnson, E. J. (2011). Visiting the decision factory: Observing cognition with MouselabWeb and other information acquisition methods. In M. Schulte-Mecklenbeck, A. Kuehberger, & R. Ranyard (Eds.), *A handbook of process methods for decision research* (pp. 21–42). New York, NY: Psychology Press.

Young, M. J., Tiedens, L. Z., Jung, H., & Tsai, M. (2011). Mad enough to see the other side: Anger and the search for disconfirming information. *Cognition and Emotion, 25(1)*, 10–21.

6

The Precision Effect

How Numerical Precision Influences Everyday Judgments

MANOJ THOMAS AND JOOWON PARK

Numerical judgments are not always based on the rules of arithmetic and logic; people often rely on heuristic inferences to make sense of numbers. In this chapter, we argue that unusually precise or sharp numbers can trigger heuristic processing and propose a model—the discrepancy attribution model—to characterize the nature of this heuristic processing. The discrepancy attribution process entails three postulates. First, we posit that atypical numbers cause processing discrepancy. Individuals have certain expectations as to how easy or difficult it will be to process numbers, and unusually round or precise numbers can render the processing easier or more difficult than expected. Second, we posit that when the processing discrepancy arises, individuals (mis)attribute this discrepancy to a salient factor. Finally, we posit that the (mis)attribution process is guided by the naive theories people have and by the contextual cues surrounding the judgment. We review several empirical studies on numerical precision that support the proposed discrepancy attribution model.

The past few years have witnessed a growing interest in numerical cognition—how people think about numbers—among the judgment-and-decision-making researchers (Bagchi & Davis, 2012; Coulter & Norberg, 2009; Denes-Raj & Epstein, 1994; Janiszewski & Uy, 2008; Monga & Bagchi, 2012; Pelham, Sumarta, & Myaskovsky, 1994; Peters et al., 2006, Pope & Simonsohn, 2011; Thomas & Morwitz, 2005, 2009; Thomas, Simon, & Kadiyali, 2010; Yaniv & Foster, 1997; Zhang & Schwarz, 2012). Researchers have identified several interesting numerical cognition effects such as the ratio bias (Denes-Raj & Epstein, 1994), the numerosity effect (Pelham, Sumarta, & Myaskovsky, 1994), and the left-digit anchoring effect (Thomas & Morwitz, 2005). There are two reasons for this growing interest in numerical cognition. First, characterizing the heuristics and biases in numerical judgments has substantive implications because numerical judgments are ubiquitous; people use numerical information every day, sometimes as recipients and sometimes as providers. Characterizing the heuristics and biases in numerical judgments will, at least to some extent, enable us to use numerical information more effectively in everyday communication. Second, and more important, numerical judgments offer a promising avenue to study the interplay of the nonconscious System 1 processes and the more deliberative System 2 processes (Kahneman & Frederick, 2002). In the case of numerical judgments, there is almost always a correct answer based on the rules of arithmetic and logic. Furthermore, in most cases people know this correct answer, and yet they systematically deviate from this correct answer in their day-to-day judgments. Thus, biases in numerical judgments often cannot be ascribed to lack of knowledge or intelligence. Indeed, recent research (Peters et al., 2006) suggests that even though the highly numerate people are less susceptible to framing effects, they are more likely to be influenced by irrelevant, affective considerations while making numerical judgments. Investigating why people systematically deviate from these correct answers has provided new insights into how nonconscious associative processes and subjective feelings surreptitiously shape our conscious judgments and decisions.

In this chapter, we focus on a novel numerical cognition effect that was unveiled quite recently: the numerical precision effect. Multi-digit numbers can be represented as precise or sharp numbers or as round numbers. How does the precision or the roundness of numbers influence people's intuitive judgments? To illustrate with an example, consider a consumer walking through the display aisles in a grocery store who has to assess which of the two discounts is more attractive:

Product A	Product B
Regular Price: $3.97	Regular Price: $4.00
Sale Price: $2.89	Sale Price: $3.00

Which of the two discounts would this consumer evaluate more favorably? The effect of precision is also relevant for providers of the numerical information because they often have to decide how to present the numerical information to elicit the most favorable response from the recipients. For example, a homeowner listing her house for sale might have to decide which of the two list prices, $380,000 or $385,875, will be more acceptable to a prospective buyer. A plaintiff seeking compensation in a medical malpractice case might have to assess whether a claim for $1 million or for $1,135,300 is more likely to seem justifiable. At first blush, these judgments seem quite straightforward. In the first example, the discount on Product A is $1.08 (38 percent) while the discount on Product B is only $1.00 (33 percent). In the second example, listing the house for $380,000 is likely to elicit a more favorable response because the alternative list price ($385,875) is higher and therefore will trigger more negotiation. In a similar vein, in the third example, the claim for $1 million is likely to be more justifiable because it is lower than the alternative.

However, empirical evidence from recent studies suggests that these naive predictions might not be correct. As noted earlier, numerical judgments are not always based on the rules of arithmetic and logic. People often rely on heuristic inferences to make sense of numbers. In this chapter, we argue that numerical precision—unusually precise or sharp numbers—can trigger heuristic processing and characterize the nature of such heuristic processing. Numerical precision triggers heuristic processing because it makes information processing, that is, the cognitive process of comparing two numbers or computing the difference between two numbers, relatively more difficult. Researchers have found that sometimes people use computational difficulty as a cue in numerical judgments: the greater the computational difficulty, the smaller is the perceived difference between two numbers (Thomas & Morwitz, 2009). If computational difficulty reduces the perceived magnitude of numerical differences, then the discount on Product A ("3.97 minus 2.89") might be incorrectly judged to be smaller than that on Product B ("4.00 minus 3.00") because the former is more difficult to process. Similarly, it has been found that unusually precise or sharp numbers can trigger heuristic inferences about the magnitude of the number or the believability of the number (Huang & Zhang, 2013; Janiszewski & Uy, 2008; Pope & Simonsohn, 2011; Thomas, Simon, & Kadiyali, 2010; Zhang & Schwarz, 2012, 2013). An atypically precise or sharp price might trigger inferences such as "this price seems low" or "the price does not seem negotiable." Such inferences can make buyers more willing to accept the precise higher list price (e.g., $385,850) rather than the round lower list price (e.g., $380,000; Janiszewski & Uy, 2008; Thomas, Simon, & Kadiyali, 2010).

We propose that the discrepancy attribution hypothesis (Whittlesea & Williams, 2000) can offer a parsimonious explanation for the effects of numerical precision on intuitive judgments. The gist of the proposal is that intuitive numerical judgments are influenced by heuristic attributions triggered by processing discrepancy. People monitor their quality of processing and when the experienced quality of processing deviates from expectation, the deviation or the discrepancy triggers an attribution process. Stated differently, processing discrepancy makes people wonder: Why is the processing discrepant? The consequent attribution process leads to inferences that are sometimes inconsistent with arithmetic rules.

In the following sections, we will first explain the discrepancy attribution framework in the context of numerical judgments and then review some factors that cause processing discrepancy in numerical judgments. We also identify unresolved issues and suggest avenues for future research to resolve some of the debates in this domain. We argue that brain-scan studies can be very useful in testing the role of processing discrepancy in biased numerical judgments because processing discrepancy can escape conscious attention, and, even when people are aware of it, self-reported measures might not be sensitive enough to capture small changes in processing discrepancy.

THE DISCREPANCY ATTRIBUTION HYPOTHESIS

The discrepancy attribution hypothesis was originally proposed by Whittlesea and Williams (2000, 2001a, 2001b) to explain the mechanisms that cause the feeling of familiarity. Traditionally, feeling of familiarity was believed to be caused by the activation of representations in memory. Per this account, if a face seems familiar, then it is probably because it matches an image activated in the perceiver's memory. This representation- or content-based account did not acknowledge the role of subjective experiences in familiarity judgments. Whittlesea and his co-authors argued that subjective feelings about the quality of processing and inferences made from such feelings play an important role in judgments of familiarity. They posited that the relationship between the feelings of familiarity and representations in memory is indirect, mediated by an unconscious attribution about the coherence of processing. They proposed that as

> people integrate various aspects of the stimulus (e.g., orthographic, semantic, and contextual properties) into a unitary construct, they also evaluate the coherence of that processing. This evaluation results in one of three perceptions: (a) that their processing is coherent; (b) that their processing contains incongruous, contradictory elements; or (c) that some aspects of their processing are in some surprising way discrepant with others.
> (Whittlesea & Williams, 2000, p. 548)

This feeling of discrepancy triggers an attribution process leading to the feeling of familiarity or unfamiliarity.

Illustrating the discrepancy attribution process with an example, Whittlesea and colleagues pointed out that a strong feeling of familiarity is seldom elicited by known stimuli. For example, one's spouse or friend seldom elicits strong feelings of familiarity. The feeling of familiarity manifests when one encounters someone from the distant past or a stranger. In such cases, it is easy to process the facial features but it is not clear why this is the case ("This person seems familiar, but I can't recall meeting him"). That is, there is a discrepancy between the expected ease of processing and the experienced ease of processing. This unexplained deviation from expectation in subjective experience is what Whittlesea and colleagues label processing discrepancy. Depending on the cues available in the context, this processing discrepancy is correctly or incorrectly attributed to salient judgment variables such as previous encounter ("Perhaps I met this person at the party last week"), similarity of features ("Perhaps this person is my classmate's brother"), or fame ("Perhaps this person is a famous movie star"; see Jacoby et al., 1989, for an example of such misattribution).

We propose that the discrepancy attribution process can also influence everyday numerical judgments. When people encounter a multi-digit number, they not only assess its magnitude based on the place values of the digits in the number but also by examining the quality of processing—whether it is unusually easy or difficult to mentally process the number. If the processing seems unusually difficult or easy, and if this deviation from expectation is surprising, then the resulting processing discrepancy will trigger an attribution process. The processing discrepancy will prompt the person to seek an explanation for the expectation violation. This could lead to biases, such as the ease-of-computation effect (Thomas & Morwitz, 2009) and the precision effect (Thomas, Simon, & Kadiyali, 2010). A putative model summarizing the discrepancy attribution model for numerical judgments is presented in Figure 6.1. As implied in Figure 6.1, the discrepancy attribution process entails three distinct postulates.

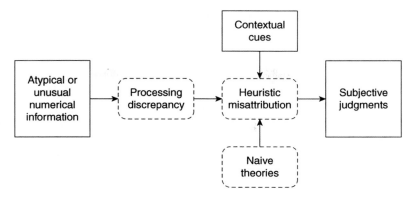

Figure 6.1 A model of discrepancy attribution effects in numerical judgments.
Note. Dotted lines represent internal processes.

Postulate 1: Atypical numbers cause processing discrepancy. For a discrepancy attribution effect to occur, first the person has to notice a discrepancy between expectation and the actual processing experience. The model assumes that while the brain processes the numerical information to make a decision, another part of the brain monitors the coherence of the cognitive process by assessing whether the actual processing experience is different from the expected processing experience.[1] Implicit in this postulate is the assumption that the brain has expectations about how easy or difficult it would be to process numbers in everyday contexts. This assumption is not unrealistic, although it does render more sophistication to brain processes than we generally assume. Several scholars have argued that metacognitive monitoring is fundamental to everyday judgment and decision making (Bless & Forgas, 2000; Kelley & Jacoby, 1998; Schwarz, 2004; Whittlesea, 1993). Metacognitive monitoring is required for the allocation of attention and processing resources and to make changes in cognitive strategy. The continuous and uninterrupted metacognitive monitoring leads to expectations about usual information formats and about the usual quality of processing. The brain learns to expect the nature of numerical information that it might encounter in different judgment contexts. At a gas station, it expects to see a precise or sharp three-digit number as the price of one gallon of gas (e.g., $3.84). In contrast, while buying a house, it expects to see six-digit numbers, often rounded to the nearest thousand (e.g., $365,000). Violation of these expectations can lead to a perception of discrepancy.

Postulate 2: People (mis)attribute the processing discrepancy to a salient factor. The model assumes that discrepancy triggers an attribution process: the mind tries to generate an explanation for the discrepancy. There are two reasons to justify the assumption that processing discrepancy triggers an attribution process. First, while making implicit judgments, the mind tries to make as much sense as possible of all salient information (Marcel, 1983; Whittlesea, 2000). Because processing discrepancy might be informative about the judgment task at hand, understanding the cause of the discrepancy is likely to facilitate a more informed judgment. Second, when the discrepancy is caused by the difficulty of encoding an unusual number (e.g., a house listed for $385,873) or the difficulty of mental calculations (3.86 minus 2.97), it creates an uneasy feeling. In such instances, processing discrepancy disrupts confidence by signaling uncertainty about the judgment. The cognitive system is inherently motivated to reduce such negative feelings by explaining away such feelings (Kahneman & Tversky, 1982; Wilson & Gilbert, 2008). Attributing the processing discrepancy to a source explains away the negative feeling and reduces the uncertainty. It is worth highlighting here that "explaining away" or attribution is not the only way to reduce processing discrepancy; sometimes people reduce processing discrepancy by changing one's cognitive strategy. It has been demonstrated that processing difficulty can induce participants to change the weights they assign to different cues in the stimulus. Specifically, processing difficulty can induce people to assign higher weight to more diagnostic cues in the stimulus (Alter, Oppenheimer, Epley, & Eyre, 2007; Bagchi & Davis, 2012).

Postulate 3: The (mis)attribution of processing discrepancy is guided by naive theories and contextual cues. Finally, the model posits that the attribution process is heuristic in nature; it is susceptible to the influence of activated naive theories and contextual cues, even when such naive theories and cues might lead to biased judgments. For example, if a person judging the magnitude of an unusually precise or sharp price believes that precise numbers are usually used for smaller magnitudes, then a higher precise price ($385,663) is likely to be judged to be lower than a comparable round price ($385,000) (Thomas, Simon, & Kadiyali, 2010). In contrast, the person assessing the rarity of caviar might infer that the caviar that has an unusually precise pack size (1.97 ounces) is rarer and more expensive than the caviar that has a regular pack size (2 ounces; Huang & Zhang, 2013). It is important to clarify that the naive theories recruited for the attribution need not be conscious beliefs that can be articulated; these naive theories could be associations that are nonconsciously formed in people's minds.

Having discussed the basic postulates of the discrepancy attribution hypothesis, we now turn our attention to some examples of discrepancy attribution effects in everyday numerical judgments.

THE EASE-OF-COMPUTATION EFFECT

The first empirical evidence for the role of processing fluency in numerical judgments was presented by Thomas and Morwitz (2009). They proposed that the ease with which one can compute the difference between two numbers can influence the perceived difference between the two numbers. They demonstrated that computationally easier differences (e.g., 5.00 − 4.00) are judged to be larger than computationally difficult differences (e.g., 4.97 − 3.96), even when the arithmetic differences are similar.

In one of their studies, the participants were told that to study how consumers evaluate discounts the experimenters have selected prices of 24 products that were on sale at a large retail store. Participants saw pairs of prices—a regular price and a sale price—one pair at a time on the computer screen. These prices varied in the discount magnitude. Participants evaluated the magnitude of the difference between the two prices on a semantic differential scale anchored at 1 = "small" and 11 = "large." Unbeknownst to the participants, the prices varied on the ease of computation. In order to study the effect of computation difficulty on magnitude judgments, the researchers used three different types of price pairs: easy, difficult–higher, and difficult–lower. The easy prices (e.g., regular price $4.00 – sale price $3.00 = discount $1.00) had single-digit formats, and the discount computations were relatively easy. The difficult–higher prices (e.g., regular price $4.97 – sale price $3.96 = discount $1.01) had nominally larger discount magnitudes than the corresponding level in the easy condition, and the discount computations were relatively difficult. Although the authors were primarily interested in comparing the easy prices with the difficult–higher prices, they also included difficult–lower prices (e.g., regular price $4.96 – sale price $3.97 = discount $0.99) to ensure that a difficult price had the same probability of being lower or higher than an easy price.

The results were consistent with their prediction. Participants incorrectly judged the easy-to-compute price differences (e.g., regular price $4.00 – sale price $3.00 = discount $1.00) to be higher than corresponding difficult–higher price differences (e.g., regular price $4.97 – sale price $3.96 = discount $1.01) as well as difficult–lower price differences (e.g., regular price $4.96 – sale price $3.97 = discount $0.99). Furthermore, mediation analysis confirmed that the bias in magnitude judgments was mediated by ease of computation. The response time for the computations mediated the effect of computational complexity on magnitude judgments.

Bagchi and Davis (2012) suggest that ease of computation can influence how consumers integrate different types of numerical information in consumption contexts. Specifically, they found that when it is difficult to do computations, consumers do not integrate different pieces of numerical information and their evaluations tend to be anchored on the most salient numeric information.

The Role of Discrepancy Attribution

As noted earlier, a key tenet of the discrepancy attribution hypothesis is that it is not fluency per se that influences subjective judgments; it is the discrepancy between expected fluency and experienced fluency that causes this effect. To test this proposition, in one study, the researchers manipulated the discrepancy between expected and experienced fluency (see Thomas & Morwitz, 2009, p. 88 for details). The manipulation, in fact, was quite simple. Before encountering each pair of prices, the participants saw a screen that had one of the two words displayed: "easy" or "difficult." These two words forewarned the participants about the ease or difficulty of the computation coming up on the subsequent screen. When the participants were forewarned, the ease of computation did not influence their subjective judgments of magnitudes. This experiment clearly shows that it is not fluency per se but the surprising or the unexpected nature of fluency or disfluency that causes the ease-of-computation effect.

The Role of Naive Theories

As illustrated in Figure 6.1, naive theory about the signaling value of processing difficulty also plays an important role in heuristic attributions. Thomas and Morwitz (2009) hypothesized that, in the absence of salient contextual cues, subjective experiences would be misattributed using naive theories about the association between processing difficulty and the discriminability of magnitudes. Naive theories are explicit or implicit beliefs about the association between two or more variables. The human mind is an intuitive statistician that automatically and effortlessly keeps track of the correlation between variables of interest. Once it discerns a pattern of association between two variables, it relies on that association to make heuristic inferences about the criterion variable using the predicting variable.

Thomas and Morwitz suggest that the following naive theory influences the ease-of-computation effect: The closer the magnitudes of two numbers, the less discriminable they are, and the greater the difficulty of judging the difference between them. The brain learns this association from everyday experiences. Usually, it is more difficult to discriminate between two bulbs of 70 and 80 watts of power than to discriminate between bulbs of 30 and 120 watts of power. Likewise, it is more difficult to discriminate between two weights or two sound pitches that are similar to each other than the two that are relatively dissimilar. Research in numerical cognition has revealed that such an association between analog magnitudes and processing fluency also manifests with numerical stimuli. Just as with light and weight, comparing two numbers that are closer to each other is relatively more difficult than comparing two numbers that are farther apart on the internal magnitude scale. For example, people take a few milliseconds more to identify that 6 is greater than 5 than to identify that 9 is greater than 5 (Moyer & Landauer, 1967). This effect, that has come to be known as the distance effect, is very robust and has been documented in several studies (Dehaene, 1997). Because of the ubiquity and the robustness of the relationship between discriminability of magnitudes and processing fluency, the human mind learns to associate processing difficulty with lower discriminability of magnitudes.

Thomas and Morwitz (2009) tested the role of this naive theory in the ease-of-computation effect in two ways. First, using a forced-choice paradigm, they assessed the existence of such a naive theory in participants' minds. They asked several college students to respond to the following forced-choice question.

> The price difference between X and Y is very small. The price difference between M and N is very large. Which of the two judgments will be easier for you?
>
> 1. Judging whether the price difference between X and Y is small or large
> 2. Judging whether the price difference between M and N is small or large.

Seventy-seven percent of the respondents (N = 56) chose the second response, suggesting the existence of a naive theory that greater processing difficulty signals that the magnitudes being compared are less discriminable.[2]

Subsequently, they tested whether manipulating the naive theory in an experimental setting can moderate the ease-of-computation effect. In one of their experiments (Experiment 3), they introduced 16 practice trials which were ostensibly designed to make the participants familiar with the task. Unbeknownst to the participants, these 16 practice trials were designed to manipulate the association between computation difficulty and the magnitude of the difference between two numbers. Of these 16 practice trials, half were computationally difficult, and the remaining trials were computationally easy. The stimuli used in these 16 practice trials differed across the two conditions in this experiment. In the smaller-is-easier condition, computationally easy prices were associated with *smaller* discounts. In the larger-is-easier condition, the association was reversed; computationally easy prices were associated with *larger* discounts. This association created in the laboratory through practice trials moderated the ease-of-computation effect. When participants learned that smaller numerical differences are easier to compute, they did not mistakenly judge the easier discounts to be larger.

THE PRECISION EFFECT

In the ease-of-computation effect, processing discrepancy was caused by surprising or unexpected computational complexity. A more frequently encountered source of processing discrepancy in numerical judgments is unusually precise or sharp numbers. For example, a buyer in the real-estate market evaluating house prices is likely to expect list prices to be rounded to the nearest thousand. So when the buyer comes across a house priced at $353,567, she is likely to find the numerical information somewhat discrepant.

Thomas et al. (2010) examined how the sharpness or precision of prices can influence subjective evaluations in the real-estate market. They hypothesized that one of the important variables in home-purchase decisions is the magnitude of the list price. If a prospective buyer feels that the magnitude of the list price is too high, then she is likely to negotiate more for the house. In contrast, if the buyer judges the magnitude to be on the lower side, then she is likely to negotiate less. How might precision or roundness of the list price influence magnitude judgments? Thomas et al. (2010) argued that an unusually precise price will trigger an inference about the magnitude of the price. Since people generally use precise numbers for small magnitudes and round numbers for larger magnitudes, buyers are likely to attribute the precision of the price to relatively smaller magnitudes.

In a series of experiments, Thomas et al. asked the participants to evaluate the magnitude of the list prices of several houses on a subjective scale. For each house, half of the participants saw a round price (e.g., $390,000) whereas the other half saw a precise price (e.g., $391,534). The precise prices were slightly higher than the comparable round prices. However, as predicted by the discrepancy attribution model, the participants paradoxically judged the precise prices to be lower than the corresponding round prices. More importantly, the authors demonstrated that list price precision can influence negotiations in actual real-estate transactions. They analyzed over 15,000 real-estate transactions in Long Island, NY and South Florida and found that when sellers use a precise list price, buyers tend to negotiate less.

Janiszewski and Uy (2008) have reported similar results, although they explain this effect using an anchoring and adjustment account.

The Role of Discrepancy Attribution

The discrepancy attribution model posits that it is the sense of uncertainty or the confidence disruption engendered by the surprising difficulty of encoding an unusual digit pattern that causes buyers to underestimate the magnitude of a precise price. (For a more detailed discussion of this point, see Step 2 of the discrepancy attribution model described in the introductory section.) This postulate implies that if the feeling of uncertainty is somehow reduced, then the magnitude of atypically precise prices would no longer be underestimated. To test this prediction, Thomas et al. (2010) directly manipulated the feeling of uncertainty in one of their experiments. In this experiment, half the participants, randomly assigned to the uncertainty/low-confidence condition, were told that "if you have some experience in real estate transactions, then you are likely to do well in this task. It has been observed that undergraduate students who have no experience in real estate transactions are usually unable to accurately evaluate real estate prices." The other half, who were assigned to the certainty/high-confidence condition, were told that "you do not need any real estate experience to do well in this task. It has been observed that most undergraduate students are able to accurately evaluate real estate prices even when they do not have any experience in real estate transactions." As predicted by the discrepancy attribution model, this manipulation moderated the effect of price precision. Only those participants who were assigned to the uncertainty/low-confidence condition incorrectly judged precise prices (e.g., $391,534) to be lower than corresponding round prices (e.g., $390,000). Magnitude judgments of participants assigned to the certainty/high-confidence condition were not influenced by price precision.

The Role of Naive Theories

The effect of price precision on magnitude judgments is based on the premise that there is a mental association between precision (or roundness) and numerical magnitudes. Indeed, there is some ecological basis for such an association. Research on the distribution of numbers has found that in spoken and written communication, when referring to large magnitudes, round numbers are more prevalent than exact or precise ones. When referring to the price of gas, people are likely to be precise to the last cent (e.g., $3.84), but when referring to the price of a car they are likely to round the number to the nearest thousand (e.g., $30,000). Dehaene and Mehler (1992) found that although the small numbers used in daily communication are not round (e.g., 1, 2, 3, 4, 5, . . ., 9), large numbers are often rounded to the nearest multiple of 10 (e.g., 10, 20, . . ., 100, 200). Stated differently, larger precise numbers (e.g., 101, 102, 103, . . ., 1011, 1012, 1013) are used relatively infrequently in daily communication (Jansen & Pollmann, 2001). Thomas et al. tested the role of the implicit association between precision and magnitude in two ways. In one study, they used a forced-choice question to elicit the association. (Note 2 explains the rationale for such questions.)

> Consider two six digit numbers, X and Y. The number X is rounded to the nearest thousand. The number Y is not rounded. Which number is likely to be smaller: X or Y?
>
> (Thomas et al., 2010, p. 184)

More than two-thirds of the respondents (69 percent) said that the number that is not rounded (Y) is likely to be smaller.

Additionally, they tested whether directly manipulating the association can moderate the precision effect. In one study, Thomas et al. (2010) manipulated the association between precision and magnitudes using a priming task. Participants were informed that they would be participating in two unrelated experiments. The first experiment was titled "Number Study," and the ostensible purpose of the experiment was to study the effect of response speed on accuracy. Unbeknownst to the participants, the actual purpose of this experiment was to prime the relationship between precision and numerical magnitude. Thirty-two numbers between 1,000 and 10,000 were presented on the computer screen, one at a time, in a random order, and participants had to quickly judge whether each number was higher or lower than 5,000. Half of the numbers were higher and the other half were lower than 5,000. Participants indicated their responses by clicking on one of the two buttons—"Higher" or "Lower"—displayed on the screen. For participants assigned to the "precise numbers are larger" condition, the numbers that were higher than 5,000 were precise (e.g., 5,563, 6,142, etc.) and the lower numbers were rounded (e.g., 4,000, 3,000, etc.). This manipulation was intended to create an expectation of larger magnitudes for precise prices. In contrast, for participants assigned to the "precise numbers are smaller" condition, the numbers that were lower than 5,000 were precise (e.g., 4,523, 3,526, etc.) and the higher numbers were rounded (e.g., 6,000, 7,000, etc.).

Consistent with the predictions of the discrepancy attribution model, priming the association between precision and number magnitude moderated the precision effect. When participants' prior experience induced them to expect lower magnitudes for precise numbers, they incorrectly judged precise prices to be lower than round prices. However, when participants' prior experience induced them to expect higher magnitudes for precise numbers, they judged precise prices to be higher than round prices.

PRECISION AND BELIEVABILITY

The precision or sharpness of numbers can not only affect magnitude judgments but it can also affect the believability of the numerical information. Schley and Peters (2013) proposed that precise numbers create greater inferences of believability about the source than round numbers. For example, when a precise number is presented (e.g., 60.37 percent), the recipient of the information infers that the number is resulting from careful calculation by a believable source. On the other hand, when a round number is presented (e.g., 60 percent), the recipient infers that the number is less carefully thought through.

In one study, participants were given a statistic about the percentage of households that recycle regularly. Half of the participants assigned to the round number condition were told that "60 percent of American households recycle regularly" while the other half assigned to the precise number condition were told that "60.37 percent of American households recycle regularly." Participants were then asked to indicate the likelihood that they would believe the statistic. Participants were also asked to attribute the statistic to one of the two pictures of men—a casually dressed unshaven man (low believability) and a formally dressed clean-cut man (high believability). Consistent with their prediction, participants presented with the precise number indicated that they were more likely to believe the given statistic compared to the participants presented with the round number. Attribution of the statistic to a source of information was also consistent with their hypothesis: Participants given the precise number were more likely to attribute the statistic to the formally dressed man.

The Role of Contextual Cues

Schley and Peters (2013) proposed that when the source of numerical information is not given, individuals use the precision of numerical information to make heuristic inferences about the source's believability using the following naive theory: A more precise number is from a source that is more believable. However, if contextual cues challenge the validity of this naive theory, then they are less likely to rely on this naive theory to interpret the processing discrepancy. That is, when individuals are reliably informed that given numerical information is presented by a believable (nonbelievable) source, they will deem the numerical information believable (nonbelievable) regardless of its precision.

They tested this prediction in an anchoring task. Participants were given several numerical anchors that they could use to answer given general knowledge questions such as the percentage of humans with blood type O+ and Gandhi's age at death. Participants were randomly assigned to one of the three conditions based on the believability of the source: ambiguous source (acquaintance), believable source (acquaintance who was a doctor), and nonbelievable source (intoxicated acquaintance). In each condition, the anchors were given either in precise or round format. As predicted, when the source of numerical anchors was ambiguous, participants used numerical precision to infer believability: The answers from participants given precise numbers were less likely to diverge from the anchor. However, the effect of numerical precision diminished when the believability of the source was made explicit. In the believable and the nonbelievable conditions, there was no effect of numerical precision on anchoring.

PRECISION AND RARITY

Product quantity information can be precise (1.97 ounces) or round (2.00 ounces), and this precision can influence evaluations of the product. Huang and Zhang (2013) proposed that a product is considered rarer and therefore to be more valuable when its weight is presented using a precise number instead of a round number. Although the authors invoke the Gricean conversational norms (Grice 1975) to account for their effect, their results are quite consistent with the proposed discrepancy attribution account.

The proposed link between precision and value was tested in one study where participants were asked to judge the quality grade of a jar of caviar. Along with the picture and product description, the quantity information was also presented to the participants. Half of the participants were told that the volume was 2 ounces while the other half of the participants were told that the volume was 1.95 ounces. As predicted, participants paradoxically considered the caviar offered in the 1.95-ounce pack to be of better quality and higher value than the caviar offered in the 2-ounce pack.

The Role of Contextual Cues

If the link between the precision of quantity and higher perceived value manifests through inference about the rarity of the product, then a more reliable contextual cue that influences this inferential process should moderate the precision effect. To test this prediction, in one study, Huang and Zhang asked participants to estimate the price of a chocolate. For half of participants (assigned to the unique chocolate condition), the chocolate was described as "hand-made in a family-owned factory in northwest Connecticut" and was "only sold in the small town where the factory is located." For the other half (assigned to the regular chocolate condition), the chocolate was described as "made in the USA" and would "soon be available at all major grocery stores across the country." In both conditions, participants saw weight information in one of the three different formats: 9.7 ounces (precise-lower), 10 ounces (round), or 10.3 ounces (precise-higher). As predicted, the effect of number format manifested only when the chocolate was described as unique. Price estimates made by participants who were told that the chocolate weighs either 9.7 ounces or 10.3 ounces were higher than those made by participants who were told that it weighs 10 ounces. However, when the chocolate was described as regular, there was no effect of precision of the quantity on the estimated price.

PRECISION AND CONFIDENCE INTERVALS

Zhang and Schwarz (2012) proposed that numerical precision can also influence confidence interval estimates. A numerical estimate can be expressed in the form of an interval or as a point estimate. For example, the price one is willing to spend on buying a used car can be expressed as "$8,000–$9,000" and the amount of time a researcher plans to work before sending a manuscript to his coauthor can be expressed as "2–3 days." When a numerical estimate is expressed in an interval format, the width of the interval implicitly signals the confidence of the information provider: the more precise the interval, the higher the perceived confidence (Yaniv & Foster, 1997). Whereas numerical estimates expressed in interval format directly convey a level of uncertainty, information recipients assume that numerical information given as a point estimate also implies a certain degree of uncertainty and width of the confidence interval. Zhang and Schwarz (2012) proposed that the numerical precision of a point estimate affects a recipient's perception of the extent of uncertainty and confidence implied by the communicator: the more precise a point estimate, the higher the confidence and the smaller the width of the confidence interval.

Zhang and Schwarz (2012) tested this hypothesis in a time-estimation context. In their study, participants were told to imagine that their car needed complicated repairs and that the dealership estimated that the repairs would take about a month. The precision of time estimation was varied across the conditions: 30 days, 31 days, or 1 month. Participants were asked to indicate their best- and worst-case estimates of the days they might have to wait. As predicted, the more fine-grained the unit, the narrower the recipient's confidence interval around the point estimate: participants who were given a 30-day or 31-day estimate were more likely to believe that the repair would be done around the projected time than the participants who were given one month as the point estimate. In another study, participants were told that a construction project would take either 1 year, 12 months, or 52 weeks. Again, participants' confidence interval was the smallest when the estimated duration was given in the smallest unit (52 weeks).

As in the studies reviewed previously, this effect is moderated by contextual cues. In one study, participants read an article about the world's largest car manufacturer developing a new vehicle. Half of the participants (assigned to knowledgeable source condition) were told that the information was from "the chief research officer of the company," while the other half (assigned to questionable source condition) were told that it is based on "a rumor spread by an auto fan website." The precision of the time estimate was also manipulated. Participants were told that the new car would be released either in two years or in 104 weeks. Participants were asked to indicate the likelihood of a timely launch of the new car and to estimate the delay in launch. As predicted, when the source of information was deemed knowledgeable, participants who were given the precise time estimate (104 weeks) were more likely to believe that the car would be successfully launched on time. Furthermore, the estimated delay was smaller when the time estimate was precise. However, both of these effects diminished when the information source was questionable.

UNRESOLVED ISSUES

Although Zhang and Schwarz's (2012) results are generally consistent with the proposed discrepancy attribution hypothesis that atypical digit patterns elicit a sense of discrepancy and the consequent attribution process that is shaped by naive theories and contextual cues, they have explained the observed effects using Gricean conversational norms (Grice, 1975). Grice stated that recipients and speakers cooperate with each other to maximize the effectiveness of their communication. He proposed four maxims of cooperativeness communication: maxims of quality, quantity, relation, and manner. Following the Gricean maxims, individuals having a conversation expect each other to convey the appropriate amount of truthful and relevant information in a clear, unambiguous manner. The Gricean maxims suggest that when numbers are not rounded and are stated precisely, recipients assume that the information provider is using the precision to serve a purpose. The recipient then tries to infer this purpose. Zhang and Schwarz (2012) argued that this inference underlies the effects of numerical precision. Grice's maxims of cooperative communication were informed by the philosophical study of language, and these maxims do not ascribe an important role to subjective experiences of processing discrepancy in linguistic inferences. In contrast, the proposed account states that the subtle evanescent feeling of processing discrepancy plays an important role in intuitive numerical judgments. The two theoretical accounts, the discrepancy attribution hypothesis and the Gricean conversational norms hypothesis, can be empirically tested by examining whether reducing the feeling of discrepancy moderates the effect of precision on intuitive judgments. The discrepancy attribution account uniquely posits that if participants are forewarned that the numbers they are going to see will be precise or sharp, then numerical precision should not influence their confidence interval estimates.

A similar approach can also test the role of the anchoring and scaling account offered by Janiszewski and Uy (2008) for the precision effect. Janiszewski and Uy (2008) have argued that the effect of numerical precision is due to a scale effect. They suggest that precision activates a more finely calibrated scale resulting in greater assimilation of judgments toward the anchor. This account also does not acknowledge the role of processing discrepancy in the effects of numerical precision on intuitive judgments. Once again, the two accounts—the discrepancy attribution account and the scaling account—can be empirically tested by forewarning the participants that the numbers they will see are precise or sharp. Only the discrepancy attribution account posits that the numerical precision effect will not manifest when the participants are forewarned about the nature of the numerical stimuli.

The Role of Neuroscience

A key postulate of the proposed discrepancy attribution account is that low-level affective responses, the feelings of unease or disquiet caused by processing discrepancy, are the core cause of the reported effects. Such low-level affective responses that last for only a fraction of a second often escape conscious attention. Furthermore, changes in subjective experiences caused by processing discrepancy are very minute. Therefore, self-reports and other such introspective methods are unlikely to be effective in delineating the role of processing discrepancy in intuitive judgments. Brain scan results can be useful in testing whether or not low-level affective responses play a role in the ease-of-computation effect and the precision effects reviewed in this chapter.

Researchers have identified specific regions of human brain that are specialized in the processing of numerical information. For instance, the horizontal part of the intraparietal sulcus (hIPS) has been shown to be activated whenever individuals are asked to attend to a number (Dehaene, 1997). This area gets activated regardless of the modality of the number; it gets activated when the number is presented as an Arabic numeral 3, written or spoken word "three," or even the presentation of three dots in a space. Interestingly, the activation of this area varies with the magnitude of numbers or the distance between the numbers. When an individual is comparing two numbers, activation is higher when the distance between the two numbers is larger. For example, hIPS activation is higher when an individual is comparing 7 and 4 than when comparing 6 and 5. It has been suggested that the activation of the hIPS area is more likely for analog judgments such as approximate magnitude judgments and less likely for symbolic rule-based processing such as mental calculations. If the ease-of-computation effect and the precision effect are indeed caused by naive theories associated with analog representations of magnitudes, then we can expect to see activations in areas such as hIPS correlated with the manifestation of these effects. Such neuroscience studies promise to unveil new insights about the human mind.

CONCLUSION

The extant body of literature has largely ignored the role of subjective feelings in everyday numerical judgments. We argue that the feeling of ease or difficulty can influence numerical judgments if such feelings are considered surprising or unexplained. We describe a model that postulates how processing discrepancy, naive theories, and contextual cues interactively influence everyday numerical judgments. We reviewed several empirical studies that support the proposed discrepancy attribution model. These studies not only augment the literature on numerical cognition and processing fluency but also offer guidelines on how to effectively use numerical information in everyday situations.

NOTES

1. We ascribe causal agency to the brain or the mind to portray that some of these processes might be occurring nonconsciously in the brain without the person's awareness or volition.
2. The first author has found that such forced-choice questions without a clear logical answer are useful in eliciting nonconscious associations that influence System 1 processing. Participants were offered only two response options in this question because offering a safer response option such as "neither" or "don't know" would have prompted them to choose the more justifiable response based on System 2 processing. When presented with such forced-choice questions to which there are no logical correct answers, participants know that they have to rely on their intuitive noetic feelings to choose a response. Reasoning is not of much use in answering such questions, and this makes it justifiable to rely on intuitions.

REFERENCES

Alter, A. L., Oppenheimer, D. M., Epley, N., & Eyre, R. N. (2007). Overcoming intuition: Metacognitive difficulty activates analytic reasoning. *Journal of Experimental Psychology: General, 136(4)*, 569–576.

Bagchi, R., & Davis, D. F. (2012). $29 for 70 items or 70 items for $29? How presentation order affects package perceptions. *Journal of Consumer Research, 39(1)*, 62–73.

Bless, H., & Forgas, J. P. (2000). The message within: Toward a social psychology of subjective experiences. In H. Bless & J. P. Forgas (Eds.), *The message within: The role of subjective experience in social cognition and behavior* (pp. 372–392). Philadelphia, PA: Psychology Press.

Coulter, K. S., & Norberg, P. (2009). The effects of physical distance between regular and sale prices on numeric difference perceptions. *Journal of Consumer Psychology, 19(2)*, 144–157.

Dehaene, S. (1997). *The number sense: How the mind creates mathematics.* New York, NY: Oxford University Press.

Dehaene, S., & Mehler, J. (1992). Cross-linguistic regularities in the frequency of number words. *Cognition, 43(1),* 1–29.

Denes-Raj, V., & Epstein, S. (1994). Conflict between intuitive and rational processing: When people behave against their better judgment. *Journal of Personality and Social Psychology, 66(5),* 819–829.

Grice, H. (1975). Logic and conversation. In P. Cole & J. Morgan (Eds.), *Syntax and semantics,* vol. III: *Speech acts* (pp. 41–58). New York, NY: Academic Press.

Huang, Y., & Zhang, Y. C. (2013). Does a better product weigh 9.7 ounce or 10? Cross-dimensional consumer inference from quantitative expressions. Working paper.

Jacoby, L. L., Kelley, C., Brown, J., & Jasechko, J. (1989). Becoming famous overnight: Limits on the ability to avoid unconscious influences of the past. *Journal of Personality and Social Psychology, 56(3),* 326–338.

Janiszewski, C., & Uy, D. (2008). Precision of the anchor influences the amount of adjustment. *Psychological Science, 19(2),* 121–127.

Jansen, C. J. M., & Pollmann, M. M. W. (2001). On round numbers: Pragmatic aspects of numerical expressions. *Journal of Quantitative Linguistics, 8(3),* 187–201.

Kahneman, D., & Frederick, S. (2002). Representativeness revisited: Attribute substitution in intuitive judgment. In T. Gilovich, D. Griffin, & D. Kahneman (Eds.), *Heuristics and biases: The psychology of intuitive judgment* (pp. 49–81). New York, NY: Cambridge University Press.

Kahneman, D., & Tversky, A. (1982). Variants of uncertainty. *Cognition, 11(2),* 143–157.

Kelley, C. M., & Jacoby, L. L. (1998). Subjective reports and process dissociation: Fluency, knowing, and feeling. *Acta Psychologica, 98(2),* 127–140.

Monga, A., & Bagchi, R. (2012). Years, months, and days versus 1, 12, and 365: The influence of units versus numbers. *Journal of Consumer Research, 39(1),* 185–198.

Moyer, R. S., & Landauer, T. K. (1967). Time required for judgment of numerical inequality. *Nature, 215(5109),* 1519–1520.

Pelham, B. W., Sumarta, T. T., & Myaskovsky, L. (1994). The easy path from many to much: The numerosity heuristic. *Cognitive Psychology, 26(2),* 103–133.

Peters, E., Västfjäll, D., Slovic, P., Mertz, C. K., Mozzocco, K., & Dickert, S. (2006). Numeracy and decision making. *Psychological Science, 17(5),* 406–413.

Pope, D., & Simonsohn, U. (2011). Round numbers as goals: Evidence from baseball, SAT takers, and the lab. *Psychological Science, V22(1),* 71–79.

Schley, D. R., & Peters, E. (2013). Precise numbers are more believable. Working paper.

Schwarz, N. (2004). Metacognitive experiences in consumer judgment and decision making. *Journal of Consumer Psychology, 14(4),* 332–348.

Thomas, M., & Morwitz, V. (2005), Penny wise and pound foolish: The left digit effect in price cognition, *Journal of Consumer Research, 32(1),* 54–64.

——(2009). The ease of computation effect: The interplay of metacognitive experiences and naïve theories in judgments of price difference. *Journal of Marketing Research, 46(1),* 81–91.

Thomas, M., Simon, D., & Kadiyali, V. (2010). The price precision effect: Evidence from laboratory and market data. *Marketing Science, 29(1),* 175–190.

Whittlesea, B. W. A. (1993). Illusions of familiarity. *Journal of Experimental Psychology: Learning, Memory, and Cognition, 19(6),* 1235–1253.

Whittlesea, B. W. A., & Williams, L. D. (2000). The source of feelings of familiarity: The discrepancy-attribution hypothesis. *Journal of Experimental Psychology: Learning, Memory, and Cognition, 26(3),* 547–565.

—— (2001a). The discrepancy-attribution hypothesis: I. The heuristic basis of feelings and familiarity. *Journal of Experimental Psychology: Learning, Memory, and Cognition, 27(3),* 3–13.

—— (2001b). The discrepancy-attribution hypothesis: II. Expectation, uncertainty, surprise, and feelings of familiarity. *Journal of Experimental Psychology: Learning, Memory, and Cognition, 27(1),* 14–33.

Wilson, D., & Gilbert, D. T. (1998). Explaining away: A model of affective adaptation. *Perspectives on Psychological Science, 3(5),* 170–386.

Yaniv, I., & Foster, D. P. (1997). Precision and accuracy of judgmental estimation. *Journal of Behavioral Decision Making, 10(1),* 21–32.

Zhang, Y. C., & Schwarz, N. (2012). How and why 1 year differs from 365 days: A conversational logic analysis of inferences from the granularity of quantitative expressions. *Journal of Consumer Research, 39(2),* 248–259.

—— (2013). The power of precise numbers: A conversational logic analysis. Working paper.

Part IV

Neuroeconomics and Neurobiology

7

Studying Decision Processes through Behavioral and Neuroscience Analyses of Framing Effects

IRWIN P. LEVIN, TODD McELROY, GARY J. GAETH,
WILLIAM HEDGCOCK, NATALIE L. DENBURG,
AND DANIEL TRANEL

In this chapter, we start by reviewing some of the basic research by brain scientists who demonstrated the crucial role of emotions in decision making. We discuss how these demonstrations helped shape current dual-process theories of decision making. After describing a variety of simple laboratory tasks designed to uncover reactions to potential gains and losses, we focus on framing effects where objectively equivalent information presented in different frames has been shown to lead to substantially different preference ratings which are accompanied by different brain activation patterns. An array of multidisciplinary tools across a growing body of literature shows that framing effects play a fundamental role in decision making. In this chapter, we explore this recent research by showing how framing effects inform current dual-process theories that describe the complementary roles of cognition and emotion/affect. Studies include a variety of laboratory tasks amenable to brain-scanning, eye-tracking, biological rhythms, and lifespan developmental techniques. These tasks include variations of the framing paradigm that differentially tap into cognitive and affective processes. Ultimately, research of this type can help us understand both group differences and individual differences in decision making.

*I*n the current chapter we focus on recent developments in decision neuroscience—the name given to the area that combines behavioral and neural science—that inform the development of theories of decision making, particularly those that consider a dual-process system that differentiates between different types of thinking style evoked by different circumstances. The careful choice of controlled tasks that focus on specific component processes in decision making is paramount. We cite a variety of tasks and measures but concentrate on those that reveal *framing effects,* the tendency for variations in emotional tone of otherwise equivalent decision problems to produce sometimes dramatic changes in preference and choice. We describe a variety of behavioral and neurological or biological markers that address what these effects reveal about the component processes of decision making, leading to systematic differences as a function of age, handedness, biological rhythm, and brain abnormality.

To this end, we focus the chapter on framing effects in decision making because evidence is accumulating at both the behavioral and neural levels that framing effects represent an appropriate setting for examining the individual and complementary roles of affect and cognition in decision making. Framing effects are ubiquitous in everyday life and thus have been a popular topic for the laboratory. We find frames impacting judgments about gambles, consumer goods and services, and medical procedures. In this chapter, we concentrate on "valence framing effects," which are particularly interesting because they represent different responses to objectively equivalent information by simply varying whether the information is expressed in positive or negative terms.

INTRODUCTION

Decision making can be a complex process involving external factors such as the availability of information about choice alternatives and internal factors such as level of maturation of brain systems that deal with stress. Thus it is not surprising that decision scientists have incorporated both the methods of the behavioral sciences and the methods of neuroscience or "brain" science. One conclusion drawn from this multidisciplinary approach is that there exist complementary roles of cognition or conscious thought and affect or emotion in decision making (e.g., Epstein et al., 1992).

Common wisdom at one time was that "cold" (emotionless) decision making was always superior to "hot" (emotional) decision making. The work of neuroscientist Antonio Damasio and colleagues changed that. Based on earlier written reports of the 1848 Phineas Gage case in which a railroad worker's temperament—but not his intellect—was dramatically changed after an explosion caused an iron rod to be blown through his skull, Damasio and colleagues found parallels in a group of patients who had suffered lesions to the brain through disease, trauma, or surgery. As revealed by neuroimaging data which allowed the researchers to identify cohorts of patients with lesions in the same location, anatomically what the patients and Mr. Gage had in common was damage to those specific parts of the brain's left frontal lobe that have been linked to the processing and expression of emotion. Behaviorally, what they had in common was the inability to appropriately use their emotions to guide behavior. For Mr. Gage, this adversely affected personal and work relations. For Damasio's patients, this led to various deficits, including the inability to learn from previous losses in a controlled laboratory task (to be described later) in which control subjects including those with lesions to other parts of the brain far outperformed the target group (Bechara et al., 1994; Damasio, 1994).

This initial study was followed by a number of studies using a variety of established laboratory tasks with the same patients where their neural impairment was shown to affect a variety of behaviors, particularly in the area of decision making (Bechara et al., 1997; Weller et al., 2007). An interesting rule of inference here is that if repeated observation reveals that damage to a particular area of the brain leads to loss of a specific function, then that area is necessary for that function. The thinking here is that if all people with injuries to the front of their brain have the same personality change, then that starts to be a pretty convincing argument that the part of the brain required for that ability has been lost.

Due to the known plasticity of the brain, converging evidence using multiple methods and populations is required and this strategy has been followed. In particular, the lesion-deficit approach has been complemented by the now popular functional magnetic imaging (fMRI) studies which detect brain activity during cognitive tasks. This technique will be illustrated later in this chapter as it applies to framing studies.

The lesson for decision-making researchers was the mounting evidence that the ability to reconstruct feelings from past successes and failures and apply them to a similar current decision can lead to more advantageous decision making such as avoiding the mistakes of the past. As we will see, current theories of decision making assign an important role to emotional (or affective) processes. This is a primary example of how the work of neuroscientists and behavioral scientists can complement each other. This chapter will provide more examples, including parallel age-related changes in behavior and the maturation and decline of specific brain structures. An important starting point is to select suitable tasks and measures for analyzing decision processes.

Tasks

In this section we sample from tasks that have desirable properties for combining behavioral and neuroscience analyses of decision making. These properties include ease of administration for researchers, intrinsic interest to participants, the ability to focus on specific questions of interest to decision scientists, and the ability to model and predict real-world decision making. Following this section, we will provide an expanded description of the use of framing paradigms.

Iowa Gambling Task   A task in which emotional involvement plays a key role is the Iowa gambling task (IGT; Bechara, 2007; Bechara et al., 1997). Because of its wide use with brain-damaged patients and in scanner research, IGT has perhaps become the prototypical "neuroscience task." Successful performance on the most widely used version of this task requires the avoidance of choices providing immediate reward but larger subsequent losses.

Participants are asked to select cards from four different decks each with its own distribution of gains and losses. No information about differences between decks is given ahead of time and participants have to learn from repeated trials which are the two "good" decks and which are the two "bad" decks. Repeated sampling from the two good decks will lead to greater gains than losses in the long run whereas sampling from the bad decks, while offering initial gains, will lead to greater losses than gains in the long run. Bechara et al. (1994, 1997) showed that patients with lesions to the ventromedial prefrontal cortex (vmPFC) were unable to learn in this task because the activation of brain mechanisms that signal potential loss based on prior experiences was dampened. Because the IGT was designed to mimic and predict actual choice behavior outside the laboratory, it combines elements of risk and ambiguity, and gain and loss. The next task separates these elements.

Cups Task   The cups task (Levin & Hart, 2003; Weller et al., 2007) was designed as a simple risky-choice task with actual gains and losses. A key feature of the cups task is the inclusion of separate trials involving risky gains and risky losses. Gain trials require the choice between an option that offers a sure gain of one quarter and another option that offers a designated probability of winning multiple quarters or no quarters, where probability information is conveyed simply by the number of cups from which to choose. This property allows the task to be administered to all age groups. Loss trials require the choice between a sure loss of one quarter and a designated probability of losing multiple quarters or no quarters.

On each trial, an array of two, three, or five cups is shown on each side of a computer screen. One array is identified as the certain or riskless side where one quarter would be gained (lost) for whichever cup was selected. The other array is designated as the risky side where the selection of one cup would lead to a designated number of quarters gained (lost) and the other cups would lead to no gain (loss). Participants select one cup from either the riskless or the risky side. By manipulating the number of cups from which to choose and the possible outcome magnitude, some trials represent "risk advantageous" choices because the expected value of a risky choice is more favorable than the sure gain or loss (e.g., one out of three chances of winning five quarters versus winning one quarter for sure, or one out of five chances of losing three quarters versus losing one quarter for sure). Conversely, other trials are "risk disadvantageous" because the expected value of a risky choice is less favorable than the sure gain or loss (e.g., one out of five chances of winning three quarters, or one out of three chances of losing five quarters).

These design features allow for comparisons across different groups (e.g., different age groups, as we will see later in this chapter) for overall risk taking to achieve gains or avoid losses, and the tendency to make risk-advantageous or -disadvantageous choices for risky gains and losses. The next task focuses on the escalation of risk over successive experiences.

Balloon Analogue Risk Task   Lejuez and colleagues developed the balloon analogue risk task (BART; Lejuez et al., 2002). BART is a computerized task that models real-world risk behavior through the conceptual frame of balancing the potential for reward and harm (Lejuez et al., 2002; White, Lejuez, & de Wit, 2007). In the task, the participant is presented with a balloon and asked to pump it by clicking a button on the screen. With each click, the balloon inflates 0.3 centimeters and money is added to the participant's temporary winnings; however, balloons also have explosion points, which can be varied both across and within studies. Before the balloon pops, participants can press "Collect $$$" which saves their earnings to a permanent bank. If the balloon pops before the participant collects the money, all earnings for that balloon are lost, and the next balloon is presented. Thus, each successive pump confers greater potential reward but also greater risk, mimicking many real-world gambling and investing decisions.

The primary BART score is the average number of pumps on unexploded balloons, with higher scores indicative of greater risk-taking propensity. In the original version of the task, each pump was worth $0.05 and there were 30 total balloons for each of three different balloon colors, with each color having a different probability of exploding on the first pump (1/8, 1/32, and 1/128, respectively). If the balloon did not explode after the first pump, the probability that the balloon would explode on the next pump increased linearly until the last pump at which the probability of an explosion was 1.00.

Participants are given no information about the breakpoints, and the absence of this information allows for the examination of participants' initial responses to the task and to changes as they experience the contingencies related to payout collections and balloon explosions. Results of the original study showed that individual differences in the average number of pumps on unexploded balloons were associated with some real-world risky behaviors occurring outside the laboratory such as smoking and substance abuse as well as with self-report measures of personality traits, including impulsivity and sensation seeking (Lauriola et al., 2014; Lejuez et al., 2003a, 2003b).

The next task focuses on the difference between "hot" and "cold" decision making.

Columbia Card Task   The Columbia card task (CCT) was developed to investigate developmental changes and individual differences in healthy individuals across the lifespan and in populations such as substance users (Figner et al., 2009). The CCT enables researchers to compare affect-based versus deliberative risky decisions and their triggering mechanisms. Applications combine behavioral methods with physiological measures, brain-imaging, and brain-stimulation techniques.

In the "hot" version of the CCT—"hot" because of its ability to arouse emotions—participants are displayed 32 cards and instructed to turn over cards for points until they wish to stop and collect the points or until a loss card is turned over and the amount of the loss is subtracted from their points. (In the original version, feedback was pre-programmed, but see below.) In the "cold" version, participants simply state how many cards they wish to turn over without actually doing so or getting any feedback about winning or losing until after they finish all rounds of the game. The absence of immediate feedback makes this version of the task less emotionally involving, thus the "cold" label.

In an important demonstration, Figner et al. (2009) found increased adolescent risk taking in the hot but not the cold condition. They then concluded that adolescents' affective system tends to override the deliberative system in states of emotional arousal. This helps explain why teens perform risky behaviors even when they know the risks.

In more recent (Figner & Weber, 2011) and current applications, a refined and shortened version of the task was developed for easier use in the fMRI scanner with unrigged feedback in the hot version to make it more incentive-compatible. This version allows for a more precise interpretation of risk-taking results and clearer operationalization of such concepts as risk and return sensitivity, risk attitude, and risk aversion. It is currently being used in an fMRI study comparing risky choices in children, adolescents, and adults (Figner, personal communication, April 20, 2013).

FRAMING TASKS

In contrast to some of the newer tasks described above, the tasks that have had the most intense history of studying decision makers' reactions to potential gains and losses are those involving framing effects. Thus we focus on these here. The history of studying framing effects is long, often traced to Tversky and Kahneman's (1981) seminal paper on the Asian disease problem. Nevertheless, new research tools have allowed us to go beyond the early demonstration of biased responding, that is, departure from normative principles, to examine in more detail when and why framing effects occur. This in turn provides deeper insight into basic decision-making processes, especially the ability to separate cognitive and affective or emotional systems.

Based on confusions in the literature at the time as to why framing effects differed across studies and investigators, we suggested that "All frames are not created equal" (Levin, Schneider, & Gaeth, 1998; see also Kühberger, 1998, and Levin et al., 2002) and laid out a scheme for classifying framing studies in terms of their operational definitions, typical findings, and possible explanations. In this chapter, we focus on two types of framing effects: "risky choice framing" and "attribute framing."

Risky choice framing, as exemplified by the Asian disease problem, requires a choice between a risky and a riskless option of equal expected value where outcomes are alternatively expressed in positive terms (e.g., lives saved by a medical procedure) or negative terms (lives lost). In the classic example, respondents are offered a treatment choice for dealing with a disease that is expected to kill 600 persons. For half the respondents (the positive frame condition) the choice is between an option that offers a sure saving of 200 lives and an option that offers a ⅓ chance of saving all 600 lives and a ⅔ chance of saving no lives. For the other half (the negative frame condition) the objectively identical choice is between an option that offers a sure loss of 400 lives and an option that offers a ⅓ chance of losing no lives and a ⅔ chance of losing all 600 lives. The most common result is that subjects are more apt to make the risky choice (selecting the option that offers a ⅓ possibility of no lives lost) in the negative condition but choose the riskless option (a sure saving of ⅓ of the lives) in the positive condition. Later work revealed a fourfold pattern of risk aversion for potential gains and risk seeking for potential losses of high probability, as in the Asian disease problem, but the opposite for losses of low probability (Tversky & Kahneman, 1992). These results are explained in terms of separate value functions for gains and losses and nonlinear weighting of probabilities in Kahneman and Tversky's (1979) prospect theory.

Attribute framing, as exemplified by the percentage lean vs. percentage fat labeling of ground beef (Levin & Gaeth, 1988), is a simpler form of framing because it involves only the alternate labeling of a single attribute of an object or event and does not require comparisons based on the element of risk. The typical finding is more favorable evaluations when alternatives are labeled in positive terms (percentage lean, success rate) rather than negative terms (percentage fat, failure rate). These results were explained in terms of associative networks primed by positive or negative labels (Levin, 1987). Levin and Gaeth (1988) found that even after consuming an identical sample of ground beef, those who were told that it was 75 percent lean ground beef gave higher ratings of healthiness and quality than did those who were told that they were tasting 25 percent fat ground beef. In an extension, Braun, Gaeth, and Levin (1997) investigated attribute framing effects in a realistic environment where the label was imbedded in an actual product package. Following a taste test, 80 percent fat-free chocolate was given higher ratings than 20 percent fat chocolate, especially by female consumers for whom the framed attribute was particularly salient.

Much of the research on attribute framing effects has emerged from controlled conditions carried out in the laboratory; however, a number of studies have demonstrated the relevance for applied decision making. For example, using practicing physicians, researchers showed that when the option of surgery was expressed in terms of "survival rate" as opposed to "mortality rate," significantly more surgeons selected surgery in the survival condition (McNeil et al., 1982). Also in the domain of health, Jasper et al. (2001) examined the effects of attribute framing on pregnant women's perceptions of fetal risk and their subsequent intentions to use a particular drug during pregnancy. Half the women received positively framed information (97–99 percent chance of having a normal child) and half received the negative version (1–3 percent chance of having a malformed child). Those in the negative condition had a significantly higher perception of risk and were significantly less likely to contemplate taking the drug.

Research has shown that attribute framing plays a profoundly influential role in many important economic decisions such as fairness in healthcare decisions (Gamliel & Peer, 2010) and allocation of resources (Gamliel & Peer, 2006). Recently, in a study involving life annuities, a team of researchers looked at how framing the question of life expectancy impacts consumers' subsequent estimate of their expected lifespan and concomitant economic decisions (Payne et al., 2012). The positive frame asks people to provide probabilities of living to a certain age or older; the negative frame asks people to provide probabilities of dying by a certain age or younger. These two answers should be complements, but Payne et al. found that estimated probabilities differed significantly in the two conditions. People in the live-to frame reported that they have a 55 percent chance of being alive at age 85, whereas people in the die-by frame reported that they have a 68 percent chance of being dead at age 85. Overall, estimated mean life expectancies, across three studies and over 2,300 respondents, were between 7.29 to 9.17 years longer when solicited in the live-to frame.

Importantly, Payne et al. showed that frame-induced life expectancies predicted behavioral intentions. Differences in life expectancies were predictive of stated preferences for life annuities, a product that provides insurance against outliving one's savings. On a process level, the authors showed that the attribute framing effect on judgments was partially mediated by the relative number of thoughts in favor of being alive at that age. This is consistent with Levin's (1987) associative model of attribute framing effects.

INDIVIDUAL DIFFERENCES

Sparked largely by the work of Stanovich and West (Stanovich, 1999; Stanovich & West, 1998a, 1998b; see also Levin, 1999), there has been a growing movement to extend aggregate-level analysis of behavioral decision making to a focus on individual differences in rational thought. For example, although we talk about "typical" findings in studies of risky choice and attribute framing, it is important to note that there are systematic variations in the magnitude and even existence of these effects as a function of specific task and situational characteristics and their interaction with individual difference factors (Lauriola & Levin, 2001; Levin et al., 2002; Mahoney et al., 2011; McElroy & Seta, 2003; Peters & Levin, 2008; Simon et al., 2004; Smith & Levin, 1996). A sampling of the findings here shows that risky-choice framing effects are largest for those scoring high on a neuroticism scale, for those scoring low on openness to new experiences, and for those displaying an experiential (heuristic) thinking style. Thinking style differences are highlighted in contemporary "dual-process" theories of decision making.

DUAL PROCESSES

Evidence is accumulating that common decision-making biases such as framing effects reveal the manner in which different thinking or processing styles are evoked. Furthermore, there is growing evidence that these processing differences can be more thoroughly understood at the neural level, particularly through the activation of affective systems in the brain (DeMartino et al., 2006; Huettel et al., 2006; Kuhnen & Knutson, 2005; Sanfey et al., 2003; Tom et al., 2007; Weller et al., 2007). Neuroscientific research suggests that because of the evolutionary importance of avoiding negative consequences, the mere presence of uncertainty induces a primary "fear" response elicited by the amygdala, which has been associated specifically with fear processing and avoidance of negative consequences — sometimes referred to as "loss aversion" (Le Doux, 2000; Phelps, 2006; Trepel, Fox, & Poldrak, 2005). This fear response activates the ventromedial prefrontal cortex (vmPFC) whose function it is to mediate decision making and to allow for more careful deliberative processes by linking together working memory and emotional systems (Damasio, 1994). Structures such as the insular cortex, which are independent of the amygdala, are also likely to impact decision making under uncertainty by providing complementary systems for dealing with potential losses (Kuhnen & Knutson, 2005; Weller et al., 2009). In a recent review, Levin et al. (2012) did in fact show that different neural systems appear to be activated in dealing with potential gains and potential losses, especially when neural activation was assessed at the crucial pre-choice stage when positive or negative possible outcomes were being considered.

The intriguing question of how humans process information in a quick, automatic fashion or a thoughtful pursuant manner traces its roots to William James and has been applied in many areas of psychology that directly relate to decision making (e.g., Epstein et al., 1992; Gilbert et al., 1991; Reyna & Brainerd, 1991; Schneider & Shiffrin, 1977; Sloman, 1996; Stanovich & West, 2000). In a more recent refined view, Kahneman and Frederick (2002; see also Kahneman, 2003, 2011) adapted a two-system approach that has many similarities with the prior contributions of Stanovich and West (2000) and also creates a new vision for the two-process model. In the Kahneman and Frederick approach, the automatic System 1 operates without attention or control processes, uses basic intuitive associations including emotional intensity, and, in the end, supplies us with quick preferences that guide most of our decision making. System 2 processing is markedly different from System 1. It is deliberative, thoughtful, and has the hallmark characteristic of requiring effort. According to this dual-process approach, either system of processing is possible, but most of our decision making is driven by System 1. This processing style allows for choices to be made with cognitive ease and factors such as emotional intensity to become the guiding principles for choice preference. However, System 2 may also be employed if the situation sufficiently motivates us and cognitive resources are available. When such situations arise, more elaborative, effortful, and time-consuming processing occurs and alternatives are considered in more depth. In System 2 processing, attention is directed to the task, alternatives are generated from memory, thoughtful (e.g., mathematical) comparisons are made, and alternatives may then be weighed in a deliberative fashion.

Before proceeding, we will briefly describe how we think the distinction between risky-choice framing and attribute framing is important for analyzing processing styles. Based on its simpler form, and our associative model of its emotional priming effects, attribute framing seems particularly amenable to System 1 processing. Specifically, attribute framing problems are comparatively simple and can be processed with relative ease. And because System 1 is the default processing style for cognitively easy tasks, it seems likely that System 1 processing will dominate for most individuals when they encounter an attribute framing task.

Conversely, because risky-choice framing has the added elements of processing numeric risk information and comparing risky and riskless options, both elements associated with System 2, we presume that System 2 processing is more likely to occur in risky-choice framing. To preview what comes later, we use this distinction to better understand why some individuals show biased responding on a risky-choice framing task but not on an attribute framing task and why different brain mechanisms are involved.

Specifically, we will show that:

1. Different types of framing manipulations evoke different levels of emotional reliance.
2. These differences are revealed in both behavioral measures and biological/neurological indicators.
3. Normal metabolic and biological fluctuations related to circadian rhythms affect decision making, as revealed by different levels of framing effects at different times of the day.

4. Naturally occurring hemispheric laterality differences as revealed by handedness impact framing effects.
5. Gaze duration as revealed by eye-tracking techniques provides further insight into attentional processes underlying framing effects.
6. The most basic of all biological processes, aging, results in changes in the balance between emotional and cognitive processes that can paradoxically lead to impaired performance on some tasks but improved performance on other tasks in the form of resistance to some forms of framing.

EMOTIONAL PROCESSING AND FRAMING EFFECTS

Emotional processing can be affected by instructions designed to either increase or decrease emotional reactions to stimuli. For example, Gross and Levenson (1993) demonstrate that emotion-suppression instructions can decrease subjective evaluations of emotional responses to films as well as decrease heart rate relative to controls. This suggests that these instructions can be used to provide information about the importance of emotional processing in decision making.

Preliminary data from a presentation by Hedgcock et al. (2012) provide evidence that attribute and risk framing are affected differently by emotion suppression. Participants in this study were presented with multiple decisions between two alternatives while type of framing (risky choice or attribute) and valence of the alternatives (positive or negative) were manipulated within-participant. Half of the participants were simply told to choose their preferred alternative while the other half were given additional instructions to avoid using emotions when making their decisions. Control participants had the typical pattern of responses: negative valence resulted in more risk seeking in risky choice and more quality seeking in attribute framing. This means that when participants are choosing between a low-quality and high-quality option of different prices, negative valence will increase their preferences for the high-quality option by making the low-quality option seem particularly unattractive. Emotion-suppression participants had a different pattern of results. Like the control participants, emotion-suppression participants increased preferences for the probabilistic option in risk framing. But, unlike the control participants, valence did not significantly affect their preferences in attribute framing. This shows that it is possible to de-bias decision making with emotion-suppression instructions in attribute framing but that these instructions may not be able to reduce bias in risk framing. This is consistent with the hypothesis that emotional processing affects these two types of framing in different ways. The next section will describe how time of day affects cognitive processing which, in turn, affects framing.

THE EFFECTS OF BRAIN METABOLIC LEVELS ON FRAMING AND OTHER EFFECTS

As we discuss, brain-imaging techniques and observations of those who suffer localized brain damage have provided insight into how specific regions of the brain may influence the input of cognition and emotion, including how these play out in different types of framing. Another physiological aspect that undoubtedly plays a role in how the brain functions is its metabolic activity. The body's metabolic activity influences all aspects of physiological and psychological functioning. Given the level of effort necessary for System 2 processing, metabolic activity should have a pronounced effect on System 2 processing while having little influence on System 1 processing. This logic should provide us with a foundation for examining the extent to which System 1 and System 2 processing is involved in risky choice and attribute framing. To explore this we focus on two main contributors to metabolic activity: circadian rhythms and glucose. Both of these factors have recently drawn the interest of decision researchers, largely because of their effects on cognitive processing.

We live in an environment that is filled with many externally regulated changes but the most profound is the day–night cycle. Not surprisingly, our bodies have developed a host of biological fluctuations that accompany variations in the diurnal cycle, all geared toward giving us specific temporal advantages. On any normal day, our internal biological clock cycles through changes in a variety of physiological functions including corporal temperature, hormones, heart rate, and blood pressure. And the list is not limited to biological functions; cognitive abilities also vary with the circadian cycle. These circadian variations occur on a roughly 24-hour cycle and appear to be controlled by an area deep within our brain, the suprachiasmatic nucleus (SCN), which acts as a circadian oscillator.

Given the important biological functions that are regulated by the circadian rhythm cycle, it seems evident that diurnal cycles will have important influences on many aspects of human behavior, including decision making. Studies investigating this topic have shown that circadian-mismatched participants (e.g., morning type in the evening) rely more on judgmental heuristics, which leads to greater stereotyping (Bodenhausen, 1990), and they have lower levels of strategic reasoning when making decisions (Dickinson & McElroy, 2010, 2012), both findings suggesting attenuation in the deliberative thought of System 2.

Recently, McElroy and Dickinson (2010) investigated how changes in deliberative thought, observed across the circadian cycle, influenced both risky choice and attribute framing. To accomplish this, they used online survey software and randomly assigned participants to specific timeslots across the full 24-hour cycle. Their findings differed for risky-choice and attribute framing. They found that risky-choice framing effects were significantly stronger during circadian off-times relative to circadian on-times and this effect was most pronounced in the losses condition. However, circadian variation had no effect on attribute framing. This highlights how the metabolic factor of circadian off-times can attenuate the cognitively effortful System 2 processing and have pronounced effects on risky-choice framing while at the same time have no effects on attribute framing.

A variety of metabolic and physiological processes operate in tune with circadian rhythm. One of these is glucose level. Blood glucose levels are intricately tied into the circadian arousal system (La Fleur, 2003). The largest benefactor of glucose utilization is the brain; it accounts for roughly 25 percent of the body's total glucose utilization.

Recently, researchers have begun to focus on how glucose levels may influence decision making. In one study, Masicampo and Baumeister (2008) manipulated whether participants were glucose deprived or enriched and then presented them with an attraction task. In this task participants are presented with two alternatives roughly equal in desirability. A third but comparatively unattractive "decoy" alternative is also presented where it has been manipulated to be more similar to one of the two focal alternatives. It has been shown that participants will shift their preference to the alternative that is most similar to the undesirable decoy (which they should rule out and disregard). In their study they found that glucose-deprived participants (compared to glucose-enriched participants) were more likely to make less optimal choices and rely on the decoy, suggesting another way in which metabolic factors influence the likelihood of System 2 processing of decisions.

In another investigation, McMahon and Scheel (2010) looked at probability learning and found that participants relied more on simple probability rules when they were glucose deprived, and, as a result, they mimicked the percentage of occurrence for each event (a less advantageous System 1 strategy) rather than choosing the event of greater likelihood. Further research by Wang and Dvorak (2010) showed that glucose enrichment reduced the rate of future discounting, suggesting a better ability to regulate expected rewards associated with System 2 type thinking. Taken together, these findings seem to indicate that glucose deprivation impedes a decision maker's ability to ignore irrelevant information, to apply more complex rules, and to consider future rewards thoughtfully, while glucose enhancement has the opposite effects. This suggests that glucose acts as circadian fuel to either inhibit or encourage more thoughtful processing of decisions, demonstrating the intricate ties between metabolic functions and behavioral outcomes.

These circadian-rhythm and glucose findings coalesce around other neurological and behavioral findings we have discussed. An emerging theme incorporating these findings is a dual-process account. Specifically, it is well established that effortful cognitive processing such as that involved in System 2 is constrained by the cognitive resources currently available (Hasher & Zacks, 1988). Behavioral research has shown that during circadian off-times cognitive resources are depleted (e.g., Schmidt et al., 2007). Further, there is neurological evidence that during circadian off-times cognitive resources are constrained because of reduced frontal-lobe functioning (e.g., Manly et al., 2002). Together, both behavioral and neurological evidence suggest that circadian off-times decrease glucose levels and inhibit cognitive resources. Consequently, deliberative, effortful System-2-type processing should be impeded during circadian off-times and advanced during on-times. This parallels the circadian effects on risky-choice framing wherein framing effects were strongest during off-times and weakest during on-times. However, circadian rhythm had no effect on attribute framing. Taken together, these findings suggest that deliberative processing central to System 2 is the key player in risky-choice framing but plays little or no role in attribute framing, thus supporting the view that risky-choice and attribute framing represent different balances of cognitive and affective processing.

Another important link between processing styles and biological processes is handedness as an observable element of right-brain/left-brain functions. There has been a great deal of research investigating how handedness differences represent underlying anatomical differences in the brain. A growing body of research has recently begun to focus on how these differences may impact decision making (e.g., Christman et al., 2007; Jasper, Barry, & Christman, 2008; Jasper & Christman, 2005). At the heart of this literature lies the belief that mixed-handers have greater interaction between the left and right hemispheres and consequently greater access to right-hemisphere processing than strong-handers (those with a dominant hand). Research based on this premise has shown that this access leads mixed-handers to demonstrate more risk propensity and stronger informational framing effects (Jasper, Fournier, & Christman, 2013).

Research has also looked at how processing differences associated with the respective hemispheres may influence risky-choice framing. Historically, hemispheric research suggests that the left hemisphere processes information in an analytic fashion, whereas the right hemisphere tends to process information in a more holistic style (e.g., Ornstein, 1972). The outcome of these respective processing styles is that left-hemisphere processing is reliant on numerically derived information and the right hemisphere is especially sensitive to context cues.

McElroy and Seta (2004) manipulated hemispheric activation through unilateral attentional direction using finger tapping and also through a monaural listening procedure wherein an auditory stimulus is presented through one channel to one ear and initially only activates the contralateral hemisphere. After selectively activating the respective hemispheres, they relied on the different hemispheric processing styles to make predictions for a traditional risky-choice framing task. Their findings revealed that the respective hemispheric processing styles had significant effects on risky-choice framing, with pronounced framing effects under holistic processing and no framing effects when analytic processing was induced. Thus, both manipulated hemispheric activation and naturally occurring differences provide converging evidence of the role of dual processing styles on risky-choice framing effects.

The following examples also illustrate how the use of framing tasks in conjunction with physiological/biological indicators can help us refine our understanding of decision processes.

NEW METHODS FOR TESTING NEW THEORIES OF DECISION MAKING

Traced back to the early work of Kahneman and Tversky (1979), prospect theory represents a psychophysical approach to describing rational choice, yet at its core it maintains a theoretical basis that is consistent with traditional approaches to decision making. The traditional approach assumes that decision makers mathematically combine quantitative information by transposing numerical amounts and probabilities into some quantitative value or utility that is then compared and contrasted across alternatives. This assumption has its foundation in some of the earliest beginnings of rational decision making (Bernoulli, 1954, originally published in 1738) and during its formative stages (e.g., Edwards, 1954).

The more recent fuzzy-trace theory (FTT; Reyna, 2012; Reyna & Brainerd, 2011), like earlier dual-process theories, involves two complementary styles that can lead decision makers to different choice preferences. However, FTT differs from prospect theory and other decision-making theories first and foremost because under most decision-making conditions it does not take a quantitative transformation approach. Rather, FTT is a dual-process, memory-based theory in which one memory system involves precise, verbatim representations of information and extracts a level of detail critical for more analytic comparisons. The other memory system extracts only vague "fuzzy" impressions but is the source of meaning and captures generalized "gist" appeal which directs an intuitive inclination toward an alternative. These two memory systems operate in parallel, each individually extracting representations from a target stimulus and then encoding and storing the information independently. The end result for decision making is that these functionally independent memory systems often lead people to different choice preferences.

According to FTT, adults normally process in as "fuzzy" and impressionistic a way as is reasonable and consequently they normally make decisions using only vague representations that capture the "gist" of the task's information. Thus, in gist processing, numeric information is extracted in a very simplified form and precise quantities are often neglected. For example, 33 percent might be extracted as "some," 67 percent as "most" and 0 percent as "none." As a consequence of this processing style, alternatives are perceived in an ordinal gist and individuals are directed by a sense of "intuition" toward the alternative with the greatest extracted value. Applying this to framing effects, in the positive framing condition of the Asian disease problem, saving some lives is more attractive than taking a chance that no lives will be saved, and, in the negative condition, losing some lives is less attractive than having a chance of losing no lives. Likewise, in the ground-beef attribute framing problem, "fat" is less desirable than "lean."

Recently, a good deal of research has set out to test FTT with prospect theory and other utility models. A means for testing these theories has emerged that involves the importance of presenting "0" (null) information to the decision maker. Because prospect theory and other standard utility models rely on a numerical transformation of the information, the presence or absence of the zero complement (e.g., ⅔ chance of saving no lives) should be irrelevant because the quantitative value of the alternative (⅓ chance of saving all 600) does not change with its presence. However, in FTT, null information is vital in gist processing as it represents a basic categorical distinction that the decision maker will use for comparison. For example, in gist processing the alternative "⅓ chance of saving all 600 lives and a ⅔ chance of saving no lives" would be encoded as "sometimes some people are saved and sometimes none are saved," which creates a strikingly different representation than when the zero complement is removed resulting in "some are saved" (Reyna et al., 2011). Kühberger and Tanner (2010) tested this theoretical assumption by manipulating whether or not participants had access to the zero complement. They found that framing effects were present when the zero complement was presented but were not observed when the zero complement was removed, thus supporting FTT assumptions.

In a recent study, McElroy et al. (2013) used eye-tracking technology during a risky-choice task to test the more quantitative processing approach of prospect theory and the memory-based processing of FTT. Eye-tracking technology allows comparative analysis of discrete eye movements and can measure gaze duration, thus allowing researchers to operationalize "processing" by associating inward cognitive processing to observational differences in eye-gaze duration. McElroy et al. (2013) hypothesize that because of prospect theory's traditional decision-making approach, numerical transformation of the quantitative information determines value and no difference in gaze duration should be observed between those who demonstrate a risky-choice framing effect and those who do not. Conversely, because zero-complement information is so important in gist processing, they predicted from FTT that gaze duration of the zero complement (i.e. the amount of time the pupil rests on the null information) should be greater for those who demonstrate risky-choice framing effects.

Their findings were consistent with FTT in the losses condition where participants who demonstrated framing effects had significantly longer gaze duration for the zero complement. However, in the gains condition no significant differences were observed, suggesting that the gains condition may lack sufficient intensity. This is consistent with the special role of loss aversion (Weller et al., 2009). Thus, in this example, eye-tracking technology is used to further corroborate behavioral data and show how physiological techniques and behavioral data can complement one another. Further, it shows how processing differences underlie risky-choice framing effects.

FRAMING EFFECTS IN SPECIAL POPULATIONS

Framing effects, or, more generally, the differential reaction to potential gains and losses of the same magnitude, differ between individuals and groups. In this section we briefly describe how group differences in framing effects shed light on fundamental differences in decision processes for special groups such as those with certain neurological disorders that affect the emotional system. We focus specifically on autism and schizophrenia.

As a starting point, DeMartino et al. (2006) found that when participants demonstrated framing effects, the amygdala was especially active, suggesting a key role for an emotional system in mediating decision biases. Moreover, across individuals, greater orbital and medial prefrontal cortex activity predicted a reduced susceptibility to the framing effect.

To follow up this line of reasoning, DeMartino et al. (2008) investigated persons with autism spectrum disorder (ASD), a disorder associated with abnormal amygdala neuronal density, using a financial task in which the monetary prospects were presented as either loss or gain. They reported both behavioral evidence that persons with ASD show a reduced susceptibility to the framing effect and psychophysiological evidence that they fail to incorporate emotional context into the decision-making process.

Participants in the study were 14 adults clinically diagnosed with autism who were approximately matched on age (mean = 35) and IQ (mean = 112) with 15 controls. Their task on each trial involved deciding whether or not to gamble with a sum of money. For example, in the gain frame they would be given a fixed amount of money and be presented with two options: Option A was to keep 40 percent;

Option B was to gamble, with a 40 percent chance of keeping the full amount and a 60 percent chance of losing everything. At other times, the participants would be presented with the loss frame, the only difference being that Option A was phrased in terms of losing money. Here, Option A was to lose 60 percent of their initial amount; Option B was the same as above.

Despite the fact that Option A was essentially the same in both gain and loss frames, the researchers found that the "control" participants—those without ASD—were more likely to gamble if the first option was to "lose" rather than "keep" money. For participants with ASD, this effect was much smaller, suggesting that this latter group was less susceptible to the framing effect—in other words, they were less likely to be guided by their emotions into making inconsistent or irrational choices. While attention to detail and a reduced influence of emotion during decision making was beneficial in this case, the researchers point out that it may be a handicap in daily life where emotional involvement is beneficial. Nevertheless, this simple laboratory framing manipulation was useful for understanding the behavioral consequences of a fundamental neurological process.

Another study used a simple gambling task involving reactions to gains and losses to support the claim of reduced emotional influence in autism. Asperger's disorder (ASP), like other ASDs, is associated with altered responsiveness to social/emotional stimuli. In a study investigating learning and responsiveness to nonsocial, but motivational, stimuli in ASP, Johnson et al. (2006) used the IGT introduced earlier in this chapter. They examined choice behavior and galvanic skin conductance responses (SCRs) during the IGT in 15 adolescents and young adults with ASP and 14 comparison participants. They used this task to examine aspects of learning, attention to wins and losses, and response style. The ASP group showed a distinct pattern of selection characterized by frequent shifts between the four IGT decks, whereas comparison participants developed clear preferences for the "good" decks. SCR results showed some evidence of reduced responsiveness in the ASP group during the IGT. In a sense, one could say that the ASP participants, unlike the controls, were not able to form an "emotional" attachment to one deck or another. According to the researchers' cognitive model, the ASP group's selections, in contrast to the comparison group's, showed less reliance on motivational cues provided by past experiences. These results thus support those of DeMartino and colleagues.

As illustrated in the studies with autism, there is special promise for using tasks that get at the emotional as well as cognitive aspects of decision making as applied to groups with known problems in the processing and expression of emotions. Schizophrenia patients show widespread impairments in several cognitive domains and emotion-based decision making. These findings are consistent with the evidence that schizophrenia reflects a dorsolateral and orbitofrontal/ventromedial prefrontal cortex dysfunction. Not surprisingly then, the IGT has been administered to patients with schizophrenia in a number of studies. Sevy et al. (2007) reviewed these studies and performed a new study with the objectives of detecting a reliable pattern of disadvantageous decision making in schizophrenics compared to controls, and detecting possible deleterious effects of cannabis use within this population.

A comprehensive battery of cognitive tests and the IGT were administered to three groups of participants:

1. 13 with DSM-IV diagnosis of schizophrenia and no concurrent substance-use disorders (mean age: 28; 54 percent males);
2. 14 with schizophrenia and concurrent cannabis-use disorders (mean age: 29; 71 percent males);
3. 20 healthy participants (mean age: 33; 60 percent males).

Compared to the healthy group, both schizophrenia groups were cognitively more impaired and did worse on IGT performance. There were no differences between patients who did and did not use cannabis on most of the cognitive tests and IGT performance. Based on the new study and their review of prior studies using the IGT, the authors concluded that schizophrenia is indeed accompanied by deficits in emotion-based decision making but that concurrent cannabis use has no compounding effect.

For the closing sections of this chapter we turn to a basic biological process—aging—and its relation to decision making in framing and other neuroeconomic tasks.

DECISION MAKING ACROSS THE LIFESPAN

Studies of the lifespan trajectory of brain functions provide insight into age-related differences in decision making, which, in turn, are associated with changes in the brain. Much of this research has focused on the early pre-adulthood ages where incomplete maturation of some brain regions leads to decision-making deficits. For example, functional maturation of the prefrontal cortex has been shown to be protracted compared to the development of subcortical reward-processing structures, and this limits the processing of fear and reward signals (Casey, Giedd, & Thomas, 2000; Crone & van der Molen, 2004; Galvan et al., 2006; Hare & Casey, 2005). The result is often inappropriate risk taking at the younger ages. These findings suggest a neurobiological basis for age-related differences in decision making.

At the other end of the spectrum, there is growing support for the "frontal lobe hypothesis" of aging (Brown & Park, 2003; Pardo et al., 2007; Resnick et al., 2003; West, 1996, 2000) whereby age-related structural declines in the prefrontal cortex, particularly the orbitofrontal and lateral prefrontal cortices, lead to declines in executive functioning tasks in the elderly that are mediated by frontal lobe functioning (West et al., 2002). However, results are not always clear-cut as to when older adults do and do not exhibit decision deficits.

Deakin et al. (2004), Denburg et al. (2005), and Weller, Levin, and Denburg (2011) all found that older adults were less sensitive to risk level than younger adults, but other researchers found that older adults performed as well as younger adults on risky decision-making tasks (Kovalchik et al., 2005; Wood et al., 2005). Bruine de Bruin, Parker, and Fischhoff (2012) explain some of these mixed results by showing that some decision-making skills decline with age while others remain unchanged or improve. One theme of the current chapter is that the net effect of this age-related mixture of skill levels depends on task demands.

In studying age-related differences in decision making, Weller et al. (2011) used the "cups" task described earlier (Levin & Hart, 2003), designed to mimic the risky-choice framing task but with actual gains and losses. Analogous to the separate gain- and loss-framed versions of the risky-choice framing task, the cups task includes separate trials involving risky gains and risky losses.

These design features allow for comparisons across age groups for overall risk taking to achieve gains or avoid losses, and the tendency to make risk-advantageous or -disadvantageous choices for risky gains and losses. Overall level of risk taking to achieve gains was shown to decrease steadily across the lifespan while risk seeking to avoid a loss was remarkably constant across age levels, a result attributed to the pervasiveness of "loss aversion" (Weller et al., 2011). All but the youngest group of five- to seven-year-olds showed the classic risky-choice framing effect of more risk taking to avoid a loss than to achieve a gain of the same magnitude (consistent with Reyna & Ellis, 1994). More interestingly, age-related differences were found in the tendency to make risk-advantageous/disadvantageous choices. The difference in number of risk-advantageous and risk-disadvantageous choices increased from childhood through young and middle adulthood but decreased for those aged 65 years and older. This demonstrates that the sensitivity to risk-relevant information decreases in older adults in a manner consistent with the frontal lobe hypothesis.

FRAMING AND TASK-RELATED DIFFERENCES IN OLDER DECISION MAKERS

Previous research demonstrated how emotional processes play a key role in the IGT (Bechara et al., 1997), how some seniors perform worse on the IGT than others (Denburg et al., 2005), and how emotion-suppression instructions affect attribute and risk framing differently (Hedgcock et al., 2012). Hypotheses in the following study were informed by these findings. Specifically, the authors predicted that performance on the IGT would predict brain activity while participants answered risk and attribute framing questions.

Hedgcock et al. (2012) had senior citizens answer risk and attribute framing questions while their brain activity was recorded using fMRI. Half of the participants had previously performed advantageously on the IGT while the other half had performed disadvantageously. Differences in brain activity while participants performed the positively versus negatively valenced versions of the task were then correlated with IGT score for both the risky-choice and attribute framing tasks.

When participants were answering attribute framing questions, their IGT scores were correlated with activity in cortical midline structures such as the ventromedial prefrontal cortex, the dorsomedial prefrontal cortex, and the anterior cingulate cortex. These areas of the brain have previously been shown to decline with age (Pardo et al., 2007; West, 1996). Further, some of these areas, such as the ventromedial prefrontal cortex, have been implicated in processing emotional stimuli (Damasio, 1994). In contrast, when participants were answering risky-choice framing questions, their IGT scores were correlated with activity only in the parietal cortex. This provides additional evidence in support of the theory that risky-choice and attribute framing are caused by different (though possibly overlapping) processes and that these differences may be related to emotional processing. Further, these results, combined with previously described findings, show how impaired emotional processing can lead to disadvantageous decisions (e.g., poor performance on the IGT), advantageous decisions (e.g., more consistent preferences in attribute framing), or relatively unchanged decisions (e.g., unchanged preferences in risk framing).

SUMMARY, CONCLUSIONS, AND FUTURE RESEARCH

In this chapter we considered the interplay of neural/biological and behavioral science in the study of decision making. We believe much can be learned from studies that link biological underpinnings with macro-level decision making. In particular, we have focused on framing effects as a tool to help us understand decision processes for several reasons:

1. Framing effects represent a well-known behavioral decision bias with important real-world consequences.
2. Framing effects have a long history of basic research in behavioral decision making and a shorter, but growing, history of research in decision neuroscience and neuroeconomics.
3. Framing effects are not an isolated phenomenon but are tied to broader decision-making principles such as loss aversion or risk aversion.
4. The simplicity of tasks that demonstrate framing effects allows for use with populations across the lifespan and involving persons with known decision impairments.
5. Framing effects can easily be studied using technologically current methods such as brain scanning or eye-tracking as well as in the traditional laboratory or online setting.

New features illustrated in the applications presented here include the identification of distinct types of framing effects combined with an examination of the intersection of cognitive processing and emotional involvement. This then allows these different paradigms to be used to address issues of broad scope, such as age-related changes in the balance of skills that lead to impaired decision making on some tasks but not on others. Another important feature illustrated here is that with proper experimental design features, framing effects can be studied not just in the aggregate but at the level of the individual decision maker. This allowed us, for example, to show which areas of the brain are differentially activated as a function of the size of the framing effect as well as differences across decision makers.

The evidence provided about the concordance of biological and behavioral factors associated with the circadian rhythm cycle came from the use of risky-choice and attribute framing tasks administered at different points in the cycle. Susceptibility to risky-choice framing effects was significantly greater during circadian off-times than during circadian on-times, and this was related to the actions of an area deep in the brain, the SCN, which governs glucose level and metabolic activity, a physiological correlate of effort. Equally insightful was the revelation that circadian cycle had no impact on attribute framing, a finding supporting our hypothesis of different processes for attribute and risky-choice framing. This demonstrates very nicely how research that integrates biological and behavioral components can contribute to both fields.

Related findings were that eye-fixation patterns were predictive of the presence versus absence of risky-choice framing effects and that right-hemispheric versus left-hemispheric processing was also related to risky-choice framing effects, each result being indicative of variations in cognitive processing. The important point for present purposes is that these demonstrations of the relation between neurological brain functions and macro-behavior using a framing paradigm serve as a tool for understanding such relations. For example, McEloy et al. (2013) were able to use their physiological measurement of gaze duration to assess the behavioral assumptions of FTT.

In a similar vein, the emotion-suppression study revealed that the two types of framing manipulations—attribute framing and risky-choice framing—do in fact call into play fundamentally different forms of decision making. Attribute framing appears to involve a purer form of emotionally driven choice, similar to System 1 processing, whereas risky-choice framing involves more deliberative analysis, similar to System 2 processing. This was confirmed in an fMRI study in which attribute framing was more closely linked to activation of brain areas associated with the emotional system than was risky-choice framing. The fMRI study with older adults not only affirmed the relation between types of framing and differential activation of brain systems but showed that those systems exhibiting age-related declines can sometimes lead to impaired performance such as on the IGT where learning from past errors is key but can sometimes lead to improved performance such as resistance to the emotional lure of attribute framing.

In this chapter we illustrate how the combination of neural/biological and decision science research can advance both fields. The illustrations here provide only a thin slice of the fascinating phenomena revealed in a systematic study of the neuroscience of human judgment and decision making. One suggestion we have for future researchers is to not consider "framing effects," "endowment effects," "sunk cost effects," and the like as contextually universal concepts but to specify how they can be operationalized in ways that can account for different results in different studies. Once viewed this way, neuro/biological tools can be useful in better explaining observed differences across individual or environmental conditions.

Finally, it is our hope that the key features illustrated here will serve future researchers investigating other phenomena that separate normatively rational behavior from the reality of the human experience. These features include the use of brain imaging, eye-tracking, and other biological measures to complement traditional behavioral measures, including both variables manipulated in the laboratory and individual difference factors. Ultimately, we hope that the combination of neuro/biological and decision-making science can help account for "why you and I make different decisions," particularly as these individual differences interact with task and real-world environmental conditions. The ultimate test of our theories may come with the better understanding, and potential improvement, in how individuals with distinctive characteristics make life-enhancing decisions.

REFERENCES

Bauer, A. S., Timpe, J. C., Edmonds, E. C., Bechara, A., Tranel, D., & Denburg, N. L. (2013). Myopia for the future or hyposensitivity to reward? Age-related changes in decision making on the Iowa Gambling Task. *Emotion, 13(1)*, 19–24.

Bechara, A. (2007). *Iowa Gambling Task (IGT) professional manual.* Lutz: Psychological Assessment Resources.

Bechara, A., Damasio, A. R., Damasio, H., & Anderson, S. W. (1994). Insensitivity to future consequences following damage to human prefrontal cortex. *Cognition, 50(1)*, 7–15.

Bechara, A., Damasio, H., Tranel, D., & Damasio, A. R. (1997). Deciding advantageously before knowing the advantageous strategy. *Science, 275(5304)*, 1293–1295.

Bernoulli, D. (1954). Exposition of a new theory on the measurement of risk. *Econometrica, 22*, 23–36. First published 1738.

Bodenhausen, G. Y. (1990). Stereotypes as judgmental heuristics: Evidence of circadian variations in discrimination. *Psychological Science, 1(5)*, 319–322.

Braun, K. A., Gaeth, G. J., & Levin, I. P. (1997). Framing effects with differential impact: The role of attribute salience. In M. Brucks & D. J. Mac Innis (Eds.), *Advances in Consumer Research, XXIV* (pp. 405–411). New York, NY: Association for Consumer Research.

Brown, S. C., & Park, D. C. (2003). Theoretical models of cognitive aging and implications for translational research. *The Gerontologist, 43(1)*, 57–67.

Bruine de Bruin, W., Parker, A. M., & Fischhoff, B. (2007). Individual differences in adult decision-making competence. *Journal of Personality and Social Psychology, 92(5)*, 938–956.

—— (2012). Explaining adult age differences in decision-making competence. *Journal of Behavioral Decision Making, 25(4)*, 352–360.

Casey, B. J., Giedd, J. N., & Thomas, K. M. (2000). Structural and functional brain development and its relation to cognitive development. *Biological Psychology, 54(1)*, 241–257.

Christman, S. D., Jasper, J. D., Sontam, V., & Cooil, B. (2007). Individual differences in risk perception versus risk taking: Handedness and interhemispheric interaction. *Brain and Cognition, 63(1)*, 51–58.

Crone, E. A., & van der Molen, M. W. (2004). Developmental changes in real life decision making: Performance on a gambling task previously shown to depend on the ventromedial prefrontal cortex. *Developmental Neuropsychology, 25(3)*, 251–279.

Damasio, A. R. (1994). *Descartes' error: Emotion, reason, and the human brain.* New York, NY: Putnam.

Deakin, J., Aitken, M., Robbins, T., & Shahakian, B. J. (2004). Risk taking during decision-making in normal volunteers changes with age. *Journal of International Neuropsychological Society, 10(4)*, 590–598.

De Martino, B., Kumaran, D., Seymour, B., & Dolan, R. J. (2006). Frames, biases, and rational decision-making in the human brain. *Science, 313(5787)*, 684–687.

De Martino, B., Harrison, N. A., Knafo, S., Bird, G., & Dolan, R. J. (2008). Explaining enhanced logical consistency during decision making in autism. *Journal of Neuroscience, 28(42)*, 10746–10750.

Denburg, N. L., Tranel, D., & Bechara, A. (2005). The ability to decide advantageously declines in some normal older persons. *Neuropsychologia, 43(7)*, 1099–1106.

Dickinson, D. L., & McElroy, T. (2010). Paper airplane producers: Morning types vs. evening types. *Annals of Improbable Research, 16(1)*, 10–12.

—— (2012). Circadian effects on strategic reasoning. *Experimental Economics, 15(3)*, 444–459.

Edwards, W. (1954). The theory of decision making. *Psychological Bulletin, 51(4),* 380–417.

Epstein, S., Lipson, A., Holstein, C., & Huh, E. (1992). Irrational reactions to negative outcomes: Evidence for two conceptual systems. *Journal of Personality and Social Psychology, 62(2),* 328–339.

Figner, B., Mackinlay, R. J., Wilkening, F., & Weber, E. U. (2009). Affective and deliberative processes in risky choice: Age differences in risk taking in the Columbia Card Task. *Journal of Experimental Psychology: Learning, Memory, and Cognition, 35(3),* 709–730.

Figner, B., & Weber, E. U. (2011). Who takes risks when and why? Determinants of risk taking. *Current Directions in Psychological Science, 20(4),* 211–216.

Galvan, A., Hare, T. A., Parra, C. E., Penn, J., Voss, H., Glover, G., & Casey, B. J. (2006). Earlier development of the accumbens relative to orbitofrontal cortex might underlie risk taking behavior in adolescents. *Journal of Neuroscience, 26(25),* 6885–6892.

Gamliel, E., & Peer, E. (2006). Positive versus negative framing affects justice judgments. *Social Justice Research, 19(3),* 307–322.

—— (2010). Attribute framing affects the perceived fairness of allocation principles. *Judgment and Decision Making, 5(1),* 11–20.

Gilbert, D. T. (1991). How mental systems believe. *American Psychologist, 46(2),* 107–119.

Gross, J. J., & Levenson, R. W. (1993). Emotion suppression: Physiology, self-report, and expressive behavior. *Journal of Personality and Social Psychology, 64(6),* 970–986.

Hare, T. A., & Casey, B. J. (2005). The neurobiology and development of cognitive and affective control. *Cognition, Brain, & Behavior, 3(3),* 273–286.

Hasher, L., & Zacks, R. T. (1988). Working memory, comprehension, and aging: A review and a new view. *The Psychology of Learning and Motivation, 22,* 193–225.

Hedgcock, W., Denburg, N., Levin, I. P., & Halfmann, K. (2012). Why older adults are impaired on some decision making tasks but not on others: Behavioral and neuroimaging evidence. Paper presented at the Annual Meeting of the Society for Judgment and Decision Making, Minneapolis, MN.

Huettel, S. (2010). Ten challenges for decision neuroscience. *Frontiers in Neuroscience, 4(171),* 1–7.

Huettel, S. A., Stowe, C. J., Gordon, E. M., Warner, B. T., & Platt, M. L. (2006). Neural signatures of economic preferences for risk and ambiguity. *Neuron, 49(5),* 765–775.

Jasper, J. D., Barry, K., & Christman, S. D. (2008). Individual differences in counterfactual production. *Personality and Individual Differences, 45(6),* 488–492.

Jasper, J. D., & Christman, S. (2005). A neuropsychological dimension for anchoring effects. *Journal of Behavioral Decision Making, 18(5),* 343–369.

Jasper, J. D., Fournier, C., & Christman, S. D. (2013). Handedness differences in information framing. *Brain and Cognition, 84(1),* 85–89.

Jasper, J. D., Goel, R., Einarson, A., Gallo, M., & Koren, G. (2001). Effects of framing on teratogenic risk perception in pregnant women. *Lancet, 358(9289),* 1237–1238.

Johnson, S. A., Yechiam, E., Murphy, R. R., Queller, S., & Stout, J. C. (2006). Motivational processes and autonomic responsivity in Asperger's disorder: Evidence from the Iowa Gambling Task, *Journal of International Neuropsychology Society, 12(5),* 668–676.

Kahneman, D. (2003). Perspective on judgment and choice: Mapping bounded rationality. *American Psychologist, 58(9),* 697–720.

—— (2011). *Thinking, fast and slow.* New York, NY: Farrer, Straus & Giroux.

Kahneman, D., & Frederick, S. (2002). Representativeness revisited: Attribute substitution in intuitive judgment. In T. Gilovich, D. Griffin, & D. Kahneman (Eds.), *Heuristics and biases: The psychology of intuitive judgment* (pp. 49–81). New York, NY: Cambridge University Press.

Kahneman, D., & Tversky, A. (1979). Prospect theory: Analysis of decision under risk. *Econometrica, 47(2)*, 263–291.

Kovalchik, S., Camerer, C. F., Grether, D. M., Plott, C. R., & Allman, J. M. (2005). Aging and decision making: A comparison between neurologically healthy elderly and young individuals. *Journal of Economic Behavior and Organization, 58(1)*, 79–94.

Kühberger, A. (1998). The influence of framing on risky decisions: A meta-analysis. *Organizational Behavior and Human Decision Processes, 75(1)*, 23–55.

Kühberger, A., & Tanner, C. (2010). Risky choice framing: Task versions and a comparison of prospect theory and fuzzy-trace theory. *Journal of Behavioral Decision Making, 23(3)*, 314–329.

Kuhnen, C. M., & Knutson, B. (2005). The neural basis of financial risk taking. *Neuron, 47(5)*, 763–770.

La Fleur, S. E. (2003). Daily rhythms in glucose metabolism: Suprachiasmatic nucleus output to peripheral tissue. *Journal of Neuroendocrinology, 15(3)*, 315–322.

Lauriola, M., & Levin, I. P. (2001). Personality traits and risky decision making in a controlled experimental task: An exploratory study. *Personality and Individual Differences, 31(2)*, 215–226.

Lauriola, M., Panno, A., Levin, I. P., & Lejuez, C. W. (2014). Individual differences in risky decision making: A meta-analysis of sensation seeking and impulsivity with the balloon analogue risk task. *Journal of Behavioral Decision Making, 27(10)*, 20–36.

LeDoux, J. E. (2000). Emotion circuits in the brain. *Annual Review of Neuroscience, 2*, 155–184.

Lejuez, C. W., Aklin, W. M., Jones, H. A., Richards, J. B., Strong, D. R., Kahler, C. W., et al. (2003a). The Balloon Analogue Risk Task (BART) differentiates smokers and nonsmokers. *Experimental and Clinical Psychopharmacology, 11(1)*, 26–33.

Lejuez, C. W., Aklin, W. M., Zvolensky, M. J., & Pedulla, C. M. (2003b). Evaluation of the Balloon Analogue Risk Task (BART) as a predictor of adolescent real-world risk-taking behaviours. *Journal of Adolescence, 26(4)*, 475–479.

Lejuez, C. W., Read, J. P., Kahler, C. W., Richards, J. B., Ramsey, S. E., Stuart, G. L., et al. (2002). Evaluation of a behavioral measure of risk-taking: The Balloon Analogue Risk Task (BART). *Journal of Experimental Psychology: Applied, 8(2)*, 75–84.

Levin, I. P. (1987). Associative effects of information framing. *Bulletin of the Psychonomic Society, 25(2)*, 85–86.

—— (1999). Why do you and I make difference decisions? Tracking individual differences in decision making. Presidential Address for Society for Judgment and Decision Making, Los Angeles, CA.

Levin, I. P., & Gaeth, G. J. (1988). How consumers are affected by the framing of attribute information before and after consuming the product. *Journal of Consumer Research, 15(3)*, 374–378.

Levin, I. P., Gaeth, G. J., Schreiber, J., & Lauriola, M. (2002). A new look at framing effects: Distribution of effect sizes, individual differences, and independence of types of effects. *Organizational Behavior and Human Decision Processes, 88(1)*, 411–429.

Levin, I. P., Gui, X., Weller, J. A., Reimann, M., Lauriola, M., & Bechara, A. (2012). A neuropsychological approach to understanding risk-taking for potential gains and losses. *Frontiers in Neuroscience, 6(15)*, 1–11.

Levin, I. P., & Hart, S. S. (2003). Risk preferences in young children: Early evidence of individual differences in reaction to potential gains and losses. *Journal of Behavioral Decision Making, 16(5)*, 397–413.

Levin, I. P., Schneider, S. L., & Gaeth, G. J. (1998). All frames are not created equal: A typology and critical analysis of framing effects. *Organizational Behavior and Human Decision Processes, 76(2)*, 149–188.

Mahoney, K. T., Buboltz, W., Levin, I. P., Doverspike, D., & Svyantek, D. J. (2011). Individual differences in a within-subjects risky-choice framing study. *Personality and Individual Differences, 51(3)*, 248–257.

Manly, T., Lewis, G. H., Robertson, I. H., Watson, P. C., & Datta, A. K. (2002). Coffee in the cornflakes: Time of day as a modulator of executive response control. *Neuropsychologia, 40(1)*, 1–6.

Masicampo, E. J., & Baumeister, R. F. (2008). Toward a physiology of dual-process reasoning and judgment: Lemonade, willpower, and expensive rule-based analysis. *Psychological Science, 19(3)*, 255–260.

McElroy, T., & Dickinson, D. L. (2010). Thoughtful days and valenced nights: How much will you think about the problem? *Judgment and Decision Making, 5(7)*, 516–523.

McElroy, T., Dickinson, C., Corbin, J., & Beck, H. (2013). Tracking risky decisions: Comparing fuzzy-trace theory and prospect theory through eye-tracking. Manuscript submitted for publication.

McElroy, T., & Seta, J. (2003). Framing effect: An analytic-holistic perspective. *Journal of Experimental Social Psychology, 39(6)*, 610–617.

——(2004). On the other hand am I rational? Hemispheric activation and the framing effect. *Brain and Cognition, 55(3)*, 572–580.

McMahon, A. J., & Scheel, M. H. (2010). Glucose promostes controlled processing: Matching, maximizing, and root beer. *Judgment and Decision Making, 5(6)*, 450–457.

McNeil, B., Pauker, S. G., Sox, H. C., & Tversky, A. (1982). On the elicitation of preferences for alternative therapies. *New England Journal of Medicine, 306(21)*, 1259–1262.

Northoff, G., & Bermpohl, F. (2004). Cortical midline structures and the self. *Trends in Cognitive Science, 8(3)*, 102–107.

Ornstein, R. (1972). *The psychology of consciousness.* New York, NY: Harcourt Brace Jovanovich.

Pardo, J. V., Lee, J. T., Sheikh, S. A., et al. (2007). Where the brain grows old: Decline in anterior cingulate and medial prefrontal function with normal aging. *Neuroimage, 35(3)*, 1231–1237.

Parker, A. M., & Fischhoff, B. (2005). Decision-making competence: External validation through an individual-differences approach. *Journal of Behavioral Decision Making, 18(1)*, 1–27.

Payne, J. W., Sagara, N., Shu, S. B., Appelt, K. C., & Johnson, E. J. (2012). Life expectancy as a constructed belief: Evidence of a live-to or die-by framing effect. Columbia Business School Research Paper No. 12–10.

Peters, E., & Levin, I. P. (2008). Dissecting the risky-choice framing effect: Numeracy as an individual difference factor in weighting risky and riskless options. *Judgment and Decision Making, 3(6)*, 435–448.

Phelps, E. A. (2006). Emotion and cognition: Insights form studies of the human amygdala. *Annual Review of Psychology, 57*, 27–53.

Resnick, S. M., Pham, D. L., Kraut, M. A., Zonderman, A. B., & Davatzikos, C. (2003). Longitudinal magnetic resonance imaging studies of older adults: A shrinking brain. *Journal of Neuroscience, 23(8)*, 3295–3301.

Reyna, V. F. (2012). A new intuitionism: Meaning, memory, and development in fuzzy-trace theory. *Judgment and Decision Making, 7(3)*, 332–359.

Reyna, V. F., & Brainerd, C. J. (1991). Fuzzy-trace theory and framing effects in choice: Gist extraction, truncation, and conversion. *Journal of Behavioral Decision Making, 4(4)*, 249–262.

——(2011). Dual processes in decision making and developmental neuroscience: A fuzzy-trace model. *Developmental Review, 31(2)*, 180–206.

Reyna, V. F., & Ellis, S. C. (1994). Fuzzy-trace theory and framing effects in children's risky decision-making. *Psychological Science, 5(5),* 275–279.

Reyna, V. F., Estrada, S. M., Demarinis, J. A., Myers, R. M., Stanisz, J. M., & Mills, B. A. (2011). Neurobiological and memory models of risky decision making in adolescents versus young adults. *Journal of Experimental Psychology: Learning, Memory, and Cognition, 37(5),* 1125–1142.

Sanfey, A. G., Rilling, J. K., Aronson, J. A., Nystrom, L. E., & Cohen, J. D. (2003). The neural basis of economic decision-making in the Ultimatum Game. *Science, 300(5626),* 1755–1758.

Schmidt, C., Collette, F., Cajochen, C., & Peigneux, P. (2007) A time to think: Circadian rhythms in human cognition. *Cognitive Neuropsychology, 24(7),* 755–789.

Schneider, W., & Shiffrin, R. M. (1977). Controlled and automatic human information processing: 1. Detection, search, and attention. *Psychological Review, 84(1),* 1–66.

Sevy, S., Visweswaraial, H., Abdelmessih, S., Lukin, M., Yechiam, E., & Bechara, A. (2007). Iowa Gambling Task in schizophrenia: A review and new data in patients with schizophrenia and co-occurring cannabis use disorders. *Schizophrenia Research, 92(1),* 74–84.

Simon, A. F., Fagley, N. S., & Halleran, J. G. (2004). Decision framing: Moderating effects of individual differences and cognitive processing. *Journal of Behavioral Decision Making, 17(2),* 77–93.

Sloman, S. A. (1996). The empirical case for two systems of reasoning. *Psychological Bulletin, 119(1),* 3–22.

Smith, S. M., & Levin, I. P. (1996). Need for cognition and choice framing effects. *Journal of Behavioral Decision Making, 9(4),* 283–290.

Stanovich, K. E. (1999). *Who is rational? Studies of individual differences in reasoning.* Mahwah, NJ: Erlbaum.

Stanovich, K. E., & West, R. F. (1998a). Cognitive ability and variation in selection task performance. *Thinking and Reasoning, 4(3),* 193–230.

——(1998b). Individual differences in rational thought. *Journal of Experimental Psychology: General, 127(2),* 161–188.

——(2000). Individual differences in reasoning: Implications for the rationality debate? *The Behavioral and Brain Sciences, 23(5),* 645–726.

Tom, S. M., Fox, C. R., Trepel, C., & Poldrack, R. A. (2007). The neural basis of loss aversion in decision-making under risk. *Science, 315(5811),* 515–518.

Trepel, C., Fox, C. R., & Poldrak, R. A. (2005). Prospect theory on the brain? Toward a cognitive neuroscience of decisions under risk. *Brain Research of the Cognitive Brain, 23(1),* 34–50.

Tversky, A., & Kahneman, D. (1981). The framing of decisions and the psychology of choice. *Science, 211(4481),* 453–458.

——(1992). Advances in prospect theory: Cumulative representation of uncertainty. *Journal of Risk and Uncertainty, 5(4),* 297–323.

Wang, X. T., & Dvorak, R. D. (2010). Sweet future: Fluctuating blood glucose levels affect future discounting. *Psychological Science, 21(2),* 183–188.

Weller, J. A., Levin, I. P., & Denburg, N. L. (2011). Trajectory of risky decision making for potential gains and losses from ages 5 to 85. *Journal of Behavioral Decision Making, 9(4),* 331–344.

Weller, J. A., Levin, I. P., Rose, J. P., & Bossard, E. (2012). Assessment of decision-making competence in preadolescence. *Journal of Behavioral Decision Making, 25(4),* 414–426.

Weller, J. A., Levin, I. P., Shiv, B., & Bechara, A. (2007). Neural correlates of adaptive decision making in risky gains and losses. *Psychological Science, 18(11),* 958–964.

—— (2009). The effects of insula damage on decision-making for risky gains and losses. *Social Neuroscience, 4(4)*, 347–358.

West, R. L. (1996). An application of prefrontal cortex function theory to cognitive aging. *Psychological Bulletin, 120(2)*, 272–292.

—— (2000). In defense of the frontal lobe hypothesis of cognitive aging. *Journal of the International Neuropsychological Society, 6(6)*, 727–729.

West, R., Murphy, K. J., Armillo, M. L., Craik, F. I. M., & Stuss, D. (2002). Lapses of intention and performance variability reveal age-related increases in fluctuations of executive control. *Brain and Cognition, 49(3)*, 402–419.

White, T. L., Lejuez, C. W., & de Wit, H. (2007). Personality and gender differences in effects of d-amphetamine on risk-taking. *Experimental and Clinical Psychopharmacology, 15(6)*, 599–609.

Wood, S., Busemeyer, J., Kolings, A., Cox, C. R., & Davis, H. (2005). Older adults as adaptive decision makers: Evidence from the Iowa gambling task. *Psychology and Aging, 20(2)*, 220–225.

8

"Hot" Cognition and Dual Systems

Introduction, Criticisms, and Ways Forward

THOMAS E. GLADWIN AND BERND FIGNER

Models distinguishing two types of processes or systems—typically one more automatic and/or affective-motivational, one more controlled and/or calculating-deliberative—are widespread in psychological science. However, such dual-process (or dual-system) models suffer from various problems and have been substantially criticized recently. In this chapter, we discuss these types of models, attempt to clarify terminology, discuss recent critiques at both empirical and theoretical levels, and suggest a more mechanistic explanation grounded in physiology and reinforcement learning of what makes "hot" processes hot. We discuss success stories and challenges related to these types of models in two illustrative fields, addiction and adolescent risk taking. Finally, we outline the basic ideas behind our R3 model—a reprocessing model grounded in reinforcement learning that conceptualizes levels of reflectivity as emergent states of one single system, rather than a separate process or system—as a possible way forward to address and overcome problems of dual-process models.

*M*odels distinguishing two types of different processes or "systems" are prominent and widespread in many fields of psychological science. However, they recently have been substantially criticized and challenged. In this chapter, we focus on so-called dual-process or dual-system models that differentiate between more automatic (often "hot" emotional-affective) versus more controlled (often "cold" cognitive-deliberative) processes. We start out with an attempt to describe and clarify different terminologies, including a clarification of the temperature metaphor of "hotness" versus "coldness." We then propose to ground and decompose the notion of "hotness" in emotion-relevant basic biological processes of the autonomic nervous system and incentive salience. Extending the scope, we then focus on two types of dual-process or dual-system models, discussing both their strengths as well as shortcomings. Finally, we suggest a diagnosis of the current state of affairs and propose possibly more fruitful directions for future research and theory-forming. As part of this, we briefly describe our R3 model, a novel model of reflectivity that here serves as a proof-of-principle thought-experiment to address several shortcomings of existing dual-process and dual-system models.

THE TEMPERATURE METAPHOR

The temperature metaphors of "hot" versus "cold" or "cool" phenomena are used widely in different forms in psychological science, typically referring to a differential involvement of processes related to affect and/or motivation on the one hand versus more controlled and/or cognitive processes on the other hand. For example, the terms "hot" versus "cold" cognition refer to cognitive processes that are relatively affect-charged versus affect-free, respectively (Abelson, 1963). However, the term "hot cognition" has been used to refer to both affective processes themselves (such as emotions or feelings) as well as phenomena such as emotional appraisal, which arguably could be considered a cognitive process (albeit one crucially relevant for affect and emotion). Thus, the mapping between hot vs. cold cognition on the one hand and affect vs. cognition on the other hand is somewhat ambiguous. Similarly to Abelson, an influential paper by Metcalfe and Mischel (1999) used the temperature metaphor to differentiate between a hot versus a cool *system*. The former refers to a system encompassing affective and motivational processes and the latter refers to a system encompassing more cognitive-deliberative processes. Grounded in a developmental perspective, Metcalfe and Mischel characterize the hot system as being under stimulus control, emotional, fast, reflexive, relatively simple, and developing relatively early during human ontogeny. In contrast, the cool system is characterized by self-control, encompasses cognitive processes, and is comparatively slow, reflective, complex, and develops relatively late during ontogeny. These and similar characteristics have been widely used to describe the two types of processes or systems often distinguished in the literature (discussed later in this chapter).

Another, somewhat different use of referring to hot vs. cold processes—which appears to be particularly prominent in research on ADHD and in developmental psychology—is the distinction between hot versus cool (or cold) *executive function* (EF) (Prencipe et al., 2011; Van den Wildenberg & Crone, 2005): The term "cold EF" is used to describe executive functions conceptualized as lacking an affective component, such as working memory and inhibition; accordingly, tasks such as backwards digit span or color word stroop are typically used to assess cold EF. The main neural substrate serving cold EF is assumed to be the dorsolateral prefrontal cortex (dlPFC). In contrast, the term "hot EF" is typically used to describe EF that involves an affective or motivational component. Typical tasks used in the literature to assess hot EF are often decision-making tasks, such as intertemporal choice tasks (also referred to as delay discounting tasks) or risky decision-making tasks, in particular the Iowa gambling task (Bechara, Damasio, Damasio, & Anderson, 1994) and variants thereof such as the hungry donkey task

(Geurts, van der Oord, & Crone, 2006; Hongwanishkul, Happaney, Lee, & Zelazo, 2005). The main neural substrates serving hot EF are assumed to be more ventral and medial regions of the prefrontal cortex, including the orbitofrontal cortex.

The idea of using performance in decision-making tasks to operationalize hot EF, however, is likely contributing to the existing variations and inconsistencies in terminology: Decision making itself is assumed to typically involve various processes, including cognitive and control processes *and* affective processes. For example the "risks-as-feeling" hypothesis (Loewenstein et al., 2001) posits that, when faced with a risky choice, we not only evaluate the available options via more cognitive and deliberative processes, but (1) also have emotional responses to characteristics of the choice options (such as their "risk," i.e. their outcome variability) and (2) that these emotional responses may have a stronger impact on choice than the more cognitive evaluations. Another role of affective processes in decision making has been termed "common currency" (Cabanac, 1992; Figner & Weber, 2011; Levy & Glimcher, 2012; Peters, Västfjäll, Gärling, & Slovic, 2006): The idea is that emotions serve as the basis to evaluate and choose among attributes, goods, and outcomes that otherwise would be incommensurable. Further complicating matters, processes of self-control to resist "hot" temptations have been shown, via experimental interference with neural processing using noninvasive brain-stimulation techniques, to causally involve the dlPFC (Figner et al., 2010; Knoch et al., 2006), which, in the framework of hot vs. cold EF, would be the main neural substrate for *cold,* not hot, EF. Finally, decision making very reliably involves neural processes in the ventromedial and orbital PFC (Carter, Meyer, & Huettel, 2010), seemingly consistent with the idea of hot EF and its neural substrates. However, in the decision neuroscience and neuroeconomics literatures, the involvement of these regions is typically not described as hot EF but as reflecting the subjective value of the presented choice options, reflecting an evaluation process that likely is at least partly affective in nature, consistent with the "common currency" idea.

At the very least these points show that using decision-making tasks as measures for hot EF can be problematic, as such tasks cannot not be considered "process-pure" measures of the underlying characteristics or processes specified by a given researcher's definition of hot EF. This touches on a more worrisome point: The differential terminology and frameworks have the potential to cause substantial misunderstanding and confusion among scientists. First, about what is being measured and observed; second, about how the results should be interpreted with respect to the involved psychological and neural processes; and, third, about what we can learn from the studies when we try to integrate results and insights across different fields, thus making it even more challenging to build more overarching models that cover a wider range of empirical work.

In the spirit of full disclosure, we should declare that one of the authors of this chapter also contributed to the already complex and confusing use of temperature metaphors, with his co-authors, and he named two versions of his risky decision-making task "hot" and "cold," respectively: namely the hot and cold Columbia card task (Figner, Mackinlay, Wilkening, & Weber, 2009a). The hot version was designed to involve substantially affective-motivational decision processes, while the cold version was designed to involve predominantly cognitive-deliberative processes. Again, both tasks naturally involve affective, deliberative, and self-control processes, however to a differential extent, and this differential involvement has inspired the use of hot and cold in the task name.

To sum up these introductory remarks, while it seems that the use of temperature metaphors is quite popular in psychological science to refer to two different types of processes or systems, these terms are not always used with the same meaning in mind, and the distinctions and implied brain regions do not always neatly line up. This is already sufficient reason to be careful to avoid creating more confusion than enlightenment when using connotations associated with hot and cold to explain psychological phenomena. But a more important goal is that we should start to lay a more solid foundation for these concepts; we suggest a possible way to do this in the next section.

FROM "HEAT" TO AUTONOMIC RESPONSES AND INCENTIVE SALIENCE

The "heat" in temperature metaphors appeals to the subjective experience of arousal and emotion—the memory, experience, and anticipation of pounding hearts, sweaty palms, rapid breathing, and so on. Such basic biological responses are patterns that prepare the body to deal with events related to survival and procreation, that is, to support fitness-enhancing behavior essential in evolution: defensive reactions to threat, or appetitive responses to attractive stimuli. For example, when confronted with threatening stimuli a "freeze" response may occur, with characteristic physiological changes such as decreased heart rate and heart-rate variability, increased skin conductance, and reduced body sway (Bracha, 2004; Dalton, Kalin, Grist, & Davidson, 2005; Jarvik & Russell, 1979; Roelofs, Hagenaars, & Stins, 2010). To some authors, it is introspectively obvious that the representation of such changes in the autonomic nervous system (ANS) is the defining feature of emotion. For instance, William James (1884, p. 451), wrote: "What kind of an emotion of fear would be left, if the feelings neither of quickened heartbeats nor of shallow breathing, neither of trembling lips nor of weakened limbs, neither of goose-flesh nor of visceral stirrings, were present, it is quite impossible to think." Accordingly, in the James–Lange theory of emotion, and its subsequent scientific lineage (Reisenzein, Meyer, & Schutzwohl, 1995), an emotion is the feeling of stimulus-evoked bodily, especially visceral, states. No consensus has been reached on the precise relationship between emotion and ANS activity, although studies, using increasingly sophisticated methods, show a close, and perhaps even emotion-specific, coupling between emotions and patterns of ANS responses over various physiological measures (Collet, Vernet-Maury, Delhomme, & Dittmar, 1997; Kreibig, 2010; Stephens, Christie, & Friedman, 2010). Here we note that from a modern neuroscientific perspective, the "autonomic" nervous system, far from being independent from the central nervous system, can be traced up to the cortex (Kreibig, 2010). A functional unit of brain regions that has been termed the central autonomic network—which includes regions with notably strong links to emotion, such as the periaqueductal gray, insula, central amygdala, anterior cingulate, and ventromedial prefrontal cortex—sends output to efferent regions of the medulla that affect sympathetic and parasympathetic ANS activity (Benarroch, 1993; Cersosimo & Benarroch, 2013; Napadow, Dhond, Conti, & Makris, 2008; Thayer & Lane, 2000).

Note that a necessary role of the central representation of ANS responses in emotion does not necessarily require a sequence of events actually involving the periphery. As with other central neuronal structures and processes, their function and meaning is ultimately derived from the biologically relevant environment. For instance, occipital regions represent visual stimuli, and motor regions represent movements; therefore, processes that involve these regions can be interpreted in terms of vision and movement, respectively, even in the absence of visual stimulation or the actual execution of muscle contraction. In our case, we are considering neurons that represent physiological states related to emotional responses. For instance, James's introspective feelings of emotions presumably most directly involve these central neural representations, rather than physiological responses that are usually connected with them. Thus, claiming that patterns of ANS activation play a core role in defining emotion refers to the consistent involvement of central neurons of which the function or representation is defined by ANS patterns. The function these neurons have, or at least would initially attempt to fulfill, in navigating the world remains the same even when they, for instance in surgical animal research or in disease, are physically disconnected from the ANS: just like visual neurons could be disconnected from the eyes or motor neurons disconnected from the limbs.

From this perspective, a definition of "hot" stimuli must include reference to "hot" physiological states, evoked due to those stimuli having evolutionary significance directly or to being linked to such significance via conditioning. Correspondingly, emotion regulation (a "hot" executive function in the distinction between hot and cold EF) would be understood to a large extent as having physiological regulation as its final outcome. Intuitively, this is what we subjectively perceive as successful regulation: When we "control," usually meaning "down-regulate," our emotions, our breathing slows, our heart rate goes down, our blood pressure drops; and presumably other visceral sensations change, which we may be less able to consciously identify.

The above focuses on the visceral part of emotion, which, although to some authors the defining feature of emotion, is clearly not the whole story of hot cognition. A foundation for understanding the more central, i.e. neural and psychological, components of "hotness" is incentive salience theory (Berridge & Robinson, 1998; LeDoux, 2012; Robinson & Berridge, 1993). This is a prominent theory on the role of dopamine in reward learning, which states that stimuli and cues that are associated with mesolimbic dopamine release acquire *incentive salience*: the ability to attract attention and act as a reward for behavior. While usually phrased in positive terms, incentive salience appears also applicable to behavior and responses based on a negative "wanting," i.e. associations with the tendency to escape or avoid aversive stimuli (although it is unclear whether the neural processes of such appetitive and aversive incentive saliency would overlap). The ability to evoke behavior aimed toward a goal involving the stimulus (termed "wanting"), measured via choice behavior, can be distinguished from the hedonic effects of a stimulus (termed "liking"), measured via observable reflections of pleasure or dislike such as facial expression and taste reactivity. One line of evidence for relating dopamine to incentive salience is that dopamine release is associated with the initiation of approach behavior rather than consumption. Further, animal research shows that depletion of dopamine in the mesolimbic system does not affect either "liking" or the learning of hedonic associations (Berridge & Robinson, 1998). An important aspect of the theory is that it explains flexible goal-directed behavior in a mechanistic fashion: What is learned via the acquisition of incentive salience is not a rigid motoric stimulus–response association, or the hedonic value of a stimulus, but the incentive value of a stimulus. Incentive value can be operationalized as the amount of work a stimulus evokes, reflecting how much effort and cost approaching or avoiding the stimulus is "worth." Incentive salience could alternatively be described as a stimulus–goal association, or as a stimulus-dependent action–outcome association (Dickinson & Balleine, 2011). Such descriptions appear to be in line with studies showing a relationship between activation in the mesolimbic system, in particular the ventral striatum, and learning how to respond in such a way as to optimize feedback (Bunge, Burrows, & Wagner, 2004; Day & Carelli, 2007; Delgado, Miller, Inati, & Phelps, 2005; O'Doherty, Hampton, & Kim, 2007; Seger, 2008; Vink, Pas, Bijleveld, Custers, & Gladwin, 2013). Ideally, the incentive value of a stimulus encodes whether the stimulus or outcome predicts, perhaps indirectly, an evolutionarily relevant event, such that it can function as reward or punishment, although the system is not perfect, as evidenced by addictive drugs, which are thought to tap relatively directly into this dopaminergic system, but without having the associated evolutionary fitness advantage. Once the goal to acquire the incentive is activated, the actions needed to achieve that goal will be determined and recruited via other processes, depending on the context and prior learning (Robbins & Everitt, 1999; Tiffany, 1990).

Addiction provides an example of incentive salience gone awry. Addictive drugs or behaviors such as gambling have been proposed to cause incentive sensitization: Repeated use leads to an increase in the mesolimbic responses underlying incentive salience, causing drugs to become increasingly "wanted" stimuli (Robinson & Berridge, 2008). In animals, exposure to drugs results in a wide range of conditioning effects including self-administration acquisition, conditioned place preference, the amount of work an animal will perform for a drug, conditioned reinforcement, and Pavlovian conditioned approach and Pavlovian instrumental transfer (the last two providing more mechanistic models for how "hot" processes can conflict with and "hijack" goal-directed "cold" processes). (For details on effects of drug exposure, see the review by Robinson and Berridge, 2008.) In humans, such research is rare, but in a placebo-controlled PET (Positron Emission Tomography) study, stimuli that have been associated with amphetamine delivery acquire the ability to release dopamine in the striatum (Boileau et al., 2007), just as the sound of a bell acquired the ability to cause salivation in Pavlov's dogs. Drug-related incentive salience can also be detected using behavioral methods. For instance, individuals who drink heavily but not in a clinically problematic way show an attentional bias toward alcohol cues (Field, Mogg, Zetteler, & Bradley, 2004; Townshend & Duka, 2007). In alcohol-dependent individuals, a more complex pattern has been shown, with initial orienting toward alcohol cues followed by attentional disengagement (Noël et al., 2006; Vollstädt-Klein, Loeber, von der Goltz, Mann, & Kiefer, 2009). Approach-avoidance biases, reflecting a stronger tendency to approach than avoid alcohol cues (although this is controversial), have also been found. One task used to assess such biases is the approach avoidance task (AAT; Enter, Colzato, & Roelofs, 2012; Rinck & Becker, 2007). In this canonical version of this task, subjects are confronted with stimuli drawn from two categories—for example, spiders and flowers. Subjects must respond to these stimuli using a joystick, with which they can execute "pull" and "push" responses which cause "zoom" effects (i.e. the pulled/pushed stimulus becomes larger/smaller mimicking actual approach/avoidance). Usually, one of the stimulus categories is expected to automatically evoke either approach or avoidance, so that trials on the AAT can be classified as congruent or incongruent: On congruent trials the instructed movement is the same as the automatic response, and on incongruent trials the instructed movement is opposite to the automatic response. For example, we would expect arachnophobes to tend to avoid stimuli depicting spiders (Rinck & Becker, 2007). The AAT can thus provide measures of performance decrements due to incongruence to measure automatic approach and avoidance tendencies for one stimulus category versus the other. Using the AAT, it has been shown that heavy drinkers with a risk gene for alcoholism are faster at pulling than pushing alcohol cues, as well as other appetitive cues (Wiers, Rinck, Dictus, & van Den Wildenberg, 2009). A conceptually similar task is the stimulus response compatibility task. In this task, a manikin is moved toward or away from a centrally located cue. Thus, incongruence can be measured as in the AAT, except with approach/avoidance involving distance between the manikin and the stimulus instead of the zoom-in/zoom-out effect of the AAT. The stimulus response compatibility task has also shown alcohol-approach biases in heavy drinkers (Field, Caren, Fernie, & De Houwer, 2011; Field, Kiernan, Eastwood, & Child, 2008). There is currently much debate on the meaning, interrelationships, replicability of published results, appropriate calculations (correction for control conditions), and optimal design of such implicit measures (Field et al., 2011). Nevertheless, such results indicate that incentive salience indeed plays a role in addiction, although the precise nature of incentive salience remains unclear: Should such effects be described in terms of stimulus attributes, or in terms of the incentive value of the outcome of an act that can be performed on the stimulus?

The link between incentive salience and physiological states has not as yet been extensively studied in humans, but stimuli with incentive salience would be expected to evoke "hot" physiological states due to their link to an original unconditioned stimulus representing an evolutionarily relevant event. The combination of fundamental biological responses and incentive salience provides a basic model for the abstract metaphor of "heat" to describe psychologial or neural processes. Decomposing the idea of "heat" by grounding it in basic biological ANS processes and incentive salience raises the possibility that perhaps effects of "heat" on, for example, response selection or decision making are effects of these general emotional processes on general selection or decision-making systems, rather than such systems having separate "hot" and "cold" variants. Imagine, for instance, that there is a single response-selection system, consisting of an interdependent set of processes such as encoding and predicting the value of outcomes, the activation of potentially relevant response options, and the outcome-based selection amongst them (Knutson & Wimmer, 2007; Seger, 2008; Wickens, Budd, Hyland, & Arbuthnott, 2007). This system could well be affected by stimuli with more versus less incentive salience. Further, such effects could well be nonlinear: Perhaps qualitatively different behaviors would arise when tasks require responses that are congruent versus incongruent with stimulus–goal associations (see, for example, work on Pavlovian versus instrumental conflict, and how this may map onto the affect versus deliberation distinction: Dayan, Niv, Seymour, & Daw, 2006). If a unitary system would indeed operate like this, the resulting patterns of behavior could lead to the incorrect assumption that this duality in behavior implies two different systems.

DUAL-PROCESS AND DUAL-SYSTEM MODELS

Models that explain behavior via the outcome of two qualitatively different and competing types of processes or systems are widespread in many fields of psychological theory (Evans, 2008; Schneider & Shiffrin, 1977; Strack & Deutsch, 2004). These processes have been described using various terms (Evans, 2008): As discussed above, the terms "hot" and "cold" are in widespread use, but many other terms have been suggested also, for example, "impulsive" versus "reflective" (Bechara, 2005; Hofmann, Friese, & Wiers, 2008; Strack & Deutsch, 2004; Wiers et al., 2007), "reflexive" versus "reflective" (Lengfelder & Gollwitzer, 2001), the "X-" versus "C-"system (Lieberman, 2007), "system I" versus "system II" (Kahneman, 2003), "top-down" versus "bottom-up" (Posner & Petersen, 1990), and "automatic" versus "controlled" (Satpute & Lieberman, 2006; Schneider & Shiffrin, 1977; Shiffrin & Schneider, 1977; Volman, Roelofs, Koch, Verhagen, & Toni, 2011). While important differences exist between these variants, the proposed dichotomies do share a family resemblance. The processes are characterized as less versus more aware, intentional, efficient, and controllable (Bargh, 1994; Moors & De Houwer, 2006), or unconscious versus conscious, implicit versus explicit, low versus high effort, parallel versus sequential (Evans, 2008). Evidence for dual processes comes from a wide variety of studies showing qualitative differences between automatized and untrained performance and uncontrollable effects of manipulations and distractions, implying the existence of automatic processes that may interfere with the controlled processes serving task goals.

There appear to be at least two broad and common types of dual-process models. (A third type of multiple-process model is fuzzy-trace theory [Reyna & Brainerd, 1995], which differentiates two representational processes—gist vs. verbatim processes—and a third that is related to emotion and inhibition; see, for example, Rivers et al., 2008, and Chick & Reyna, 2011.) First, there is a general information-processing viewpoint, with roots in cognitive psychology, exemplified by the seminal work of Schneider and Shiffrin (1977). They defined automatic versus controlled processing in the context of a model in which memory is conceived of a network of extremely abstract "nodes," which represent any unit of elements related to information processing (e.g., associative connections, response programs, and directions for the processing of information by other nodes). The set of activated nodes is described as being "in working memory," although notably this does not necessarily refer to a separate *system* in these models. This working memory has a limited capacity; only a subset of nodes can be active at once. An automatic process is a sequence of activation of nodes that occurs in response to an initial input configuration of activation and that progresses without needing control or attention. A controlled process is a sequence of activation of nodes that requires attention, or, that is dependent on "processing-directives" nodes that need to be active in working memory. A classic series of experiments on automatic versus controlled processes from this perspective compared the effects of automatization in visual search tasks (Schneider & Shiffrin, 1977; Shiffrin & Schneider, 1977): subjects learn to automatically detect stimuli after extensive training. The Stroop task provides another example of automatization: the automatic process of reading words leads to performance deficits when having to name the color in which the word is printed, if the word itself is a conflicting color word (Stroop, 1935). Simon tasks (Simon & Rudell, 1967) and Flanker tasks (Eriksen & Eriksen, 1974) provide further examples of flexible but slow and vulnerable controlled processes, versus reliable and fast but rigid and hence possibly task-inappropriate automatic processes. A difference between these latter tasks and the Stroop task and Schneider and Shiffrin's search tasks is that the involved automatic processes are due to inherent properties of the human attentional system rather than a learning process.

Notably, the above conception of dual-process research does not focus on emotion or motivation (or other "hot" processes); the automatization process is described in highly abstract terms and the tasks involve stimuli and responses that appear highly unlikely to evoke defensive or appetitive physiological responses. In a second line of dual-process research, automatic (or impulsive) processes are far more closely related to emotion and motivation (Strack & Deutsch, 2004). The model underlying such research is closely related to the "horse and rider" metaphor (Hofmann, Friese, & Strack, 2009): Our emotional "animal" drives pull us to immediate reward and away from imminent punishment without regard for long-term consequences, and our rational self must control them and steer us toward virtuous—or, in terms of the lab setting, task-relevant—behavior. As already discussed, the broad class of approach-avoidance tasks shows performance deficits when subjects have to avoid an attractive stimulus such as a drug cue, or approach an aversive stimulus such as an angry face (Volman et al., 2011), or a spider in an individual with arachnophobia (Rinck & Becker, 2007). Emotional Stroop tasks (Frings, Englert, Wentura, & Bermeitinger, 2010; Williams, Mathews, & MacLeod, 1996) provide evidence for task-irrelevant processes that cause distraction when subjects are exposed to emotional words of which they are instructed to name the color. A task that has been very extensively used to study automatic processes related to evaluation is the Implicit Association Test (IAT; Greenwald, McGhee, & Schwartz, 1998; Greenwald, Poehlman, Uhlmann, & Banaji, 2009). This is a classification task: subjects must press one or another button to indicate to which of two possible categories a presented stimulus belongs. An IAT typically involves two classification pairs: an evaluative classification, e.g., "good" versus "bad," and a target classification, e.g., "spider" versus "flower." In the essential part of the IAT, subjects have to perform both classifications in one block. However, they can only use two buttons, so that one response represents one of the target classes as well as one of the evaluative classes, and the other button represents the other target class as well as the other evaluative class. This results in congruence versus incongruence between target words and evaluative words assigned to the same response button. Thus, in the classic example, spiders and insects can be shown to be automatically evaluated more negatively than flowers because of increased errors and slower reaction times in the incongruent (insects–positive on one response; flowers–negative on the other) blocks than in the congruent (insects–negative; flowers–positive) blocks. Such congruence effects have been used to study automatically activated associations and attitudes involving race, food, politicians, and so forth. We briefly note that it is debated whether IAT scores purely reflect underlying evaluative associations, or whether they may also be due to, e.g., which categories are more salient, or to the selection of exemplars of stimulus categories (Blanton & Jaccard, 2006; Conrey, Sherman, Gawronski, Hugenberg, & Groom, 2005; Fiedler, Messner, & Bluemke, 2006; Olson & Fazio, 2004).

The dual-process models discussed above, in particular the emotion-based models, have been applied to theories of addiction, in which the paradox of persistent behavior against the person's own interests and explicit desires has been described as an inability of reflective processes to sufficiently modulate the effects of impulsive processes (Bechara, 2005; Deutsch & Strack, 2006; Stacy, Ames, & Knowlton, 2004; Wiers et al., 2007). The studies discussed above in the context of incentive salience in addiction can often be interpreted in dual-process terms: Biases are due to automatic processes evoked by the drug-related stimuli, which lead to impulsive responses or task attentional shifts that conflict with explicit task goals. In line with the incentive salience account, alcohol cues appear to be relatively easy to condition: Consistently selecting an alcohol stimulus in a forced-choice task leads to strong automatization in more heavily drinking subjects, as reflected by performance costs when subjects are instructed *not* to select that stimulus (Gladwin & Wiers, 2012). A sufficiently effective reflective system would be needed to minimize the effects of this conflict between conditioning and task goals, for instance via top-down reduction of the salience of drug cues (Finn, 2002). Of particular interest from a dual-process perspective is that alcohol cues may actively interfere with controlled processing (Gladwin & Wiers, 2011b), potentially leading to a vicious cycle in combination with incentive salience. Dual-process models have received more specific support from findings showing that higher working memory capacity (Grenard et al., 2008; Thush et al., 2008) and interference control capacity (Houben & Wiers, 2009; Wiers, Beckers, Houben, & Hofmann, 2009) weaken the impact of automatic processes on behavior. It appears to be necessary to have both strong associations and weak executive control to show drug-related biases.

Another research domain in which dual-process models—with a strong focus on neural processes—are currently influential is adolescent behavior, particularly when explaining changes in risky and other possibly problematic behaviors that occur during the transitions from childhood to adolescence and from adolescence to adulthood. From real-world statistics, it is known that adolescents and young adults, compared to both children and older adults, show increased levels of risk-taking behaviors in the form of risky driving, unsafe sex, criminal behavior, and experimentation with and initiation of substance use (Reyna & Farley, 2006). The respective dual-process models of adolescent risk taking share many commonalities with models to explain substance use and addiction, as we have explicitly discussed in Gladwin, Figner, Wiers, and Crone (2011). These frontostriatal neurodevelopmental models of adolescent decision making posit a potential for an imbalance between strong motivational-affective bottom-up processes and relatively weak controlling top-down processes (Blakemore & Robbins, 2012; Crone & Dahl, 2012; Richards, Plate, & Ernst, 2013; Somerville, Jones, & Casey, 2010; Steinberg, 2010). The assumption of a developmentally transient imbalance during adolescence is grounded both in animal work (Spear, 2011) and insights from human neuroanatomical development (Giedd, 2008). However, it is important to state that the current empirical evidence that investigated risk taking in children, adolescents, and adults behaviorally and/or neurally is both generally sparse and not unequivocal in supporting or refuting this "imbalance" model: First, the inverted-U developmental trajectory in risk-taking levels across the relevant age range—both observed in real-world statistics and predicted by the imbalance model—appears to be elusive in controlled laboratory situations, as only very few studies observed such a trajectory (Burnett, Bault, Coricelli, & Blakemore, 2010; Figner, Mackinlay, Wilkening, & Weber, 2009b). Consistent with this more anecdotal observation, such a trajectory was also not observed in a formal meta-analysis of the existing risky decision-making studies in the relevant age range (Defoe, Dubas, Figner, & van Aken, submitted). Second, the (still very few) fMRI studies investigating the neural age differences predicted by the imbalance model in both subcortical and cortical neural responses do not provide consistent results: Some studies find evidence consistent with the model (e.g., striatal "hyperreactivity" to rewards in adolescents: Chein, Albert, O'Brien, Uckert, & Steinberg, 2011; Cohen et al., 2010), but others report an absence of age differences or patterns opposite of what the model would predict (e.g., no age differences or striatal "hyporeactivity" to rewards in adolescents: Bjork et al., 2004; Bjork, Smith, Chen, & Hommer, 2010; Paulsen, Carter, Platt, Huettel, & Brannon, 2011; see also, for example, Pfeifer & Allen, 2012, and Reyna et al., 2011; and for an early behavioral study, see Reyna & Ellis, 1994). Finally, in Reyna and Farley (2006), risky behaviors were not predicted by impulsivity but by explicit ratings of risk and benefit. It is thus currently difficult to draw any firm conclusions on the imbalance model of adolescence.

Despite the success and/or popularity of dual-process models illustrated in these two illustrative domains of addiction and adolescence—and there are of course many more domains in which such models are widely accepted—we will argue here that the step from the observation of "dualistic" patterns in behavior or brain activation to an underlying model involving dual processes or systems is hazardous. This is especially true for the second kind of emotion-based dual-process models, which explicitly attempt to incorporate motivation and emotion in their "systems," unlike the more abstract information-processing models (although a criticism of these latter models could be that they are so abstract that they leave much to be explained, thereby evading the problems that the models criticized in this section at least attempt to address). First, the fact that task-irrelevant processes can influence performance does not mean that there exist consistent sets of task-relevant versus task-irrelevant processes. The most careful interpretation of the evidence appears to be simply that cognition is not immune to task-irrelevant effects. Individuals' differences in how badly they are affected are similarly not necessarily due to their having one system that is strong relative to another system; perhaps, for instance, some kind of automatic process that inhibits distracting information leads to high scores on executive control tasks as well as weak effects of task-irrelevant processes. Second, the characteristics that define automatic versus controlled processes do not consistently respond to manipulations as a unit, as would be expected if they reflect a common type of process or the function of one system. In contrast, for instance, a process may be efficient (a property of automatic processes) but still may be dependent on volition and intentions (a property of controlled processes) (Bargh, 1994; Evans, 2008; Moors & De Houwer, 2006). An example given by Bargh is driving: Although many components of driving are automatic, drivers do not automatically start driving when seated at the wheel, and where they drive is dependent on where they want to go. This suggests that a simple binary division of the processes underlying behavior into automatic or controlled is untenable. One response to this is to claim that no task or task manipulation aimed at detecting automatic or controlled processes is process-pure (Conrey et al., 2005): All behavior depends on some mixture of controlled and automatic processes; or, every mental process can have some, perhaps varying, attributes of automaticity and control. However, such a degree of nuances strongly diminishes the parsimony and falsifiability of dual-process models. That is, models with too many "moving parts" provide less and less advantage over simply considering the features attributed to one or the other type of process by themselves, without clustering them into coherent constellations. Third, models positing dual (cognitive or neural) systems have been shown to have far weaker evidence than often assumed (Keren & Schul, 2009; Pfeifer & Allen, 2012). For instance, the finding of brain activation differentially related to one or the other type of processing cannot logically be taken as evidence for separable processing systems. In the elegant model of the X- and C-neural systems (Lieberman, 2007), referring roughly to refleXive and refleCtive processing, regions that were initially attributed to the X-system, such as the basal ganglia, are for instance also involved in executive control—a function of the C-system (Frank, Loughry, & O'Reilly, 2001; Hazy, Frank, & O'Reilly, 2007; Persson, Larsson, & Reuter-Lorenz, 2013; Van Hecke et al., 2010). Such falsifiability, at least of the details of the model, was predicted by Lieberman and is in principle a scientific strength of the X- and C-model—a good model needs to be falsifiable, and there is clearly room for refinements that could use new information. But the model must also allow a more rigorous falsification, namely of the adequacy of the basic division into dual systems. For example, the "X-system" could be reformulated to consist of networks that implement the fast detection of salience and defensive reactions, such as the amygdala and periaqueductal gray (Hermans, Henckens, Roelofs, & Fernández, 2012), or regions that re-establish stored information-processing procedures, such as the hippocampus and, of potentially central importance to this question, the cerebellum (Marvel & Desmond, 2010). However, it is unclear from this perspective what the C-system would be, and whether it would actually still form a "dual system"—rather than an opposing system, it would consist of processes that fundamentally rely on the input from the X-system to function at all. Finally, the attribution of motivation and emotion to only one of the systems or sets of processes leads to what has been termed the motivational homunculus problem: That is, when controlled processing is required to "do the right thing" given a certain task, context, or set of long-term contingencies, it must be explained why the control exerted by the subject should be task-appropriate or have a long-term positive expected outcome. Evidently, motivation and control must be interwoven, as opposed to functioning as competing processes. Indeed, there has been increasing interest in the integration of motivation and reinforcement on the one hand and controlled processing on the other (Gladwin, Figner, Crone, & Wiers, 2011; Hazy, Frank, & O'Reilly, 2006; Kouneiher, Charron, & Koechlin, 2009; Pessoa, 2009; Robbins, 2007). However, this again blurs the lines between dual systems.

THE FUTURE: ASKING BETTER QUESTIONS

The models discussed above describe interesting and important phenomena, but suffer from concerning flaws. The general underlying problem appears to be premature abstraction: "Hotness" is an intuitively appealing abstraction from physiological states and mesolimbic functions, but studies appear to use the term only as a vague abstraction, without resolving the metaphor to concrete, precise relationships. Similarly, positing the existence of "systems" suggests that we have some knowledge of what these systems are, what they consist of, what set of equations describes them, etc. In contrast, again, they appear to be used more as suggestive placeholders, appealing to common sense and intuition. Due to premature abstraction, studies will be aimed at answering badly defined questions, will be unable to specify precise measures and operationalizations, and hence will be unlikely to converge on a clear theory. This may play a role in the general methodological problems of psychological research that have recently come under scrutiny. If we don't really know what we're looking for, we are far more likely to commit some form of data-snooping or method-snooping—and have far more freedom to do so—to at least find *something*.

Of course, many researchers have recognized these problems and attempted to deal with them. One question that has been raised concerning dual-process models is whether there are, perhaps, a *different* number of systems—one, or three, or more. While this skepticism concerning the duality of models is commendable, perhaps we should be questioning the use of "systems" itself. Is defining a system for this and a system for that, a system with these features and a system with those, the best way to understand decision making, response selection, emotion, etc? We briefly note some general approaches that may lead to important alternative ways forward. First, frameworks of dual-process theories could be built more rigorously on conditioning processes (de Wit & Dickinson, 2009; Dickinson & Balleine, 2011), which may provide insight into conflict between well-defined processes related to types of conditioning, for instance by reinterpreting affective versus deliberative processes as Pavlovian-instrumental interactions (Dayan et al., 2006). Second, computational modeling of controlled and automatic processes forces researchers to at least make explicit what we do and do not know and what theories say in exact terms; such models have for instance made clear how working memory may be related to reinforcement (Hazy et al., 2006). Third, we may need the creative generation of novel fundamental types of processes such as iterative reprocessing (Cunningham, Zelazo, Packer, & Van Bavel, 2007), as explored in the next section.

R3: THE REPROCESSING AND REINFORCEMENT MODEL OF REFLECTIVITY

We have previously suggested a broad class of model, termed the Reprocessing and Reinforcement model of Reflectivity (or R3 model; Figure 8.1), in an attempt to address criticisms of dual-process models (Gladwin et al., 2011; Wiers, Gladwin, Hofmann, Salemink, & Ridderinkhof, 2013). The core of the model is a cyclical process of response selection based on prior reinforcement, in particular of act–outcome associations (de Wit & Dickinson, 2009; Dickinson & Balleine, 2011). In the basic "step" of the model, current-state representations activate a set of associated responses, which activate associated outcomes given the state, which in turn are used to select responses. "Responses" in the model are highly abstract, in the tradition of Schneider and Shiffrin's (1977) nodes, and include all kinds of behavioral and cognitive responses. A response node could include functions traditionally termed executive or controlled, such as an attentional shift, search for information, or update of information in working memory. We emphasize the time-dependence of activation in the selection process due to iterative reprocessing (Cunningham et al., 2007). The available set of responses may change over time passed since stimulus presentation; and the incentive value of the predicted outcome of an act may also change over time, and is assumed to also be dependent on the state. As an example showing the potential relevance of iterative reprocessing and time-dependence, recall that the attentional bias toward and away from alcohol cues in alcohol-dependent patients was highly time-dependent, moving from an initial approach to a possibly more reflective avoidance bias (Noël et al., 2006). Control, or reflectivity, is defined within the model as *the effective time the response selection process is given to converge by the parameters of the system.* That is, reflective processing means that sufficient time is given to allow time-dependent processes affecting response options and incentive values to converge on a stable optimum, which would not be replaced if more processing cycles were completed. Impulsive behavior occurs when responses are executed after a "too short" reprocessing time, although in certain situations external constraints would make reflective processing disadvantageous.

The R3 model, beyond attempting to capture the nature of reflective or controlled processing, serves as a thought-experiment intended to make four main points. First, the model addresses the motivational homunculus problem: Assuming a purely cold, unemotional control system, the question arises why such a system would serve our interests, why it would be aimed at achieving positive outcomes, even if at longer delays. Our reflective behavior has to be motivated by emotion and incentive as much as our impulsive behavior. The R3 model shows a system in which emotion and motivation, in the form of the incentive value of

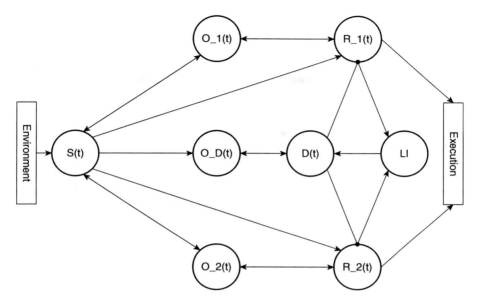

Figure 8.1   Illustration of the R3 model. The basic function of the unified system of the R3 model is the selection of the response (R_*i*) associated with the optimal outcome (O_*i*), given the current state (S). We show a simple case with only two activated responses. The essential feature of the model is that the activation of responses and the value of the associated outcomes vary over time. This implies that different responses could be selected at different time points following an event. A delay parameter (D) allows the selection process time to settle on non-impulsive responses that require longer to win the competition, represented here via simple lateral inhibition (LI). In the figure, arrows show (often bidirectional) effects on interaction between nodes; arrowheads represent, roughly, activating effects while blunt line-endings represent inhibitory effects. In this abstraction, the output of outcome nodes is assumed to be signed: positive for reinforcing outcomes and negative for punishing outcomes. Delay here shown to be dependent on the State and the amount of conflict, encoded in the activation of the Lateral Inhibition node. Thus, simply changing the delay parameter can shift processing from a more impulsive to a more reflective state, without needing to assume separate systems. Each node may involve various brain networks. Reflectivity, however, is defined as an emergent property of the system as a whole, and is not assigned to any element within the system. Note further that delay is itself a response with an expected outcome (O_D) that must be associated to appropriate situations via reinforcement.

outcomes, are part of every response selection or decision. "Hot" stimuli could well disrupt the reprocessing cycles within the model, but note that these disruptions take place in the same system that would serve response selection in a "cold" situation with little immediate arousal (but nevertheless always some value to giving the correct response). Second, we used the model to illustrate category mistakes that can be made by ignoring what we term levels of emergence. Features that are relevant to behavioral patterns or subjective thought should not be attributed to elements of a model containing underlying processes. That is, no *process* is either reflective or reflexive, or controlled or automatic: The system as a whole functions in a more or less reflective state, depending on certain parameters—in particular the time allowed for reprocessing (note that this essential delaying is a *response* itself, subject to selection and learning processes; it is therefore not a "delaying homunculus," and could well be tuned incorrectly). One could say that every subprocess is "automatic," as reflectivity or control is only defined, or only exists, at the level of the system as a whole. Third, the time allotment serves as an illustration of a single parameter that determines how reflective response selection will be. That is, the model shows that we can have reflective and impulsive states of processing without any kind of conflict between a reflective and impulsive system and without having to distinguish subsets of types of processes that can be classified as either automatic or controlled. Possibly interesting from this perspective is that no single brain area, such as the dlPFC, which is strongly related to working memory, should contain "control." Recent brain stimulation work provides a possibly interesting illustration of this point. Transcranial direct current stimulation (tDCS) of the dlPFC has been found to enhance performance in working-memory tasks (Fregni et al., 2005; Ohn et al., 2008); we recently replicated and extended this basic finding using a Sternberg task involving distraction (Gladwin, den Uyl, Fregni, & Wiers, 2012). However, the same stimulation protocol failed to reduce the congruence bias on an insects-and-flowers IAT (Gladwin, den Uyl, & Wiers, 2012). Even more surprisingly, dlPFC stimulation actually selectively enhanced performance on congruent trials, on which there was no conflict involving evaluation but there was the need to apply a stimulus–response rule. Although this line of research is only starting, such studies start to show that the function of the stimulated region is not "control" but a specific subprocess that could either aid or hinder the efficiency of reflective processing. Finally, the model changes the focus from an unspecific "strength" metaphor to a learning perspective that emphasizes how successful reflective processing at least partly results from an individual's reinforcement history. Has an individual been rewarded for responding to certain situations with, for example, delaying responses, or with a slow memory search strategy to look for downsides to immediate response options? Does an addict, beyond being burdened with fast and easily available drug-seeking responses associated with high incentive value, have any reinforced alternatives to which response selection could converge given sufficient time? The model appears to fit very well with the "Tools of the Mind" approach (Diamond, Barnett, Thomas, & Munro, 2007) for reinforcing the use of executive function in young children, and is perfectly illustrated by the "Think About the Answer Don't Tell Me" song (FWIChannel, 2012). We briefly mention that the model also extends the "binding" concept (the need to temporarily associate elements in memory) from stimulus features and stimulus–responses connections to act–outcome associations. This is beyond the scope of this chapter, but may connect dual-process models to psychophysiological methods and results involving phase coding and synchrony (Gladwin, 't Hart, & de Jong, 2008; Gladwin, Lindsen, & de Jong, 2006; Jensen & Lisman, 1998).

To summarize, we first aimed to clarify terminology by describing the various uses of temperature metaphors and attempted to decompose "hotness" into basic biological responses and incentive salience. We then extended the scope to discuss dual-process and dual-system models. These models are highly success-ful (surely also in the sense of being popular) but nevertheless need to be viewed with scientific skepticism, which we discussed next. Importantly, changes to the models and subsequent lines of research may have implications for a wide variety of applications, such as cognitive bias modification protocols in addiction and other psychopathology (Wiers et al., 2013), in our understanding of adolescent behavior (Pfeifer & Allen, 2012), or in theory- and evidence-based approaches in education (Diamond et al., 2007). Finally, we briefly presented some possible ways forward, including our own R3 model. Regardless of the routes researchers will choose, we believe that the time is ripe for models to more often become objects of critical study rather than accepted assumptions.

REFERENCES

Abelson, R. P. (1963). Computer simulation of "hot cognition." In S. Tomkins & S. Messick (Eds.), *Computer simulation of personality* (pp. 277–302). New York, NY: Wiley.

Bargh, J. A. (1994). The four horsemen of automaticity: Awareness, intention, efficiency and control in social cognition. In R. Wyer & T. Srull (Eds.), *Handbook of social cognition* (2nd ed., pp. 1–40). Hillsdale, NJ: Erlbaum.

Bechara, A. (2005). Decision making, impulse control and loss of willpower to resist drugs: a neurocognitive perspective. *Nature Neuroscience, 8(11)*, 1458–1463.

Bechara, A., Damasio, A. R., Damasio, H., & Anderson, S. W. (1994). Insensitivity to future consequences following damage to human prefrontal cortex. *Cognition, 50(1–3)*, 7–15.

Benarroch, E. E. (1993). The central autonomic network: Functional organization, dysfunc-tion, and perspective. *Mayo Clinic Proceedings, 68(10)*, 988–1001.

Berridge, K. C., & Robinson, T. E. (1998). What is the role of dopamine in reward: Hedonic impact, reward learning, or incentive salience? *Brain Research Reviews, 28(3)*, 309–369.

Bjork, J. M., Knutson, B., Fong, G. W., Caggiano, D. M., Bennett, S. M., & Hommer, D. W. (2004). Incentive-elicited brain activation in adolescents: Similarities and differ-ences from young adults. *Journal of Neuroscience: The Official Journal of the Society for Neuroscience, 24(8)*, 1793–1802.

Bjork, J. M., Smith, A. R., Chen, G., & Hommer, D. W. (2010). Adolescents, adults and rewards: Comparing motivational neurocircuitry recruitment using fMRI. *PLoS ONE, 5(7)*, e11440.

Blakemore, S.-J., & Robbins, T. W. (2012). Decision-making in the adolescent brain. *Nature Neuroscience, 15(9)*, 1184–1191.

Blanton, H., & Jaccard, J. (2006). Postscript: Perspectives on the reply by Greenwald, Rud-man, Nosek, and Zayas (2006). *Psychological Review, 113(1)*, 166–169.

Boileau, I., Dagher, A., Leyton, M., Welfeld, K., Booij, L., Diksic, M., & Benkelfat, C. (2007). Conditioned dopamine release in humans: A positron emission tomography [11C]raclopride study with amphetamine. *Journal of Neuroscience: The Official Journal of the Society for Neuroscience, 27(15)*, 3998–4003.

Bracha, H. S. (2004). Freeze, flight, fight, fright, faint: Adaptationist perspectives on the acute stress response spectrum. *CNS Spectrums, 9(9)*, 679–685.

Bunge, S. A., Burrows, B., & Wagner, A. D. (2004). Prefrontal and hippocampal contribu-tions to visual associative recognition: Interactions between cognitive control and epi-sodic retrieval. *Brain and Cognition, 56(2)*, 141–152.

Burnett, S., Bault, N., Coricelli, G., & Blakemore, S.-J. (2010). Adolescents' heightened risk-seeking in a probabilistic gambling task. *Cognitive Development, 25(2)*, 183–196.

Cabanac, M. (1992). Pleasure: The common currency. *Journal of Theoretical Biology, 155(2)*, 173–200.

Carter, R., Meyer, J., & Huettel, S. (2010). Functional neuroimaging of intertemporal choice models: A review. *Journal of Neuroscience, Psychology, and Economics, 3(1)*, 27–45.

Cersosimo, M. G., & Benarroch, E. E. (2013). Central control of autonomic function and involvement in neurodegenerative disorders. In R. M. Buijs and D. F. Swaab (Eds.), *Autonomic nervous system: Handbook of clinical neurology 117* (pp. 45–57). San Diego, CA: Elsevier Science & Technology Books.

Chein, J., Albert, D., O'Brien, L., Uckert, K., & Steinberg, L. (2011). Peers increase adolescent risk taking by enhancing activity in the brain's reward circuitry. *Developmental Science, 14(2)*, F1–10.

Chick, C. F. & Reyna, V. F. (2011). A fuzzy-trace theory of adolescent risk taking: Beyond self-control and sensation seeking. In V. F. Reyna, S. Chapman, M. Dougherty, & J. Confrey (Eds.), *The adolescent brain: Learning, reasoning, and decision making* (pp. 379–428). Washington, DC: American Psychological Association.

Cohen, J. R., Asarnow, R. F., Sabb, F. W., Bilder, R. M., Bookheimer, S. Y., Knowlton, B. J., & Poldrack, R. A. (2010). A unique adolescent response to reward prediction errors. *Nature Neuroscience, 13(6)*, 669–671.

Collet, C., Vernet-Maury, E., Delhomme, G., & Dittmar, A. (1997). Autonomic nervous system response patterns specificity to basic emotions. *Journal of the Autonomic Nervous System, 62(1–2)*, 45–57.

Conrey, F. R., Sherman, J. W., Gawronski, B., Hugenberg, K., & Groom, C. J. (2005). Separating multiple processes in implicit social cognition: The quad model of implicit task performance. *Journal of Personality and Social Psychology, 89(4)*, 469–487.

Crone, E. A., & Dahl, R. E. (2012). Understanding adolescence as a period of social-affective engagement and goal flexibility. *Nature Reviews: Neuroscience, 13(9)*, 636–650.

Cunningham, W. A., Zelazo, P. D., Packer, D. J., & Van Bavel, J. J. (2007). The iterative reprocessing model: A multilevel framework for attitudes and evaluation. *Social Cognition, 25(5)*, 736–760.

Dalton, K. M., Kalin, N. H., Grist, T. M., & Davidson, R. J. (2005). Neural-cardiac coupling in threat-evoked anxiety. *Journal of Cognitive Neuroscience, 17(6)*, 969–980.

Day, J. J., & Carelli, R. M. (2007). The nucleus accumbens and Pavlovian reward learning. *The Neuroscientist: A Review Journal Bringing Neurobiology, Neurology and Psychiatry, 13(2)*, 148–159.

Dayan, P., Niv, Y., Seymour, B., & Daw, N. D. (2006). The misbehavior of value and the discipline of the will. *Neural Networks: The Official Journal of the International Neural Network Society, 19(8)*, 1153–1160.

De Wit, S., & Dickinson, A. (2009). Associative theories of goal-directed behaviour: A case for animal–human translational models. *Psychological Research, 73(4)*, 463–476.

Delgado, M. R., Miller, M. M., Inati, S., & Phelps, E. A. (2005). An fMRI study of reward-related probability learning. *NeuroImage, 24(3)*, 862–873.

Deutsch, R., & Strack, F. (2006). Duality models in social psychology: From dual processes to interacting systems. *Psychological Inquiry, 17(3)*, 166–172.

Diamond, A., Barnett, W. S., Thomas, J., & Munro, S. (2007). Preschool program improves cognitive control. *Science, 318(5855)*, 1387–1388.

Dickinson, A., & Balleine, B. (2011). Motivational control of instrumental action motivational action control of instrumental. *Current Directions in Psychological Science, 4(5)*, 162–167.

Enter, D., Colzato, L. S., & Roelofs, K. (2012). Dopamine transporter polymorphisms affect social approach-avoidance tendencies. *Genes, Brain, and Behavior, 11(6)*, 671–676.

Eriksen, B. A., & Eriksen, C. W. (1974). Effects of noise letters upon the identification of a target letter in a nonsearch task. *Perception and Psychophysics, 16(1),* 143–149.

Evans, J. S. B. T. (2008). Dual-processing accounts of reasoning, judgment, and social cognition. *Annual Review of Psychology, 59,* 255–278.

Fiedler, K., Messner, C., & Bluemke, M. (2006). Unresolved problems with the "I," the "A," and the "T": A logical and psychometric critique of the Implicit Association Test (IAT). *European Review of Social Psychology, 17(1),* 74–147.

Field, M., Caren, R., Fernie, G., & De Houwer, J. (2011). Alcohol approach tendencies in heavy drinkers: Comparison of effects in a relevant stimulus–response compatibility task and an approach/avoidance Simon task. *Psychology of Addictive Behaviors, 25(4),* 697–701.

Field, M., Kiernan, A., Eastwood, B., & Child, R. (2008). Rapid approach responses to alcohol cues in heavy drinkers. *Journal of Behavior Therapy and Experimental Psychiatry, 39(3),* 209–218.

Field, M., Mogg, K., Zetteler, J., & Bradley, B. P. (2004). Attentional biases for alcohol cues in heavy and light social drinkers: The roles of initial orienting and maintained attention. *Psychopharmacology, 176(1),* 88–93.

Figner, B., Knoch, D., Johnson, E. J., Krosch, A. R., Lisanby, S. H., Fehr, E., & Weber, E. U. (2010). Lateral prefrontal cortex and self-control in intertemporal choice. *Nature Neuroscience, 13(5),* 538–539.

Figner, B., Mackinlay, R. J., Wilkening, F., & Weber, E. U. (2009a). Affective and deliberative processes in risky choice: Age differences in risk taking in the Columbia Card Task. *Journal of Experimental Psychology: Learning, Memory, and Cognition, 35(3),* 709–730.

——(2009b). Risky choice in children, adolescents, and adults: Affective versus deliberative processes and the role of executive functions. In *Proceedings of the Society for Research in Child Development.* Denver, CO: Society for Research in Child Development, National Research Council.

Figner, B., & Weber, E. U. (2011). Who takes risks when and why? Determinants of risk taking. *Current Directions in Psychological Science, 20(4),* 211–216.

Finn, P. R. (2002). Motivation, working memory, and decision making: A cognitive-motivational theory of personality vulnerability to alcoholism. *Behavioral and Cognitive Neuroscience Reviews, 1(3),* 183–205.

Frank, M. J., Loughry, B., & O'Reilly, R. C. (2001). Interactions between frontal cortex and basal ganglia in working memory: A computational model. *Cognitive, Affective and Behavioral Neuroscience, 1(2),* 137–160.

Fregni, F. F., Boggio, P. S., Nitsche, M. A., Bermpohl, F., Antal, A., Feredoes, E., et al. (2005). Anodal transcranial direct current stimulation of prefrontal cortex enhances working memory. *Experimental Brain Research, 166(1),* 23–30.

Frings, C., Englert, J., Wentura, D., & Bermeitinger, C. (2010). Decomposing the emotional Stroop effect. *Quarterly Journal of Experimental Psychology (2006), 63(1),* 42–49.

FWI Channel (2012). Diamond—Day Night Presentation.mpg [video file]. Retrieved April 11, 2013 from www.youtube.com/watch?v=DbszNVN3OO4, June 20.

Geurts, H. M., van der Oord, S., & Crone, E. A. (2006). Hot and cool aspects of cognitive control in children with ADHD: Decision-making and inhibition. *Journal of Abnormal Child Psychology, 34(6),* 813–824.

Giedd, J. N. (2008). The teen brain: Insights from neuroimaging. *Journal of Adolescent Health: Official Publication of the Society for Adolescent Medicine, 42(4),* 335–343.

Gladwin, T. E., 't Hart, B. M., & de Jong, R. (2008). Dissociations between motor-related EEG measures in a cued movement sequence task. *Cortex, 44(5),* 521–536.

Gladwin, T. E., den Uyl, T. E., & Wiers, R. W. (2012). Anodal tDCS of dorsolateral prefontal cortex during an Implicit Association Test. *Neuroscience Letters, 517(2)*, 82–86.

Gladwin, T. E., Figner, B., Crone, E. A., & Wiers, R. W. (2011). Addiction, adolescence, and the integration of control and motivation. *Developmental Cognitive Neuroscience, 1(4)*, 364–376.

Gladwin, T. E., Lindsen, J. P., & de Jong, R. (2006). Pre-stimulus EEG effects related to response speed, task switching and upcoming response hand. *Biological Psychology, 72(1)*, 15–34.

Gladwin, T. E., den Uyl, T., Fregni, F. F., & Wiers, R. W. (2012). Enhancement of selective attention by tDCS: Interaction with interference in a Sternberg task. *Neuroscience Letters, 512(1)*, 33–37.

Gladwin, T. E., & Wiers, R. W. (2011). How do alcohol cues affect working memory? Persistent slowing due to alcohol-related distracters in an alcohol version of the Sternberg task. *Addiction Research and Theory, 20(4)*, 284290.

——(2012). Alcohol-related effects on automaticity due to experimentally manipulated conditioning. *Alcoholism: Clinical and Experimental Research, 36(5)*, 895–899.

Greenwald, A. G., McGhee, D. E., & Schwartz, J. L. (1998). Measuring individual differences in implicit cognition: The implicit association test. *Journal of Personality and Social Psychology, 74(6)*, 1464–1480.

Greenwald, A. G., Poehlman, T. A., Uhlmann, E. L., & Banaji, M. R. (2009). Understanding and using the Implicit Association Test: III. Meta-analysis of predictive validity. *Journal of Personality and Social Psychology, 97(1)*, 17–41.

Grenard, J., Ames, S. L., Wiers, R. W., Thush, C., Sussman, S., & Stacy, A. W. (2008). Working memory capacity moderates the predictive effects of drug-related associations on substance use. *Psychology of Addictive Behaviors, 22(3)*, 426–432.

Hazy, T. E., Frank, M. J., & O'Reilly, R. C. (2006). Banishing the homunculus: Making working memory work. *Neuroscience, 139(1)*, 105–118.

——(2007). Towards an executive without a homunculus: Computational models of the prefrontal cortex/basal ganglia system. *Philosophical Transactions of the Royal Society of London. Series B, Biological Sciences, 362(1485)*, 1601–1613.

Hermans, E. J., Henckens, M. J. A. G., Roelofs, K., & Fernández, G. (2012). Fear bradycardia and activation of the human periaqueductal grey. *NeuroImage, 66C*, 278–287.

Hofmann, W., Friese, M., & Strack, F. (2009). Impulse and self-control from a dual-systems perspective. *Perspectives on Psychological Science, 4(2)*, 162–176.

Hofmann, W., Friese, M., & Wiers, R. W. (2008). Impulsive versus reflective influences on health behavior: A theoretical framework and empirical review. *Health Psychology Review, 2(2)*, 111–137.

Hongwanishkul, D., Happaney, K. R., Lee, W. S. C., & Zelazo, P. D. (2005). Assessment of hot and cool executive function in young children: Age-related changes and individual differences. *Developmental Neuropsychology, 28(2)*, 617–644.

Houben, K., & Wiers, R. W. (2009). Response inhibition moderates the relationship between implicit associations and drinking behavior. *Alcoholism, Clinical and Experimental Research, 33(4)*, 626–633.

Jarvik, L. F., & Russell, D. (1979). Anxiety, aging and the third emergency reaction. *Journal of Gerontology, 34(2)*, 197–200.

Jensen, O., & Lisman, J. (1998). An oscillatory short-term memory buffer model can account for data on the Sternberg task. *Journal of Neuroscience, 18(24)*, 10688–10699.

Kahneman, D. (2003). A perspective on judgment and choice: Mapping bounded rationality. *American Psychologist, 58(9)*, 697–720.

Keren, G., & Schul, Y. (2009). Two is not always better than one: A critical evaluation of two-system theories. *Perspectives on Psychological Science, 4(6)*, 533–550.

Knoch, D., Gianotti, L. R. R., Pascual-Leone, A., Treyer, V., Regard, M., Hohmann, M., & Brugger, P. (2006). Disruption of right prefrontal cortex by low-frequency repetitive transcranial magnetic stimulation induces risk-taking behavior. *Journal of Neuroscience, 26(24)*, 6469–6472.

Knutson, B., & Wimmer, G. E. (2007). Splitting the difference: How does the brain code reward episodes? *Annals of the New York Academy of Sciences, 1104(1)*, 54–69.

Kouneiher, F., Charron, S., & Koechlin, E. (2009). Motivation and cognitive control in the human prefrontal cortex. *Nature Neuroscience, 12(7)*, 939–945.

Kreibig, S. D. (2010). Autonomic nervous system activity in emotion: A review. *Biological Psychology, 84(3)*, 394–421.

LeDoux, J. (2012). Rethinking the emotional brain. *Neuron, 73(4)*, 653–676.

Lengfelder, A., & Gollwitzer, P. M. (2001). Reflective and reflexive action control in patients with frontal brain lesions. *Neuropsychology, 15(1)*, 80–100.

Levy, D. J., & Glimcher, P. W. (2012). The root of all value: A neural common currency for choice. *Current Opinion in Neurobiology, 22(6)*, 1027–1038.

Lieberman, M. D. (2007). The X- and C-systems: The neural basis of automatic and controlled social cognition. In E. Harmon-Jones and P. Winkielman (Eds.), *Social neuroscience: Integrating biological and psychological explanations of social behavior* (pp. 290–315). New York: Guilford Press.

Marvel, C. L., & Desmond, J. E. (2010). The contributions of cerebro-cerebellar circuitry to executive verbal working memory. *Cortex, 46(7)*, 880–895.

Metcalfe, J., & Mischel, W. (1999). A hot/cool-system analysis of delay of gratification: Dynamics of willpower. *Psychological Review, 106(1)*, 3–19.

Moors, A., & De Houwer, J. (2006). Automaticity: A theoretical and conceptual analysis. *Psychological Bulletin, 132(2)*, 297–326.

Napadow, V., Dhond, R., Conti, G., & Makris, N. (2008). Brain correlates of autonomic modulation: Combining heart rate variability with fMRI. *Neuroimage, 42(1)*, 169–177.

Noël, X., Colmant, M., Van Der Linden, M., Bechara, A., Bullens, Q., Hanak, C., & Verbanck, P. (2006). Time course of attention for alcohol cues in abstinent alcoholic patients: The role of initial orienting. *Alcoholism, Clinical and Experimental Research, 30(11)*, 1871–1877.

O'Doherty, J. P., Hampton, A., & Kim, H. (2007). Model-based fMRI and its application to reward learning and decision making. *Annals of the New York Academy of Sciences, 1104(1)*, 35–53.

Ohn, S. H., Park, C.-I., Yoo, W.-K., Ko, M.-H., Choi, K. P., Kim, G.-M., et al. (2008). Time-dependent effect of transcranial direct current stimulation on the enhancement of working memory. *Neuroreport, 19(1)*, 43–47.

Olson, M. A., & Fazio, R. H. (2004). Reducing the influence of extrapersonal associations on the Implicit Association Test: Personalizing the IAT. *Journal of Personality and Social Psychology, 86(5)*, 653–667.

Paulsen, D. J., Carter, R. M., Platt, M. L., Huettel, S. A., & Brannon, E. M. (2011). Neurocognitive development of risk aversion from early childhood to adulthood. *Frontiers in Human Neuroscience, 5*, 1–17.

Persson, J., Larsson, A., & Reuter-Lorenz, P. A. (2013). Imaging fatigue of interference control reveals the neural basis of executive resource depletion. *Journal of Cognitive Neuroscience, 25(3)*, 338–351.

Pessoa, L. (2009). How do emotion and motivation direct executive control? *Trends in Cognitive Sciences, 13(4)*, 160–166.

Peters, E., Västfjäll, D., Gärling, T., & Slovic, P. (2006). Affect and decision making: A "hot" topic. *Journal of Behavioral Decision Making, 19(2),* 79–85.

Pfeifer, J. H., & Allen, N. B. (2012). Arrested development? Reconsidering dual-systems models of brain function in adolescence and disorders. *Trends in Cognitive Sciences, 16(6),* 322–329.

Posner, M. I., & Petersen, S. E. (1990). The attention system of the human brain. *Annual Review of Neuroscience, 13,* 25–42.

Prencipe, A., Kesek, A., Cohen, J., Lamm, C., Lewis, M., & Zelazo, P. (2011). Development of hot and cool executive function during the transition to adolescence. *Journal of Experimental Child Psychology, 108(3),* 621–637.

Reisenzein, R., Meyer, W., & Schutzwohl, A. (1995). James and the physical basis of emotion: A comment on Ellsworth, *Psychological Review, 102(4),* 757–761.

Reyna, V. F., & Brainerd, C. J. (1995). Fuzzy-trace theory: An interim synthesis. *Learning and Individual Differences, 7(1),* 1–75.

Reyna, V. F., & Ellis, S. C. (1994). Fuzzy-trace theory and framing effects in children's risky decision making. *Psychological Science, 5(5),* 275–279.

Reyna, V. F., Estrada, S. M., DeMarinis, J. A., Myers, R. M., Stanisz, J. M., & Mills, B. A. (2011). Neurobiological and memory models of risky decision making in adolescents versus young adults. *Journal of Experimental Psychology: Learning, Memory, and Cognition, 37(5),* 1125–1142.

Reyna, V. F., & Farley, F. (2006). Risk and rationality in adolescent decision making: Implications for theory, practice, and public policy. *Psychological Science in the Public Interest, 7(1),* 1–44.

Richards, J. M., Plate, R. C., & Ernst, M. (2013). A systematic review of fMRI reward paradigms used in studies of adolescents vs. adults: The impact of task design and implications for understanding neurodevelopment. *Neuroscience and Biobehavioral Reviews, 37(5),* 976–991.

Rinck, M., & Becker, E. S. (2007). Approach and avoidance in fear of spiders. *Journal of Behavior Therapy and Experimental Psychiatry, 38(2),* 105–120.

Rivers, S. E., Reyna, V. F., & Mills, B. A. (2008). Risk taking under the influence: A fuzzy-trace theory of emotion in adolescence. *Developmental Review, 28(1),* 107–144.

Robbins, T. W. (2007). Shifting and stopping: Fronto-striatal substrates, neurochemical modulation and clinical implications. *Philosophical Transactions of the Royal Society of London. Series B, Biological Sciences, 362(1481),* 917–932.

Robbins, T. W., & Everitt, B. J. (1999). Drug addiction: Bad habits add up. *Nature, 398(6728),* 567–570.

Robinson, T. E., & Berridge, K. C. (1993). The neural basis of drug craving: An incentive-sensitization theory of addiction. *Brain Research Reviews, 18(3),* 247–291.

—— (2008). Review. The incentive sensitization theory of addiction: Some current issues. *Philosophical Transactions of the Royal Society of London. Series B, Biological Sciences, 363(1507),* 3137–3146.

Roelofs, K., Hagenaars, M. A., & Stins, J. (2010). Facing freeze: Social threat induces bodily freeze in humans. *Psychological Science, 21(11),* 1575–1581.

Satpute, A. B., & Lieberman, M. D. (2006). Integrating automatic and controlled processes into neurocognitive models of social cognition. *Brain Research, 1079(1),* 86–97.

Schneider, W., & Shiffrin, R. M. (1977). Controlled and automatic human information processing: I. Detection, search, and attention. *Psychological Review, 84(1),* 1–66.

Seger, C. A. (2008). How do the basal ganglia contribute to categorization? Their roles in generalization, response selection, and learning via feedback. *Neuroscience and Biobehavioral Reviews, 32(2),* 265–278.

Shiffrin, R. M., & Schneider, W. (1977). Controlled and automatic human information processing: II. Perceptual learning, automatic attending and a general theory. *Psychological Review, 84(2)*, 127–190.

Simon, J. R., & Rudell, A. P. (1967). Auditory S–R compatibility: The effect of an irrelevant cue on information processing. *Journal of Applied Psychology, 51(3)*, 300–304.

Somerville, L. H., Jones, R. M., & Casey, B. J. (2010). A time of change: Behavioral and neural correlates of adolescent sensitivity to appetitive and aversive environmental cues. *Brain and Cognition, 72(1)*, 124–133.

Spear, L. P. (2011). Rewards, aversions and affect in adolescence: Emerging convergences across laboratory animal and human data. *Developmental Cognitive Neuroscience, 1(4)*, 392–400.

Stacy, A. W., Ames, S. L., & Knowlton, B. J. (2004). Neurologically plausible distinctions in cognition relevant to drug use etiology and prevention. *Substance Use and Misuse, 39(10–12)*, 1571–1623.

Steinberg, L. (2010). A dual systems model of adolescent risk-taking. *Developmental Psychobiology, 52(3)*, 216–224.

Stephens, C. L., Christie, I. C., & Friedman, B. H. (2010). Autonomic specificity of basic emotions: Evidence from pattern classification and cluster analysis. *Biological Psychology, 84(3)*, 463–473.

Strack, F., & Deutsch, R. (2004). Reflective and impulsive determinants of social behavior. *Personality and Social Psychology Review, 8(3)*, 220–247.

Stroop, J. (1935). Studies of interference in serial verbal reactions. *Journal of Experimental Psychology, 18(6)*, 643–662.

Thayer, J. F., & Lane, R. D. (2000). A model of neurovisceral integration in emotion regulation and dysregulation. *Journal of Affective Disorders, 61(3)*, 201–216.

Thush, C., Wiers, R. W., Ames, S. L., Grenard, J., Sussman, S., & Stacy, A. W. (2008). Interactions between implicit and explicit cognition and working memory capacity in the prediction of alcohol use in at-risk adolescents. *Drug and Alcohol Dependence, 94(1–3)*, 116–124.

Tiffany, S. T. (1990). A cognitive model of drug urges and drug-use behavior: Role of automatic and nonautomatic processes. *Psychological Review, 97(2)*, 147–168.

Townshend, J. M., & Duka, T. (2007). Avoidance of alcohol-related stimuli in alcohol-dependent inpatients. *Alcoholism, Clinical and Experimental Research, 31(8)*, 1349–1357.

Van den Wildenberg, W., & Crone, E. (2005). Development of response inhibition and decision-making across childhood: A cognitive neuroscience perspective. In J. R. Marrow (Ed.), *Focus on child psychology research* (pp. 23–42). Hauppauge, NY: Nova Science Publishers.

Van Hecke, J., Gladwin, T. E., Coremans, J., Destoop, M., Hulstijn, W., & Sabbe, B. (2010). Prefrontal, parietal and basal activation associated with the reordering of a two-element list held in working memory. *Biological Psychology, 85(1)*, 143–148.

Vink, M., Pas, P., Bijleveld, E., Custers, R., & Gladwin, T. E. (2013). Ventral striatum is related to within-subject learning performance. *Neuroscience, 250*, 408–16.

Vollstädt-Klein, S., Loeber, S., von der Goltz, C., Mann, K., & Kiefer, F. (2009). Avoidance of alcohol-related stimuli increases during the early stage of abstinence in alcohol-dependent patients. *Alcohol and Alcoholism, 44(5)*, 458–463.

Volman, I., Roelofs, K., Koch, S., Verhagen, L., & Toni, I. (2011). Anterior prefrontal cortex inhibition impairs control over social emotional actions. *Current Biology, 21(20)*, 1766–1770.

Wickens, J. R., Budd, C. S., Hyland, B. I., & Arbuthnott, G. W. (2007). Striatal contributions to reward and decision making: Making sense of regional variations in a reiterated processing matrix. *Annals of the New York Academy of Sciences, 1104(1)*, 192–212.

Wiers, R. W., Bartholow, B. D., van den Wildenberg, E., Thush, C., Engels, R. C. M. E., Sher, K. J., et al. (2007). Automatic and controlled processes and the development of addictive behaviors in adolescents: A review and a model. *Pharmacology, Biochemistry, and Behavior, 86(2)*, 263–283.

Wiers, R. W., Beckers, L., Houben, K., & Hofmann, W. (2009). A short fuse after alcohol: Implicit power associations predict aggressiveness after alcohol consumption in young heavy drinkers with limited executive control. *Pharmacology, Biochemistry, and Behavior, 93(3)*, 300–305.

Wiers, R. W., Gladwin, T. E., Hofmann, W., Salemink, E., & Ridderinkhof, K. R. (2013). Cognitive bias modification and cognitive control training in addiction and related psychopathology: Mechanisms, clinical perspectives, and ways forward. *Clinical Psychological Science, 1(2)*, 192–212.

Wiers, R. W., Rinck, M., Dictus, M., & van den Wildenberg, E. (2009). Relatively strong automatic appetitive action-tendencies in male carriers of the OPRM1 G-allele. *Genes, Brain, and Behavior, 8(1)*, 101–106.

Williams, J. M., Mathews, A., & MacLeod, C. (1996). The emotional Stroop task and psychopathology. *Psychological Bulletin, 120(1)*, 3–24.

9

Neuroeconomics and Dual Information Processes Underlying Charitable Giving

STEPHAN DICKERT, DANIEL VÄSTFJÄLL,
AND PAUL SLOVIC

Every year, billions of dollars are donated to charity organizations for a wide range of causes. However, the underlying mechanisms of charitable giving are not well understood. The seemingly contradictory motives of helping others while at the same time following egoistic goals present a challenge for both practical as well as theoretical perspectives in the social sciences. In the current chapter, we outline how the concept of dual information processing and insights from neuroeconomics can help explain some of the behavioral deviations from rational assumptions in the domain of donation decisions. Specifically, we show how affective information processing and the influence of emotions can lead to effects like pseudo-inefficacy, magnitude insensitivity, identifiability, and proportion dominance. Neuroscientific evidence strengthens the viewpoint that the interaction of affect and deliberation is a key ingredient in understanding why people sometimes help and sometimes fail to help others in need.

When made aware of the misfortune of others, we are often inclined to offer help. While we do not always follow such impulses, offering help to those in need seems to be a common phenomenon in most societies. There are many ways in which one can alleviate the suffering of others, and donating to charitable causes is one way to do this. Prosocial behavior organized on a larger scale often takes the form of charity organizations soliciting financial contributions from potential donors. While it is also possible to donate time, clothes, or other consumer goods, many nongovernmental organizations (NGOs) are specifically interested in acquiring financial contributions. Every year billions of dollars are donated to charity organizations in the USA alone for a wide range of causes, including domestic and international aid programs for humanitarian as well as environmental causes (National Philanthropic Trust, 2012). Some donors are responding to current catastrophes like Hurricane Sandy in the USA while others focus on more permanent crises (e.g., endeavors to help starving people in Africa, saving the rain forest and endangered species, and reducing environmental pollution). These examples highlight that the study of charitable giving is closely related to the practical challenges faced by NGOs that rely on donations to fund charitable projects. However, at the heart of the endeavors to secure financial aid is a question that has a rich theoretical background and longstanding history: Why do people help others in distress?

For many centuries, philosophers (e.g., Plato, Descartes, Hume, Kant) have studied and debated the fundamental question of what motivates a person to help someone else. Part of this ongoing discussion revolves around normative moral aspects (e.g., moral obligations to help others, moral dilemmas and how they should be resolved), while other parts delineate the societal, political, and economic implications of redistributions of wealth. More recently, other disciplines (such as psychology, economics, and neuroscience) have addressed this question as one of the main challenges in their fields of research.

A careful and comprehensive review of the economic literature on philanthropy (Andreoni, 2006) documents the hundreds of articles on this topic in the past 40 years, many seeking to reconcile the seemingly unselfish and altruistic behavior of philanthropists with the assumption of self-interest and egoistic motives central to economics. Economic theory posits that people are rational and seek to maximize their utility, which is often conceptualized in terms of personal welfare and profit. One of the central assumptions is based on the idea of *homo economicus*, the rational man, who is concerned about his own payoff and does not care about others' welfare as long as it does not affect his own. According to this reasoning, people with the narrow self-interest of maximizing their own utility would not benefit from sharing their resources with others if they get nothing in return. Much of traditional economic theory is based on this assumption and contrasted by more recent accounts that include social or other-regarding preferences (e.g., Fehr & Schmidt, 1999; Loewenstein, Thompson, & Bazerman, 1989).[1] These recent accounts show that one's utility can be dependent on the state of others' welfare and highlight that social comparisons influence economic decisions.

Studies on charitable giving, regardless of whether they are done in a controlled laboratory setting or conducted as field research, are often concerned with the moderating influences and factors that determine when someone is willing to contribute to a good cause. Many methods are available to measure such influences on charitable giving, including straight requests for donations either through mail solicitations (Karlan, List, & Shafir, 2011) or telephone calls (Shang, Reed, & Croson, 2008), and several economic "games" that measure cooperation and trade-offs in social and moral dilemmas (e.g., prisoner's dilemma games, give-some games, trust games, public goods dilemmas).

Psychologists have also been interested in the role of altruistic vs. selfish motives in prosocial behavior. For example, research has found contradicting results regarding the importance of altruism (e.g., Batson, 1990) and egoism (e.g., Cialdini et al., 1987; Schaller & Cialdini, 1988) in charitable giving. Based on more recent evidence, some scholars believe that both factors are operating together in a circular and mutually reinforcing relationship, such that people who are happier give more to charity and that, in turn, giving makes people happier (Dunn, Aknin, & Norton, 2008). A defining feature of recent psychological research on giving is the specific focus on the affective and cognitive processes underlying these different motivations and the resulting valuations of human lives. This approach seems to be quite promising, as charitable giving is usually not determined by simple, monocausal reasons. On the contrary, in a recent review of over 500 scholarly articles, Bekkers and Wiepking (2011) concluded that the reasons for charitable giving are numerous, multifaceted, and usually the result of multiple mechanisms working at once. Understanding the underlying processes might shed some light on the otherwise isolated effects that are associated with decisions to help others.

In this chapter, we aim to provide insights into recent psychological and neuroeconomic developments in research on charitable giving. Specifically, we will build on a dual processing perspective to explain some of the behavioral effects prevalent in donation decisions. We conclude with a neuropsychological perspective on the role of brain activation underlying the different processes.

THE DUAL PROCESSING FRAMEWORK

Several theories of human information processing point toward two qualitatively different yet interconnected processing modes (e.g., Chaiken & Trope, 1999; Epstein, 1994; Evans, 2008; Kahneman, 2003, 2011; Kahneman & Frederick, 2002; Reyna, 2004; Sloman, 1996; Stanovich & West, 2000). Although research on dual processing has generated different labels for the two processes, important commonalities exist. One mode is characterized by relatively quick, automatic, effortless, associative, concrete, and affective processing. The other is thought to be slower, more effortful, rule-based, controlled, and abstract. Even though the specific content of the different dual-process theories varies to some extent, all have the assumption in common that reality can be mentally represented in two distinct ways. While fuzzy-trace theory (FTT; Reyna & Brainerd, 1995) posits that information can be processed on the basis of verbatim vs. gist representations, the conceptualization by Kahneman (2003, 2011) stresses the slow vs. fast distinction of the thinking process underlying different judgment and decision biases. Sloman (2002) suggests that two forms of conceptually different mental computations are performed by the associative system and the rule-based system. In the present chapter, we will use the terminology of Stanovich and West (2000), who distinguish "System 1" from "System 2." System 1 is sensitive to perceptual similarities of the features in one's environment, where information is processed based on the degree to which it can be meaningfully grouped into a coherent set of clusters that reflect one's perceptual reality. System 2, on the other hand, processes information on the bases of abstractions and logical, rule-based reasoning. This formulation is largely compatible with Epstein's (1994) suggestion that information can be processed in an experiential way and an analytical way. Table 9.1 summarizes some of the

Table 9.1   Two modes of information processing.

Information Processing Mode	
System 1	**System 2**
Fast	Slow
Automatic	Controlled
Parallel	Serial
Effortless	Effortful
Associative	Rule-based
Affective	Deliberative

characteristics of the two systems (for a more detailed summary, see Evans, 2008). The two processes are thought to inform and influence each other. For example, System 2 is suggested to control output from System 1 and is capable of overriding the resulting conclusions and preferences if better decision alternatives exist (Kahneman, 2011).

Nonetheless, it is also important to mention that the dual processing framework has its critics who point out that these theories infer different processing modes merely from different choice behavior and may suffer from circularity. For example, if people react differently when put under time pressure, proponents of the standard dual processing framework interpret this finding as evidence that System 2 did not have enough time to control output from System 1. Accordingly, when deprived of sufficient time to reflect on the choice options and weigh the pros and cons deliberatively, other aspects of the decision gain in importance (e.g., the affective appeal of a choice option). However, even if these critics point to the possibility of just one process instead of two (and, for example, construct beautiful computational neural network models to prove this), it remains clear that reality can be interpreted and mentally represented in distinctly different ways. This becomes most evident in choice dilemmas in which people prefer one option if they listen to their heart (i.e. feelings) and another, diametrically opposite option when they listen to their head (i.e. their thoughts). Although useful for imitating some cognitive processes, computational models that focus exclusively on simulating neural activity may fall short in conceptualizing the meaning of information to the individual and how it is subjectively perceived.

In the psychological domain, the proposition for a separation between affective and cognitive processing was prominently advanced by Zajonc (1980), who suggested that (unconscious) emotions sometimes precede cognitions.[2] Contrary to the viewpoint that all emotions require prior cognitive appraisals (Lazarus, 1991),[3] Zajonc argued that emotions substantially influence preferences and do not need to depend on conscious cognitive representations. Evidence from neuroscience that utilizes brain imaging techniques and lesion studies further supports a distinction between two systems of information processing (Bechara, Damasio, Tranel, & Damasio, 1997; Bush, Luu, & Posner, 2000; Damasio, 1994). Specifically, Damasio and colleagues found that neurological damage to specific brain regions (ventromedial prefrontal cortex; Brodmann's areas 10 and 11) impedes affective processing without impairing deliberative ability. Yet affective processing seems necessary to do well on experience-based decision-making tasks (e.g., the Iowa gambling task) that require the integration of affective information into people's preferences. Using a variant of the Iowa gambling task and controlling for working-memory ability, Peters and Slovic (2000) found that people with higher affective reactivity did better in learning to make good choices and stay away from bad choices. Further evidence for separate affective vs. cognitive information processing is provided by a review on the neural activity in the anterior cingulate cortex, which found dorsal pathways for cognitive tasks (e.g., a counting Stroop task) vs. more ventral pathways for affective tasks (e.g., an affective Stroop task; Bush et al., 2000).

The characteristics of the dual information processing modes that are probably most useful for the study of charitable giving revolve around the distinction between affective vs. deliberative information processing. As we will show below, the reason for this is based on the fact that charitable giving is often motivated by emotional reactions to the suffering of others. Similarly, deliberate thinking can motivate or de-motivate helping, for example by facilitating or inhibiting emotional reactions.

THE ROLE OF EMOTIONS AND COGNITIONS IN CHARITABLE GIVING

Emotions play a special role in motivating prosocial behavior. Humans are equipped with the capacity to empathize and feel someone else's suffering. When we are exposed to the misery of others, we often also feel bad in response.[4] The empathic concern for someone else, often expressed as compassion or sympathy, seems to be a key emotional experience associated with helping (Batson, 1990). However, a second cluster of emotions that can also lead to helping responses is related to the perceiver (Cialdini et al., 1987; Dickert, Sagara, & Slovic, 2011). Feelings of guilt, shame, or regret are examples of emotions that motivate people to engage in prosocial activities in order to reduce the experienced empathic distress. It is unclear which type of emotion is more potent in motivating people's willingness to contribute money to people in need. However, in our studies (e.g., Dickert, 2008; Dickert et al., 2011), we found that self-focused emotions (e.g., anticipated regret) are often the better predictors for helping responses (especially the frequency of helping). Only under specific circumstances was sympathy and compassion related to helping. In one study we found that when participants' cognitive capacity was reduced (i.e. under high cognitive load), donation amounts were predicted by the expressed sympathy for the person(s) in need. Conversely, under low cognitive load participants' donation amounts were only related to how donors felt about themselves (e.g., how much better they would feel if they donated). Similar results emerged in a different study, where priming participants to process information affectively (i.e. by having participants express emotions to unrelated material; see also Hsee & Rottenstreich, 2004; and Small, Loewenstein, & Slovic, 2007) increased the relationship between other-focused emotions and helping responses. When participants were primed to process information deliberatively (by doing math problems prior to the donation decision; Hsee & Rottenstreich, 2004), only self-focused emotions predicted helping responses. Additionally, when the decision to help is split into two consecutive decisions (one being the initial willingness to contribute anything at all and the other being the actual amount of money people are willing to donate), only self-focused emotions are related to people's initial willingness to contribute. Based on these results, we proposed a two-stage model of donation decisions in which the impact of egoistic motivations (i.e. mood management) is separable from the impact of altruistic motivations springing from empathic concern.[5]

Whereas the facilitating effects of empathic emotions usually influence charitable giving in similar ways (i.e. if people feel more empathic concern, they are more likely to donate money), the role of thoughts and deliberations seems to be more complex. The decision to help others can also stem from careful deliberations and analytical reasoning without strong empathic concern. For example, the decision whether to give to charity might depend on thoughts about how much money can be spared[6] or how effective a donation would be. However, in recent depictions of information processing underlying donation decisions, deliberative reasoning is thought to reduce the willingness to help because it distracts from the feelings otherwise needed to motivate helping (Loewenstein & Small, 2007; Slovic, 2010). Compelling evidence for this proposition comes from research done by Small, Loewenstein, and Slovic (2007) who found that adding information that is difficult to process affectively reduced people's willingness to help starving children. In one study, participants were willing to give higher donations to an individual life when it was presented without statistical information on how many lives are at risk. Another study demonstrated that priming participants to calculate (rather than focus on their feelings) also reduced donations to identifiable people in need. Later studies by Dickert et al. (2011) replicated these results and confirmed that the sympathy and compassion toward the people in need was reduced when information was processed deliberatively.

BEHAVIORAL BIASES IN VALUATIONS OF LIVES

When valuing the lives of others, people are prone to exhibit similar biases as in other decision domains, including framing effects (Li, Vietri, Galvani, & Chapman, 2010) and preference reversals (Dickert, Västfjäll, Kleber, & Slovic, 2012). Both affective and cognitive processes are involved in creating these biases. Moreover, these valuations are influenced by individual differences such as numeric ability (e.g., Dickert, Kleber, Peters, & Slovic, 2011) and just-world belief (Kogut, 2011). Of specific interest for the current chapter are behavioral biases leading to helping responses that might seem strange or at odds with normative approaches to the study of giving. What is normative, of course, depends either on what is commonly accepted to be the norm or what is dictated by logical reasoning (Baron, 2008; Dickert et al., 2012). Although the search for deviations from normative valuations is still ongoing and far from being complete, we will highlight the effects of psychophysical numbing, magnitude insensitivity, identifiability, pseudo-inefficacy, and proportion dominance on charitable giving.

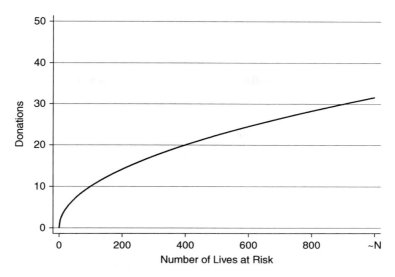

Figure 9.1   Psychophysical numbing function.

PSYCHOPHYSICAL NUMBING

Although many people would probably agree to the maxim that every (statistical) life should be valued equally, empirical data support the notion that donations to people in need are not linearly related to the number of lives at risk (Fetherstonhaugh, Slovic, Johnson, & Friedrich, 1997). Valuations of lives often follow a curvilinear relationship as the number of lives at risk increases, a nonnormative phenomenon that Fetherstonhaugh and colleagues termed "psychophysical numbing" (see Figure 9.1). The decreasing marginal increase in valuations depicts diminished sensitivity to changes in lives at risk against the backdrop of a larger tragedy. In other words, the psychophysical properties of this function imply that each individual life becomes less valuable as the number of people at risk increases.

The psychophysical response to an increase in the number of lives at risk is closely related to a decreasing affective sensitivity when large groups of people are in danger (Slovic, 2007). In fact, the apathetic response to human tragedies on a greater scale (such as genocides) speaks to the importance of affect as a motivating force in helping others.[7]

MAGNITUDE INSENSITIVITY

When people are asked to set a price for a market good, economic theory suggests that the quantity of this good figures into the valuation thereof. Similarly, for nonmarket goods (e.g., human lives, environmental protection, and preservation of endangered species) the magnitude should also have consequences for its valuation. For nonmarket goods, researchers have developed a method to measure how much preserving nonmarket and public goods is worth to the individual (i.e. contingent valuation; Mitchell & Carson, 1989; Venkatachalam, 2004). While contingent valuation might work in principle, critics (e.g., Frederick & Fischhoff, 1998) point out that the method falls short when the nonmarket good is characterized by multiple units (instead of one person in need or one cause). For example, Desvouges et al. (1993) found that participants are willing to pay about the same amount for saving 2,000, 20,000, or 200,000 birds from drowning in oil ponds. Moreover, Frederick and Fischhoff (1998) found that participants were willing to pay similar amounts for saving endangered wild wolves in Maine, Wisconsin, or both States altogether. This insensitivity to changes in magnitude has also been found with other elicitation methods, and is not limited to nonmarket goods. For example, Hsee and Rottenstreich (2004) found that participants were not only willing to pay similar amounts to save one vs. four pandas; they were also insensitive to changes in the number of CDs to be bought from a friend. Importantly, Hsee and Rottenstreich point out that this insensitivity is stronger when the good to be valued is processed affectively: When people focus on their feelings, they are generally more insensitive (but see Gong & Baron, 2011).

According to one explanation for magnitude insensitivity (Kahneman & Frederick, 2005), people substitute an extensional attribute (e.g., the number of lives at risk) with a nonextensional one (e.g., a picture of a prototype of the group at risk). Envisioning a prototype should not differ depending on the size of the group. Such a prototype heuristic suggests that people do not answer the question of how much they value saving 20,000 oil soaked birds (which are arguably very difficult to mentally imagine), but instead use the image of a single oil soaked bird as a proxy for evaluating the different number of birds. This could explain why Desvouges and colleagues (1993) found virtually no difference in valuations across different sizes of bird flocks.

Further evidence for magnitude insensitivity comes from a number of studies that asked participants to state a willingness to contribute to a single person vs. a group in need (Kogut & Ritov, 2005a, 2005b, 2007). These studies attempt to raise money for children in need of financial help to survive. The number of lives at risk is varied and participants express their willingness to donate along with their emotional reaction. Kogut and Ritov found that under certain conditions single donation recipients are preferred, receive higher donation amounts, and elicit stronger feelings than groups of recipients (even when the single recipient is part of the larger group). Findings like this "singularity effect" cannot easily be explained by the prototype heuristic, as it constitutes a different form of magnitude insensitivity. In fact, participants were not insensitive to the magnitude as participants were in the Hsee and Rottenstreich (2004) studies. According to the prototype heuristic explanation, no differences in valuations between single and multiple people in need would have been expected. It seems more likely that the mechanisms behind the singularity effect are related to Gestalt principles of perception, such as how entitative (i.e. unitary and cohesive; Campbell, 1958) a group of needy people is perceived (Dickert, 2008; Kogut & Ritov, 2005a, 2005b; Slovic, 2007; Smith, Faro, & Burson, 2012). For example, Smith and colleagues (2012) report that presenting children as part of a unitary and cohesive family increases charitable giving. An additional explanation for the singularity effect is based on attentional mechanisms underlying the generation of feelings (Dickert & Slovic, 2009; Slovic, 2007). Single individuals are easier to visually focus on than groups, which in turn can influence the generation of empathic emotions.

Finally, the selective retrieval of values can exacerbate or ameliorate magnitude insensitivity (Reyna & Casillas, 2009). For example, while values related to the equality of all people could potentially increase magnitude sensitivity, values related to nationalism or family could have the opposite effect when lives of strangers or foreigners are at risk. Also, when sacred values are invoked (e.g., Baron & Spranca, 1997), people are less willing to make utilitarian trade-offs (which usually require magnitude sensitivity).

IDENTIFIABILITY

Another factor that leads valuations of human lives to deviate from normative expectations is related to the identifiability of the person in need (i.e. the identifiability effect). We tend to value identified lives more than unidentified or statistical lives (Jenni & Loewenstein, 1997; Schelling, 1968; Small & Loewenstein, 2003). Identified people in need generally receive more attention, provoke stronger emotions, and receive more money in charity requests. This can be problematic in the case of catastrophes affecting large numbers of people, most of whom remain unidentified and are depicted by statistics. Humanitarian aid organizations sometimes try to circumvent this problem by making use of representative single, identified individuals who can function as a prototype. Moreover, the same principle is applied in sponsorships for individual children, where donors are informed in detail about the sponsored child's needs and background. It feels better to give to someone who is identified. It also feels worse to not help someone who is identified. Some of the underlying causes of identifiability are related to feelings of responsibility (Cryder & Loewenstein, 2012) and donor efficacy (Cryder, Loewenstein, & Scheines, 2013; Erlandsson, Björklund, & Bäckström, 2013). As would be expected, donors were more likely to contribute to a charitable cause when that cause was described in more detail, which Cryder and colleagues (2013) attribute to the effectiveness of a donation and not the emotions that these details are generating. Although donor efficacy is an important concept in explaining charitable giving, it remains unclear to what extent this explanation can supplant the earlier idea that giving to charity is primarily driven by affective motivations. For example, Dickert (2008) found that donors were more likely to feel better about giving when they judged the donation to have a significant effect on the recipient.

PSEUDO-INEFFICACY AND PROPORTION DOMINANCE

Another striking example of how valuations of lives can deviate from normative considerations can be found in situations where the presence of people at risk who *cannot* be helped reduces donors' willingness to contribute to people who *can* be helped. Such situations arise when too many lives are at risk (and donors face budget constraints) or when other factors hinder the dispersion of aid (e.g., political instability in specific regions hit by catastrophes). Obviously, it can be argued that under normative (and rational) considerations decisions to help should not depend on information about those who cannot be helped. Västfjäll and Slovic (2011) termed this decline in motivation to help "pseudo-inefficacy," as it makes potential donors feel less effective in helping. They propose that the negative feeling of not helping demotivates by reducing the positive feeling associated with giving. The influence of lives not saved on donation decisions can also be seen (although less clearly) in studies that pit absolute vs. proportional help against each other and use preference scales instead of willingness to contribute paradigms (Bartels, 2006). Here participants tended to prefer higher proportional help over higher absolute help even though they indicated that this was not a normative response. Higher proportions usually entail smaller numbers of people who are not helped. More-over, proportions are usually easier to evaluate and have affective meaning, some-thing that absolute numbers often lack (Slovic, 2007; Slovic, Finucane, Peters, & MacGregor, 2002, 2004).

We propose that the presented behavioral biases in the valuation of human lives (i.e. psychophysical numbing, magnitude insensitivity, identifiability, pseudo-inefficacy, and proportion dominance) can best be understood by the underly-ing information processing in relation to the prosocial emotions that they elicit (Dickert et al., 2012). Valuations of human lives, expressed as donations, show a non-linear relationship when critical emotional processes are not triggered or are hampered by cognitive considerations (Loewenstein & Small, 2007). We will now turn to a brief overview of how neuroscience can inform the study of charitable giving in light of the dual processes underlying the behavioral biases in donation decisions.

NEUROECONOMIC PERSPECTIVES ON GIVING

Even though the neuroscientific study of charitable giving is still in its infancy (e.g., Mayr, Harbaugh, & Tankersley, 2009), it already offers several important insights. Among the questions that research in neuroeconomics seeks to answer are (1) why and when people donate, (2) the economic "puzzle" of selfless (pure altruism) vs. selfish (warm glow) giving and whether "giving" is rational, as well as (3) whether specific donation decisions recruit more affective or cognitive information pro-cessing. A few qualifying remarks are in order for these questions, however. First, the added benefit of neuroimaging studies for addressing the causes of people's donation decisions comes primarily from the fact that neuroscientists are able to correlate brain activation with donation decisions. The ability to inspect brain acti-vations and use them to predict when people decide to donate money is a valuation step forward, however since these activations are often responses to behavioral and situational manipulations they sometimes merely serve as reinforcement of behavioral theories already in place. Nonetheless, these verifications can still be an important part in the search for parsimonious explanations for charitable giv-ing. Secondly, the question of whether charitable giving is motivated primarily by selfless or selfish motives is often context dependent and also varies by donor. Research in neuroeconomics pays special attention to these different motives while also recognizing a third alternative: impure altruism, which combines both sets of motives. Depending on the situation and variance between individuals, the neural data support all three possibilities. Finally, with regard to the separation of affective and deliberative processes it should be noted that a strict division of these processes is most likely an oversimplification. Both affective and deliberative processes are involved in most charitable giving decisions (Dickert, 2008; Loewenstein & Small, 2007). Nonetheless, brain imaging helps identify the neural circuits and brain structures typically associated with one or another kind of information processing.

The insights offered by neuroeconomics regarding people's decisions to give to charity are closely linked to the processing of rewards. The act of giving is related to activations in reward areas with dopaminergic connections, including the ventral striatum, nucleus accumbens, insulae, and select parts of the orbitofrontal cortex (OFC). So-called "reward centers" and dopaminergic projections in the subcortical midbrain regions (e.g., Schultz, 2009) are a vital part in valuations of how good or rewarding something is (Balleine, Daw, & O'Doherty, 2009), and neural activity in these areas is responsive to both concrete primary rewards (such as food or drugs) as well as more abstract secondary rewards (Knutson & Cooper, 2005; O'Doherty, 2004). The integration of positive and negative reward signals into more abstract representations seems to involve the ventromedial prefrontal cortex and the OFC (Shenhav & Greene, 2010). Moreover, these same areas are involved in processing rewards for the self as well as for others (Harbaugh, Mayr, & Burghart, 2007; Moll, et al., 2006). It is therefore conceivable that the motivation to donate money is strongly linked to activations of the neural reward circuitry. This would complement the behavioral findings that donating money increases the well-being of the donor (Dunn et al., 2008). In fact, a study by Harbough and colleagues (2007) suggests that activations in the ventral striatum (which is associated with emotional and motivational aspects of behavior and features many dopaminergic connections) can be used to predict the amount given to charity. When participants received money, stronger activation in the ventral striatum (among other related regions) predicted that these participants were less likely to give money to charity on other trials. Conversely, stronger neural activation in trials when the charity received money (at no cost to the participant) predicted participants' giving on other trials.

The second important contribution revolves around the (economic) debate of whether charitable giving constitutes rational behavior based on utility calculations and whether it is borne out of selfish or selfless motivations. As we mentioned at the beginning of the chapter, philanthropy may be difficult to explain with classical economic theory and the viewpoint of purely self-interested rational individuals (unless one allows for differences in social preferences; Fehr & Schmidt, 1999). Neuroeconomics has touched on this debate as well. For example, Mayr et al. (2009) conclude that the neural evidence supports a rational choice model of giving, such that people only give to charity if the utility they receive from that outweighs the costs of giving (for behavioral evidence, see also Rubaltelli & Agnoli, 2012). Arguments like these are compelling since the neural data suggest that similar brain areas are active when people receive and give money (e.g., Harbaugh et al., 2007). However, whether giving is really rational (regardless of selfish or selfless motivations) is debatable (Dickert et al., 2012). As long as one pits utilities derived from giving against the utilities derived from keeping the money (as in cost–benefit analyses) it seems easy to declare that giving is in the rational self-interest of the donor (if benefits > costs). It is unclear how the behavioral anomalies that we discussed above fit into this view. For example, magnitude insensitivity and the singularity effect lead to donation behavior that often favors saving fewer lives (at similar costs) even though saving more should give higher utilities. Likewise, pseudo-inefficacy is an example of how seemingly irrelevant information can reduce the utility of giving. Regardless of its input into the rationality debate of charitable giving, the neural data from Harbaugh et al. (2007) do provide evidence for both selfless giving (as proposed by Batson, 1990) as well as selfish giving (as proposed by Cialdini et al., 1987), which could be subsumed under a theory of impure altruism. Also, Mayr et al. (2009) suggest that the neural activation in the ventral striatum underlying selfish motivations does not monotonically increase when the number of people in need increases. Recent neuroscientific evidence shows that activation in the striatum is higher for identified victims, and that this activation predicts donation amounts (Genevsky, Västfjäll, Slovic, & Knutson, 2013). This would be in line with arguments regarding people's emotional apathy when confronted with victims of catastrophes (Slovic, 2007, 2010).

The third contribution (and perhaps the most relevant for the current chapter) is related to the question of affective vs. deliberative information processing in charitable giving. Seminal work on the neural correlates of affective vs. deliberative processing has been conducted using various forms of moral dilemmas (e.g., Greene, Nystrom, Engell, Darley, & Cohen, 2004; Greene, Sommerville, Nystrom, Darley, & Cohen, 2001). In many regards the decision to donate is quite similar to moral (and also social) dilemmas. Both situations involve difficult tradeoffs between the advantages and disadvantages of helping others. For example, donors with limited budgets will have to decide which of many available humanitarian aid projects is worthy of financial support. Additionally, both moral judgments and decisions about charitable giving seem to recruit similar neural circuitry (Mayr et al., 2009), and the same brain regions are also involved in calculations about losses of lives as in economic expected value calculations about payoffs (Shenhav & Greene, 2010; see also Montague & Berns, 2002). These valuations include, among other structures, the subcortical regions (striatum, thalamus, and amygdala) as well as the more cortical regions (cingulate cortex, insula, and vmPFC) (Hare, Camerer, Knoepfle, & Rangel, 2010; Knutson, Taylor, Kaufman, Peterson, & Glover, 2005).

Investigating the neural activations for cognitive conflicts in moral dilemmas such as the trolley and footbridge dilemmas sheds light on the underlying mechanisms of charitable giving. In the trolley dilemma, participants are faced with the situation in which a trolley is heading toward five workers on the tracks who will be killed by the trolley. Participants have to decide whether they save the lives of the five people by pulling a switch that redirects the trolley onto a different track, sacrificing the live of another person who is working on the other track. The footbridge dilemma is a variant of this, where participants have to decide whether they push a person off a footbridge to be killed by the trolley (and thereby saving the five other lives). Some moral judgments are resolved via socio-emotional responses, while others are resolved with utilitarian considerations. Greene et al.

(2004) suggest that the socio-emotional responses, which tend to be triggered by personally framed dilemmas (e.g., when information about the lives at risk is vivid and emotionally engaging), map best onto deontological approaches to moral dilemmas. Conversely, utilitarian responses, which tend to be triggered by more impersonally framed dilemmas (e.g., when information about lives at risk is abstract and difficult to imagine vividly), map onto consequential approaches.[8] Also, personally framed dilemmas (e.g., pushing another person off the footbridge vs. throwing a switch) recruit socio-emotional neural circuitry (e.g., activations in the ventral striatum and medial prefrontal cortex) whereas impersonally framed dilemmas recruit more "cognitive" neural circuits (e.g., activations in the dorsolateral prefrontal cortex; Greene et al., 2001). Automatic emotions often interfere with utilitarian judgments (Greene et al., 2004). This is further supported by lesion studies that found persons with damage to the orbitofrontal cortex (which has been implicated in emotional processing; Damasio, 1994) to be more "rational" in the trade-offs of lives (Koenigs et al., 2007). It thus seems reasonable to assume that framing charitable requests as more personal, with more vivid and emotionally engaging material, recruits brain regions that are typically involved in emotional processing. A more "cognitive" donation decision (e.g., based on effectiveness considerations) might recruit the dlPFC, a more "emotional" donation decision (e.g., based on sympathy) that most likely involves subcortical structures related to dopaminergic projections (e.g., ventral striatum). A direct consequence of this reasoning would be to assume that emotional donation decisions are linked to experiencing rewards, whereas cognitive donation decisions would not be related to subjectively experienced rewards.

Additionally, neuroscientific evidence supports the notion that emotion regulation plays an important part in the resolution of dilemmas and charitable giving. For example, humanizing the victims of catastrophes is likely to engage more brain activity related to emotional regulation (Majdandzic et al., 2012). In terms of affect regulation, activity in the dlPFC predicts more utilitarian judgments and less emotional judgments (Greene et al., 2004). This is in line with evidence that the dlPFC is involved in deliberative thought processes (e.g., Beer, Knight, & D'Esposito, 2006) and was also found to be engaged in regulating emotional input in social decision making (Sanfey et al., 2003).[9] The conflict between utilitarian and nonutilitarian solutions activates the anterior cingulate cortex (ACC), which is commonly thought to be involved in the processing of conflict and error detection (Posner & Raichle, 1994). Greene and colleagues (2004) suggest that the ACC could be involved in conflict resolution that arises in difficult moral dilemmas where utilitarian vs. deontological approaches clash (i.e. when the decision to help is answered differently by deliberative and utilitarian reasoning vs. affective information processes).

SUMMARY

In the present chapter we outlined the usefulness of a dual information processing framework and neuroeconomics to understand the psychological mechanisms underlying charitable giving. While donating to charity is often multi-causal and multi-determined, research points to the importance of emotions such as sympathy and compassion to motivate giving. The role of deliberative thought has been depicted as interfering with the generation of emotions. However, it should be noted that deliberative reasoning can also lead to charitable giving. As in most complex decisions, it can be expected that both deliberative and affective emotion processing is involved. Some recently discovered behavioural "anomalies," such as psychophysical numbing, magnitude insensitivity and singularity effects, identified victim effects, as well as pseudo-inefficacy and proportion dominance demonstrate that charitable giving does not always follow normative or rational considerations. Finally, we presented neuroscientific evidence to show that affective processes indeed seem to recruit different neural activity than more deliberative, utilitarian processes in donation decisions. The question why people donate money to charity will continue to stimulate research, and we believe that the underlying affective and deliberative processes are central in the search for answers.

NOTES

1. This viewpoint is related to the concept of *homo reciprocans*, depicted as a person who values cooperation and gains utility from improving others' welfare.
2. The proposition that "reasons" and "passions" are separable and often have contradictory influences on behavior dates back more than 2,500 years in Western philosophy in the works of Aristotle (cited in Zajonc, 2004).
3. This alternative account proposes that emotions are based on appraisals, which are inherently cognitive in nature. Thus, emotions such as fear of a spider would arise due to the cognitive appraisal that a spider bite might be poisonous and should be avoided at all cost.
4. Interestingly, we feel compassion toward animals as well and are willing to spend significant portions of money for their rescue should they be in danger. For example, to save a dog stranded on a tanker adrift in the Pacific Ocean the coast guard spent more than $300,000 (reported in Vedantam, 2010).
5. This is in line with reasoning on dual information processing in Reyna and Casillas (2009), who argue that categorical decisions in the form of none vs. some (i.e. no donation vs. some donation) are governed by different mental representations than ordinal decisions (e.g., some donation vs. some higher donation).
6. The fact that money can only be given to charity if potential donors are financially able to donate is obvious and only worth mentioning here because it is sometimes used as an argument to distract from the importance of studying the underlying motivations to give.
7. An alternative account to affective insensitivity is offered by Reyna and Casillas (2009), who point out that the highest sensitivity to lives at risk occurs when making a qualitative change from no life at risk to some life at risk, and that people are somewhat less sensitive to quantitative changes (e.g., from some lives at risk to some more lives at risk).
8. A deontological perspective would solve moral dilemmas by referring to general moral values that hold true regardless of the circumstances. A consequentialist would solve moral dilemmas by choosing the course of action that benefits the greater good, even if this means violating firmly held, general moral values.
9. However, one needs to be careful to not equate utilitarian judgment with a purely cognitive thought process. Emotions seem to be very important in utilitarian and rational judgments as well (e.g., Damasio, 1994; Slovic, 2007).

REFERENCES

Andreoni, J. (2006). Philanthropy. In S.-C. Kolm & J. M. Mercier (Eds.), *Handbook of the economics of giving, altruism and reciprocity* (pp. 1201–1269). Amsterdam: Elsevier/North-Holland.

Balleine, B. W., Daw, N. D., & O'Doherty, J. P. (2009). Multiple forms of value learning and the function of dopamine. In P. W. Glimcher, C. F. Camerer, E. Fehr, & R. A. Poldrack (Eds.), *Neuroeconomics: Decision making and the brain* (pp. 367–389). London: Elsevier.

Baron, J. (2008). *Thinking and deciding* (4th ed.). Cambridge: Cambridge University Press.

Baron, J., & Spranca, M. (1997). Protected values. *Organizational Behavior and Human Decision Processes, 70(1)*, 1–16.

Bartels, D. M. (2006). Proportion dominance: The generality and variability of favoring relative savings over absolute savings. *Organizational Behavior and Human Decision Processes, 100(1)*, 76–95.

Batson, C. D. (1990). How social an animal? The human capacity for caring. *American Psychologist, 45(3)*, 336–346.

Bechara, A., Damasio, H., Tranel, D., & Damasio, A. R. (1997). Deciding advantageously before knowing the advantageous strategy. *Science, 275(5304)*, 1293–1295.

Beer, J. S., Knight, R. T., & D'Esposito, M. (2006). Controlling the integration of emotion and cognition: The role of frontal cortex in distinguishing helpful from hurtful emotional information. *Psychological Science, 17(5)*, 448–453.

Bekkers, R., & Wiepking, P. (2011). A literature review of empirical studies of philanthropy: Eight mechanisms that drive charitable giving. *Nonprofit and Voluntary Sector Quarterly, 40(5)*, 924–973.

Bush, G., Luu, P., & Posner, M. (2000). Cognitive and emotional influences in anterior cingulate cortex. *Trends in Cognitive Sciences, 4(6)*, 215–221.

Campbell, D. T. (1958). Common fate, similarity, and other indices of the status of aggregates of persons as social entities. *Behavioral Science, 3(1)*, 14–25.

Chaiken, S., & Trope, Y. (1999). *Dual-process theories in social psychology*. New York, NY: Guilford Press.

Cialdini, R. B., Schaller, M., Houlihan, D., Arps, K., Fultz, J., & Beaman, A. L. (1987). Empathy-based helping: Is it selflessly or selfishly motivated? *Journal of Personality and Social Psychology, 52(4)*, 749–758.

Cryder, C., & Loewenstein, G. (2012). Responsibility: The tie that binds. *Journal of Experimental Social Psychology, 48(1)*, 441–445.

Cryder, C., Loewenstein, G., & Scheines, R. (2013). The donor is in the details. *Organizational Behavior and Human Decision Processes, 120(1)*, 15–23.

Damasio, A. R. (1994). *Descartes' error: Emotion, reason, and the human brain*. New York, NY: Avon.

Desvouges, W. H., Johnson, F., Dunford, R., Hudson, S., Wilson, K., & Boyle, K. (1993). Measuring natural resource damages with contingent valuation: Tests of validity and reliability. In J. A. Hausman (Ed.), *Contingent valuation: A critical assessment* (pp. 91–164). Amsterdam: North Holland.

Dickert, S. (2008). Two routes to the perception of need: The role of affective and deliberative information processing in pro-social behavior. Doctoral dissertation, University of Oregon, OR.

Dickert, S., Kleber, J., Peters, E., & Slovic, P. (2011). Numeric ability as a precursor to pro-social behavior: The impact of numeracy and presentation format on the cognitive mechanisms underlying donations. *Judgment and Decision Making, 6(7)*, 638–650.

Dickert, S., Sagara, N., & Slovic, P. (2011). Affective motivations to help others: A two-stage model of donation decisions. *Journal of Behavioral Decision Making, 24(4)*, 361–376.

Dickert, S., & Slovic, P. (2009). Attentional mechanisms in the generation of sympathy. *Judgment and Decision Making, 4(4)*, 297–306.

Dickert, S., Västfjäll, D., Kleber, J., & Slovic, P. (2012). Valuations of human lives: Normative expectations and psychological mechanisms of (ir)rationality. *Synthese, 189(1)*, 95–105.

Dunn, E. W., Aknin, L. B., & Norton, M. I. (2008). Spending money on others promotes happiness. *Science, 319(5870)*, 1687–1688.

Epstein, S. (1994). Integration of the cognitive and the psychodynamic unconscious. *American Psychologist, 49(8)*, 709–724.

Erlandsson, A., Björklund, F., & Bäckström, M. (2013). Perceived utility (not sympathy) mediates the proportion dominance effect in helping decisions. *Journal of Behavioral Decision Making, 27(1)*, 37–47.

Evans, J. St. B. T. (2008). Dual-processing accounts of reasoning, judgment, and social cognition. *Annual Review of Psychology, 59*, 255–278.

Fehr, E., & Schmidt, K. M. (1999). A theory of fairness, competition, and cooperation. *The Quarterly Journal of Economics, 114(3)*, 817–868.

Fetherstonhaugh, D., Slovic, P., Johnson, S. M., & Friedrich, J. (1997). Insensitivity to the value of human life: A study of psychophysical numbing. *Journal of Risk and Uncertainty, 14(3)*, 283–300.

Frederick, S. W., & Fischhoff, B. (1998). Scope (in)sensitivity in elicited valuations. *Risk, Decision, and Policy, 3(2)*, 109–123.

Genevsky, A., Västfjäll, D., Slovic, P., & Knutson, B. (2013). Neural underpinnings of the identifiable victim effect: Affect shifts preferences for giving. *Journal of Neuroscience, 33(43)*, 17188–17196.

Gong, M., & Baron, J. (2011). The generality of the emotion effect on magnitude sensitivity. *Journal of Economic Psychology, 32(1)*, 17–24.

Greene, J. D., Nystrom, L. E., Engell, A.D., Darley, J. M., & Cohen, J. D. (2004) The neural bases of cognitive conflict and control in moral judgment. *Neuron, 44(2)*, 389–400.

Greene, J. D., Sommerville, R. B., Nystrom, L. E., Darley, J. M., & Cohen, J. D. (2001). An fMRI investigation of emotional engagement in moral judgment. *Science 14(5537)*, 2105–2108.

Harbaugh, W. T., Mayr, U., & Burghart, D. R. (2007). Neural responses to taxation and voluntary giving reveal motives for charitable donations. *Science, 316(5831)*, 1622.

Hare, T. A., Camerer, C. F., Knoepfle, D. T., & Rangel, A. (2010). Value computations in ventral medial prefrontal cortex during charitable decision making incorporate input from regions involved in social cognition. *Journal of Neuroscience, 30(2)*, 583–590.

Hsee, C. K., & Rottenstreich, Y. (2004). Music, pandas, and muggers: On the affective psychology of value. *Journal of Experimental Psychology-General, 133(1)*, 23–30.

Jenni, K. E., & Loewenstein, G. (1997). Explaining the "identifiable victim effect." *Journal of Risk and Uncertainty, 14(3)*, 235–257.

Kahneman, D. (2003). A perspective on judgment and choice: Mapping bounded rationality. *American Psychologist, 58(9)*, 697–720.

——(2011). *Thinking, fast and slow*. New York, NY: Farrar, Straus & Giroux.

Kahneman, D., & Frederick, S. (2002). Representativeness revisited: Attribute substitution in intuitive judgment. In T. Gilovich, D. Griffin, & D. Kahneman (Eds.), *Heuristics and biases: The psychology of intuitive judgment* (pp. 49–81). New York, NY: Cambridge University Press.

—— 2005. *A model of heuristic judgment*. In K. J. Holyoak & R. G. Morrison (Eds.), *The Cambridge handbook of thinking and reasoning* (pp. 267–293). New York, NY: Cambridge University Press.

Karlan, D., List, J. A., & Shafir, E. (2011). Small matches and charitable giving: Evidence from a natural field experiment. *Journal of Public Economics, 95(5)*, 344–350.

Knutson, B., & Cooper, J. C. (2005). Functional magnetic resonance imaging of reward prediction. *Current Opinion in Neurology, 18(4)*, 411–417.

Knutson, B., Taylor, J., Kaufman, M., Peterson, R., & Glover, G. (2005). Distributed neural representation of expected value. *Journal of Neuroscience, 25(19)*, 4806–4812.

Koenigs, M., Young, L., Adolphs, R., Tranel, D., Cushman, F., Hauser, M., & Damasio, A. (2007). Damage to the prefrontal cortex increases utilitarian moral judgements. *Nature, 446(7138)*, 908–911.

Kogut, T. (2011). Someone to blame: When identifying a victim decreases helping. *Journal of Experimental Social Psychology, 47(4)*, 748–755.

Kogut, T., & Ritov, I. (2005a). The "identified victim" effect: An identified group, or just a single individual? *Journal of Behavioral Decision Making, 18(3)*, 157–167.

—— (2005b). The singularity effect of identified victims in separate and joint evaluations. *Organizational Behavior and Human Decision Processes, 97(2)*, 106–116.

—— (2007). "One of us": Outstanding willingness to help save a single identified compatriot. *Organizational Behavior and Human Decision Processes, 104(2)*, 150–157.

Lazarus, R. S. (1991). Cognition and motivation in emotion. *American Psychologist, 46(4)*, 352–367.

Li, M., Vietri, J., Galvani, A. P., & Chapman, G. B. (2010). How do people value life? *Psychological Science, 21(2)*, 163–167.

Loewenstein, G., & Small, D. A. (2007). The scarecrow and the tin man: The vicissitudes of human sympathy and caring. *Review of General Psychology, 11(11)*, 112–126.

Loewenstein, G., Thompson, L., & Bazerman, M. (1989). Social utility and decision making in interpersonal contexts. *Journal of Personality and Social Psychology, 57(3)*, 426–441.

Majdandžić, J., Bauer, H., Windischberger, C., Moser, M., Engl, E., & Lamm, C. (2012). The human factor: Behavioral and neural correlates of humanized perception in moral decision making. *PLoS ONE, 7(10)*, 1–14.

Mayr, U., Harbaugh, W., & Tankersley, D. (2009). Neuroeconomics of charitable giving and philanthropy. In P. W. Glimcher, C. F. Camerer, E. Fehr, & R. A. Poldrack (Eds.), *Neuroeconomics: Decision making and the brain* (pp. 303–320). London: Elsevier.

Mitchell, R. C., & Carson, R. T. (1989). *Using surveys to value public goods: The contingent valuation method*. Washington, DC: Resource for the Future.

Moll, J., Krueger, F., Zahn, R., Pardini, M., de Oliveira-Souza, R., & Grafman, J. (2006). Human fronto-mesolimbic networks guide decisions about charitable donation. *Proceedings of the National Academy of Sciences, 103(42)*, 15623–15628.

Montague, P., & Berns, G. (2002). Neural economics and the biological substrates of valuation. *Neuron, 36(2)*, 265–284.

National Philanthropic Trust (2012). *Charitable giving statistics*. Retrieved December 10, 2013, from www.nptrust.org/philanthropic-resources/charitable-giving-statistics.

O'Doherty, J. P. (2004). Reward representations and reward-related learning in the human brain: Insights from neuroimaging. *Current Opinion in Neurobiology, 14(6)*, 769–776.

Peters, E., & Slovic, P. (2000). The springs of action: Affective and analytical information processing in choice. *Personality and Social Psychology Bulletin, 26(12)*, 1465–1475.

Posner, M. I., & Raichle, M. E. (1994). *Images of mind*. New York, NY: Scientific American Books.

Reyna, V. F. (2004). How people make decisions that involve risk: A dual-processes approach. *Current Directions in Psychological Science, 13(2)*, 60–66.

Reyna, V. F., & Brainerd, C. J. (1995). Fuzzy-trace theory: An interim synthesis. *Learning and Individual Differences, 7(1)*, 1–75.

Reyna, V. F., & Casillas, W. (2009). Development and dual processes in moral reasoning: A fuzzy-trace theory approach. In B. H. Ross (Series Ed.) & D. M. Bartels, C. W. Bauman, L. J. Skitka, & D. L. Medin (Eds.), *Psychology of learning and motivation*, vol. L: *Moral judgment and decision making* (pp. 207–239). San Diego, CA: Elsevier Academic Press.

Rubaltelli, E., & Agnoli, S. (2012). The emotional cost of charitable donations. *Cognition and Emotion, 26(5)*, 769–785.

Sanfey, A. G., Rilling, J. K., Aronson J. A., Nystrom L. E., & Cohen, J. D. (2003). The neural basis of economic decision making in the Ultimatum Game. *Science, 300(5626)*, 1755–1758.

Schaller, F., & Cialdini, R. B. (1988). The economics of empathic helping: Support for a mood management motive. *Journal of Experimental Social Psychology, 24(2)*, 163–181.

Schelling, T. C. (1968). The life you save may be your own. In S. B. Chase (Ed.), *Problems in public expenditure analysis* (pp. 127–176). Washington, DC: The Brookings Institute.

Schultz, W. (2009). Midbrain dopamine neurons: A retina of the reward system. In P. W. Glimcher, C. F. Camerer, E. Fehr, & R. A. Poldrack (Eds.), *Neuroeconomics: Decision making and the brain* (pp. 323–330). London: Elsevier.

Shang, J., Reed, A., & Croson, R. (2008). Identity congruency effects on donations. *Journal of Marketing Research, 45(3)*, 351–361.

Shenhav, A., & Greene, J. D. (2010). Moral judgments recruit domain-general valuation mechanisms to integrate representations of probability and magnitude. *Neuron, 67(4)*, 667–677.

Sloman, S. (1996). The empirical case for two systems of reasoning. *Psychological Bulletin, 119(1)*, 3–22.

Slovic, P. (2007). "If I look at the mass I will never act": Psychic numbing and genocide. *Judgment and Decision Making, 2(2)*, 79–95.

——(2010). The more who die, the less we care. In E. Michel-Kerjan & P. Slovic (Eds.), *The irrational economist: Making decisions in a dangerous world* (pp. 30–40). New York, NY: Public Affairs.

Slovic, P., Finucane, M., Peters, E., & MacGregor, D. G. (2002). The affect heuristic. In T. Gilovich, D. Griffin, & D. Kahneman (Eds.), *Heuristics and biases: The psychology of intuitive judgment* (pp. 397–420). New York, NY: Cambridge University Press.

——(2004). Risk as analysis and risk as feelings: Some thoughts about affect, reason, risk, and rationality. *Risk Analysis, 24(2)*, 311–322.

Small, D. A., & Loewenstein, G. (2003). Helping a victim or helping the victim: Altruism and identifiability. *Journal of Risk and Uncertainty, 26(1)*, 5–16.

Small, D. A., Loewenstein, G., & Slovic, P. (2007). Sympathy and callousness: The impact of deliberative thought on donations to identifiable and statistical victims. *Organizational Behavior and Human Decision Processes, 102(2)*, 143–153.

Smith, R. W., Faro, D., & Burson, K. A. (2013). More for the many: The influence of entitativity on charitable giving. *Journal of Consumer Research, 39(5)*, 961–976.

Stanovich, K. E., & West, R. F. (2000). Individual differences in reasoning: Implications for the rationality debate? *Behavioral and Brain Sciences, 23(5)*, 645–665.

Västfjäll, D., & Slovic, P. (2011). Pseudo-inefficacy: When awareness of those we cannot help demotivates us from aiding those we can help. Working paper.

Vedantam, S. (2010). *The hidden brain: How our unconscious minds elect presidents, control markets, wage war, and save our lives*. New York, NY: Random House Publishing Group.

Venkatachalam, L. (2004). The contingent valuation method: A review. *Environmental Impact Assessment Review, 24(1)*, 89–124.

Zajonc, R. B. (1980). Feeling and thinking: Preferences need no inferences. *American Psychologist, 35(2)*, 151–175.

——(2000). Feeling and thinking: Closing the debate over the independence of affect. In J. P. Forgas (Ed.), *Feeling and thinking: The role of affect in social cognition* (pp. 31–58). New York, NY: Cambridge University Press.

Part V

Developmental and Individual Differences

10

Risky Choice from Childhood to Adulthood

Changes in Decision Strategies, Affect, and Control

ANNA C. K. VAN DUIJVENVOORDE,
BRENDA R. J. JANSEN, AND HILDE M. HUIZENGA

This chapter discusses developmental changes in decision making under risk from a multidisciplinary perspective. That is, to enhance understanding of children's and adolescents' decision making, we include findings from the judgment and decision-making literature, from developmental psychology, and from neuroimaging studies. We focus on two key aspects of decision making: (1) the use of different decision strategies and (2) the influences of affect and control in decision making. First, studies on the use of different decision strategies show that both normative and heuristic responding may increase with age, and that individual differences in decision strategy are pronounced. These individual differences have been linked to underlying neural activation in the medial and lateral prefrontal cortices in adult populations. These findings illustrate the need to further characterize and consider the use of different decision strategies in developmental (imaging) studies. Second, affect and control, and the balance between these processes, may change profoundly across childhood and adolescence. Such changes have been related to distinct maturational trajectories of subcortical and cortical brain regions. Here, we discuss studies that address how decision context may influence affect and control processes, and in this way interact with age-related differences in decision making. Additionally, we highlight approaches that characterize individual differences in risky decision making. Together, this multidisciplinary framework identifies key issues and future aims for the study of risky choice across development.

*D*ecision making is ubiquitous in daily life. Think of a typical day in which you are faced with a stream of decisions such as what to have for breakfast, how to travel to work, whether to accept that new job offer, whether to spend or save your money, whether to join that party or study, and so on. An important feature is that with many—if not most—decisions, the decision outcome carries a degree of uncertainty, i.e. a desired outcome may only occur with a certain probability. These types of decisions are commonly called decisions under risk.[1] This chapter discusses research on decision making under risk with a specific focus on developmental changes occurring across childhood and adolescence.

As a complex process, decision making can be broken down into basic subprocesses. For instance, think about a possible job offer you could be contemplating: You need to represent this decision problem, analyze the choice options, select an appropriate action, and eventually you will evaluate the outcomes of your choice (Rangel, Camerer, & Montague, 2008). These processes of decision making have been studied in many fields, ranging from economics and finance, to both cognitive and developmental psychology, as well as, most recently, neuroscience (Sharp, Monterosso, & Montague, 2012). Whereas economics and finance contribute models that describe decision making under risk, neuroscience investigates brain activation underlying decision making under risk (Fehr & Rangel, 2011). Psychology, on the other hand, provides theories on learning and choice behavior, and developmental psychology has focused on the maturational trajectories of decision making. Nowadays, eclectic fields have emerged, such as (developmental) neuroeconomics, that combine knowledge and integrate insights across these fields (Camerer, 2008).

In developmental psychology, there has been a long-lasting interest in the development of risky-choice behavior (e.g., Hall, 1904). For example, adolescence—the period defined by the start of puberty (around ages 10 to 12) up to the gaining of independence in early adulthood—presents an interesting paradox: While cognitive as well as physical capacities improve, mortality rates also increase. It is suggested that these fatalities may be partly attributed to poor choices, risky actions, and/or heightened emotionality (Eaton et al., 2008). However, adolescence is not only described as a period of pitfall to dangerous behavior and "risky" decision making (Casey, Getz, & Galvan, 2008; Somerville, Jones, & Casey, 2010) but also as a period of potential for flexibility, learning, and adaptive decision making (Crone & Dahl, 2012; Dahl, 2004). Changes in brain maturation are thought to underlie these specific sensitivities across development (Casey et al., 2008; Crone & Dahl, 2012). Taken together, there has been growing interest in studying the development of risky decision making, and understanding the neural maturational changes that underlie these developmental patterns.

In this chapter we discuss developmental changes in decision making under risk by highlighting insights from judgment and decision making, developmental psychology, and neuroimaging studies. We focus on two key aspects of decision making under risk: the use of different decision strategies and the influences of affect and control in decision making. Within these topics, we aim to present key findings from a multidisciplinary perspective.

DECISION STRATEGIES

Integrative Strategies and the Use of Heuristics

Finance and economics traditionally aim to explain and predict people's choice behavior under risk. A prominent framework in these fields is that people's choice behavior can be explained based on an integrated value strategy (Von Neumann & Morgenstern, 1944). That is, during choice, people assign a value to the available choice options, in which the option with the highest value is generally chosen. In (monetary) economic choice tasks, the value of an option is typically defined by the expected value of the option (i.e. the products of the probability and the gain/loss of each option) or its transformation, the expected utility of the option. Such economics models assume a certain "rationality" in choice behavior. That is, decision makers are assumed to have consistent beliefs and consistent preferences (Von Neumann & Morgenstern, 1944).

In contrast to economic theories, the very influential (and Nobel Prize-winning) prospect theory of risky decision making focuses on systematic biases and observed violations of utility-based models in people's decision making (Kahneman & Tversky, 1979). Prospect theory specified separate value functions for gains and losses, with the function for losses being steeper than that for gains, resulting in an effect known as loss aversion (i.e. losses loom larger), relative to a reference point (usually the status quo), and the change in value diminishes with the distance from this reference point (i.e. diminishing sensitivity). A second addition is the subjective evaluation of probability, to account for the fact that people tend to overweigh small probabilities (near 0; e.g., people's enthusiasm for lotteries, and also their need for insurance for incidents with low prevalence) but underweigh medium or high probabilities (near 1; e.g., the difference between a probability of .99 versus 1 looms larger than the difference between probabilities of .10 and .11). Third, it is also assumed that people engage in editing operations of choice. For instance, decision makers tend to simplify a choice option by rounding off numbers or by cancellation (i.e. cancel the shared components of options that are offered together) (Trepel, Fox, & Poldrack, 2005).

Prospect theory presents a flexible model for describing individuals' choice behavior under risk compared to more traditional financial models, however, it still demands an integration of subjective value (gains and losses) and subjective probability to determine choice behavior. An alternative view is that risky decisions may not rely on an integrative process but can be based on a set of comparative processes, such as the use of decision heuristics (Gigerenzer & Goldstein, 1996; Russo & Dosher, 1983; Tversky & Kahneman, 1974; Vlaev, Chater, Stewart, & Brown, 2011). Heuristics are "rules of thumb" that simplify the decision process by comparing options on a limited set of attributes. Heuristics may lead to biases in people's behavior, but heuristics have also been called fast and frugal, as they would yield faster choices which are sometimes equivalent to normative ones (Brandstätter, Gigerenzer, & Hertwig, 2006; Gigerenzer & Gaissmaier, 2011). In general, heuristics are non-integrative (do not involve an integration of attributes such as probability and value) and noncompensatory (negative values on one attribute cannot be compensated by positive values on another attribute). Different heuristics have been described in the literature. For example, in the "Take the Best" or the "Lexicographic" heuristic, attributes are sorted in order of importance and options are compared per attribute in a sequential manner. When a sufficiently large difference between attributes is detected, a choice is made (Brandstätter et al., 2006; Tversky & Slovic, 1988). The use of different decision heuristics has been tested by structural modeling approaches and process-tracing techniques (e.g., Payne, Bettman, & Johnson, 1988).

Developmental Trajectories of Integrative vs. Heuristic Strategies

Adults are typically characterized as competent decision makers, and, consistently, developmental research focused on maturational changes toward an end state of integrative (normative) decision strategies. This developmental trajectory fits a traditional Piagetian framework (Piaget & Inhelder, 1975). This framework states that children's problem solving is a progression through a series of suboptimal stages (comparable to heuristics) before the correct strategy is used (comparable to a normative, integrative, strategy; Siegler, 1996).

A famous problem-solving task that illustrates a progression toward normative responding is the balance-scale task (Siegler, 1981, 1996). In this task various weights are placed at various distances on both arms, and children are asked to predict whether the balance will tip to the left, to the right, or will remain in balance. Children may use various rules to solve this balance-scale task. A simple, one-dimensional rule would involve a comparison of the numbers of weights only. A two-dimensional rule would be to first consider the weights, and if these are equal to consider the distances from the fulcrum. A correct decision is, however, only made when weights and distances are integrated correctly (weights × distance). A rule-based analysis showed a developmental increase across childhood from one-dimensional reasoning to integrative problem solving (Jansen & van der Maas, 2002).

The hypothesis that such reasoning is also applied in decision making when confronted with multiple choice attributes (gains, losses, probabilities) was tested by Huizenga, Jansen, and Crone (2007) using the Iowa gambling task (IGT). This task is a so called experience-based decision task, in which outcomes need to be learned given repeated sampling. Huizenga and colleagues used a latent mixture approach to detect different decision strategies across age groups varying from 8 to 25 years of age (Fraley & Raftery, 2002). Results showed that younger children were more inclined to use only one of the attributes to make a decision (a primary focus on probability of loss), whereas older children were able to use a two-dimensional strategy, focusing first on the probabilities, and if these were equal between options choosing on the basis of amount of loss. Eventually, a small group of adults attained integrative decision making, in which decision attributes were correctly integrated (into expected value). Thus, in accordance with a Piagetian framework, children were more prone to use simple decision strategies, and the complexity of such strategies (i.e. the number of attributes considered and integration) increased with age.

Jansen, van Duijvenvoorde, and Huizenga (2012) elaborated on these findings by using a risky-choice paradigm optimized to distinguish between different types of nonintegrative decision strategies versus a normative, integrative, decision strategy. Participants (ages 8 to 17) were asked to make a series of choices between two options. These options explicitly displayed the probability of loss, amount of gain, and the amount of loss, and no immediate outcomes were experienced. Moreover, the presented choices varied such that the favorability of one, two, or all of these decision-attributes differed between options, in which decision-attributes could present conflicting information on the option's favorability (i.e. one option may have a lower loss, while the other has a higher gain). A latent-class analysis (LCA; McCutcheon, 1987) was used to find subgroups of participants with comparable decision strategies. Jansen and colleagues showed that children aged eight to nine focused primarily on minimizing probability of loss. With increasing age, more attributes were taken into account, such as a sequential consideration of probability of loss, amount of loss, and amount of gain. This developmental trajectory resembles the one found on the balance-scale task and is consistent with Piagetian theory. However, this study also observed large individual differences between children from the same age group. For example, some of the youngest children chose according to a type of integrative decision strategy, whereas some adults responded in accordance with sequential, i.e. "heuristic," strategies.

Biases in adult reasoning have been well documented (e.g., Reyna & Brainerd, 2011) and studies using judgment and reasoning paradigms indicated two types of developmental change (Jacobs & Klaczynski, 2002). That is, studies comparing younger and older adolescents show a growth in normative (i.e. logically coherent) reasoning from early to middle adolescence (Klaczynski, 2005). However, studies also suggest that biases and the use of heuristics increase with age (for reviews, see Albert & Steinberg, 2011; Jacobs & Klaczynski, 2002; Reyna & Farley, 2006). This developmental increase in reasoning biases has been described by dual-process systems, defining a developmental increase not only in logical competence (i.e. the "analytic" system) but also of the experiential system (i.e. the heuristic system), leading to a combination of normative reasoning and biases in adults (Jacobs & Klaczynski, 2002; Klaczynski, 2005). Similarly, fuzzy-trace theory (Reyna & Brainerd, 1995, 2011; Reyna & Ellis, 1994) distinguishes between analytical thinking based on verbatim representation of the pros and cons, and intuition based on gist operation, capturing the essence of a situation. This theory states that both processes develop during childhood, but that gist-based intuitions are thought to be preferred with increasing age (Rivers, Reyna, & Mills, 2008; Reyna & Farley, 2008).

Taken together, given the variety of decisions strategies observed within age groups, the maturation of decision strategies is seemingly more diverse than a simple normative end-state. This may suggest that adolescents' typical poor-choice behavior is not *necessarily* the result from a yet underdeveloped normative (or analytic) processing style but may result from changes in both analytical and heuristic processing (Jacobs & Klaczynski, 2002). In addition, the findings discussed so far indicate that not only developmental changes *between* age groups are of importance but that individual differences in decision strategies *within* age groups as well. Individual difference measures, model-based analyses, and statistical techniques (e.g., LCA, mixtures) can be important tools for such purposes.

Decision Neuroscience

Decision neuroscience (or "neuroeconomics") focuses on the neural mechanisms that reflect the processes of decision making, including the deviations and mistakes people make in their choices (Fehr & Rangel, 2011). A general approach of decision neuroscience has been to study key components in decision making, such as the representation of reward, loss, and integrated value. Neuroscientists have identified a "reward-network" in the brain which centers around evolutionary old, subcortical structures, including dopamine-rich areas in the midbrain, such as the (ventral) striatum (Schultz, Dayan, & Montague, 1997). The striatum has been implicated in anticipating and processing different types of rewards (Knutson, Taylor, Kaufman, Peterson, & Glover, 2005), but to some extent also losses (Tom, Fox, Trepel, & Poldrack, 2007), as well as in producing learning signals indicating whether an outcome is better or worse than expected (Cohen et al., 2010; Schultz et al., 1997). Neural representations of integrated utility have been associated primarily with activation in the ventral medial prefrontal cortex (PFC), a region that is linked to value anticipation and value comparisons between choice options (Rushworth, Mars, & Summerfield, 2012; Rushworth, Noonan, Boorman, Walton, & Behrens, 2011). Regions such as the ventral medial PFC, lateral orbitofrontal cortex, and dorsal medial PFC are thought to constitute a valuation network in the PFC that drives choice toward the highest valued option and that learns to optimize behavior based on the experienced value of outcomes (Rushworth et al., 2012). Finally, signals of risk have been particularly associated with neural activation in regions coding more negative emotions and uncertainty, such as the anterior cingulate cortex (ACC), the dorsal medial PFC, and the insula (Mohr, Biele, & Heekeren, 2010; Preuschoff, Bossaerts, & Quartz, 2006).

There are only a handful of neuroimaging studies that looked into the coding of integrative versus heuristic decision strategies in the brain. For instance, Venkatraman and colleagues (Venkatraman, Payne, Bettman, Luce, & Huettel, 2009) presented participants with a mixed gamble with five potential outcomes. Participants could decide between two possible improvements, of which one would maximize the overall probability of winning, and the other would minimize the magnitude of the largest monetary loss or maximize the magnitude of the largest monetary gain. A simplifying, heuristic, choice was linked to probability-maximizing, whereas a gain-maximizing or loss-minimizing choice was interpreted as consistent with integrative models such as expected utility maximization. Functional magnetic resonance imaging (fMRI) results indicated that brain activation in the dorsal medial PFC was linked to choices that were inconsistent with a participant's preferred strategy and that functional connectivity with other brain regions, such as the parietal cortex and insular cortex, predicted individual variability in strategy preferences. Thus, it was concluded that the dorsal medial PFC is a critical region for exercising strategic control in order to switch between decision strategies in an adaptive manner (e.g., Venkatraman & Huettel, 2012).

Other fMRI studies have also related the dorsal medial PFC to experienced conflict when using a noncompensatory strategy (De Neys, Vartanian, & Goel, 2008), and to the conflict that is experienced between a generally preferred emotional heuristic response and a more rational analytic choice (De Martino, Kumaran, Seymour, & Dolan, 2006). Other regions, such as the dorsolateral PFC, a key region for top-down control (e.g., Miller & Cohen, 2001), have been linked to executing control in overriding a heuristic response (De Neys et al., 2008) and in evaluating choice-attributes from memory (Khader et al., 2011) in heuristic (i.e. nonintegrative) decision making. However, much is still unknown on the neural processes underlying different decision strategies. A further delineation and consideration of the presence of different decision strategies is relevant in future neuroimaging studies.

It will be a challenge to further characterize the development of different decision strategies, and their associated neural mechanisms. The literature discussed up to here focused specifically on a more cognitive appraisal of different decision strategies. However, over the past decades there has been an increase in research and theorizing that focused on the importance of affective processes in decision making. The influence of the development of affect and control will therefore be discussed in the next section.

AFFECT AND CONTROL: A DUAL-SYSTEM ACCOUNT

The dual-system account, which has been very influential in psychology and neuroscience, describes behavior as the outcome of affective impulses aimed toward obtaining (immediate) rewards, and cognitive control processes aimed toward regulating behavior in favor of long-term goals (Miller & Cohen, 2001). Cognitive control abilities start to emerge in early childhood and gradually improve over childhood and through adolescence. Central concepts of cognitive control are processes such as inhibition and working memory (see, for overviews, Crone, 2009; Garon, Bryson, & Smith, 2008; Geier & Luna, 2009), where inhibition is described as the ability to suppress more reflexive responses, and working memory is described as the ability to retain and manipulate relevant information.

Cognitive control processes are thought to mature steadily into young adulthood, although different control processes may have slightly diverging maturational trajectories. For instance, working memory is shown to have a more protracted development than inhibition (Huizinga, Dolan, & van der Molen, 2006). In contrast, affective impulses may specifically intensify during adolescence compared to childhood and adulthood. This intensification of emotions may occur because of surging hormones (Ernst & Fudge, 2009; Spear, 2011) as well as changes in dopamine levels, and these changes may impact decision making and learning. For instance, advanced pubertal levels (when corrected for age) have been linked to risk-taking behaviors such as alcohol use (De Water, Braams, Crone, & Peper, 2013), and changes in dopamine levels have been linked to the motivational aspects of rewarding and aversive stimuli (see Spear, 2011, for an overview).

More specifically, adolescence has been described as a period of imbalance between a cognitive control system and an emotional, affective system, which has been linked to differential structural maturation of brain areas (Casey et al., 2008). Specifically, subcortical, affective regions (such as the striatum) mature earlier in comparison to frontal, control regions (such as the PFC). For example, the increase in cortical gray matter volume with maturation appears to peak latest in higher association areas such as the prefrontal cortex, inferior parietal cortex, and superior temporal gyrus relative to other cortical areas (Gogtay et al., 2004). Also, white-matter connections between brain regions continue to strengthen across adolescence, though this is not complete until early adulthood (e.g., Tamnes et al., 2010). The coherence of these connections is shown to correlate with developing abilities, such as the increasing ability to inhibit a response (Liston, Matalon, Hare, Davidson, & Casey, 2006) and the potential to wait for a delayed reward (Peper et al., 2012; but see Berns et al., 2009).

Accordingly, developmental fMRI studies in adolescence have focused primarily on the overactive adolescent reward system that would be associated with an approach bias encouraging risky behavior, since high rewards (e.g., more money, status, or fun) are usually associated with a riskier course of action. A range of decision-making and learning tasks showed indeed a heightened striatal response toward a received reward in adolescents (Cohen et al., 2010; Galvan, Hare, Voss, Glover, & Casey, 2007; Galvan et al., 2006; Van Leijenhorst et al., 2010), and this greater reward-related subcortical activation predicted self-report of everyday risk-taking behaviors (Galvan et al., 2007). On the other hand, other studies have reported little adolescent-specific increases in neural activation associated with receiving rewards (May et al., 2004; Paulsen, Carter, Platt, Huettel, & Brannon, 2012), and some have even demonstrated a decrease in neural activation in adolescents compared to adults when anticipating rewards (Bjork et al., 2004; Geier, Terwilliger, Teslovich, Velanova, & Luna, 2010). Recent overviews highlight that these mixed findings may be due to differences in the decision phase under study (for extensive reviews, see Galvan, 2010; Richards, Plate, & Ernst, 2013), decision context, and individual differences in reward sensitivity. The next section further discusses current findings on decision context and individual differences in reward sensitivity across development.

Context

One way in which context may influence risk taking is the affective engagement of a certain task. It is suggested that adolescents are specifically prone, compared to other age groups, to use less advantageous decision strategies in a so-called "hot" decision context. "Hot" contexts are situations in which adolescents' emotions are enhanced by external sources such as an immediate outcome and/or the presence of respected peers (see, for reviews on social influences in decision making, Albert, Chein, & Steinberg, 2013; Steinberg et al., 2008).

Figner and colleagues (Figner, Mackinley, Wilkening, & Weber, 2009) developed the Columbia card task, which manipulates the immediacy of outcomes. In this way, different decision contexts (i.e. "hot" and "cold" contexts) can be directly compared. Self-reports and assessments of electrodermal activity confirmed a heightened involvement of affective processes in the "hot" compared to the "cold" decision context. Results showed increased risk taking, coupled with simplified information use, in the "hot" decision context (i.e. with immediate outcomes) in adolescents compared to adults, whereas in the "cold" decision context (i.e. without immediate outcomes) adolescents showed the same level of risk taking and information use as adults. These findings indicate that specifically in adolescence a "hot" decision context diminishes more deliberative, and more advantageous, choice behavior. Similarly, a study into decision strategies in a mid-adolescent sample (van Duijvenvoorde, Jansen, Visser, & Huizenga, 2010) showed that in a "cold" decision context, i.e. without immediate outcomes, only a small subgroup of adolescents showed a simple, disadvantageous, decision rule, and the majority of adolescents were capable of using a relatively advantageous, complex decision strategy. However, in a "hot" decision context, in which actual gains and losses were experienced, the majority of adolescents showed an impoverished strategy and were merely driven by minimizing the probability of loss. Moreover, strategy use in the "cold" context was not predictive for strategy use in the "hot" decision context, indicating the need to understand risky decision making in context.

Besides differences in emotional engagement, a recent study suggested that the explicitness of the decision situation may profoundly influence risky decision making across development. That is, Tymula and colleagues (2012) presented adolescents (12 to 17 years of age) and adults (30 to 50 years of age) with choices between a guaranteed amount versus a risky option. The crucial manipulation was that some of these choice outcomes were played in a "risky" context (i.e. outcome probability was precisely specified), and others were played in an "ambiguous" context (i.e. outcome probability was hidden). Adolescents were specifically more ambiguity tolerant, but also more risk averse, compared to adults (i.e. taking more risks in ambiguous contexts but less risk in risky contexts compared to adults). Also, adolescents that reported more frequent reckless behaviors were significantly more ambiguity tolerant. These findings should be replicated in further studies, but they highlight that specifically ambiguity tolerance may drive risky behavior in adolescence. This ambiguity tolerance is suggested to be adaptive for learning to explore an uncertain environment (Tymula et al., 2012).

The aforementioned results indicate that such factors as affective engagement and outcome ambiguity may influence observed developmental changes of risky decision making from childhood to adulthood. These factors may be particularly relevant because of their representativeness of real-world decision making. That is, real-world decision making often occurs in affectively laden conditions (high arousal, peer pressure, real consequences; Figner & Weber, 2011) and in ambiguous decision situations, in which at least to some extent the exact probabilities of a risky choice are unknown. Future studies may benefit from behavioral and imaging studies that provide a more precise delineation of these influences across development.

Individual Differences

Another possible source of mixed findings in decision making under risk is individuals' sensitivity to rewards and risks. For instance, several studies reported that adolescents' reward-related activation in the ventral striatum (VS) was positively associated with self-reported reward sensitivity as measured by the behavioral approach system (BAS) scale (van Duijvenvoorde, Op de Macks, Overgaauw, Gunther-Moor, Dahl, & Crone, 2014), and sensation seeking, as measured by the brief sensation-seeking scale (Bjork, Knutson, & Hommer, 2008). These personality differences in reward-related response tendencies may explain why some adolescents are more responsive to rewards than others.

A model-based approach is a promising starting point for studying individual differences in risky decision making across development and contexts. An example of such a model is the *risk-return model*, which describes an individual's risk-taking behavior as a result of a trade-off between the expected return and the expected risk of a choice (Mohr et al., 2010; Weber, Shafir, & Blais, 2004). Other model-based approaches which are applied to decompose risky decision making along with an individual-difference characterization are prospect theory (Engelmann et al., 2013; Tom et al., 2007) and reinforcement-learning models (Cohen et al., 2010; van den Bos, Cohen, Kahnt, & Crone, 2011) that study prediction-error signaling. A prediction error signals a mismatch between expected and obtained outcomes and is therefore positive if outcomes are better than expected and negative if outcomes are worse than expected. For instance, positive prediction-error signaling (unexpected rewards) has been shown to be larger in adolescents compared with children and adults (Cohen et al., 2010). This study is a compelling example of how a model-based approach may increase our understanding of the processes underlying risky choice along with characterizing the extent of individual differences within age groups.

Affect and Control: Learning to Make Good Decisions

Learning from gains and losses is an important component in many decision tasks and relies heavily on the interaction between affect and control processes. That is, outcomes may give rise to immediate affective reactions (e.g., Figner & Weber, 2011; Loewenstein, Weber, Hsee, & Welch, 2001), but also need to be used effectively to adjust future behavior. A range of studies indicate that *probabilistic* learning environments are specifically difficult for children and adolescents (Eppinger, Mock, & Kray, 2009; van den Bos, Cohen, Kahnt, & Crone, 2012). In a probabilistic environment outcomes are not directly mapped to behavior. For instance, an optimal response may only be positively reinforced in 70 percent of the cases. The difficulty in learning may arise because a probabilistic environment requires individuals to attend to the long-term consequences and override the reactive tendency to respond directly to local outcomes.

Studies indicated that relative to adults, children and adolescents show a heightened tendency to continuously change responses after an occasional loss, which results in lower overall performance in a range of probabilistic decision tasks (Carlson, Zayas, & Guthormsen, 2009; Crone, Bunge, Latenstein, & van der Molen, 2005; Jansen, van Duijvenvoorde, & Huizenga, 2013; van Duijvenvoorde, Jansen, Bredman, & Huizenga, 2012). In a two-choice probabilistic learning task, adults were able to switch from a lose–shift to a lose–stay strategy once the correct option was learned (van Duijvenvoorde et al., 2013), whereas adolescents and children failed to do so. This ability to control choice behavior in response to gains and losses may depend specifically on the prefrontal cortex and its connections, a brain region that is important for controlling goal-directed behavior and which is still maturing in children and adolescents (see also Hämmerer & Eppinger, 2012).

Whether lowering the load on cognitive control processes influences children's and adolescent's decision making was studied by van Duijvenvoorde and colleagues (2012, 2013). Here, children and adolescents were presented with two versions of a probabilistic feedback task: one in which choice outcomes were essential for learning the value of different options, and one in which the probabilities and outcomes were explicitly presented. It was assumed that (working) memory load was low in the latter condition relative to the former. Consistent with less mature control and prefrontal structures, children's and adolescent's choice behavior improved profoundly from the noninformed to the informed situation and a reactive lose–shift strategy was largely, but not fully, diminished (van Duijvenvoorde et al., 2012). These findings suggest that storing and updating value representations (working and long-term memory) are key components that constrain the learning and decision making of children and adolescents in probabilistic tasks. These findings may indicate a promising road for interventions in decision making across development in which lowering working memory load may be a way to improve learning in uncertain environments.

CONCLUSION

In this chapter we discussed two key aspects of decision making under risk: the usage of different decision strategies across development and the influence of the development of affect and control in decision making. These aspects were studied by combining insights from neuroeconomics, developmental psychology, and the more traditional judgment and decision-making literature. Across these studies, a few general conclusions emerge. First, it is apparent that when studying decision making, consideration of decision context is crucial. Here we focused on literature discussing the influences of emotional engagement (triggered by, for instance, the immediateness of outcomes) and the explicitness of choice information. Understanding in which contexts risk taking occurs, and how that is predictive of behavior in real life, is a necessary target for future research. Second, studies and methods that illustrate individual differences are becoming increasingly important in the field of risky decision making. For instance, although adolescence may generally be a phase of heightened emotionality, not all adolescents are risk takers. Similarly, a focus on mean performance between age groups may hide the use of different decision strategies within age groups. The analysis and measurement tools (e.g., LCA, model-based approaches) used to characterize such individual differences are therefore an important addition to the field. Moreover, when used in combination with neuroimaging studies, this allows the investigation of neural mechanisms that underlie individual differences in risky choice.

We argue that advancing the understanding of developmental changes in risky decision making is important for providing crucial input into ambitious "next steps" such as finding tools to optimize children's and adolescents' decisions. As is apparent from the mixture of theories and methods discussed in this chapter, this is both an exciting and a challenging research field. But who said decision making (or decision-making research) was ever easy?

ACKNOWLEDGEMENT

The authors would like to thank Chris Warren for his careful reading and constructive comments on an earlier draft of this manuscript.

NOTE

1. Note that the definition of "decision making under risk" or "risky decision making" in the developmental literature commonly refers to choices that are associated with a probability, known or unknown, of undesirable outcomes. In economics/finance, however, it refers to situations in which outcomes occur with known probabilities. This is in contrast to ambiguous decision making, which refers to situations in which outcomes occur with unknown probabilities.

REFERENCES

Albert, D., Chein, J., & Steinberg, L. (2013). The teenage brain peer influences on adolescent decision making. *Current Directions in Psychological Science, 22(2)*, 114–120.

Albert, D., & Steinberg, L. (2011). Judgment and decision making in adolescence. *Journal of Research on Adolescence, 21(1)*, 211–224.

Berns, G. S., Moore, S., & Capra, C. M. (2009). Adolescent engagement in dangerous behaviors is associated with increased white matter maturity of frontal cortex. *PLoS ONE, 4(8)*, e6773.

Bjork, J. M., Knutson, B., Fong, G. W., Caggiano, D. M., Bennett, S. M., & Hommer, D. W. (2004). Incentive-elicited brain activation in adolescents: Similarities and differences from young adults. *Journal of Neuroscience, 24(8)*, 1793–1802.

Bjork, J. M., Knutson, B., & Hommer, D. W. (2008). Incentive-elicited striatal activation in adolescent children of alcoholics. *Addiction, 103(8)*, 1308–1319.

Brandstätter, E., Gigerenzer, G., & Hertwig, R. (2006). The priority heuristic: Making choices without tradeoffs. *Psychological Review, 113(2)*, 409–432.

Camerer, C. F. (2008). Neuroeconomics: Opening the gray box. *Neuron, 60(3)*, 416–419.

Carlson, S., Zayas, V., & Guthormsen, A. (2009). Neural correlates of decision making on a gambling task. *Child Development, 80(4)*, 1076–1096.

Casey, B. J., Getz, S., & Galvan, A. (2008). The adolescent brain. *Developmental Review, 28(1)*, 62–77.

Cohen, J. R., Asarnow, R. F., Sabb, F. W., Bilder, R. M., Bookheimer, S. Y., Knowlton, B. J., & Poldrack, R. A. (2010). A unique adolescent response to reward prediction errors. *Nature Neuroscience, 13(6)*, 669–671.

Crone, E. A. (2009). Executive functions in adolescence: Inferences from brain and behavior. *Developmental Science, 12(6)*, 825–830.

Crone, E. A., Bunge, S. A., Latenstein, H., & van der Molen, M. W. (2005). Characterization of children's decision making: Sensitivity to punishment frequency, not task complexity. *Child Neuropsychology, 11(3)*, 245–263.

Crone, E. A., & Dahl, R. E. (2012). Understanding adolescence as a period of social-affective engagement and goal flexibility. *Nature Reviews Neuroscience, 13(9)*, 636–650.

Dahl, R. E. (2004). Adolescent brain development: A period of vulnerabilities and opportunities. Keynote address. *Annals of the New York Academy of Sciences, 1021(1)*, 1–22.

De Martino, B., Kumaran, D., Seymour, B., & Dolan, R. J. (2006). Frames, biases, and rational decision-making in the human brain. *Science, 313(5787)*, 684–687.

De Neys, W., Vartanian, O., & Goel, V. (2008). Smarter than we think when our brains detect that we are biased. *Psychological Science, 19(5)*, 483–489.

De Water, E., Braams, B. R., Crone, E. A., & Peper, J. S. (2013). Pubertal maturation and sex steroids are related to alcohol use in adolescents. *Hormones and Behavior, 63(2)*, 392–397.

Engelmann, J. B., Moore, S., Capra, C. M., & Berns, G. S. (2013). Differential neurobiological effects of expert advice on risky choice in adolescents and adults. *Social, Cognitive, Affective Neuroscience, 7(5)*, 557–567.

Eppinger, B., Mock, B., & Kray, J. (2009). Developmental differences in learning and error processing: Evidence from ERPs. *Psychophysiology, 46(5)*, 1043–1053.

Ernst, M., & Fudge, J. L. (2009). A developmental neurobiological model of motivated behavior: Anatomy, connectivity and ontogeny of the triadic nodes. *Neuroscience and Biobehavioral Reviews, 33(3)*, 367–382.

Fehr, E., & Rangel, A. (2011). Neuroeconomic foundations of economic choice: Recent advances. *Journal of Economic Perspective, 25(4)*, 3–30.

Figner, B., Mackinlay, R., Wilkening, F., & Weber, E. (2009). Affective and deliberative processes in risky choice: Age differences in risk taking in the Columbia Card Task. *Journal of Experimental Psychology: Learning, Memory and Cognition, 35(3)*, 709–730.

Figner, B., & Weber, E. (2011). Who takes risk when and why? Determinants of risk taking. *Current Directions in Psychological Science, 20(4)*, 211–216.

Fraley, C., & Raftery, A. E. (2002). Model-based clustering, discriminant analysis, and density estimation. *Journal of the American Statistical Association, 97(458)*, 611–631.

Galvan, A. (2010). Adolescent development of the reward system. *Frontiers in Human Neuroscience, 4(6)*. www.ncbi.nlm.nih.gov/pmc/articles/PMC2826184/ Dec 1, 2013.

Galvan, A., Hare, T. A., Parra, C. E., Penn, J., Voss, H., Glover, G., & Casey, B. J. (2006). Earlier development of the accumbens relative to orbitofrontal cortex might underlie risk-taking behavior in adolescents. *Journal of Neuroscience, 26(25)*, 6885–6892.

Galvan, A., Hare, T., Voss, H., Glover, G., & Casey, B. J. (2007). Risk-taking and the adolescent brain: Who is at risk? *Developmental Science, 10(2)*, F8–F14.

Garon, N., Bryson, S., & Smith, I. (2008). Executive function in preschoolers: A review using an integrative framework. *Psychological Bulletin, 134(1)*, 31–60.

Geier, C., & Luna, B. (2009). The maturation of incentive processing and cognitive control. *Pharmacology Biochemistry and Behavior, 93(3)*, 212–221.

Geier, C., Terwilliger, R., Teslovich, T., Velanova, K., & Luna, B. (2010). Immaturities in reward processing and its influence on inhibitory control in adolescence. *Cerebral Cortex, 20(7)*, 1613–1629.

Gigerenzer, G., & Gaissmaier, W. (2011). Heuristic decision making. *Annual Review of Psychology, 62*, 451–482.

Gigerenzer, G., & Goldstein, D. G. (1996). Reasoning the fast and frugal way: Models of bounded rationality. *Psychological Review, 103(4)*, 650–669.

Gogtay, N., Giedd, J., Lusk, L., Hayashi, K., Greenstein, D., Vaituzis, A., et al. (2004). Dynamic mapping of human cortical development during childhood through early adulthood. *Proceedings of the National Academy of Sciences, 101(21)*, 8174–8179.

Hämmerer, D., & Eppinger, B. (2012). Dopaminergic and prefrontal contributions to reward-based learning and outcome monitoring during child development and aging. *Developmental Psychology, 48(3)*, 862–874.

Huizinga, M., Dolan, C., & van der Molen, M. (2006). Age-related change in executive function: Developmental trends and a latent variable analysis. *Neuropsychologia, 44(11)*, 2017–2036.

Jacobs, J. E., & Klaczynski, P. A. (2002). The development of judgment and decision-making during childhood and adolescence. *Current Directions in Psychological Science, 11(4)*, 145–149.

Jansen, B. R. J., & van der Maas, H. (2002). The development of children's rule use on the balance scale task. *Journal of Experimental Child Psychology, 81(4)*, 383–416.

Jansen, B. R. J., van Duijvenvoorde, A. C. K., & Huizenga, H. M. (2013). Development and gender related differences in response switches after non-representative negative feedback. *Developmental Psychology, 50(1)*, 237–246.

——(2012). Development of decision making: Sequential versus integrative rules. *Journal of Experimental Child Psychology, 111(1)*, 87–100.

Kahneman, D., & Tversky, A. (1979). Prospect theory: An analysis of decision under risk. *Econometrica, 47(2)*, 263–292.

Khader, P. H., Pachur, T., Meier, S., Bien, S., Jost, K., & Rösler, F. (2011). Memory-based decision-making with heuristics: Evidence for a controlled activation of memory representations. *Journal of Cognitive Neuroscience, 23(11)*, 3540–3554.

Klaczynski, P. A. (2001). Analytic and heuristic processing influences on adolescent reasoning an decision-making. *Child Development, 72(3)*, 844–861.

—— (2005). Metacognition and cognitive variability: A dual-process model of decision making and its development. In J. Jacobs & P. Klaczynski (Eds.), *The development of judgment and decision making in children and adolescents* (pp. 39–76). Mahwah, NJ: Erlbaum.

Knutson, B., Taylor, J., Kaufman, M., Peterson, R., & Glover, G. (2005). Distributed neural representation of expected value. *Journal of Neuroscience, 25(19)*, 4806–4812.

Liston, C., Matalon, S., Hare, T. A., Davidson, M. C., & Casey, B. J. (2006). Anterior cingulate and posterior parietal cortices are sensitive to dissociable forms of conflict in a task-switching paradigm. *Neuron, 50(4)*, 643–653.

Loewenstein, G. F., Weber, E. U., Hsee, C. K., & Welch, N. (2001). Risk as feelings. *Psychological Bulletin, 127(2)*, 267–286.

May, J. C., Delgado, M. R., Dahl, R. E., Stenger, V. A., Ryan, N. D., Fiez, J. A., & Carter, C. S. (2004). Event-related functional magnetic resonance imaging of reward-related brain circuitry in children and adolescents. *Biological Psychiatry, 55(4)*, 359–366.

McCutcheon, A. C. (1987). *Latent class analysis.* Beverly Hills, CA: Sage.

Miller, E., & Cohen, J. (2001). An integrative theory of prefrontal cortex function. *Annual Review of Neuroscience, 24(1)*, 167–202.

Mohr, P. N., Biele, G., & Heekeren, H. R. (2010). Neural processing of risk. *Journal of Neuroscience, 30(19)*, 6613–6619.

Paulsen, D. J., Carter, R. M., Platt, M. L., Huettel, S. A., & Brannon, E. M. (2011). Neurocognitive development of risk aversion from early childhood to adulthood. *Frontiers in Human Neuroscience, 5.* http://journal.frontiersin.org/Journal/10.3389/fnhum.2011.00178/full Dec 1, 2013.

Payne, J. W., Bettman, J. R., & Johnson, E. J. (1988). Adaptive strategy selection in decision making. *Journal of Experimental Psychology: Learning, Memory, and Cognition, 14(3)*, 534–552.

Peper, J. S., Mandl, R. C. W., Braams, B. R., De Water, E., Heijboer, A. C., Koolschijn, P. C. M. P., & Crone, E. A. (2013). Delay discounting and frontostriatal fiber tracts: A combined DTI and MTR study on impulsive choices in healthy young adults. *Cerebral Cortex, 23(7)*, 1695–1702.

Piaget, J., & Inhelder, B. (1975). *The origin of the idea of chance in children.* Oxford: Norton.

Preuschoff, K., Bossaerts, P., & Quartz, S. R. (2006). Neural differentiation of expected reward and risk in human subcortical structures. *Neuron, 51(3)*, 381–390.

Rangel, A., Camerer, C., & Montague, P. R. (2008). A framework for studying the neurobiology of value-based decision making. *Nature Reviews Neuroscience, 9(7)*, 545–556.

Reyna, V. F., & Brainerd, C. J. (1995). Fuzzy-trace theory: An interim synthesis. *Learning and Individual Differences, 7(1)*, 1–75.

—— (2011). Dual processes in decision making and developmental neuroscience: A fuzzy-trace model. *Developmental Review, 31(2)*, 180–206.

Reyna, V., & Farley, F. (2006). Risk and rationality in adolescent decision making: Implications for theory, practice, and public policy. *Psychological Science in the Public Interest, 7(1)*, 1–44.

Richards, J. M., Plate, R. C., & Ernst, M. (2013). A systematic review of fMRI reward paradigms in adolescents versus adults: The impact of task design and implications for understanding neurodevelopment. *Neuroscience and Biobehavioral Reviews, 37(5)*, 976–991.

Rivers, S., Reyna, V., & Mills, B. (2008). Risk taking under the influence: A fuzzy-trace theory of emotion in adolescence. *Developmental Review, 28(1)*, 107–144.

Rushworth, M., Mars, R. B., & Summerfield, C. (2012). General mechanisms for making decisions? *Current Opinion in Neurobiology, 19(1)*, 75–83.

Rushworth, M., Noonan, M. P., Boorman, E. D., Walton, M. E., & Behrens, T. E. (2011). Frontal cortex and reward-guided learning and decision-making. *Neuron, 70(6)*, 1054–1069.

Russo, J. E., & Dosher, B. A. (1983). Strategies for multiattribute binary choice. *Journal of Experimental Psychology:Learning, Memory and Cognition, 9(4)*, 676–696.

Schultz, W., Dayan, P., & Montague, P. R. (1997). A neural substrate of prediction and reward. *Science, 275(5306)*, 1593–1599.

Sharp, C., Monterosso, J., & Montague, P. R. (2012). Neuroeconomics: A bridge for translational research. *Biological Psychiatry, 72(2)*, 87–92.

Siegler, R. (1981). Developmental sequences within and between concepts. *Monographs of the Society for Research in Child Development, 46* (Serial No. 189).

—— (1996). *Emerging minds: The process of change in chidren's thinking.* New York, NY: Oxford University Press.

Somerville, L. H., Jones, R. M., & Casey, B. J. (2010). A time of change: Behavioral and neural correlates of adolescent sensitivity to appetitive and aversive environmental cues. *Brain and Cognition, 72(1)*, 124–133.

Spear, L. P. (2011). Rewards, aversions and affect in adolescence: Emerging convergences across laboratory animal and human data. *Developmental Cognitive Neuroscience, 1(4)*, 392–400.

Steinberg, L. (2008). A social neuroscience perspective on adolescent risk taking. *Developmental Review, 28(1)*, 78–106.

Tamnes, C. K., Østby, Y., Fjell, A. M., Westlye, L. T., Due-Tønnessen, P., & Walhovd, K. B. (2010). Brain maturation in adolescence and young adulthood: Regional age-related changes in cortical thickness and white matter volume and microstructure. *Cerebral Cortex, 20(3)*, 534–548.

Tom, S. M., Fox, C. R., Trepel, C., & Poldrack, R. A. (2007). The neural basis of loss aversion in decision-making under risk. *Science, 315(5811)*, 515–518.

Trepel, C., Fox, C. R., & Poldrack, R. A. (2005). Prospect theory on the brain? Toward a cognitive neuroscience of decision under risk. *Brain Research Cognitive Brain Research, 23(1)*, 34–50.

Tversky, A., & Kahneman, D. (1974). Judgment under uncertainty: Heuristics and biases. *Science, 185(4157)*, 1124–1131.

—— (1981). The framing of decisions and the psychology of choice. *Science, 211(4481)*, 453–458.

Tversky, A., & Slovic, P. (1988). Contingent weighting in judgment and choice. *Psychological Review, 95(3)*, 371–384.

Tymula, A., Belmaker, L. A. R., Roy, A. K., Ruderman, L., Manson, K., Glimcher, P. W., & Levy, I. (2012). Adolescents' risk-taking behavior is driven by tolerance to ambiguity. *Proceedings of the National Academy of Sciences, 109(42)*, 17135–17140.

Van den Bos, W., Cohen, M. X., Kahnt, T., & Crone, E. A. (2012). Striatum-medial prefrontal cortex connectivity predicts developmental changes in reinforcement learning. *Cerebral Cortex, 22(6)*, 1247–1255.

Van Duijvenvoorde, A. C. K., Jansen, B. R. J., Bredman, J. C., & Huizenga, H. M. (2012). Age-related changes in decision making: Comparing informed and noninformed situations. *Developmental Psychology, 48(1)*, 192–203.

Van Duijvenvoorde, A. C. K., Jansen, B. R. J., Griffioen, E., van der Molen, M. W., & Huizenga, H. M. (2013). Decomposing developmental differences in probabilistic feedback learning: Indices of heart-rate and behavior. *Biological Psychology, 93(3)*, 175–183.

Van Duijvenvoorde, A. C. K., Jansen, B. R. J., Visser, I., & Huizenga, H. M. (2010). Affective and cognitive decision-making in adolescents. *Developmental Neuropsychology, 35(5)*, 539–554.

Van Duijvenvoorde, A. C. K., Op de Macks, Z. A., Overgaauw, S., Gunther Moor, B., Dahl, R. E., & Crone, E. A. (2014). A cross-sectional and longitudinal analysis of reward-related brain activation: Effects of age, pubertal stage and reward sensitivity, *Brain and Cognition*.

Van Leijenhorst, L., Gunther Moor, B., Op de Macks, Z. A., Rombouts, S. A., Westenberg, P. M., & Crone, E. A. (2010). Adolescent risky decision-making: Neurocognitive development of reward and control regions. *Neuroimage, 51(1)*, 345–355.

Venkatraman, V., & Huettel, S. A. (2012). Strategic control in decision-making under uncertainty. *European Journal of Neuroscience, 35(7)*, 1075–1082.

Venkatraman, V., Payne, J. W., Bettman, J. R., Luce, M. F., & Huettel, S. A. (2009). Separate neural mechanisms underlie choices and strategic preferences in risky decision making. *Neuron, 62(4)*, 593–602.

Vlaev, I., Chater, N., Stewart, N., & Brown, G. D. (2011). Does the brain calculate value? *Trends in Cognitive Sciences, 15(11)*, 546–554.

Von Neumann, J., & Morgenstern, O. (1944). *Theory of games and economic behavior.* Princeton, NJ: Princeton University Press.

Weber, E. U., Shafir, S., & Blais, A. R. (2004). Predicting risk sensitivity in humans and lower animals: Risk as variance or coefficient of variation. *Psychological Review, 111(2)*, 430–445.

11

Individual Differences in Decision-Making Competence across the Lifespan

WÄNDI BRUINE DE BRUIN, ANDREW M. PARKER,
AND BARUCH FISCHHOFF

Throughout their lives, people make decisions that affect their health, finances, and overall well-being. Their competence to make those decisions may vary across the lifespan, including adolescence and adulthood. To assess individuals' decision-making competence, and whether strategies for improving it are effective, researchers need a validated individual-differences measure of decision-making competence. This chapter covers recent developments towards assessing individual differences in decision-making competence across the lifespan. We discuss how these efforts have been based on traditional behavioral decision research, which defined the normative standards and methodological approaches for evaluating people's decisions, as well as on initial individual-differences studies with adolescents and older adults. We also highlight new research questions that can be explored now that validated individual-differences measures of decision-making competence are available. Specifically, we discuss opportunities to examine which skills contribute to people's ability to make sound decisions, to study how aspects of decision-making competence change with adult age, as well as to develop and evaluate communications, decision aids, behavioral-skills training, and other efforts to improve decision making.

Throughout their lives, people make decisions that affect their health, finances, and overall well-being, and their competence to make those decisions may vary across life stages such as adolescence and late adulthood. When people have trouble making decisions, policy makers and practitioners can provide communications, decision aids, or training. Policies may also be designed to influence decisions through "nudges" toward a specific option or through out-right enforcement. At the extreme, individuals with insufficient decision-making competence may need a proxy to decide for them.

To assess individuals' decision-making competence, researchers need a validated individual-differences measure of decision-making competence. Individual differences, however, have not been a major emphasis of decision research. The main focus has generally been on identifying common decision biases in people's decisions and understanding the situational causes. Therefore, most studies have been run in psychological laboratories, so as to control decision contexts. Furthermore, research participants have tended to be undergraduate students, under the assumption that the human psychology of decision making would generalize to populations of different ages, education, and cognitive ability.

This chapter covers recent developments toward assessing individual differences in decision-making competence across the lifespan. We discuss the traditional research that has defined the normative standards and methodological approaches for examining people's decisions, and initial studies of adolescents' and older adults' decision making that inspired individual-differences research. After a brief description of two efforts to develop and validate measures of decision-making competence, we highlight new research questions that can be explored now that a validated individual-differences measure of decision-making competence is available.

DEFINING DECISION-MAKING COMPETENCE

Traditional decision research has developed *normative* theories that identify the decision processes that should on average yield the best outcomes, and *descriptive* research methods to evaluate people's actual performance against normative standards. Without normative criteria, attempts to evaluate (or improve) people's decisions remain atheoretical and subjective. Without descriptive methods for assessing decision performance, researchers revert to asking people for self-reports of how they make decisions (Appelt et al., 2011). This section describes the normative and descriptive approaches that have defined decision-making competence. Both can inform prescriptive strategies for improving people's decisions, which will be discussed in the final section of this chapter.

Normative Theories: How Should People Make Decisions?

Normative decision theories prescribe how people should be making decisions, emphasizing four fundamental processes (Edwards, 1954; Parker & Fischhoff, 2005):

1. *Belief assessment* involves judging the likelihood of experiencing specific outcomes as a result of choosing a decision option.
2. *Value assessment* involves evaluating these outcomes in terms of how well they meet one's goals.
3. *Integration* involves combining assessed beliefs and values to choose the option that is most likely to meet one's goals.
4. *Metacognition* refers to knowing the extent of one's abilities.

DECISION MAKING ACROSS THE LIFESPAN 221

Normative criteria have been developed for evaluating processes within each set.

Normatively sound decision processes may defensibly lead to different choices, if individuals have different beliefs and values. Without knowing people's beliefs and values, it is therefore difficult to judge the quality of their decision processes. Nevertheless, the quality of a specific decision can (and arguably should) be judged by its process rather than by its outcome (Keren & Bruine de Bruin, 2003). Good decision processes may yield undesirable outcomes due to chance, but individuals who are objectively better at applying normatively correct decision processes should on average obtain better decision outcomes. Normative approaches to belief assessment, value assessment, integration, and metacognition are described below.

Belief Assessment   To make informed decisions, people need the ability to assess the probability that their choices will yield desirable outcomes and avoid undesirable ones. Normatively, belief assessment can be evaluated in terms of *correspondence* with an external criterion or *coherence* with other beliefs. Consider individuals' beliefs about their personal survival, which are relevant to decisions about retirement savings and other life plans (Hurd, 2009). Correspondence rules posit that the judged probability of living until a certain age should be in line with estimates from statistical life tables. Coherence rules posit that judged probabilities should follow probability theory, such that probabilities about mutually exclusive events such as living and dying should add up to 100 percent, and the probability of subset events such as dying in a terrorist attack should be lower than the probability of the superset event such as dying at all (Bruine de Bruin et al., 2007).

Value Assessment   To make informed decisions, people need the ability to assess the values of the possible outcomes of their choices. For example, correspondence norms state that value assessments should follow the sunk-cost rule, which posits that options should be valued for their expected future outcomes, independent of whether prior investments were made. Indeed, it is normatively incorrect to continue investments in options that are no longer beneficial (Arkes & Blumer, 1985). Value assessments can also be evaluated according to coherence norms. For example, the norm of descriptive invariance posits that the evaluation of a decision option should be unaffected by how that option is described, such that a medical treatment should be equally attractive whether it is said to be "95 percent effective" or "5 percent ineffective" (Levin et al., 1988).

Integration   Making good decisions also requires the ability to compare options by evaluating the associated outcomes in terms of assessed beliefs and values, and selecting the option that is expected to yield the best personal value. Normative decision theories compute the expected value of each decision option by multiplying the associated probabilistic belief and the judged values. Traditional normative strategies require that decision makers systematically consider the available information about all of the possible options and all of their attributes (Payne et al., 1993). If these normative strategies are accurately applied, they should follow standards of coherence. For example, according to the principle of transitivity choosing option A over B and B over C implies choosing A over C (Kahneman et al., 1982).

Metacognition   Good decision makers need to understand the limitations of their own decision-making processes, knowledge, and abilities, so that they realize when to seek information or advice from others. That ability has typically been assessed by comparing confidence in knowledge with performance on a knowledge test (Klayman et al., 1999). A decision maker is said to be well calibrated when confidence is in line with overall performance. For example, being on average 70 percent confident is appropriate when overall performance is also 70 percent.

Descriptive Research: Do People Violate Normative Rules When Making Decisions?

Descriptive research in judgment and decision making has studied when and why people violate normative rules (Kahneman et al., 1982). Systematic decision errors have been revealed in belief assessment, value assessment, integration, and metacognition.

Belief Assessment   To evaluate people's belief assessments, descriptive research has used survey questions that ask people to judge the probability of specific events happening in their lives. For example, respondents may be asked for the probability that they will live until a certain age, or be diagnosed with a life-threatening disease. People commonly show unrealistic optimism, by overestimating their likelihood of experiencing positive events and underestimating their likelihood of experiencing negative events, even after seeing the official statistics (Rothman et al., 1996). This optimism may reflect wishful thinking, as well as cognitive processes: People are more likely to judge lower risks for themselves than for others when considering common and controllable events, because they know how they but not how others would protect themselves (Kruger & Burrus, 2004).

Violations of coherence, as defined by probability rules, reflect systematic biases in quantitative judgments (Poulton, 1989). For example, people fail to realize that their probability of dying includes the probability of dying from various causes (Tversky & Koehler, 1994). As a result, their probability judgments of mutually exclusive events may not add up to 100 percent, and their probability judgments of specific vivid events such as dying in a terrorist attack may be larger than their probability judgments of dying at all.

Value Assessment   Descriptive research has also identified systematic violations of correspondence and coherence norms in people's value assessments. For example, people violate the sunk-cost rule, which posits that decision options should be valued for their expected future outcomes regardless of prior investments that are lost regardless of how the decision maker proceeds. Descriptive studies have presented research participants with hypothetical choices between continuing or discontinuing a failing course of action. Results show that people often hesitate to quit, due to concerns about wasting their prior investments (Arkes & Blumer, 1985). Coherence errors have also been identified in people's value assessments. Classic studies presented descriptions that vary in specific wording but provide normatively equivalent information about decision options. They found violations of description invariance, because people do consider medical treatments more attractive when they are described as 95 percent effective rather than 5 percent ineffective (Levin et al., 1988), perhaps because they assume that the wording reflects the messenger's opinion (McKenzie, 2004).

Integration   Descriptive research into people's ability to apply decision rules has also identified violations of normative theories. Participants have been asked to choose between decision options that vary along different attributes. Results have shown a failure to use the normative strategy of comparing all options along their different attributes. Rather, people often use simple strategies, by selecting the option with the best value on the one attribute they value the most, or the first option that seems good enough to meet their minimum requirements (Payne et al., 1993). Although these heuristics save time and effort, they risk selecting an option that is less than optimal, violating coherence norms.

Metacognition   Classic descriptive research on metacognition has asked people to answer knowledge questions such as "Which is further north, New York or Rome?" and then express their confidence in that answer (50 percent = just guessing; 100 percent = certainty). Findings show that mean confidence across items tends to be higher than the overall percent correct, and this overconfidence increases with the difficulty of the task (Klayman et al., 1999). Overconfidence partly results from people's tendency to generate reasons that confirm rather than disconfirm each reported answer (Koriat et al., 1980), which may be exacerbated in groups (Strauss et al., 2011; Zamoth & Sniezek, 1997) and advisory settings, due to people equating confidence with expertise (Price & Stone, 2003).

DECISION-MAKING COMPETENCE ACROSS THE LIFESPAN

Although decision research has typically enrolled undergraduate research participants, a few studies have focused on adolescents or older adults, comparing their decision-making competence to that of other groups (Bruine de Bruin et al., 2012; Fischhoff, 2008; Peters & Bruine de Bruin, 2012; Strough et al., 2011). This research has also been extended to children, often using more age-appropriate decision tasks (Jacobs & Potenza, 1991; Levin et al., 2007). Because these studies have aimed to understand developmental trajectories in decision-making competence, they have inspired theories about the cognitive and emotional skills that underlie decision-making competence and have informed approaches to measuring individual differences in decision-making competence.

   A primary reason for studying decision-making competence in adolescents and older adults has been that some negative events are more common in these age groups. For example, adolescents are more likely to experience motor vehicle accidents (Turner & McClure, 2003), alcohol dependency (Grant & Dawson, 1997), and HIV diagnoses (CDC, 2004). Older adults file for bankruptcy (Thorne et al., 2009) and fail to take prescribed medications (Park et al., 1992) at disturbing rates. Yet normative theories posit that even good decision makers sometimes experience poor outcomes. Normatively, choices should depend on preferences for risks and benefits, which may vary with age. The unpredictable or uncontrollable environments faced by specific age groups may also make it harder to make good decisions.

Nevertheless, age groups may vary in cognitive ability and experience, both of which contribute to good performance on commonly studied decision tasks (Bruine de Bruin et al., 2012; Reyna, 2004; Stanovich & West, 2008). There are concerns that the young may have mature cognitive skills but lack experience, while the old may be experienced but face age-related cognitive decline (Bruine de Bruin, 2012; Peters & Bruine de Bruin, 2012; Reyna & Farley, 2006; Strough et al., 2011). Research on age and decision making can test these theories and inform evaluations of whether individuals have the competence to make autonomous decisions, with legal implications for their ability to give medical consent, make financial commitments, and stand trial.

Comparing Adolescent to Adult Decision-Making Competence

Adolescence is the developmental stage between childhood and adulthood, including the teenage years and early twenties. Adolescents need good decision-making competence, because they are asked to make important decisions for the first time, producing lasting habits and consequences (Reyna & Farley, 2006). Cognitive development peaks in the late teens, but critics have noted that adolescents may lack the life experience and emotional maturity relevant to make good decisions (Reyna & Farley, 2006). Nevertheless, developmental claims should be based on comparisons of adolescents to adults, who (as noted above) are also prone to decision errors.

Belief Assessment As noted, beliefs may be evaluated in terms of correspondence to external criteria, or coherence across reported beliefs. Few studies have examined the developmental trajectory of individuals' ability to assess coherent beliefs. Findings suggest that children actually become more likely to violate normative probability rules as they age, possibly because they learn heuristics to assess probabilities by their vividness (Klaczynski, 2001). Adolescents' ability to assess beliefs has also been evaluated against objective criteria. In 1997, the National Longitudinal Study of Youth (NLSY) asked US adolescents to judge probabilities of experiencing different events happening in the next year and by age 20. On average, their responses seemed reasonable, with for example mean judged probabilities for getting a high-school diploma by age 20 being in line with the official statistical estimates from 1997 and reports of whether or not they were enrolled in school that year (Fischhoff et al., 2000). Adolescents who had judged higher probabilities in 1997 were significantly more likely to report experiencing the event in the next year or by age 20 (Bruine de Bruin et al., 2007)—although self-reported behaviors (e.g., 1997 enrollment in school) may have better predictive ability (Persoskie, 2013; see Bruine de Bruin et al., 2010, for an exception). The main problem was with the probability of dying, which many teens incoherently judged to be the same for the next year and by age 20 and seriously overestimated as compared to statistical life tables and actual death rates in the NLSY cohort (Bruine de Bruin et al., 2007; Fischhoff et al., 2000). Thus, although adolescents had valid beliefs for most events, they did not show adults' ability to assess coherent beliefs for an emotional event such as dying (Hurd, 2009), perhaps due to their increased worry about health and safety threats (Fischhoff et al., 2010).

Lack of experience may also play a role. Adolescents are more likely than adults to overestimate the probability of experiencing negative consequences from risky behaviors such as unsafe sex and alcohol use (Cohn et al., 1995; Millstein & Halpern-Felsher, 2002; Quadrel et al., 1993). As adolescents gain experience with risky behaviors, they may learn that they were too worried and their risk perceptions become more realistic (Gerrard et al., 1996; Halpern-Felsher et al., 2001).

Assessing Values   Few developmental studies have examined adolescents' ability to assess values. Some show positive developmental progression, with adults being more likely than adolescents to adhere to the sunk-cost rule when assessing decision options with irrecoverable investments (Klaczynski, 2001; Klaczynski & Cottrell, 2004). Adolescents may be less able than adults to generate possible consequences of actions not taken, leading to less appreciation of both sunk costs and opportunity costs (Beyth-Marom et al., 1993; Fischhoff, 1996). However, adults do make sunk-cost errors (Arkes & Blumer, 1985) and may be outperformed by five- to six-year-olds (Arkes & Ayton, 1999). Framing errors tend to increase with age, with adolescents being worse than four- to five-year-olds (Reyna & Ellis, 1994) and better than adults (Reyna et al., 2011; Weller et al., 2011). Whether value assessments improve with age may depend on whether normative rules are easy to learn from experience or require more deliberate training (Stanovich & West, 2008). With age, people may also learn the norm of not wasting their time and effort and then incorrectly overgeneralize the idea to sunk-cost problems (Arkes & Ayton, 1999).

Integration   The few studies that have examined adolescents' ability to apply decision rules for integrating their beliefs and values suggest that they are worse than adults. Adolescents consider fewer risks and benefits of decision options (Beyth-Marom et al., 1993; Halpern-Felsher & Cauffman, 2001). Adolescents may have the cognitive ability to make logical evaluations of their perceptions of risks and benefits but lack the experience to resist the social and emotional influences that sway their cognitive deliberations (Gerrard et al., 2008; Reyna & Farley, 2006).

Metacognition   Studies on metacognition are not in agreement. Reports of age-related declines of overconfidence in knowledge (Klaczynski, 2001) may explain why adolescents are less likely than adults to seek advice (Halpern-Felsher & Cauffman, 2001). However, adolescents and their parents have similar confidence in their knowledge about risky behaviors (Beyth-Marom & Fischhoff, 1997). The result may depend on whether adolescents have experience with the topic.

Comparing Older Adults' with Younger Adults' Decision-Making Competence

Older adults need good decision-making competence because they face complex decisions about their finances and health care. Moreover, poor decision outcomes may be harder to overcome in older age, due to fewer opportunities for supplementing income and reduced family safety nets. Age-related cognitive declines threaten the quality of complex decisions about healthcare plans (Finucane & Gullion, 2010; Finucane et al., 2002, 2005). However, decision making is likely to be more than just a cognitive exercise and may require experience and emotional maturity that improve with age (Peters & Bruine de Bruin, 2012; Reyna, 2004).

Belief Assessment   There are few studies on adult age and the ability to assess beliefs. Adults' probability judgments seem to correspond appropriately with their life experiences, but older adults may be somewhat overoptimistic about their probabilities of surviving until a target age, perhaps due to having outlived their peers (Hurd, 2009). There is no evidence of adult age differences in the ability to provide coherent responses across related sets of probability questions, such as stating lower likelihood of dying in a terrorist attack than of dying at all (Bruine de Bruin et al., 2012). Perhaps older adults have experience-based abilities that help them to judge risks consistently despite experiencing age-related cognitive declines.

Value Assessment   Descriptive research on value assessment shows mixed relationships of performance with age. One study found that older adults were more likely to commit framing errors (Bruine de Bruin et al., 2007, 2012). Others showed the opposite or no age effect (Kim et al., 2005; Mayhorn et al., 2002; Mikels & Reed, 2009; Rönnlund et al., 2005; Weller et al., 2011). The conflicting results may be due to the cognitive demands of the specific tasks. Studies of individual differences typically present each participant with both frames in a pair, making it more likely that they will recognize the second frame as similar to the first and alter their responses to be consistent. Recognizing frames as related is less likely when they are separated by filler tasks (LeBoeuf & Shafir, 2003), which increases demands on memory skills that decline with age. However, even framing studies with between-subject designs found conflicting results on aging, suggesting variation in the extent to which the studies tapped other skills that change with age.

More consistent results have been found for the relationship between adult age and the ability to resist sunk costs. Adherence to the normative sunk-cost rule improves with age, in part because the task is not cognitively demanding (Bruine de Bruin et al., 2007, 2012; Strough et al., 2008, 2011). Older adults may also be better than younger adults at avoiding sunk-cost errors because they regulate emotions better and dwell less on irrecoverable losses (Strough et al., 2011).

Integration   There is a negative correlation between adult age and the ability to apply decision rules, which is mediated by age-related declines in cognitive ability (Bruine de Bruin et al., 2007, 2012). This finding is consistent with prior studies showing that, when selecting their own choice strategies, older adults are more likely than younger adults to use noncompensatory ones that reduce cognitive effort by using fewer comparisons (Johnson, 1990). However, age differences in performance depend on the decision context. Older adults perform at least as well as younger adults when applying decision rules in the grocery store, a context in which they have more experience (Kim & Hasher, 2005; Tentori et al., 2001).

Metacognition   Depending on the study, older adults may be less overconfident than younger adults (Kovalchik et al., 2005), more overconfident (Crawford &

Stankov, 1996), or no different (Bruine de Bruin et al., 2012). The result may depend on the cognitive demands of the confidence assessment method and the degree to which older adults have experience with the specific topic (Hansson et al., 2008).

DEVELOPING AND VALIDATING A COMPREHENSIVE MEASURE OF DECISION-MAKING COMPETENCE

In this section, we discuss the need for a validated and comprehensive measure of individual differences in decision-making competence, our efforts to design and validate such a measure, and a framework of the antecedents and consequences of decision-making competence.

The Need for a Validated Individual-Differences Measure of Decision-Making Competence

Descriptive decision research has typically used paper-and-pencil tasks to identify errors in people's decisions. Because they present hypothetical decisions with no real-world consequences, the question remains how well performance on these tasks predicts real-world performance. A related threat to the validity of paper-and-pencil tasks is that they are seemingly ill defined. Violations of sunk-cost rules may occur because recipients question the scenarios and generate defensible reasons for violating normative rules about sunk costs (Frisch, 1993). Framing errors may be defensible when descriptions affect how people experience their choices, with diners enjoying ground beef more when it is described as "75 percent lean" than as "25 percent fat" (Levin & Gaeth, 1988). Moreover, unjustified confidence may help to overcome hesitance to take those financial risks that lead to more retirement savings (Parker et al., 2012). Finally, normative strategies for integrating beliefs and values have been criticized for being too difficult without guaranteeing a better outcome than simple heuristics (Payne et al., 1993; Schwarz et al., 2002).

Reports of age-related changes in decision-making competence have also been questioned. Some critics have argued that adolescents may perform well on paper-and-pencil tasks in the psychological laboratory but behave less wisely in the real world due to heightened emotions and peer pressure (see Reyna & Farley, 2006). Others have argued that older adults may perform worse on paper-and-pencil tasks than in the real world where they can rely on their experience (see Peters & Bruine de Bruin, 2012). Indeed, the relationship between adult age and decision-making competence tends to be negative when tasks are cognitively demanding, while performance on more experience-based tasks may be unaffected by or improve with age (Bruine de Bruin et al., 2012).

Development and Validation of Individual-Differences Measures of Decision-Making Competence

Despite questions about the external validity of decision-making tasks, there is increasing evidence that better decision-making competence on seemingly unrealistic paper-and-pencil tasks is related to real-world antecedents and consequences of poor decision making. Because decision making has traditionally been seen as a cognitive exercise, several studies have examined the association between decision-making competence and cognitive abilities. Individuals with better performance on measures of fluid cognitive ability and executive functions are indeed more resistant to common decision-making biases such as overconfidence and framing effects (Bruine de Bruin et al., 2007; Del Missier et al., 2010, 2012; Finucane & Gullion, 2010; Finucane et al., 2002, 2005; Parker & Fischhoff, 2005; Stanovich & West, 2008).

Our first study focused on measuring decision-making competence in adolescents from diverse backgrounds (Parker & Fischhoff, 2005). Tasks included consistency in risk perception, resistance to sunk costs, resistance to framing, applying decision rules, and under/overconfidence. Because decision-making competence reflects a mutually supporting set (or "positive manifold") of skills (Stanovich & West, 2008), batteries of decision-making competence may vary in their portfolio of paper-and-pencil tasks, as long as they comprehensively represent the main processes (belief assessment, value assessment, integration, and metacognition) and are reliable and valid. In our studies, although some individual tasks showed relatively low internal consistency, overall performance across tasks was sufficiently reliable to warrant the computation of an aggregate measure. Furthermore, this overall decision-making competence score correlated with better cognitive ability and less maladaptive risk taking (e.g., delinquency) even after controlling for cognitive ability, suggesting external validity.

Our second study focused on adult decision-making competence (Bruine de Bruin et al., 2007). It built on the first study by adapting its items for adults, while using larger item sets and methods refined to improve their reliability. Adults of diverse ages showed relatively consistent performance within and across the component tasks. The validity of the component tasks and of their overall score emerged in significant correlations with measures of cognitive ability, socioeconomic status, and cognitive styles. Most importantly, performance on individual tasks and overall performance across tasks were related to avoiding negative decision outcomes, even after controlling for cognitive ability and other characteristics. The decision outcomes were self-reported on the Decision Outcome Inventory (DOI), which gave individuals credit for avoiding negative controllable life experiences, such as sexually transmitted infections, if they had made decisions that could have led to those experiences (e.g., if they had had sex). While the selected outcomes may not always result from poor decision making, they should be more common among poor decision makers than among good decision makers. Indeed, we found that participants with better decision-competence scores were less likely to report poor outcomes on individual DOI items as well as on the set as a whole. These results support other findings that traditional paper-and-pencil tasks are reliable and valid measures of decision-making competence (Finucane & Gullion, 2010; Finucane et al., 2002, 2005).

Framework for Considering the Antecedents and Consequences of Decision-Making Competence

Figure 11.1 summarizes the literature we have reviewed thus far, presenting a simple overview of the relationships that are emerging. Following theoretical models

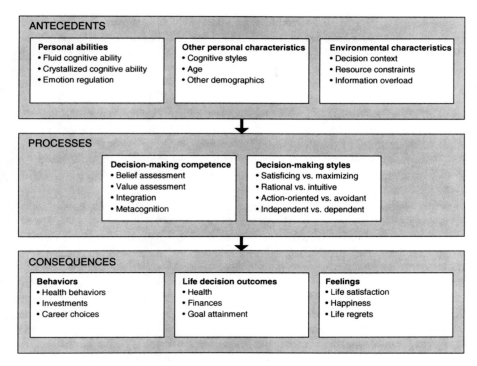

Figure 11.1   Antecedents, processes, and consequences of decisions.

proposed by Yates (2003) and others, Figure 11.1 suggests that personal and environmental *antecedents* shape decision-making *processes,* in turn leading to specific decision-making *consequences.*

Antecedents   Personal abilities, other personal characteristics, and environmental characteristics are possible antecedents of decision-making competence. Personal abilities include fluid cognitive ability, which has been associated with better performance on decision tasks (Bruine de Bruin et al., 2007, 2012; Del Missier et al., 2012; Stanovich & West, 2008). The relatively low correlations of fluid cognitive ability with resistance to sunk costs suggest that this task poses low cognitive demand (Bruine de Bruin et al., 2007; Strough et al., 2008). Decision tasks for which performance shows low correlations with fluid cognitive ability may require experience-related knowledge about how to execute the task or emotion-regulation skills that prevent normatively incorrect affective responses (Stanovich & West, 2008).

Research on the contribution of other personal abilities has been relatively limited, due to validated measures being less readily available than for fluid cognitive ability. These other personal abilities with plausible relationships include crystallized intelligence, defined as knowledge and skills acquired through training or age-related life experience. Age and vocabulary (which improves with age) have been used as a proxy for crystallized intelligence (Bruine de Bruin et al., 2012; Parker & Fischhoff, 2005). Self-reports of having taken formal courses covering normative decision making are correlated with performance on sunk-cost tasks (Larrick et al., 1993). Older, and hence more experienced, decision makers may develop efficient heuristics that reduce the cognitive complexity of their decisions (Reyna, 2004; Stanovich & West, 2008). As noted, the ability to cope with irrecoverable losses and better emotion regulation may also be correlated with better sunk-cost decisions (Strough et al., 2011). These initial results support theories of decision making across the lifespan, which hold that decision performance depends on fluid cognitive skills that improve until adolescence and then show age-related decline, as well as experience and emotional maturity which improve with age (Peters & Bruine de Bruin, 2012; Reyna, 2004; Reyna & Farley, 2006; Strough et al., 2011).

Other personal characteristics may also contribute to making good decisions. Cognitive styles such as need for cognition have sometimes been associated with making fewer framing errors (Smith & Levin, 1996) and sometimes not (LeBeouf & Shafir, 1993; Levin et al., 2002). Age-related changes in decision-making competence were reviewed above (Peters & Bruine de Bruin, 2012; Reyna, 2004; Reyna & Farley, 2006; Strough et al., 2011). Other demographic variables include socioeconomic status, with individuals of disadvantaged backgrounds performing worse on decision-making tasks (Bruine de Bruin et al., 2007; Parker & Fischhoff, 2005), possibly because they are less likely to have life experiences that develop their potential.

Antecedents of decision-making competence also include environmental characteristics. Decision researchers have extensively documented how normatively irrelevant variations in decision context cause decision errors (Kahneman et al., 1982). The descriptive research reviewed in this chapter highlighted the effects of framing, or normatively irrelevant variations in how an option is described, as well as the effects of the presence of sunk costs, or normatively irrelevant past investments of time or money in an option (Arkes & Blumer, 1985). Resource constraints such as time pressure lead decision makers to use faster and more efficient decision strategies, which may sometimes improve and sometimes threaten the quality of decisions (Payne et al., 1993). Information overload may also lead people to feel overburdened, leading to effort-saving deviations from normative theories, and even to choice paralysis or decision avoidance (Schwarz et al., 2002). Naturally, these environmental characteristics may interact with individual characteristics. As noted, familiar contexts may help older adults to rely on their experience (Kim & Hasher, 2005; Tentori et al., 2001).

Processes   The use of specific decision processes is likely shaped by decision-making competence and decision-making styles. Decision-making styles may affect tendencies to use specific decision processes, such as maximizing or searching for the best option rather than satisficing or selecting an option that is good enough (Parker et al., 2007; Schwartz et al., 2002). A decision styles battery by Scott and Bruce (1995) involves self-reported tendencies to make rational, intuitive, avoidant, dependent, and spontaneous decisions. A recent review has noted that, unlike measures of decision-making competence, measures of decision-making styles often lack validation or grounding in decision theory (Appelt et al., 2011). Yet some decision styles, such as the tendency to satisfice rather than maximize, have been validated by being linked with greater life satisfaction and better decision outcomes (Bruine de Bruin et al., 2007; Parker et al., 2007; Schwarz et al., 2002).

Consequences   Finally, consequences of decisions include *behaviors* observed in the real world, such as health behaviors, investments, and career choices, *life decision outcomes* such as better health, finances, and goal attainment, and *feelings* such as life satisfaction, happiness, and life regrets. Validation studies have suggested that individuals with better decision-making competence do indeed report more positive self-reported behaviors and outcomes, even after controlling for fluid cognitive ability (Bruine de Bruin et al., 2007; Parker & Fischhoff, 2005). Decision-making competence has also been associated with reduced feelings of regret, even after controlling for regret-inducing decision styles such as maximizing (Parker et al., 2007).

While not explicitly noted in our literature review or shown in Figure 11.1, there are likely dynamic interactions and feedback loops among the various stages of this simple model. For example, decision outcomes may change environmental situations: A particularly poor decision at work could result in loss of employment, whereas a particularly good series of relationship choices could result in a successful long-term relationship. Both good and bad decisions can provide experiences that change decision-making competence and decision-making styles.

NEXT STEPS

Until recently, individual-differences research has received relatively little attention in the field of decision making. Having access to validated and comprehensive individual-differences measures of decision-making competence has inspired new research and promises theoretical and practical advances. We expect that individual-differences research will grow in three main directions. First, the availability of validated comprehensive measures provides the opportunity to systematically test which skills underlie people's ability to make sound decisions. The Adult Decision-Making Competence battery has been added to longitudinal panel studies such as the Betula project in Sweden, facilitating research on its relationship with specific memory skills (Del Missier et al., in press). Second, a validated assessment of overall decision-making competence and its various components will facilitate research on age-related changes in decision making. Ultimately, data from national samples could be used to create norms for decision-making competence, helping to establish empirically-driven legal benchmarks for whether specific individuals have the ability to make sound decisions. Third, access to a validated measure will facilitate the evaluation of communication materials, decision aids, behavioral-skills training, and other efforts that aim to teach better decision making. In the absence of such measures, little can be learned from attempts to teach better decision making (Beyth-Marom et al., 1991). For example, a recent study found that a high-school history curriculum that was augmented with decision education and discussion of historical decisions showed greater improvement in student' decision-making competence than did the standard curriculum (Jacobson et al., 2012). Intervention design should benefit from the two lines of research on underlying skills and aging-related changes. Indeed, if adolescents are found to be swayed from making sound decisions in situations with which they lack experience, interventions may focus on providing initial experience in a protective environment. For example, a video-based intervention that provided adolescents with models for how to negotiate safer strategies with their sexual partners was found to increase periods of having no sex, condom use among those who did choose to have sex, and lower rates of sexually transmitted infections (Downs et al., 2004). Analogously, if older adults are found to make poor decisions due to age-related cognitive declines, then interventions may need to provide training in cognitive skills, cognitive aids, simplified information, or increasing reliance on previous personal experience (Park et al., 1992; Peters & Bruine de Bruin, 2012). Finally, interventionists could employ decision-making competence assessments for tailoring provided information and skills training to individuals' specific needs.

In summary, this chapter shows how individual-differences research has built on normative theories that prescribe how to make decisions and descriptive research on common violations of normative decision rules. With the development of validated comprehensive measures of decision-making competence, decision research now provides the theoretical approach and the methodological tools needed to understand how decision-making competence develops across the lifespan, relates to downstream consequences, and varies with individuals' cognitive and emotional skills, experience, other personal characteristics, environment, and person–environment interactions. It should facilitate helping people to improve their decision-making competence, by identifying and building on their strengths and overcoming their weaknesses.

AUTHOR NOTE

We gratefully acknowledge funding from the European Union Seventh Framework Programme (Marie Curie Career Integration Grant 618522), the National Institute on Aging (P01AG026571), the National Institute on Drug Abuse (P50DA05605), and the National Science Foundation (SES-0213782).

REFERENCES

Appelt, K. C., Milch, K. F., Handgraaf, M. J. J., & Weber, E. U. (2011). The decision making individual differences inventory and guidelines for the study of individual differences in judgment and decision making research. *Judgment and Decision Making, 6(3)*, 252–262.
Arkes, H. R., & Ayton, P. (1999). The sunk cost and Concorde effects: Are humans less rational than lower animals? *Psychological Bulletin, 5(5)*, 591–600.
Arkes, H. R., & Blumer, C. (1985). The psychology of sunk cost. *Organizational Behavior and Human Decision Processes, 35(1)*, 124–140.
Beyth-Marom, R., Austin, L., Fischhoff, B., Palmgren, C., & Jacobs-Quadrel, M. J. (1993). Perceived consequences of risky behaviors: Adults and adolescents. *Developmental Psychology, 29(3)*, 549–563.

Beyth-Marom, R., & Fischhoff, B. (1997). Adolescents' decisions about risks: A cognitive perspective. In J. Schulenburg, J. L. Maggs, & K. Hurrelmann (Eds.), *Health risks and developmental transitions during adolescence* (pp. 110–135). New York, NY: Cambridge University Press.

Beyth-Marom, R., Fischhoff, B., Quadrel, M. J., & Furby, L. (1991). Teaching adolescents decision making. In J. Baron & R. Brown (Eds.), *Teaching decision making to adolescents* (pp. 19–60). Hillsdale, NJ: Erlbaum.

Bruine de Bruin, W. (2012). Judgment and decision making in adolescents. In M. K. Dhami, A. Schlottmann, & M. Waldmann (Eds.), *Judgment and decision making as a skill: Learning, development, and evolution* (pp. 85–112). New York, NY: Cambridge University Press.

Bruine de Bruin, W., Downs, J. S., Murray, P. M., & Fischhoff, B. (2010). Can female adolescents tell whether they will test positive for Chlamydia infection? *Medical Decision Making, 30(2)*, 189–193.

Bruine de Bruin, W., Parker, A. M., & Fischhoff, B. (2012). Explaining adult age differences in decision-making competence. *Journal of Behavioral Decision Making, 25(4)*, 352–360.

—— (2007a). Individual differences in adult decision-making competence. *Journal of Personality and Social Psychology, 92(5)*, 938–956.

—— (2007b). Can teens predict significant life events? *Journal of Adolescent Health, 41(2)*, 208–210.

Centers for Disease Control and Prevention (2004). Youth risk behavior surveillance: United States, 2003. *Morbidity and Mortality Weekly Report, 53(2)*, 1–96.

Cohn, L., Macfarlane, S., Yanez, C., & Imai, W. (1995). Risk-perception: Differences between adolescents and adults. *Health Psychology, 14(3)*, 217–222.

Crawford, J. D., & Stankov, L. (1996). Age differences in the realism of confidence judgments: A calibration study using tests of fluid and crystallized intelligence. *Learning and Individual Differences, 2(2)*, 83–103.

Del Missier, F., Mäntylä, T., & Bruine de Bruin, W. (2010). Executive functions in decision making: An individual differences approach. *Thinking and Reasoning, 16(2)*, 69–97.

—— (2012). Decision-making competence, executive functioning, and general cognitive abilities. *Journal of Behavioral Decision Making, 25(4)*, 331–351.

Del Missier, F., Mäntylä, T., Hansson, P., Bruine de Bruin, W., & Parker, A. M. (2013). The multifold relationship between memory and decision making: An individual differences study. *Journal of Experimental Psychology: Learning, Memory, and Cognition, 39(5)*, 1344–1364.

Downs, J. S., Murray, P. J., Bruine de Bruin, W., White, J. P., Palmgren, C., & Fischhoff, B. (2004). Interactive video behavioral intervention to reduce adolescent females' STD risk: A randomized controlled trial. *Social Science and Medicine, 59(8)*, 1561–1572.

Edwards, W. (1954). The theory of decision making. *Psychological Bulletin, 51(4)*, 380–417.

Finucane, M. L., & Gullion, C. M. (2010). Developing a tool for measuring the decision-making competence of older adults. *Psychology and Aging, 25(2)*, 271–288.

Finucane, M. L., Mertz, C. K., Slovic, P., & Schmidt, E. S. (2005). Task complexity and older adults' decision-making competence. *Psychology and Aging, 20(2)*, 71–84.

Finucane, M. L., Slovic, P., Hibbard, J. H., Peters, E., Mertz, C. K., & Macgregor, D. G. (2002). Aging and decision-making competence: An analysis of comprehension and consistency skills in older versus younger adults. *Journal of Behavioral Decision Making, 15(2)*, 141–164.

Fischhoff, B. (1996). The real world: What good is it? *Organizational Behavior and Human Decision Processes, 65(3)*, 232–248.

—— (2008). Assessing adolescent decision-making competence. *Developmental Review, 28(1)*, 12–28.

Fischhoff, B., Bruine de Bruin, W., Parker, A. M., Millstein, S. G., & Halpern-Felsher, B. L. (2010). Adolescents' perceived risk of dying. *Journal of Adolescent Health, 46(3)*, 265–269.

Fischhoff, B., Parker, A. M., Bruine de Bruin, W., Downs, J. S., Palmgren, C., Dawes, R., & Manski, C. (2000). Teen expectations for significant life events. *Public Opinion Quarterly, 64(2)*, 189–205.

Gerrard, M., Gibbons, F. X., Houlihan, A. E., Stock, M. L., & Pomery, E. A. (2008). A dual-process approach to health risk decision making: The prototype willingness model. *Developmental Review, 28(1)*, 29–61.

Grant, B. F., & Dawson, D. A. (1997). Age at drinking onset and its association with DSM-IV alcohol use and problem behavior in late adolescence: Results from the National Longitudinal Alcohol Epidemiologic Survey. *Journal of Substance Abuse, 9*, 103–110.

Halpern-Felsher, B. L., & Cauffman, E. (2001). Costs and benefits of a decision: Decision-making competence in adolescents and adults. *Journal of Applied Developmental Psychology, 22(3)*, 257–273.

Halpern-Felsher, B. L., Millstein, S. G., Ellen, J. M., Adler, N. E., Tschann, J. M., & Biehl, M. (2001). The role of behavioral experience in judging risks. *Health Psychology, 20(2)*, 120–126.

Hansson, P., Rönnlund, M., Juslin, P., & Nilsson, L. G. (2008). Adult age differences in the realism of confidence judgments: Overconfidence, format dependence, and cognitive predictors. *Psychology and Aging, 23(3)*, 531–544.

Hurd, M. D. (2009). Subjective probabilities in household surveys. *Annual Review of Economics, 1*, 543–562.

Jacobs, J. E., & Potenza, M. (1991). The use of judgment heuristics to make social and object decisions: A developmental perspective. *Child Development, 62(1)*, 166–178.

Jacobson, D., Parker, A., Spetzler, C., Bruine de Bruin, W., Hollenbeck, K., Heckerman, D., & Fischhoff, B. (2012). Improved learning in U.S. history and decision competence with decision-focused curriculum. *PLoS ONE, 7(9)*, 1–3.

Johnson, M. M. (1990). Age differences in decision making: A process methodology for examining strategic information processing. *Journal of Gerontology, 45(2)*, 75–78.

Kahneman, D., Slovic, P., & Tversky, A. (1982). *Judgment under uncertainty: Heuristics and biases.* New York, NY: Cambridge University Press.

Keren, G., & Bruine de Bruin, W. (2003). On the assessment of decision quality: Considerations regarding utility, conflict, and accountability. In D. Hardman & L. Macchi (Eds.), *Thinking: Psychological perspectives on reasoning, judgment and decision making* (pp. 347–363). New York, NY: Wiley.

Kim, S., Goldstein, D., Hasher, L., & Zacks, R. T. (2005). Framing effects in younger and older adults. *Journal of Gerontology: Psychological Sciences, 60B(4)*, 215–218.

Kim, S., & Hasher, L. (2005). The attraction effect in decision making: Superior performance by older adults. *Quarterly Journal of Experimental Psychology, 58A(1)*, 120–133.

Klaczynski, P. A. (2001). Analytic and heuristic processes influences on adolescent reasoning and decision making. *Child Development, 72(3)*, 844–861.

Klaczynski, P. A., & Cottrell, J. M. (2004). A dual-process approach to cognitive development: The case of children's understanding of sunk cost decisions. *Thinking and Reasoning, 10(2)*, 147–174.

Klayman, J., Soll, J. B., González-Vallejo, C., & Barlas, S. (1999). Overconfidence: It depends on how, what and whom you ask. *Organizational Behavior and Human Decision Processes, 79(3)*, 216–247.

Koriat, A., Lichtenstein, S., & Fischhoff, B. (1980). Reasons for confidence. *Journal of Experimental Psychology: Human Learning and Memory, 6(2)*, 107–118.

Kruger, J., & Burrus, J. (2004). Egocentrism and focalism in unrealistic optimism. *Journal of Experimental Social Psychology, 40(3)*, 332–340.

Larrick, R. P., Nisbett, R. E., & Morgan, J. N. (1993). Who uses the cost-benefit rules of choice? Implications for the normative status of microeconomic theory. *Organizational Behavior and Human Decision Processes, 56(3)*, 331–347.

LeBoeuf, R. A., & Shafir, E. (2003). Deep thoughts and shallow frames: On the susceptibility to framing effects. *Journal of Behavioral Decision Making, 16(2)*, 77–92.

Levin, I. P., & Gaeth, G. J. (1988). How consumers are affected by the framing of attribute information before and after consuming the product. *Journal of Consumer Research, 15(3)*, 374–378.

Levin, I. P., Gaeth, G. J., Schreiber, J., & Lauriola, M. (2002). A new look at framing effects: Distribution of effect sizes, individual differences, and independence of types of effects. *Organizational Behavior and Human Decision Processes, 88(1)*, 411–429.

Levin, I. P., Schnittjer, S. K., & Thee, S. L. (1988). Information framing effects in social and personal decisions. *Journal of Experimental Social Psychology, 24(6)*, 520–529.

Levin, I. P., Weller, J. A., Pederson, A. A., & Harshman, L. A. (2007). Age-related differences in adaptive decision making: Sensitivity to expected value in risky choice. *Judgment and Decision Making, 2(4)*, 225–233.

Mayhorn, C. B., Fisk, A. D., & Whittle, J. D. (2002). Decisions, decisions: Analysis of age, cohort, and time of testing on framing of risky decision options. *Human Factors, 44(4)*, 515–521.

McKenzie, C. R. M. (2004). Framing effects in inference tasks—and why they are normatively defensible. *Memory and Cognition, 32(6)*, 874–885.

Mikels, J. A., & Reed, A. E. (2009). Monetary losses do not loom large in later life: Age differences in the framing effect. *Journal of Gerontology: Psychological Sciences, 64B(4)*, 457–460.

Park, D. C., Morwell, R. W., Frieske, D., & Kincaid, D. (1992). Medication adherence behaviors in older adults: Effects of external cognitive supports. *Psychology and Aging, 7(2)*, 252–256.

Parker, A. M., Bruine de Bruin, W., & Fischhoff, B. (2007). Maximizers vs. satisficers: Decision-making styles, competence, and outcomes. *Judgment and Decision Making, 2(6)*, 342–350.

Parker, A. M., Bruine de Bruin, W., Yoong, J., & Willis, R. (2012). Inappropriate confidence and retirement planning: Four studies with a national sample. *Journal of Behavioral Decision Making, 4(4)*, 382–389.

Parker, A. M., & Fischhoff, B. (2005). Decision-making competence: External validation through an individual-differences approach. *Journal of Behavioral Decision Making, 18(1)*, 1–27.

Payne, J. W., Bettman, J. R., & Johnson, E. J. (1993). *The adaptive decision maker.* New York, NY: Cambridge University Press.

Persoskie, A. (2013). How well can adolescents really judge risk? Simple, self reported risk factors out-predict teens' self estimates of personal risk. *Judgment and Decision Making, 8(1)*, 1–6.

Peters, E. M., & Bruine de Bruin, W. (2012). Aging and decision skills. In M. K. Dhami, A. Schlottmann, & M. Waldmann (Eds.), *Judgment and decision making as a skill: Learning, development, and evolution* (pp. 113–140). New York, NY: Cambridge University Press.

Poulton, E. C. (1989). *Bias in quantifying judgment.* Hillsdale, NJ: Lawrence Erlbaum.

Price, P. C., & Stone, E. R. (2003). Intuitive evaluation of likelihood judgment producers: Evidence for a confidence heuristic. *Journal of Behavioral Decision Making, 17(1)*, 39–57.

Reyna, V. F. (2004). How people make decisions that involve risk: A dual-processes approach. *Current Directions in Psychological Science, 13(2)*, 60–66.

Reyna, V. F., & Ellis, S. C. (1994). Fuzzy-trace theory and framing effects in children's risky decision making. *Psychological Science, 5(5)*, 275–279.

Reyna, V. F., Estrada, S. M., DeMarinis, J. A., Myers, R. M., Stanisz, J. M., & Mills, B. A. (2011). Neurobiological and memory models of risky decision making in adolescents versus young adults. *Journal of Experimental Psychology: Learning, Memory, and Cognition, 37(5)*, 1125–1142.

Reyna, V. F., & Farley, F. (2006). Risk and rationality in adolescent decision making: Implications for theory, practice and public policy. *Psychological Science in the Public Interest, 7(1)*, 1–44.

Rönnlund, M., Karlsson, E., Laggnäs, E., Larsson, L., & Lindström, T. (2005). Risky decision making across three arenas of choice: Are younger and older adults differently susceptible to framing effects? *Journal of General Psychology, 132(1)*, 81–92.

Rothman, A. J., Klein, W. M., & Weinstein, N. D. (1996). Absolute and relative biases in estimations of personal risk. *Journal of Applied Social Psychology, 26(14)*, 1213–1236.

Schwartz, B., Ward, A., Monterosso, J., Lyubomirsky, S., White, K., & Lehman, D. R. (2002). Maximizing versus satisficing: Happiness is a matter of choice. *Journal of Personality and Social Psychology, 83(5)*, 1178–1197.

Scott, S. G., & Bruce, R. A. (1995). Decision making style: The development and assessment of a new measure. *Educational and Psychological Measurement, 55(5)*, 818–831.

Smith, S. M., & Levin, I. P. (1996). Need for cognition and choice framing effects. *Journal of Behavioral Decision Making, 9(4)*, 283–290.

Strough, J., McKarns, T. E., & Schlossnagle, L. (2011). Decision-making heuristics and biases across the life span. *Annals of the New York Academy of Sciences, 1235(1)*, 57–74.

Strough, J., Mehta, C. M., McFall, J. P., & Schuller, K. L. (2008). Are older adults less subject to the sunk-cost fallacy than younger adults? *Psychological Science, 19(7)*, 650–652.

Tentori, K., Osherson, D., Hasher, L., & May, C. (2001). Wisdom and aging: Irrational preferences in college students but not older adults. *Cognition, 81(3)*, 87–96.

Thorne, D., Warren, E., & Sullivan, T. A. (2009). Increasing vulnerability of older Americans: Evidence from the bankruptcy court. *Harvard Law and Policy Review, 3*, 87–101.

Turner, C., & McClure, R. (2003). Age and gender differences in risk taking behaviour as an explanation for high incidence of motor vehicle crashes as a driver in young males. *Injury Control and Safety Promotion, 10(3)*, 123–130.

Tversky, A., & Koehler, D. J. (1994). Support theory: A nonexistensional representation of subjective probability. *Psychological Review, 101(4)*, 547–567.

Weller, J. A., Levin, I. P., & Denburg, N. (2011). Trajectory of adaptive decision making for risky gains and losses from ages 5 to 85. *Journal of Behavioral Decision Making, 24(4)*, 331–344.

Yates, J. F. (2003). *Decision management: How to assure better decisions in your company.* San Francisco, CA: Jossey-Bass.

Zarnoth, P., & Sniezek, J. A. (1997). The social influence of confidence in group decision making. *Journal of Experimental Social Psychology, 33(4)*, 345–366.

Part VI

Improving Decisions

12

Predictors of Risky Decisions

Improving Judgment and Decision Making Based on Evidence from Phishing Attacks

JULIE S. DOWNS, DONATO BARBAGALLO, AND ALESSANDRO ACQUISTI

Neuroeconomic approaches to judgment and decision making require precision in operationalization and measurement, separating individual predictors from the behaviors or judgments being studied. We describe divergent predictive relationships between multi-faceted variables and different qualities of downstream outcomes in the domain of information security. We analyze behavioral responses to phishing attacks (fraudulent email requests for sensitive information), and consider the interdependent relationships between predictors such as awareness, different kinds of knowledge, perceptions of severity and susceptibility to risk, costs, and ability to distinguish between the effectiveness of different protective strategies. We test how well these factors predict measures of both intentions and behavior. We find that increased awareness predicts improvements in procedural and, especially, declarative knowledge about phishing attacks, and that both kinds of knowledge predict a tempering of perceived susceptibility to risk. Of particular interest, we find that declarative knowledge predicts an ability to identify which protective strategies are weaker, but that procedural knowledge predicts an ability to actually protect oneself from phishing attacks without a commensurate rise in false alarms to legitimate emails, a distinction that was not identified by measures of intentions. Indeed, measures of intentions revealed only overall variability in approach versus avoidant strategies, without respect for the riskiness of the situation. This pattern affirms the importance of measuring constructs beyond the self-awareness required for direct self-reports, and measuring relationships between variables that may reveal processes not accessible to conscious reports. Neuroeconomic approaches to measurement hold great promise to expand our ability to disentangle such relationships.

*U*nderstanding how individuals make decisions should include an accounting of the factors that predict those decisions. The precision of measurement required by a neuroeconomic approach, in order to pinpoint neural mechanisms, must be accompanied by methodological strategies to isolate and operationalize inputs to decisions that will allow differentiation between them. Here, we use behavioral and self-report data to explore how decision makers incorporate relevant pieces of information into a judgment about the risks associated with different behaviors, and how those judgments combine to predict decisions.

We use the domain of information security to study so-called phishing attacks, in which fraudulent email messages are used to elicit passwords and other private information from unsuspecting individuals. This behavior is of great importance to organizations and policy makers, which have devoted significant efforts to improving the technical security of information systems, although end users often remain the weak link in the security chain (Herath & Rao, 2009; Williams, 2008). Because decision content and behavior in this domain are relatively easily defined and measured, phishing attacks provide a good arena to explore basic processes that are relevant to a broader set of risky decisions.

As with many risky domains (Jacobsen & Jacobsen, 2011), primary educational efforts against phishing attacks aimed at lowering risk have focused on raising awareness about the risk, and then offering behavioral solutions (Albrechtsen & Hovden, 2010; D'Arcy et al., 2009; McCoy & Fowler, 2004; Shaw et al., 2009). Indeed, the Organisation for Economic Co-operation and Development (OECD) identified awareness as a fundamental principle in information security (OECD, 2002) and one that can affect attitudes, intentions, and norms (Dinev & Hu, 2007). However, informed decisions in most domains require more than mere awareness, and information security is no exception, with many familiar factors emerging as relevant, including trust (Sug & Han, 2003), accessibility of understanding (Cranor & Garfinkel, 2005), cognitive and behavioral biases (Acquisti, 2004; Engelman et al., 2009), and attention to trade-off processes (Hann et al., 2007). Previous research has found very low discrimination between legitimate emails and phishing attacks (Downs et al., 2006), or in interpreting warnings or cues provided by system architecture as opposed to easily spoofed cues in the content itself (Dhamija et al., 2005, 2006), suggesting that mere awareness in this domain will be no more effective on its own than in other risky domains.

One can imagine multiple, interrelated steps required for optimal information security decision making, just as is the case in financial, health, and career domains. Neglecting or misunderstanding any step along the way can thwart protection against the threat, potentially exposing oneself to risk—a progression leading some experts to conclude that end users cannot be sufficiently educated (Gorling, 2006). Imagine, for example, receiving an email from your bank with instructions to immediately log on to your account and change your online bank credentials. Awareness that such a message may pose a threat provides a cue for more in-depth processing and engaging in protective strategies, but perhaps only if the potential risk is not viewed as trivial.

As in many domains, severity of the threat and heightened risk perceptions are popular targets for intervention (Asgharpour et al., 2007; Mcilwraith, 2006).

Perceived severity may be sufficient to galvanize a threat response (Ng et al., 2009; Sipponen, 2000), but in the absence of an effective action plan it is unlikely to translate into effective prevention of risk (Witte, 1992). Indeed, also as in many domains, the perceived severity of the consequences of phishing is not a great predictor of the use of effective protective strategies against it (Downs et al., 2007). Knowledge of how to reduce risk is necessary for severity to produce results (Witte & Allen, 2000).

Promoting knowledge has been central to many educational efforts aimed at helping computer users avoid these risks (Ferguson, 2005; Jagatic et al., 2007; New York State Office of Cyber Security and Critical Infrastructure Coordination, 2005; Sheng et al., 2007; Spagat, 2009), although most do not take a decision-analytic approach. Cues are offered to users in the forms of warnings and toolbar options, often using terms that are not well understood or trusted (Wu et al., 2006), leaving people with inadequate comprehension of their choices as they try to comply with instructions or at least make messages go away. The cues provided by protection systems may be directly contradicted by the fraudulent message, creating dissonance in interpreting the threat. Unfortunately, naive computer users often cannot differentiate between valid and fraudulent cues or, worse yet, find the fraudulent cues easier to make sense of (Dhamija et al., 2006).

Understanding how to distinguish these types of cues requires both declarative knowledge (e.g., understanding the term "chrome" to represent the borders, frames, and menus of a web browser, so as to understand instructions provided by websites), and effective procedural knowledge (e.g., understanding how to interpret URLs to determine their trustworthiness; Kumaraguru et al., 2006). Procedural knowledge that is too shallow, such as knowing how to identify simple indicators of fraud, can undermine risk prevention by relying too much on generalization from inappropriate gist knowledge (Reyna & Adam, 2003). Such simple strategies risk obsolescence and, ironically, can increase risk if these very strategies are hijacked by attackers (Srikwan & Jakobsson, 2008). For example, basic strategies for interpreting website content, such as looking for a padlock icon on the page, predict poor performance in discriminating phishing from nonphishing websites, in contrast to more sophisticated strategies that incorporate scrutiny of URLs, security indicators, and icons in the browser chrome, which predict much better discrimination (Dhamija et al., 2006). However, sufficient knowledge to identify effective protective techniques still requires a decision to engage such strategies, which may be time-consuming or otherwise costly, leading to an implicit cost–benefit analysis of whether to follow security advice (Bellovin, 2008; Herley, 2009).

These are some potential factors that may lead people to fail to engage in sufficient protective strategies, possibly contributing to the so-called "privacy paradox," the contradictory behavior of users who voice a preference for privacy but voluntarily disclose personal information for marketing (Norberg et al., 2007), service personalization (Awad & Krishnan, 2006), social networks (Acquisti & Gross, 2006; Barnes, 2006), or small rewards (Acquisti & Grossklags, 2005). Indeed, these disclosures tend to be better predicted by trust perceptions than by risk perceptions (Cranor et al., 1999; Schoenbachler & Gordon, 2002), suggesting that privacy concerns may be trumped by mitigating factors. In many ways this discrepancy reflects intention–behavior gaps that have emerged in a wide variety of domains (Sheeran, 2002) as documented in most models of risky behavior, including the Health Belief Model (Rosenstock, 1966), the Theory of Planned Behavior (Ajzen, 2002), its precursor the theory of reasoned action (TRA; Fishbein & Ajzen, 1980), and an application of these theories in the domain of information systems, the technology acceptance model (TAM; Davis, 1989). Intentions tend to be poorer measures of behavior to the extent that they are more distal measures of the behavior itself (Sutton, 1998), with potentially divergent predictors. The degree to which intentions are stable over time and situation contributes to their ability to predict behavior (Sheeran & Abraham, 2003). However, attention to privacy varies in response to environmental cues or events (Joinson et al., 2008), and may be conceived of relatively abstractly (Schwartz, 1968), undermining its ability to translate reliably into behavior.

In this chapter we aim to illuminate how decision factors predict intentions and behavior, as well as the relationships between them, with additional exploration of the degree to which self-reports can capture these factors. These relationships are particularly important for application to the neuroeconomics of decision making, by refining constructs that are relevant to decisions and defining them concisely enough that they might be mapped onto measures of neural activity. In the data presented here, we used a behavioral role-play exercise to assess nondeclarative behavior in a simulated environment and followed that with a survey to systematically assess self-reported intentions and the other decisional factors described above. In addition to behavior and intentions, we consider self-reported awareness, tests of knowledge (declarative and procedural), perceived susceptibility to

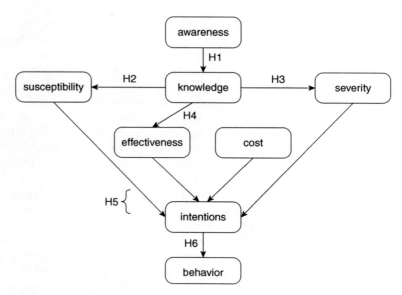

Figure 12.1   A predictive model of behavior for protection against risky email.

risk, perceived severity of risk, anticipated costs of protective behavior, and perceived effectiveness of different kinds of protective strategies, testing predicted relationships as depicted in Figure 12.1.

EMPIRICAL SUPPORT

We recruited 451 participants through various online methods. Participants varied widely in age (mean = 34; range: 16 to 78) and internet experience (range: 3 to 23 years) but were predominantly female (79 percent) and well educated (67 percent with at least college degree, and 21.4 percent reporting some postgraduate education).

The task was presented online, with no initial discussion of information security, starting with distractor questions about typing behavior and office etiquette. These questions set the stage for a role-play exercise about an office worker responding to and managing emails, using validated materials (Downs et al., 2007) to frame the task as one of mundane email management, as a means to reduce demand characteristics that would accompany unusual tasks (Stanton et al., 1956). Finally, participants completed a survey instrument assessing the suite of predictors and intentions to engage in protective behavior.

The role play consisted of nine emails, the first two of which were legitimate office correspondence and social emails, followed by a mix of five phishing emails (one targeted), one email containing a suspicious .exe file, and one more legitimate email. All phishing and legitimate emails included a link to a website. For each, participants were asked to choose from eight possible, nonexclusive actions:

1. reply by email;
2. contact the sender by phone or in person;
3. delete the email;
4. save the email;
5. click on the link;
6. copy and paste the URL;
7. type the URL into a browser window;
8. indicate any other action.

Most open-ended responses consisted of more sophisticated actions, such as reporting the email as fraud, which had purposefully been omitted from the provided list in order to avoid signaling the purpose of the task. Between 3 percent and 17 percent of respondents gave open-ended answers to any given email. All responses, including open-ended, were coded to determine whether the participant would follow the link, whether valid or fraudulent. (For example, an open-ended response to the eBay phishing email of "pay the auction" was coded as following, and a response of "I would check to see if I had the same message in my messages on my eBay account" was coded as not following; only a very small number of these responses qualified as following the link, as most expressed suspicion about the emails.) Participants who followed each email's link were presented with an image of the website that they would reach and asked to choose from five possible, nonexclusive actions:

1. click one or more links on the page;
2. enter requested data
3. bookmark, save, or archive the page;
4. visit another (related) webpage;
5. leave or close the website.

All responses were coded to determine whether the participant would provide requested information. Each predictor is defined and operationalized below, in turn.

Awareness was assessed as the sum of responses to three direct questions at the conclusion of the survey asking whether the participant had known about the existence of phishing scams prior to participating in the study (Cronbach's $\alpha = 0.68$).

Knowledge was divided into two constructs: understanding of terms (declarative knowledge) and ability to determine URL legitimacy (procedural knowledge). The former was measured as a proportion of correct answers to 15 terminology questions about computer security jargon (e.g., cookie, spam) and security symbols (e.g., lock icons, https; Cronbach's $\alpha = 0.76$). The latter was assessed as the proportion of correct answers to nine questions testing the subject's ability to determine trustworthiness about a set of URLs, some legitimate and some fraudulent (Eraut, 1994; Cronbach's $\alpha = 0.72$).

Perceived susceptibility was measured with a single question asking how easy participants thought it would be for them to fall for a phishing attack, asked on a seven-point scale.

Perceived severity was assessed with nine items (Cronbach's $\alpha = 0.82$) asking about possible outcomes from phishing attacks, ranging from identity theft to an increase in spam, each assessed on a seven-point scale.

Behavioral intentions were operationalized within the context of 11 protective strategies, generated from qualitative research (Downs et al., 2006) representing the more common techniques used to combat phishing, ranging considerably in their efficacy. The same strategies were also used to assess perceived costs and effectiveness, described below. Intentions to engage in each of the 11 strategies were assessed on a seven-point scale. To reduce the number of strategies to a more manageable and interpretable set, we conducted a principal component analysis with Varimax rotation on the intentions questions, revealing two categories: stronger strategies (e.g., using Google to search the company name instead of clicking on a link) and weaker ones, generally considered by experts to be ineffective or outdated (e.g., looking to see whether the email was addressed personally). The resulting groupings produced reliable indices for intentions to use stronger strategies (Cronbach's $\alpha = 0.85$, seven items) and to use weaker ones (Cronbach's $\alpha = 0.81$, four items).

Perceived effectiveness. Each of the 11 strategies was also assessed on a seven-point scale in terms of its perceived effectiveness in preventing phishing attacks. Participants were permitted to indicate that they were not familiar with each strategy. Using the groupings described above produced reliable indices for perceived effectiveness of stronger strategies (Cronbach's α = 0.82) and of weaker ones (Cronbach's α = 0.87).

Perceived costs of each of the same 11 strategies were assessed on a seven-point scale, specifying that costs could include time or money. A principal component analysis suggested a single factor (Cronbach's α = 0.94).

Behavior was assessed using choices made in the role-play exercise. Using contextualized real behaviors precludes measurement of behavioral strategies that map directly onto intentions (e.g., whether the participant was actually looking for spelling errors in the email). Thus, our proxy for strategy-specific behaviors—and indeed possibly the gold standard for assessing the value of their behaviors—was the action taken, represented by the outcome that would have been experienced based on choices made in the role-play section of our study. We identified the outcomes for the different possible actions in response to each message, measuring the proportion of phishing emails in which the respondent provided the requested information on the website (mean = 22 percent, range: 0–80 percent), and the proportion of legitimate emails on which the respondent provided the appropriate information (mean = 51 percent, range: 0–100 percent).

We identify predictions for the relationships between these variables, as indicated in Figure 12.1, which we test in the form of six hypotheses using linear regressions for univariate outcomes and multivariate analysis of variance (MANOVA) when more than one variable is being predicted, e.g., for the two kinds of knowledge being measured.

H1: Increased awareness is positively related to increased knowledge. Without awareness, there is little opportunity or incentive to develop knowledge, thus we hypothesize that those who are more aware of phishing risk will also have more (accurate) knowledge about the problem. Self-reported awareness of the possibility of fraud through email was very high, with 77 percent of participants indicating awareness of all three kinds of threats. In contrast, performance on the knowledge tests revealed more limited understanding of terms for declarative knowledge (mean = .63, Standard Deviation [SD] = .31) or procedural knowledge, in terms of ability to determine trustworthiness of URLs (mean = .22, SD = .24). Indeed, although 64 percent indicated that they were pretty sure the simple URL www.amazon.com was trustworthy, only 8 percent could make the same determination from a site beginning with http://cgi.ebay.com, and 29 percent thought they could be pretty sure that a URL starting with http://128.237.226.112/ebay was trustworthy, suggesting a fundamental lack of ability to parse URLs for much of our sample. The two forms of knowledge were only moderately correlated (r = .22,

$p = .001$), suggesting some degree of independence between understanding what phishing is and knowing how to determine if a link is a phishing attack. Using a MANOVA analysis we find support for H1, that awareness positively predicts knowledge, $F(2,393) = 8.50$, $p < .001$, with a stronger relationship for declarative knowledge, $F(1,394) = 15.04$, $p < .001$, partial $\eta^2 = .037$, than for procedural knowledge, $F(1,394) = 4.69$, $p = .04$, partial $\eta^2 = .012$.

H2: Perceived susceptibility decreases with more knowledge. Knowledge about a risk can affect perceived susceptibility in complex ways, increasing susceptibility for risks perceived as uncontrollable but decreasing it for more controllable ones (Slovic, 2000) such as ecommerce (Bhatnagar et al., 2000) and Internet security (Furnell et al., 2007). We find overall support for this hypothesis, $F(2,390) = 4.59$, $p = .01$, $R^2 = .015$, but with each type of knowledge predicting susceptibility with only marginal statistical significance. Declarative knowledge predicts reduced perceived susceptibility, $t(390) = -1.87$, $p = .06$, as does procedural knowledge, $t(390) = -1.92$, $p = .06$. These results suggest some, but not overwhelming, support for the idea that understanding more about phishing and how to protect oneself from it can reduce perceptions of susceptibility to it. Whether or not this perception is accurate, of course, depends on the actual measures taken to reduce the risk (Brewer et al., 2004).

H3: Perceived severity decreases with more knowledge. More familiarity with a risk tends to decrease estimates of its severity (Slovic, 2000). However, our measure of severity did not decrease as a function of knowledge, $F(2,389) = 1.54$, $p = .22$. Our measures focused on a list of actual, potential outcomes of phishing (e.g., how bad would a stolen identity be) rather than on how bad phishing itself is, potentially disrupting the anticipated relationship.

H4: Increased knowledge is positively related to better ability to discriminate among strategies' effectiveness. The importance of knowledge for downstream outcomes depends in part on the complexity of the behavior involved. In some cases, appropriate behavior requires little knowledge (e.g., compliance with seatbelt laws: Fahs et al., 1999). However, in the domain of phishing, many strategies are available to protect against risk, ranging from nearly airtight to hopelessly misguided (Dhamija et al., 2006; Fette et al., 2007; Wu et al., 2006). We explore here whether declarative and procedural knowledge can distinguish between the effectiveness of strong and weak strategies. Judgments of the effectiveness of protection strategies were similar overall for the stronger set of strategies (M = 4.97) than for the weaker, discredited set (M = 4.93), $t(388) = .52$, $p = .60$. We find partial support for this relationship, with effectiveness ratings predicted by both declarative, $F(2,383) = 5.91$, $p < .01$, and procedural knowledge, $F(2,383) = 6.10$, $p < .01$. However, both types of knowledge predicted effectiveness estimates only for the weaker set of strategies, with greater declarative knowledge being associated with a decrease in effectiveness ratings of these strategies, $F(1,384) = 11.33$, $p = .001$, partial $\eta^2 = .029$, and greater procedural knowledge being, surprisingly, associated with higher effectiveness ratings of these poor strategies, $F(1,384) = 11.56$, $p = .001$, partial $\eta^2 = .029$. Effectiveness ratings of the stronger strategies were not predicted by either declarative, $F(1,384) = 1.58$, $p = .21$, partial $\eta^2 = .004$, or procedural knowledge, $F(1,384) = 1.42$, $p = .23$, partial $\eta^2 = .004$. This pattern may suggest that the kind of knowledge indicating better understanding of the risks affords people with a sense of why poor strategies may not work, rather than a particular affinity toward the stronger strategies.

H5: Stated intentions to use stronger and weaker strategies should be predicted overall by increased perceived susceptibility, severity, and cost, and the relative use of the different types should be predicted by the perceived effectiveness of each. Perceived risk has been linked to intentions or behaviors for health (Ajzen, 2002; Rosenstock, 1966), e-commerce (Dinev & Hart, 2006; Malhotra et al., 2004), social networking (Krasnova & Veltri, 2010), computer security (Ng et al., 2009), and phishing attacks (Sheng et al., 2010). All else equal, perceived effectiveness of the different strategies should translate into increasing intentions to engage in associated behaviors (Ajzen, 2002; Davis, 1989; Pavlou & Fygenson, 2006). However, the costs associated with different approaches may create barriers, thus inhibiting intentions (e.g., Rosenstock, 1966), with costs being exogenously determined based on perceptions of steps required. However, little research has examined whether end users routinely make such trade-offs in the course of their naive behaviors, as captured in this study (Dinev & Hart, 2006; Krasnova & Veltri, 2010). We hypothesize that intentions to choose stronger strategies rely on perceptions of the risk, augmented by a cost–benefit analysis.

Overall, participants indicated stronger intentions to use the weaker set of strategies (M = 5.97) compared to the stronger set (M = 4.54), $t(389) = 18.36$, $p < .001$, although the two measures were highly correlated, $r(390) = .49$, $p < .001$. The stronger strategies were also perceived as more costly (M = 2.71) compared to the weaker set (M = 2.04), $t(384) = 13.19$, $p < .001$, although given the high correlation between these measures, $r(385) = .84$, it was not feasible to determine whether they would differentially predict intentions. We find considerable support for this hypothesis, with overall intentions to use protective strategies predicted by estimates of the effectiveness of both strong, $F(2,376) = 89.55$, $p < .001$, and weak strategies, $F(2,376) = 20.03$, $p < .001$, and by both susceptibility, $F(2,376) = 7.73$, $p = .001$, and severity, $F(2,376) = 4.17$, $p = .02$, but not cost, $F(2,376) = 2.21$, $p = .11$. Interestingly, perceived susceptibility and severity predicted only intentions to use the stronger strategies: $F(1,377) = 14.66$, $p < .01$, partial $\eta^2 = .037$ and $F(1,377) = 8.22$, $p = .04$, partial $\eta^2 = .021$, respectively. Neither predicted intentions to use the weaker strategies: $F(1,377) = 0.04$, $p = .83$, partial $\eta^2 = .000$, and $F(1,377) = 1.37$, $p = .24$, partial $\eta^2 = .004$, respectively. Perceived effectiveness of the stronger strategies predicted intentions to use either type: $F(1,377) = 177.52$, $p < .001$, partial $\eta^2 = .320$ for using the stronger strategies and $F(1,377) = 26.77$, $p < .001$, partial $\eta^2 = .066$ for using the weaker ones. Perhaps most telling, perceived effectiveness of the weaker strategies only predicted intentions to use those weaker ones, $F(1,377) = 36.12$, $p < .001$, partial $\eta^2 = .087$, not the stronger ones, $F(1,377) = 0.05$, $p = .83$, partial $\eta^2 = .000$.

H6: Intentions to use stronger strategies predict more appropriate behaviors than those to use weaker strategies. One of the key shortcomings in understanding human decision making has been the limited power of intentions to account for behavior (Sutter, 2007). Behaviors indicating falling for phishing scams were positively correlated with behaviors for appropriate response to legitimate emails, $r(451) = .33$, $p < .001$, suggesting a generally inefficient process of distinguishing between the two, but variability in caution toward phishing and legitimate emails collectively. Behavioral outcomes corresponding to responding to both phishing and legitimate emails were predicted by intentions to use both strong, $F(1,387) = 11.09$, $p = .001$, partial $\eta^2 = .028$, and weak strategies, $F(1,387) = 4.85$, $p = .04$, partial $\eta^2 = .012$, suggesting that strong strategies were generally better at promoting resistance to phishing but at the expense of more false alarms to legitimate emails. Neither intention measure interacted with the outcomes, suggesting that neither use of the stronger strategies, $F(1,387) = 0.00$, $p = .99$, partial $\eta^2 = .000$, nor the weak strategies, $F(1,387) = 0.23$, $p = .63$, partial $\eta^2 = .001$, were effective at discriminating between phishing and legitimate emails.

Adding knowledge to this model produces some interesting results. Although declarative knowledge does little to predict outcomes, $F(1,384) = 1.02$, $p = .31$, partial $\eta^2 = .003$, procedural knowledge actually interacts with outcome type, $F(1,387) = 5.20$, $p = .03$, partial $\eta^2 = .013$, such that increased ability to determine whether URLs are trustworthy predicts better actual protection against phishing, $r_{partial}(393) = -.14$, $p = .01$, with no associated reduction in failure to follow through with legitimate emails, $r_{partial}(393) = .00$, $p = .96$.

DISCUSSION

These data suggest complex relationships between the precursors of behavior in protection against phishing emails. Knowledge, in particular, has a multifaceted role, which depends on how it is conceptualized and measured. Declarative knowledge, in the form of ability to recognize and describe aspects of the phishing problem, was related sensibly to most self-reported predictors. However, procedural knowledge, which tended to be more weakly related to people's insight into decision factors—even predicting less useful assessments of strategies' effectiveness—turned out to be the only factor that actually predicted the ability to enact adaptive behaviors. This finding suggests the importance of delving beyond people's assessments of their own attitudes, knowledge, and intentions, into decisions that may not map cleanly onto self-reported constructs.

This separation of self-reports from objective measures underscores the importance of assessing true decisions or behaviors rather than hypothetical ones. There are many trade-offs to consider in this endeavor. The use of a role-play methodology in this study removes participants from the real-world demands of their computer environments, potentially reducing the environmental demands on their time. However, it allows for a more direct observation of behavior than self-reports or intentions. Previous validation of the role-play technique used in this study suggests that it is correlated with, but more conservative than, real-world email behavior. Here it is useful as a measurable and validated proxy of otherwise difficult-to-measure behavior (Downs et al., 2007), if an imperfect one (Schechter et al., 2007).

These results speak to an important separation in memory and knowledge that may account for the different predictive patterns for self-reported versus behavioral responses. Measures of declarative knowledge, indicating familiarity with terms and definitions, were relatively good predictors of self-reports of other associated variables, including awareness, susceptibility, and intentions. These relationships may reflect a type of knowledge that is not easily applied to decision making. In contrast, the measure of procedural knowledge was more poorly predictive of self-reports, in some cases even being negatively associated, but appeared to tap some element of deeper understanding, perhaps not as easily verbalized (Reyna, 2008). These results also have implications for the effects of risk-reduction approaches. Raising awareness is a popular approach across many domains of risk, but one that often fails to achieve behavior change. Consistent with these results, in other work we have found that attention to a more procedural approach of understanding how strategies work and knowing when to apply them can translate more directly into behavior change (Downs, 2004).

New methods and approaches developed as part of the burgeoning field of neuroeconomics hold great promise to expand upon our existing literature, and perhaps better explain underlying relationships between decisions and their predictors. As the field advances, it will be important for researchers to define variables clearly and cleanly, and to acknowledge interim processes that might affect relationships. Incorporating both self-reports and more objective measurements, indeed even comparing the two, has the potential to reveal profound insights into our understanding of how decisions are made. The increased attention to central and peripheral cognitive processes may help to further refine this focus.

REFERENCES

Acquisti, A. (2004). Privacy in electronic commerce and the economics of immediate gratification. In *Proceedings of the 5th ACM Conference on Electronic Commerce* (pp. 21–29). New York, NY: Association for Computing Machinery.

Acquisti, A., & Gross, R. (2006). Imagined communities: Awareness, information sharing, and privacy on Facebook. In G. Danezis and P. Golle (Eds.), *Proceedings of Privacy Enhancing Technologies Workshop (PET)* (pp. 36–58). Berlin: Springer.

Acquisti, A., & Grossklags, J. (2005). Privacy and rationality in decision making. *IEEE Security and Privacy*, 3(1), 26–33.

Ajzen, I. (2002). Perceived behavioral control, self-efficacy, locus of control, and the theory of planned behavior. *Journal of Applied Social Psychology*, 32(4), 665–683.

Albrechtsen, E., & Hovden, J. (2010). Improving information security awareness and behaviour through dialogue, participation and collective reflection: An intervention study. *Computer and Security*, 29(4), 432–445.

Asgharpour, F., Liu, D., & Camp, L. J. (2007). Mental models of computer security risks. In R. Sion (Ed.), *Financial cryptography and data security* (pp. 367–377). New York, NY: Springer.

Awad, N. F., & Krishnan, M. S. (2006). The personalization privacy paradox: An empirical evaluation of information transparency and the willingness to be profiled online for personalization. *MIS Quarterly, 30(1),* 13–28.

Barnes, S. B. (2006). A privacy paradox. *First Monday, 11(9),* http://firstmonday.org/article/view/1394/131211/22/2013.

Bellovin, S. (2008). Security by checklist. *IEEE Security and Privacy, 6(2),* 88.

Bhatnagar, A., Misra, S., & Rao, H. R. (2000). On risk, convenience, and Internet shopping behavior. *Communications of the ACM, 43(11),* 98–105.

Brewer, N., Weinstein, N. D., Cuite, C. L., Herrington, J., & Hayes, N. (2004). Measuring risk perception and its relation to risk behavior. *Annals of Behavioral Medicine, 27(4),* 125–130.

Cranor, L. F., & Garfinkel, S. (2005). *Security and usability: Designing secure systems that people can use.* Sebastopol, CA: O'Reilly Media.

Cranor, L. F., Reagle, J., & Ackerman, M. S. (1999). Beyond concern: Understanding net users' attitudes about online privacy. AT&T Labs Research Technical Report, TR99.4.3. Retrieved November 14, 2013, from www.research.att.com.

D'Arcy, J., Hovav, A., & Galletta, D. (2009). User awareness of security countermeasures and its impact on information systems misuse: A deterrence approach. *Information Systems Research, 20(1),* 79–98.

Davis, F. D. (1989). Perceived usefulness, perceived ease of use, and user acceptance of information technology. *MIS Quarterly, 13(3),* 319–340.

Dhamija, R., & Tygar, J. D. (2005). The battle against phishing: Dynamic security skins. In *Proceedings of the 2005 Symposium on Usable Privacy and Security, Pittsburgh, PA, July 6–8, 2005* (vol. 93, pp. 77–88). New York, NY: Association for Computing Machinery.

Dhamija, R., Tygar, J. D., & Hearst, M. (2006). Why phishing works. In *Proceedings of the SIGCHI Conference on Human Factors in Computing Systems (CHI '06)* (pp. 581–590). New York, NY: Association for Computing Machinery.

Dinev, T., & Hart, P. (2006). An extended privacy calculus model for e-commerce transactions. *Information Systems Research, 17(1),* 61–80.

Dinev, T., & Hu, Q. (2007). The centrality of awareness in the formation of user behavioral intention toward protective information technologies. *Journal of the Association for Information Systems, 8(7),* 386–408.

Downs, J. S., Bruine de Bruin, W., Murray, P. J., & Fischhoff, B. (2004). When "it only takes once" fails: Perceived infertility predicts condom use and STI acquisition. *Journal of Pediatric and Adolescent Gynecology, 17(3),* 224.

Downs, J. S., Holbrook, M., & Cranor, L. F. (2006). Decision strategies and susceptibility to phishing. In *Proceedings of the Second Symposium on Usable Privacy and Security, Pittsburgh, PA, July 12–14, 2006* (vol. 149, pp. 79–90). New York, NY: Association for Computing Machinery.

——(2007). Behavioral response to phishing risk. In *Proceedings of the Anti-Phishing Working Groups Second Annual eCrime Researchers Summit, Pittsburgh, PA, October 4–5, 2007)* (vol. 269, pp. 37–44). New York, NY: Association for Computing Machinery.

Eraut, M. (1994). *Developing professional knowledge and competence.* London and New York: Routledge.

Fahs, P. S., Smith, B. E., Atav, A. S., Britten, M. X., Collins, M. S., Lake Morgan, L. C., & Spencer, G. A. (1999). Integrative research review of risk behaviors among adolescents in rural, suburban, and urban areas. *Journal of Adolescent Health, 24(4),* 230–243.

Ferguson, A. J. (2005). Fostering e-mail security awareness: The West Point carronade. *EDUCASE Quarterly*, *28(1)*, 54–57.

Fette, I., Sadeh, N., & Tomasic, A. (2007). Learning to detect phishing emails. In *Proceedings of the Sixteenth International Conference on the World Wide Web* (pp. 649–656). New York, NY: Association for Computing Machinery.

Fishbein, M., & Ajzen, I. (1980). *Understanding attitudes and predicting social behavior*. Englewood Cliffs, NJ: Prentice-Hall.

Furnell, S. M., Bryant, P., & Phippen, A. D. (2007). Assessing the security perceptions of personal internet users. *Computer and Security*, *26(5)*, 410–417.

Gorling, S. (2006). The myth of user education. In *Proceedings of the Sixteenth Virus Bulletin International Conference, October 2006* (vol. 11, pp. 13–16). Abingdon: Virus Bulletin Ltd.

Hann, I., Hui, K., Lee, S., & Png, I. (2007). Overcoming online information privacy concerns: An information-processing theory approach. *Journal of Management Information Systems*, *24(2)*, 13–42.

Herath, T., & Rao, H. R. (2009). Encouraging information security behaviors in organizations: Role of penalties, pressures and perceived effectiveness. *Decision Support Systems*, *47(2)*, 154–165.

Herley, C. (2009). So long, and no thanks for the externalities: The rational rejection of security advice by users. In *Proceedings of the 2009 Workshop on New Security Paradigms Workshop, Oxford, September 8–11, 2009* (pp. 133–144). New York, NY: Association for Computing Machinery.

Jacobsen, G. D., & Jacobsen, K. H. (2011). Health awareness campaigns and diagnosis rates: Evidence from National Breast Cancer Awareness Month. *Journal of Health Economics*, *30(1)*, 55–61.

Jagatic, T., Johnson, N., Jakobsson, M., & Menczer, F. (2007). Social phishing. *Communications of the ACM*, *50(10)*, 94–100.

Joinson, A. N., Paine, C., Buchanan, T., & Reips, U. D. (2008). Measuring self-disclosure online: Blurring and non-response to sensitive items in web-based surveys. *Computers in Human Behavior*, *24(5)*, 2158–2171.

Krasnova, H., & Veltri, N. F. (2010). Privacy calculus on social networking sites: Explorative evidence from Germany and USA. In *Proceedings of the Forty-Third Hawaii International Conference on System Sciences, January 2010* (pp. 1–10). Los Alamitos, CA: IEEE Computer Society Press.

Kumaraguru, P., Acquisti, A., & Cranor, L. F. (2006). Trust modelling for online transactions: A phishing scenario. In *Proceedings of the 2006 International Conference on Privacy, Security and Trust: Bridge the Gap between PST Technologies and Business Services* (vol. 380, pp. 1–9). New York, NY: Association for Computing Machinery.

Malhotra, N. K., Sung, S., Kim, S. S., & Agarwal, J. (2004). Internet users' information privacy concerns (IUIPC): The construct, the scale, and a causal model. *Information Systems Research*, *15(4)*, 336–355.

McCoy, C., & Fowler, R. T. (2004). "You are the key to security": Establishing a successful security awareness program. In *Proceedings of the Thirty-Second Annual ACM SIGUCCS Conference on User Services, Baltimore, MD, October 10–13, 2004* (pp. 346–349). New York, NY: Association for Computing Machinery.

McIlwraith, A. (2006). *Information security and employee behaviour: How to reduce risk through employee education, training and awareness*. Aldershot and Burlington, VT: Gower.

New York State Office of Cyber Security and Critical Infrastructure Coordination (2005). Gone phishing . . . A briefing on the anti-phishing exercise initiative for New York State government: Aggregate exercise results for public release.

Ng, B. Y., Kankanhalli, A., & Xu, Y. (2009). Studying users' computer security behavior: A health belief perspective. *Decision Support Systems, 46(4)*, 815–825.

Norberg, P. A., Horne, D. R., & Horne, D. R. (2007). The privacy paradox: Personal information disclosure intentions versus behaviors. *Journal of Consumer Affairs, 41(1)*, 100–126.

Organisation for Economic Co-operation and Development (2002). *OECD guidelines for the security of information systems and networks: Towards a culture of security*. Paris: Organisation for Economic Co-operation and Development.

Pavlou, P. A., & Fygenson, M. (2006). Understanding and predicting electronic commerce adoption: An extension of the theory of planned behavior. *Management Information Systems Quarterly, 30(1)*, 115–143.

Reyna, V. F. (2008). A theory of medical decision making and health: Fuzzy trace theory. *Medical Decision Making, 28(6)*, 850–865.

Reyna, V. F., & Adam, M. B. (2003). Fuzzy-trace theory, risk communication, and product labeling in sexually transmitted diseases. *Risk Analysis, 23(2)*, 325–342.

Rosenstock, I. M. (1966). Why people use health services. *Milbank Memorial Fund Quarterly, 44(3)*, 94–127.

Schechter, S. E., Dhamija, R., Ozment, A., & Fischer, I. (2007). The emperor's new security indicators. In *Proceedings of the 2007 IEEE Symposium on Security and Privacy, May 20–23, 2007, Washington, DC*, pp. 51–65.

Schoenbachier, D. D., & Gordon, G. L. (2002). Trust and customer willingness to provide information in database-driven relationship marketing. *Journal of Interactive Marketing, 16(3)*, 2–16.

Schwartz, B. (1968). The social psychology of privacy. *American Journal of Sociology, 73(6)*, 741–752.

Shaw, R. S., Chen, C. C., Harris, A. L., & Huang, H. (2009). The impact of information richness on information security awareness training effectiveness. *Computers and Education, 52(1)*, 92–100.

Sheeran, P. (2002). Intention–behavior relations: A conceptual and empirical review. *European Review of Social Psychology, 12(1)*, 1–36.

Sheeran, P., & Abraham, C. (2003). Mediator of moderators: Temporal stability of intention and the intention–behavior relation. *Personality and Social Psychology Bulletin, 29(2)*, 205–215.

Sheng, S., Magnien, B., Kumaraguru, P., Acquisti, A., Cranor, L. F., Hong, J., & Nunge, E. (2007). Anti-Phishing Phil: The design and evaluation of a game that teaches people not to fall for phish. In *Proceedings of the Third Symposium on Usable Privacy and Security, Pittsburgh, PA, July 18–20, 2007* (vol. 229, pp. 88–89). New York, NY: Association for Computing Machinery.

Sipponen, M. T. (2000). A conceptual foundation for organizational information security awareness. *Information Management and Computer Security, 8(1)*, 31–41.

Slovic, P. (2000). *The perception of risk*. Sterling, VA: Earthscan Publications Ltd.

Spagat, E. (2009). Justice department hoaxes employees. Retrieved January 29, 2009 from http://news.yahoo.com/s/ap/20090129/ap on go ca st pe/justice hoax.

Stanton, H., Back, K. W., & Litwak, E. (1956). Role-playing in survey research. *American Journal of Sociology, 62(2)*, 172–176.

Srikwan, S., & Jakobsson, M. (2008). Using cartoons to teach internet security. *Cryptologia, 32(2)*, 137–154.

Sutter, M. (2007). Outcomes versus intentions: On the nature of fair behavior and its development with age. *Journal of Economic Psychology, 28(1)*, 69–78.

Sutton, S. (1998). Predicting and explaining intentions and behavior: How well are we doing? *Journal of Applied Social Psychology, 28(15)*, 1317–1338.

Williams, P. A. (2008). In a "trusting" environment, everyone is responsible for information security. *Information Security Technical Report, 13(4)*, 207–215.

Witte, K. (1992). Putting the fear back into fear appeals: The extended parallel process model. *Communications Monographs, 59(4)*, 329–349.

Witte, K., & Allen, M. (2000). A meta-analysis of fear appeals: Implications for effective public health campaigns. *Health Education and Behavior, 27(5)*, 591–615.

Wu, M., Miller, R. C., & Garfinkel, S. L. (2006). Do security toolbars actually prevent phishing attacks? In R. Grinter, T. Rodden, P. Aoki, E. Cutrell, R. Jeffries, & G. Olson (Eds.), *Proceedings of the SIGCHI Conference on Human Factors in Computing Systems, Montréal, April 22–27, 2006* (pp. 601–610). New York, NY: Association for Computing Machinery.

13

Improving Judgments and Decisions by Experiencing Simulated Outcomes

ROBIN M. HOGARTH AND EMRE SOYER

It is well established that probabilistic inferences are affected by presentation format. Consequently, much attention has been directed at determining transparent task descriptions that lead to accurate judgments. However, since it is difficult to generalize from approaches already suggested, we propose an alternative that exploits the human ability to encode sequentially experienced frequency data. That is, instead of static descriptions, we provide decision makers the opportunity to observe — dynamically — sequences of outcomes from the underlying process as represented by a simulation. We summarize a research program that tests this approach in three areas: classical puzzles in probability theory; an investment decision; and assessing the chances of winning a competition. In all cases, sequentially simulated experience leads to more accurate responses than standard formats; users relate well to the method; and differences due to statistical sophistication are small. We conclude with specific implications for further research.

An extensive literature in judgment and decision making has documented many kinds of errors that people make in their intuitive judgments and forecasts. They are inconsistent when reasoning probabilistically (Kahneman, Slovic, & Tversky, 1982), intuitive predictions are often erroneous (Tversky & Kahneman, 1974), overconfidence is prevalent (Moore & Healy, 2008), and people are subject to biases such as illusory correlation and the use of confirming information to test hypotheses (Plous, 1993). The impression generated by this literature is that humans have great difficulty in matching their assessments of uncertainty with empirical realities.

On the other hand, there are many judgmental tasks that people perform each day with remarkable accuracy. For example, consider skills of locomotion that depend heavily on predictive judgment. It is rare that people bump into each other when crossing a busy street (Zakay & Block, 1997), and we can plan and execute the path to exit a room by a particular door with ease and accuracy. As stated many years ago by the late Japanese psychologist Masanao Toda, "Man and rat are both incredibly stupid in an experimental room. On the other hand, psychology has paid little attention to the things they do in their normal habitats; man drives a car, plays complicated games, and organizes society, and rat is troublesomely cunning in the kitchen" (1962, p. 165).

From both theoretical and practical viewpoints, the important issue is to understand the conditions under which people do or do not make good judgments (which, as we will show, do not just involve the issue of external validity highlighted by Toda). In turn, this requires identifying the match between human judgmental characteristics and task demands (Brunswik, 1952; Simon, 1956).

To highlight the relevance of this issue, consider the task faced by experts who must decide how to present information to others. As examples, consider physicians discussing test results with patients or financial advisers explaining risks to naive investors. Clearly the presentation format should not bias decision makers to choose specific options. Instead, this should allow them to understand fully the implications of the data and thereby reach their own conclusions (Hogarth & Soyer, in press). The goal of this chapter is to illuminate one way of achieving such understanding and it is organized as follows.

We first briefly describe strengths and weaknesses of the human cognitive system from an information processing perspective. In particular, we emphasize mechanisms that humans have evolved to overcome some of their processing limitations. Second, we provide a framework for conceptualizing the characteristics of judgmental tasks that involves two dimensions. One is whether tasks are structured such that they are transparent or opaque to the individual. The other is whether people have or acquire information about the task in the form of a description or, alternatively, whether they have learned about task characteristics through experience. Moreover, we distinguish between experience that can help or impede accurate learning of task features. Third, we exploit the implications of our analysis to identify conditions under which human processing abilities and task demands are and are not well matched. Fourth, we describe an experimental research program in which we have tested these ideas. Our results suggest that when individuals are provided with sequentially simulated outcomes of complex decision process, (1) they easily relate to this technology; (2) they prefer this format to synthetic descriptions; and (3) their judgments improve. Finally, we conclude with implications and suggestions for further research.

HUMAN INFORMATION PROCESSING: STRENGTHS AND WEAKNESSES

With each passing year, psychologists and neuroscientists unravel many wonderful and surprising features of the complexities of the human information processing system and its capacity for dealing with a wide range of problems. However, although intrinsically sophisticated, the human information processing system is still less complex than the environment in which it operates. Moreover, although it has evolved to meet the challenges of the natural environment, today many important judgmental tasks involve artificial settings (Simon, 1996) that have emerged as a result of human actions but for which evolution has had insufficient time to develop appropriate responses. For one striking example, consider economic activity. Although we have some knowledge about how this works, we are still unable to engineer steady growth rates and full employment, let alone forecast and handle financial crises.

From the perspective of judgment and decision making, limitations on attention and short-term memory are among the most important constraints. There are several consequences. First, subtle shifts in the attention that people can afford to pay to different aspects of information greatly influence the judgments and choices they make (see, e.g., Tversky & Kahneman, 1981). In short, people are sensitive to how information is presented and different information displays can induce different responses, even if objective features of the underlying problem are identical.

Second, people have at their disposal a variety of simple-to-use rules for making judgments and decisions that allow speedy responses to even quite complex tasks. These rules—also called heuristics—typically reduce the amount of information that can be processed by focusing on and extrapolating from a selective subset. In other words, they ignore part of the information. Whereas much literature on judgment has demonstrated that heuristics can lead to systematic biases (Kahneman et al., 1982), other work has stressed their advantages. Heuristics can be effective, often even leading to better judgments than so-called optimal models (Gigerenzer, Todd, & the ABC Research Group, 1999). Closely related to these themes is work on how people acquire and exhibit expertise in specific domains (Ericsson & Charness, 1994). The key is that people learn what information to select—and what to ignore—and thereby reach speedy conclusions. Moreover, these kinds of processes also characterize intuitive reactions in everyday life in which people develop skills in understanding the "gist" of situations or problems they encounter (Reyna, 2012).

Third, the use of heuristics in decision making is complemented by two important, related cognitive skills. One is the ability to identify patterns; the other is recognition memory (Goldstein & Gigerenzer, 2002). Our cognitive system is highly attuned to identifying patterns (as opposed to making calculations), and we have an uncanny ability to recognize what we have seen or heard before.

Fourth, an important mechanism that people use to overcome cognitive limitations is sequential processing. Instead of trying to process all of the information relevant to an issue at one moment in time, people use sequential strategies that involve partial answers being updated as more information is considered. Whereas such strategies can lead to biases due to order effects (see, for example, Hogarth & Einhorn, 1992), they represent how we process large amounts of information. Indeed, in a naturally occurring environment, a sizeable part of the information we have can be thought of as resulting from samples that we have experienced across time.

Fortunately, people are able to encode accurately information experienced across time and particularly the frequencies of different events. As a simple demonstration, imagine that you are asked how many times you have been to the cinema in the past three months. Most people can answer this question without difficulty and fairly accurately. And yet, they did not know they were going to be asked the question, nor did they maintain specific counts for this particular or other possible events. The research on frequency encoding has been well summarized by Hasher and Zacks (1979, 1984) and Zacks and Hasher (2002). They point out that, in addition to its accuracy and reliability, this ability requires little by way of attention or intention and is invariant to learning, age, and many individual differences. Moreover, the possibility that it has a long evolutionary history is supported by the fact that the basic skill is shared by several nonhuman species.

THE STRUCTURE OF JUDGMENTAL TASKS

There are many ways in which one could characterize judgmental tasks. In our work, we have found it useful to distinguish two dimensions on which tasks can be conceptualized. One is the extent to which the task is transparent or opaque to the individual. By transparent we mean that the task is described in a way that the person can "see through" the description and understand the correct implications. Typically, transparent tasks are simple in form, but not necessarily so. For example, when a simple choice is framed as, say, a loss as opposed to a gain (Tversky & Kahneman, 1981), this task would not be transparent to a decision maker who does not realize that choice should not be affected by framing in terms of losses or gains. A related point is that whether a task is transparent or opaque depends on characteristics of the individual concerned. For example, many problems in probability theory might be opaque to all but a group of expert statisticians.

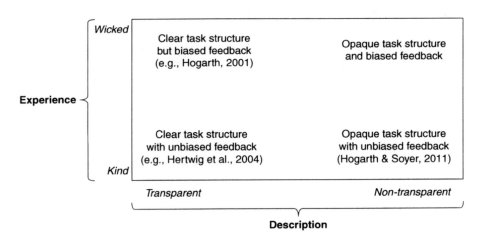

Figure 13.1   Characterizations of decision tasks by description and experience. Task structures can vary on description (the horizontal axis) from transparent to nontransparent (i.e. from clear to opaque). Experience (on the vertical axis) can vary from kind to wicked (i.e. with feedback that varies from being unbiased to biased). From Figure 1 in Hogarth and Soyer (2011, p. 435). Copyright 2011 by the American Psychological Association. Adapted with permission.

The second dimension is the contrast between having, on the one hand, a description of the task or, on the other hand, learning about the task through experience (cf., Hertwig, Barron, Weber, & Erev, 2004; Yechiam & Busemeyer, 2005). Such learning, of course, depends on receiving feedback across time and thus also raises an issue about the quality of feedback. Was the feedback sufficient and unbiased so that the person has an accurate representation of the task, or was it incomplete and/ or biased in some manner? If the former, we describe the task as involving *kind* experience; if the latter, we say that it is *wicked* (Hogarth, 2001, 2010).

Figure 13.1 depicts our characterization of tasks. If people have descriptions of tasks, these may vary on the dimension of transparency—the horizontal axis of the figure. If they learn about the tasks through experience—the vertical axis of the figure—then these will vary on the extent to which they are kind or wicked.

MATCHING PEOPLE AND TASKS: IMPLICATIONS

As discussed above, the "story" of judgment and decision making to date revolves around the fact that responses depend crucially on how tasks are described. Thus, the emphasis in helping people make better judgments and decisions has been on matching people and tasks by rendering descriptions of the latter transparent. A good example is the work of Gigerenzer and Hoffrage (1995) who have pioneered the use of frequency data (or "natural frequencies") to simplify the task of Bayesian updating.

For example, consider a Bayesian updating problem of the following type:

Assume you conduct breast-cancer screening using mammography in a certain region. You know the following information about the women in this region:

The probability that a woman has breast cancer is 1% (prevalence).
If a woman has breast cancer, the probability that she tests positive is 90% (sensitivity).
If a woman does not have breast cancer, the probability that she nevertheless tests positive is 9% (false-positive rate).

A woman, chosen at random, gets breast screening, and the test results show that she has cancer. What is the probability that she has cancer?

1. The probability that she has breast cancer is about 81%.
2. Out of 10 women with a positive mammogram, about 9 have breast cancer.
3. Out of 10 women with a positive mammogram, about 1 has breast cancer.
4. The probability that she has breast cancer is about 1%.
        (Gigerenzer, Gaissmaier, Kurz-Milcke, Schwartz, & Woloshin, 2007, p. 55)

Most people find this problem hard to solve. Indeed, only 34 out of 160 (or 21 percent) gynecologists to whom Gigerenzer et al. (2007) posed this question selected the correct answer of 1 out of 10 (option 3). However, when these same gynecologists were trained to transform the probabilistic information provided into a natural frequency format, 139 (or 87 percent) chose the correct answer. The distinction between standard and natural frequency formats is illustrated in

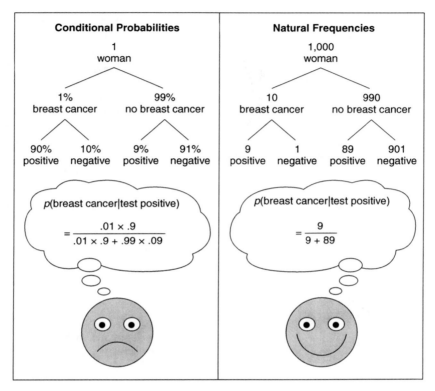

Figure 13.2   Two ways of calculating the probability that a woman who tests positive in mammography screening actually has breast cancer (positive predictive value). The left side illustrates the calculation with conditional probabilities, and the right side with natural frequencies. The four probabilities at the bottom of the left tree are conditional probabilities, each normalized on base 100. The four frequencies at the bottom of the right tree are natural frequencies. The calculation using natural frequencies is simpler (smiling face) because natural frequencies are not normalized relative to base rates of breast cancer, whereas conditional probabilities (or relative frequencies) are, and need to be multiplied by the base rates. (The formula to calculate the positive predictive value is known as Bayes's rule.) Adapted from Figure 3 in Gigerenzer et al. (2007, p. 56). Copyright 2007 by Sage Publications. Reprinted by permission of Sage Publications.

Figure 13.2—the standard format on the left, the natural frequency format on the right. Clearly, for most people presenting this problem in the natural frequency format renders it transparent.

Whereas the performance of the natural frequency approach in this particular case is impressive, a question remains: Can people transform most probabilistic reasoning problems into natural frequency formats, or do different types of problems require specific transformations? Tests on the effectiveness of such transformations have revealed that in other contexts (e.g., conjunction problems that involve nested relationships), the advantages are less evident (Evans, Handley, Perham, Over, & Thompson, 2000; Koehler & Macchi, 2004; Sloman, Over, Slovak, & Stibel, 2003). In light of these findings, we seek a more general method.

Our approach is to exploit the human ability to encode accurately sequentially experienced frequency data, such as in the example of recalling cinema visits discussed above.[1] Thus, we present decision tasks by experience as opposed to description (see Figure 13.1). That is, instead of providing a description of a problem (e.g., in standard or natural frequency format), we enable people to sample sequentially outcomes of the process about which they are asked to make inferences. Specifically, we create a simulation of the process, ask people to interact with the simulation (by observing many trials), and then ask them to make estimates based on their experience.

As an example of such a process, consider Figure 13.3, which illustrates a simulation in which the participant estimates the probability of heads when tossing a coin (assuming it is not known whether the coin is fair or not). Preparing the underlying simulation model requires, of course, somebody to set the parameter

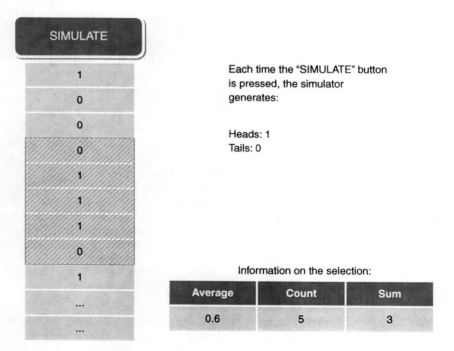

Figure 13.3   A coin toss simulator. In this particular model, each time the SIMULATE button is clicked, a coin toss is simulated producing a 1 (heads) or 0 (tails). The figure depicts the outcomes of nine clicks of which five have been selected (dashed area). Summary statistics of this subsample are shown in the table provided. This model lets users sample as many outcomes as they wish and to obtain statistical summaries of subsamples they select. From Figure 2 in Hogarth and Soyer (2011, p. 437). Copyright 2011 by the American Psychological Association. Adapted with permission.

of the Bernoulli process that generates outcomes. But from the viewpoint of the individual making the judgment, all that is seen is a sequence of simulated "heads" and "tails"—one outcome for each press of the simulation button. Parenthetically, we note that the simplicity of the coin toss example can be misleading in that the person setting up the simulation would know the precise answer to the problem that the individual is being asked to estimate. However, and as we illustrate below, in many simulations the person who constructs the simulation does not have to be fully aware of the probabilistic implications of the underlying model. That is, there may be several probabilistic parameters that combine to generate simple outcomes.

In summary, our approach to matching tasks to human cognitive abilities is to provide individuals with simulated experience of the outcomes of the processes about which they are asked to make inferences. Moreover, even when the underlying probabilistic structures of the problems faced are complicated, building simulations does not require more information than is needed to provide descriptions of the same problems. Simulations make interpreting experience as simple as observing a sequence of coin tosses.

TESTING SIMULATED EXPERIENCE: OVERVIEW OF A RESEARCH PROGRAM

We have investigated the accuracy of people's judgments in probabilistic problems when they have the opportunity to observe sequentially simulated outcomes similar to the coin toss example illustrated above. We describe three types of experiments.

Probabilistic Problems

In the first experiments (Hogarth & Soyer, 2011), we selected seven probabilistic problems for which people's answers, based on the usual descriptive formats, have typically been erroneous. These are the Bayesian updating problem described above (Gigerenzer et al., 2007), the birthday problem (where respondents typically underestimate the probability that two people in a group share the same birthday), the conjunction problem, the Linda problem (Tversky & Kahneman, 1983), the hospital problem (Tversky & Kahneman, 1974), regression toward the mean (where extreme events tend to be followed by less extreme ones), and the Monty Hall problem (Friedman, 1998; Krauss & Wang, 2003; see Hogarth & Soyer, 2011, for full details).

Experimental participants saw two versions of all problems. One was the typical descriptive format; the other involved experiencing sequentially simulated outcomes. Thus, for example, for the Bayesian problem, participants saw a version in the same standard format as Gigerenzer et al.'s participants (2007; see above), and also observed outcomes of a simulation model. To instruct participants in how to use and interpret the simulation model, we first demonstrated the coin toss simulator described above and allowed them to interact with it. For the simulation of the Bayesian problem, we told them that this model allows them to "toss" patients, given the probabilistic structure underlying the problem. The interface revealed whether a simulated woman with a positive test result really had cancer or not. We emphasized that in all tasks participants were free to sample as many trials as they wished. As they sampled more and more cases with a positive test result, they became aware that false positives were more prevalent than true positives.

The experiment involved two different populations of respondents, one of which was relatively sophisticated in terms of statistical expertise, while the other was relatively naive. The first consisted of 62 advanced undergraduate students at Universitat Pompeu Fabra who had taken courses in probability and statistics. The second involved 20 members of the general public, university-educated but without specialist statistical knowledge.

From each participant, we elicited three responses for each problem:

1. an answer based on the standard descriptive statement of the problem—denoted "Analytic";
2. an answer reached after experiencing simulated outcome—denoted "Experience";
3. a final answer—denoted "Final."

Half of the undergraduates saw the standard version before the simulation, and for the other half this order was reversed (i.e. simulation first, standard version second). The remuneration of the undergraduates depended on the accuracy of their final answers.

Results of the experiment are summarized in Table 13.1. Overall they demonstrate strong effects of simulated experience. For example, for the Bayesian problem almost all participants chose the correct answer after experiencing simulated outcomes. However, having also attempted to answer the problem in the standard format has a negative impact in that the final answers are not as accurate as those based on experience. This is also true for all of the other problems and raises the issue as to whether one should only present people with problems in the form of sequentially sampled outcomes. We will return to this issue below.

Investments

To test our ideas in a domain other than well-known problems in probability theory, we investigated whether people could use a simulation model in an investment task to make correct inferences concerning expected returns.

There were two conditions in this experiment. In one, participants responded using the output of a statistical model (as a control group); in the other, participants were provided with a simulation model (the treatment group). The scenario and the problems read as follows:

You have 40 euro and can invest in two different opportunities, I_1 and I_2. How much would you invest so that you can expect to obtain 45 euro?

Given your choice:

1. What is the probability that you will end up with less than 40 euro?
2. What is the probability that you will end up with less than 45 euro?

Table 13.1 Percentages of correct answers to well-known probabilistic problems by experimental conditions. From Hogarth and Soyer (2011, p. 441, Table 2). Copyright 2011 by the American Psychological Association. Adapted with permission.

	Sophisticated		Naive	Mean
	A-E[a]	E-A[a]		
1. Bayesian updating problem				
Analytic	17	42	20	27
Experience	97	97	100	98
Final	79	58	70	69
2. Birthday problem				
Analytic	3	13	0	6
Experience	55	61	65	60
Final	35	61	30	44
3. Conjunction problem				
Analytic	55	52	25	47
Experience	74	77	75	75
Final	77	77	75	77
4. Linda problem				
Analytic	10	32	10	18
Experience	97	97	90	95
Final	65	71	60	66
5. Hospital problem				
Analytic	39	61	25	44
Experience	97	97	100	98
Final	81	68	65	72
6. Regression toward mean				
Analytic	32	45	25	35
Experience	68	90	70	77
Final	55	65	35	54
7. Monty Hall problem				
Analytic	31	48	15	34
Experience	93	97	95	95
Final	69	58	55	61
n =	31[b]	31	20	

[a] A-E is short for Analytic-Experience and E-A is short for Experience-Analytic. These denote the order in which the tasks were completed.
[b] The number of observations for the Sophisticated A-E was 29 for the Bayesian updating problem.

Thank you for participating in this experiment. It is anonymous; please do not write your name.

Here you will be asked to make an investment decision. You are given 40 credits. You can allocate these 40 credits in 3 ways:

I_1: You can invest some in "Investment 1"
I_2: You can invest some in "Investment 2"
N: You can choose not to invest some of it.

You can choose how much to put in each of these 3 options, provided that your choices add up to 40. The relationship between the investments and their effect on the outcome is given by the following linear equation:

$$\Delta Y_i = \alpha + \beta_1 I_{1,i} + \beta_2 I_{2,i} + e_i$$

Where "ΔY" is the **change** in resulting credits, "I_1" is the amount invested in Investment 1, "I_2" is the amount invested in Investment 2, "β_1" and "β_2" are the effects of investments on the change in credits, and "e" is the random perturbation.

The return to each investment is estimated through historical data. Past 1,000 investments were taken into account for each investment, and an OLS regression was conducted to compute the relationship between each investment and its return.

The sample statistics for the data are as follows:

Variable	Mean	Standard deviation
ΔY	8.4	7.9
I_1	11.1	5.8
I_2	9.6	5.2

The OLS estimation results are as follows:

	Dependent variable: ΔY	
I_1	0.5	$(0.20)^{\circ\circ}$
I_2	0.3	$(0.05)^{\circ\circ}$
Constant	−0.1	(0.15)
R^2	0.21	
n	1,000	

Standard errors in parentheses.
°°Significant at 95% confidence level.
n is the number of observations.

This means that both the investments are estimated to have positive and significant effects on the change in one's returns. Specifically, in the average, "Investment 1" is expected to generate a 50% increase and "Investment 2" is expected to generate a 30% increase over the invested amount.

Figure 13.4   Set-up for the control group in the experiment involving the Investment task (OLS = ordinary least squares). From Hogarth and Soyer (2011, Figure 5, p. 445). Copyright 2011 by the American Psychological Association. Adapted with permission.

3. What is the probability that you will end up with more than someone investing $I_1 = 0$ and $I_2 = 0$?

The control group consisted of 26 graduate students in economics at Universitat Pompeu Fabra, and Figure 13.4 displays the details of the regression model provided to them for answering the questions. There were in fact two types of participants in the treatment group and both had available the same simulation model to answer the questions, illustrated in Figure 13.5. One of these sub groups consisted of 28 graduate students in economics at Universitat Pompeu Fabra, denoted

Please insert your investment choices in boxes "I_1" and "I_2", and press "SIMULATE" to see the prediction of the model.

Even for the same investment choices, the model might predict different outcomes at each press due to uncertainty.

You can try as many investment strategies as you wish before giving an answer to Question 1. You can also select and summarize subsamples of predictions for investments.

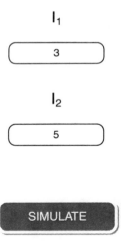

I_1	I_2	Outcome
0	5	42
0	5	37
0	5	49
0	5	39
0	5	35
3	5	44
3	5	40
3	5	40
3	5	39
...	...	
...	...	

Information on the selection:

Average	Count
43	4

Figure 13.5   Set-up for the experience group in the experiment involving the Investment task. Functions are similar to the coin toss simulation shown in Figure 13.3. Each time the SIMULATE button is clicked, a predicted outcome is shown based on both the user's inputs and the parameters of the model. Participants in the experiment were free to sample as many outcomes as they wished and to obtain statistical summaries of subsamples they selected with the mouse (I = investment). From Hogarth and Soyer (2011, p. 446, Figure 6). Copyright 2011 by the American Psychological Association. Adapted with permission.

"economists," while the other involved 18 members of the general public, with university education but no special knowledge of statistics or regression analysis, denoted "noneconomists."

Results are provided in Table 13.2. This shows that the quality of responses achieved after using the simulation model is high and that the noneconomists are as accurate as the economists. Whereas on average participants in both control and treatment groups made approximately correct guesses about the average returns to their investments, treatment groups did a better job in identifying uncertainties inherent in the outcomes, given their actions. In particular, the economists in the control group inflated the correct answer to Question 3 by 24 percent on average, while the absolute deviation from the correct answer was only 6 percent on average for the noneconomists using the simulations. (For further details, see Hogarth & Soyer, 2011.)

Table 13.2 Means and standard deviations for all the groups in the experiment involving the Investment task (I = investment and <SD>). From Hogarth and Soyer (2011, p. 447, Table 3). Copyright 2011 by the American Psychological Association. Adapted with permission.

Condition	Analytic group	Experience groups	
		Economists	Noneconomists
(n =	26	28	18)
Decisions			
I_1	3.5	5.7	6.7
	<4.6>	<3.9>	<5.9>
I_2	12.3	7.8	9.8
	<7.0>	<4.5>	<7.7>
Expected outcome			
Y	45.5	45.2	46.3
	<0.9>	<1.6>	<2.1>
Prob $(Y < 40)$			
Question 1: | Response − Correct|	17%	8%	8%
	<7%>	<7%>	<7%>
Proportion with (Response < Correct)	88%	61%	22%
Prob $(Y < 45)$			
Question 2: | Response − Correct |	2%	8%	8%
	<5%>	<8%>	<8%>
Prob$(Y \mid I_1, I_2) >$ Prob$(Y \mid$ no investment)			
Question 3: | Response − Correct |	24%	11%	6%
	<10%>	<9%>	<5%>
Proportion with (Response > Correct)	100%	53%	67%

Competitive Behavior

Our third test of the simulation methodology involved a decision problem where people had to assess the probability of being successful in a competition (Hogarth, Mukherjee, & Soyer, 2013). The scenario in this experiment read as follows:

> Imagine that Abyz is a popular skill-based computer game that you like to play. The game is played enthusiastically by thousands of young people like you. You know that different people have different playing skills; some are experts while there are others who are just learning the game. You estimate your own skill level to be better than **50 percent** and worse than **50 percent** of the Abyz playing population. Suppose there is an Abyz competition where **ten** contestants are selected at random by lottery from the large number of people who play the game and you are one of the selected contestants. Estimate your chances of winning the competition when **three** of the **ten** contestants are winners.[2]

There were four experimental groups, each of which answered nine variations of this problem. First, 20 participants had to give answers without any aid—the control group. In the second group, 22 participants were provided with the responses of a consultant, an "expert statistician." The third and fourth groups each had 20 participants, and both were provided with simulation tools. One of these tools had no "memory" (i.e. the model did not show or summarize past outcomes); but the other did (i.e. the model both showed and summarized previously observed outcomes). Participants were all undergraduate students at Universitat Pompeu Fabra. Thus, in this study, we investigated not only the effectiveness of simulation against standard responses but the effectiveness of simulated experience relative to receiving expert opinion as well as different features of simulation models, that is, with and without a memory aid.

In all groups, participants were first required to answer the nine questions in standard format without any aid. Next, they received their respective aids (except for the control group), and then they gave their final responses, the accuracy of which determined their remuneration.

Figure 13.6 summarizes the main results. Clearly, receiving the opinion of an expert makes a big difference. In fact, the expert did provide the correct answers and the accuracy of participants' judgments increased from 35 percent to 74 percent after receiving this advice. Simulation also increased accuracy of responses: from 44 percent to 54 percent for the tool without memory, and from 38 percent to 64 percent for the tool with memory.

DISCUSSION

We have demonstrated, across a range of problems, that probabilistic inferences can be improved by allowing people to experience sequences of outcomes generated by simulation models. Moreover, people seem quite comfortable in using such models, the use of which can be explained in a few minutes. Indeed, we noted no great differences in the results achieved by participants varying in levels of statistical sophistication.

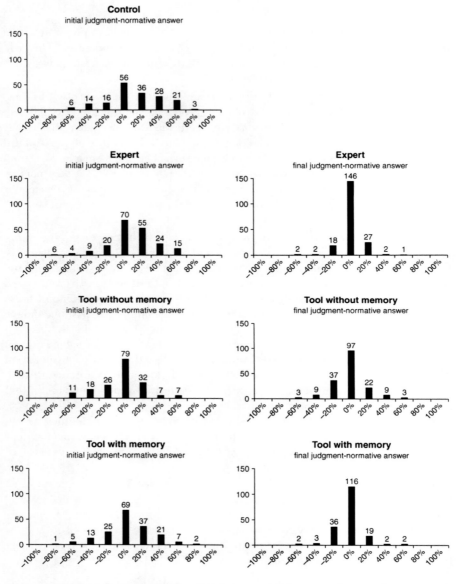

Figure 13.6 Distributions of differences between judgments and normative answers in the experiment involving competitions. From top to bottom, the histograms on the left display differences between initial judgments and normative answers in the control condition ($n = 180$), the expert condition (n = 188), the tool without memory condition ($n = 180$), and the tool with memory condition ($n = 180$). From top to bottom, the histograms on the right display differences between final judgments and normative answers for the same conditions except for the control condition, where the initial judgments are also the final ones. From Hogarth, Mukherjee, and Soyer (2013, p. 446, Figure 8). Copyright 2013 by the American Psychological Association. Adapted with permission.

Whereas simulated experience undoubtedly improved the accuracy of probabilistic inferences relative to unaided judgment, it still leaves room for improvement. Our results and experience with the method suggest several avenues of investigation. First is the question as to whether people should view probabilistic inference problems in different formats—for example, both through standard descriptions and as experience-based outputs of a simulation. On the one hand, it could be argued that people should look at problems from different perspectives. Against this, however, is the argument that it is pointless to use a presentation format if it is known to lead to errors.

In a related investigation (Soyer & Hogarth, 2012), we presented results of a simple regression analysis to academic economists using three different formats and asked them to make several inferences. There were three conditions. In one, respondents saw results of the analysis in the tabular format that is typically used in the economics profession. The second group saw both the analysis and a scatter plot of the data. The third group only saw the scatter plot. The first two groups were inaccurate in their inferences (they underestimated uncertainty). However, although respondents in the third group were quite accurate, they complained bitterly about not having enough information to answer the questions appropriately. Clearly, it is important that people making inferences should trust and have confidence in their information. Future research should identify problem formats that inspire both confidence and accuracy.

Several procedural details of the simulation methodology should also be investigated. First, in all our work we instructed participants to simulate as many trials as they wanted. We gave no hints as to what we thought might be suitable samples of experience. In general, in our first experiments (the probability problems) the more sophisticated participants averaged some 65 trials per question whereas their more naive counterparts averaged close to 50. In other work involving sampling in order to make decisions for laboratory gambles, participants have been observed to use far smaller samples—medians of around 15 (Hertwig et al., 2004). An important issue for future research therefore centers on understanding the cues people use to determine when to stop sampling.

A second point centers on the amount and nature of information that a simulated experience contains. For instance, in the experiments involving probability problems, we only let participants see binary outputs (1s or 0s) that corresponded to outcomes of the different problems (e.g., heads/tails in the coin toss displayed in Figure 13.3 or cancer/no cancer in the Bayesian updating problem). On the other hand, the investment scenario provided the participants with actual outcomes, i.e. the exact amounts they gained or lost through their actions (as shown in Figure 13.5). Whereas the binary content is easier to track and summarize, showing actual values reveals more clearly the rise-and-fall pattern due to randomness that is inherent in the outcomes.

Consider as an example a situation involving regression toward the mean. Imagine that a group of 100 people take a standard test, where performance is mainly based on skill (correlation between skill and performance is .75). What would be the likelihood that a person, who ranked 5th among 100, obtains a lower ranking in a subsequent test conducted on the same group? The analytical solution to this problem involves the use of cumulative distribution functions and probability densities, which lead to the answer of 65 percent. A simulation, on the other hand, lets a decision maker observe the possible outcomes in subsequent tests, without requiring the knowledge about the calculations that provide a precise answer. However, as Figure 13.7 shows, the simulated outcomes can be featured in a variety of ways, which reveal different aspects of the process. Whereas a binary sequence (higher ranked = 1; lower ranked = 0) leads to an understanding of chances for better or worse rankings, a tool that simulates and also includes the potential ranking information would make the distribution of potential outcomes more transparent.

Another related issue involves the difference between simulation tools that do or do not provide participants with the ability to summarize outcomes mechanically, that is, a memory aid. In our competitive paradigm we investigated the effect of such a tool and found that it did improve accuracy. At one level, this result might appear obvious. However, we suggest that, taken to its extreme, systematically summarizing outcomes could obviate people having to experience sequences of outcomes and this might affect understanding and confidence in using simulation tools.

In our work we explicitly compared responses of groups of respondents that varied in statistical sophistication and found little differences in accuracy following the experience of simulated outcomes. This finding raises two questions: One is whether there would still be little difference if both groups had extensive experience with simulated outcomes (i.e. the methodology was presumably new to both groups in our experiments). It could be that the statistically sophisticated might adapt faster to a higher level of accuracy; the second is whether the experience of sampling outcomes leads by itself to a higher level of statistical sophistication.

Subsequent evaluations	1	2	3	4	5	6	7	8	9	10	11	12	13	14	15
Simulated outcomes	0	0	0	0	0	0	1	1	1	0	0	1	0	1	1
Simulated rankings without underlining	7	12	17	6	8	13	4	1	4	7	7	1	22	2	4
Simulated rankings with underlining	7	12	17	6	8	13	4	1	4	7	7	1	22	2	4

Figure 13.7   Simulation results of subsequent outcomes of a person who ranked 5th in the first trial in a task where the correlation between skill and performance is .75. The "Simulated outcomes" row only features binary outcomes representing a better or equal ranking (1) and a worse one (0). The "Simulated rankings without underlining" row provides the information on potential subsequent rankings. The "Simulated rankings with underlining" row combines the information provided by the above two rows by providing ranking information while signaling its position with respect to the realized outcome (5th), i.e., if the outcome is better than or the same as the realized case, the simulated outcome is underlined, and is not if otherwise.

Although we observed some improvement in analytical responses of participants who were previously exposed to simulated experience on the same problem (in the experiment featuring probabilistic problems), we believe this was mainly an anchoring effect. Hence, more experience with the methodology is required to determine whether simulation really has a positive effect on analytical ability.

One of our experiments involved an investment decision and we emphasize that we are not alone in promoting the use of simulation tools for these kinds of decisions (Goldstein, Johnson, & Sharpe, 2008; Kaufmann, Weber, & Haisley, 2013). Basically, users of such tools are asked to observe how choices of different portfolios result in different distributions of returns (means and variances). The key idea is that users can gain insights into what outcomes can result from different investment strategies. An important applied issue is whether such tools affect people's attitudes toward risk. In particular, since in making decisions by experience, as opposed to description, people have been found to underweight as opposed to overweight small probabilities (Hertwig et al., 2004), simulation might lead people to be less risk averse (because it leads them to underweight unlikely events). Although there is some evidence of this possibility (Kaufmann et al., 2013), the issue needs to be explored in greater depth. To do so, however, we need to answer an important question: What is the standard for determining the decision maker's attitude toward risk?

Finally, one interpretation of our use of sequentially simulated experience is that this exploits people's intuitive information processing abilities. Moreover, since the information people observe involves *kind* experience, their responses should be accurate (Hogarth, 2001, 2010). A more complete investigation of the ideas presented here would include an understanding of how different forms of *wicked* experience might influence responses and whether people can learn to correct for these effects.

NOTES

1. We note that the concept of natural frequencies pioneered by Gigerenzer et al. (2007) has its justification in the same literature that we cite demonstrating that humans are effective at encoding sequentially experienced frequency data. In Gigerenzer et al.'s work, however, it is important to recognize that frequency data are summarized for participants and not experienced sequentially. Moreover, transforming probabilistic representations into frequency formats might not always be feasible.

2. The numbers in bold varied for different stimuli. Moreover, the participants went through a test phase where the mechanism of the game was explained in more detail. In particular, participants were shown what we meant by a skill-based game. We told them that "once a sample of players is selected, they are sorted according to their skill levels and the few most skilled are the winners." (Numbers depended on the specific cases.)

REFERENCES

Brunswik, E. (1952). *The conceptual framework of psychology*. Chicago, IL: University of Chicago Press.

Ericsson, K. A., & Charness, N. (1994). Expert performance: Its structure and acquisition. *American Psychologist, 49(8),* 725–747.

Evans, J. S. B., Handley, S. J., Perham, N., Over, D. E., & Thompson, V. A. (2000). Frequency versus probability formats in statistical word problems. *Cognition, 77(3)*, 197–213.

Friedman, D. (1998). Monty Hall's three doors: Construction and deconstruction of a choice anomaly. *American Economic Review, 88(4)*, 933–946.

Gigerenzer, G., Gaissmaier, W., Kurz-Milcke, E., Schwartz, L. M., & Woloshin, S. (2007). Helping doctors and patients make sense of health statistics. *Psychological Science in the Public Interest, 8(2)*, 53–96.

Gigerenzer, G., & Hoffrage, U. (1995). How to improve Bayesian reasoning without instructions: Frequency formats. *Psychological Review, 102(4)*, 684–704.

Gigerenzer, G., Todd, P. M., & The ABC Research Group. (1999). *Simple heuristics that make us smart*. New York, NY: Oxford University Press.

Goldstein, D. G., & Gigerenzer, G. (2002). Models of ecological rationality: The recognition heuristic. *Psychological Review, 109(1)*, 75–90.

Goldstein, D. G., Johnson, E. J., & Sharpe, W. F. (2008). Choosing outcomes versus choosing products: Consumer-focused retirement investment advice. *Journal of Consumer Research, 35(3)*, 440–456.

Hasher, L., & Zacks, R. T. (1979). Automatic and effortful processes in memory. *Journal of Experimental Psychology: General, 108(3)*, 356–388.

——(1984). Automatic processing of fundamental information: The case of frequency occurrence. *American Psychologist, 39(12)*, 1372–1388.

Hertwig, R., Barron, G., Weber, E. U., & Erev, I. (2004). Decisions from experience and the effect of rare events in risky choice. *Psychological Science, 15(8)*, 534–539.

Hogarth, R. M. (2001). *Educating intuition*. Chicago, IL: University of Chicago Press.

——(2010). Intuition: A challenge for psychological research on decision making. *Psychological Inquiry, 21(4)*, 338–353.

Hogarth, R. M., & Einhorn, H. J. (1992). Order effects in belief updating: The belief-adjustment model. *Cognitive Psychology, 24(1)*, 1–55.

Hogarth, R. M., & Soyer, E. (2011). Sequentially simulated outcomes: Kind experience vs. non-transparent description. *Journal of Experimental Psychology: General, 140(3)*, 434–463.

——(in press). Communicating forecasts: The simplicity of simulated experience. *Journal of Business Research*.

Hogarth, R. M., Mukherjee, K., & Soyer, E. (2013). Assessing the chances of success: Naïve statistics versus kind experience. *Journal of Experimental Psychology: Learning, Memory, and Cognition, 39(1)*, 14–32.

Kahneman, D., Slovic, P., & Tversky, A. (Eds.) (1982). *Judgment under uncertainty: Heuristics and biases*. New York, NY: Cambridge University Press.

Kaufmann, C., Weber, M., & Haisley, E. (2013). The role of experience sampling and graphical displays on one's investment risk appetite. *Management Science, 59(2)*, 323–340.

Koehler, J. J., & Macchi, L. (2004). Thinking about low-probability events: An exemplar-cuing theory. *Psychological Science, 15(8)*, 540–546.

Krauss, S., & Wang, X. T. (2003). The psychology of the Monty Hall problem: Discovering psychological mechanisms for solving a tenacious brain teaser. *Journal of Experimental Psychology: General, 132(1)*, 3–22.

Moore, D. A., & Healy, P. J. (2008). The trouble with overconfidence. *Psychological Review, 115(2)*, 502–517.

Plous, S. (1993). *The psychology of judgment and decision making*. New York, NY: McGraw-Hill.

Reyna, V. F. (2012). A new intuitionism: Meaning, memory, and development in fuzzy-trace theory. *Judgment and Decision Making, 7(3)*, 332–359.

Simon, H. A. (1956). Rational choice and the structure of environments. *Psychological Review, 63(2)*, 129–138.

——(1996). *The sciences of the artificial* (3rd ed.). Cambridge, MA: MIT Press.

Sloman, S. A., Over, D., Slovak, L., & Stibel, J. M. (2003). Frequency illusions and other fallacies. *Organizational Behavior and Human Decision Processes, 91(2)*, 296–309.

Soyer, E., & Hogarth, R. M. (2012). The illusion of predictability: How regression statistics mislead experts. *International Journal of Forecasting, 28(3)*, 695–711.

Toda, M. (1962). The design of a fungus eater: A model of human behavior in an unsophisticated environment. *Behavioral Science, 7(2)*, 164–183.

Tversky, A., & Kahneman, D. (1974). Judgment under uncertainty: Heuristics and biases. *Science, 185(4157)*, 1124–1131.

—— (1981). The framing of decisions and the psychology of choice. *Science, 211(4481)*, 453–458.

—— (1983). Extensional versus intuitive reasoning: The conjunction fallacy in probability judgment. *Psychological Review, 90(4)*, 293–315.

Yechiam, E., & Busemeyer, J. R. (2005). Comparison of basic assumptions embedded in learning models for experience-based decision making. *Psychonomic Bulletin and Review, 12(3)*, 387–402.

Zacks, R. T., & Hasher, L. (2002). Frequency processing: A twenty-five year perspective. In P. Sedlmeier & T. Bestch (Eds.), *Etc.: Frequency processing and cognition* (pp. 21–36). New York, NY: Oxford University Press.

Zakay, D., & Block, R. A. (1997). Temporal cognition. *Current Directions in Psychological Science, 6(1)*, 12–16.

Index